# HAILING THE STATE

# HAILING

## LISA
## MITCHELL

# THE

## STATE

### INDIAN DEMOCRACY BETWEEN ELECTIONS

Duke University Press
Durham and London
2023

Library of Congress Cataloging-in-Publication Data
Names: Mitchell, Lisa, [date] author.
Title: Hailing the state : Indian democracy between elections /
Lisa Mitchell.
Description: Durham : Duke University Press, 2023. | Includes
bibliographical references and index.
Identifiers: LCCN 2022043119 (print)
LCCN 2022043120 (ebook)
ISBN 9781478018766 (paperback)
ISBN 9781478016120 (hardcover)
ISBN 9781478023395 (ebook)
ISBN 9781478093589 (ebook other)
Subjects: LCSH: Democracy—India. | Political participation—India. |
Elections—India. | India—Politics and government—21st century. |
BISAC: POLITICAL SCIENCE / World / Asian | SOCIAL SCIENCE /
Anthropology / Cultural & Social
Classification: LCC JQ281 .M565 2023 (print) | LCC JQ281 (ebook) |
DDC 323/.0420954—dc23/eng/20221205
LC record available at https://lccn.loc.gov/2022043119
LC ebook record available at https://lccn.loc.gov/2022043120

COVER ART: Students staging a *dharna* in front of the district collector's office in Khammam to draw attention to the inadequate supply of textbooks, July 3, 2010. Photo by G. N. Rao/ *The Hindu.*

The author was supported by the Department of South Asia Studies at the University of Pennsylvania, the European Union's Horizon 2020 research and innovation programme under grant agreement No 853051, and the Max Planck Institute for Social Anthropology, and this title is freely available in an open access edition thanks to the generous support from these institutions.

*To Leela and Rohan,*
*with the hope that they will know a world that protects freedom*
*of speech, freedom of the press, and freedom of assembly*

The English people thinks it is free; it is greatly mistaken, it is free only during the election of Members of Parliament; as soon as they are elected, it is enslaved, it is nothing.—JEAN-JACQUES ROUSSEAU, "Of Deputies and Representatives," *The Social Contract*, 1762

Sumati, a serpent is powerful, but it can be killed by many tiny ants. A similar fate awaits a strong man who does not care for other people and behaves with them rudely. A strong man cannot always depend on his strength and behave in an arrogant fashion with others. A horde of weaker people may defeat and destroy him.—BADDENA, *Sumati Śatakamu* (A Hundred Moral Verses), thirteenth century

If a group of jute strands are braided together, it becomes a rope and you tie an elephant with that rope; so, too, a union is also like that.—TIRUNAGARI RAMANJANEYULU, *Saṅgaṃ: Telaṅgāṇā Pōrāṭa Navala* (The Union: A Novel of Telangana Struggle), 1986

Words from Indian languages that are commonly recognized in English, contemporary place names, and personal names have been transliterated without diacritics. For all other terms transliterated from Indian languages, long vowels are marked (*ā* as in *hot*; *ī* as in *deep*; *ū* as in *fool*; *ē* as in *fade*; *ō* as in *hope*), and short vowels—half the length of their long counterparts—are left unmarked (*a* as in *hut*; *i* as in *dip*; *u* as in *full*; *e* as in *fed*; *o* as in the first *o* in *oh-oh*). An underdot beneath a consonant (*ṭ, ṭh, ḍ, ḍh, ṇ, ṣ, ḷ*) indicates a retroflex consonant, pronounced by curling the tip of the tongue back toward the palate and flipping it forward, except for *ṛ*, which indicates a vowel sound similar to the *ri* in *merrily*. *Ś* is pronounced as the English *sh*. For consistency and to assist English readers, I have departed from conventional Telugu transliteration practices in using *ch* (rather than *c*) to indicate the English *ch* sound and *chh* to indicate an aspirated *ch*. Within quotations, I have kept an author's original transliteration scheme and markings. All translations from Telugu are my own unless otherwise indicated.

This book's release into the world has taken far longer than I ever intended, and I have accrued countless debts in the process. The competing obligations and administrative responsibilities of a mid-career life collided perilously with a project that kept taunting me to expand its scope, not to mention a global pandemic that began the same month I submitted the manuscript. I doubt that I will ever feel that this book is truly finished, but nonetheless I hope that, despite its flaws, it may serve as a stimulus for debate and future research on the mechanisms for holding elected officials accountable to their campaign promises between elections and on the relationships between collective assembly, political recognition, and representation in the history of democracy. Although it would be impossible to mention everyone who has contributed directly and indirectly to my thinking and to the making of this book, I would like to acknowledge the following people.

In Hyderabad, R. Bhagya Lakshmi offered friendship, introductions, and research assistance of every imaginable sort. To her, to her mother, and to Varun Kumar, Shishira, Swaroopa, Thambi, Vamshi, and Dolly, I will forever be indebted. A. Suneetha and R. V. Ramana Murthy have intertwined the pleasures of friendship with the joys of research from our days as doctoral students in Hyderabad in the 1990s to the present. Laxman Aeley, Seenu Amudala, Anil Battula, Uma Maheswari Bhrugubanda, Bhangya Bhukya, Mrunalini Chunduri, Shyamala Gogu, Dileep Konatham, M. Kondandaram, Yamini Krishna, K. Lalita, Ram Mohan, Atluri Murali, M. Parthasarathi, P. Pavana, Satish Poduval, M. Madhava Prasad, Pillalamarri Ramulu, Jagan Reddy, K. Sajaya, V. Sandhya, Adapa Satyanarayana, K. Satyanarayana, Chandra Sekhar, Sujatha Surepally, N. Venugopal, and K. Vimala offered lively conversation and enriched my vision and thinking. Smita Rawat shared warm friendship and facilitated crucial introductions in both Hyderabad and Lucknow. Gandra Mohan Rao assisted me in gaining access to statistics regarding arrests during the Telangana movement. I am also grateful to Dr. Zareena Parveen and Saraswathi at the Andhra Pradesh (now Telangana) State Archives; to the librarians at the Sundarayya Vignana Kendram; to the many activists, politicians, and political party members who helped me better understand how railway, road, and other public spaces are used to communicate with representatives of the state; and to the numerous administrators at Sanchalan Bhavan, Railway Nilayam, and the Secunderabad Railway Station who took time from their busy schedules to speak with me. Most importantly, the nearly three and a half decades of friendship with the extended family of Glory Premila and Sunil Kumar Bernard have made Hyderabad into a permanent home away from home for me, daily enriched by the kindness, generosity, and celebratory cooking of the late Vijay Kumar, Shoba, Komal, Anjali, Sunand, Prajakta, and Matthew. The sudden loss of Vijay to COVID-19 leaves a hole that can never be filled.

In Delhi, I am grateful to Dr. Bhashyam Kasturi, Mr. Mahajan, librarian Gopa Sengupta, and former director Mridula Mukherjee at the Nehru Memorial Museum and Library for providing me with affiliation in 2008–9; Dineshwar Kumar and Jaya at the National Archives of India; Mayank Tewari, Adarsha Sharma, O. P. Tyagi, and T. S. Hanspal at the National Rail Museum Archives; the staff of the Central Secretariat Library; Vijaya Laxmi, Mr. Khanna, and Mr. Venkat in the Sahitya Akademi Library Reading Room; Purnima Mehta, Mini Kumar, P. Bilimale, Ravinder Kumar, and Mr. Arora of the American Institute of Indian Studies; and Eswaran Sridharan and Tishya Sethi at the University of Pennsylvania Institute for the Advanced Study of India (UPIASI). I also want to thank Shahid Amin, Jyoti Atwal, Saumya Gupta, Gopal Guru, Chitra Joshi, Lora Krishnamurthi Prabhu, Sunil Prabhu, Chandra Bhan Prasad, Meera Prasad, and Ravikant for their friendship and rich conversation. Alan Chadwick, Rohan D'Souza, Snehalata Gupta, Holly Higgins, Joseph Mathai, and Yu Sasaki made Delhi feel like yet another home.

In Lucknow, thanks are due to B. M. S. Bisht, Ashima Singh, Indu Dubey, and the late Ram Advani, as well as to the many railway administrators in the Northern Railways and North Eastern Railways who graciously agreed to talk with me. In Warangal, Prof. Burra Ramulu, Kaloji Narayana Rao, and a range of activists and political party workers took time to educate me. In Nellore, I am grateful to Amburu Subramanyam, the late V. Anantha Ramaiah, Chandra Latha, V. Anthony Jayaraju, Md. Jaffar, A. Malakondaiah, K. Kothaiah, and the staff at the Zamin Ryot office, especially T. Vanamali, Rahim, Haneef, and Faiz, for allowing me access to their newspaper archives. And in Chennai, many thanks go to A. R. Venkatachalapathy,

C. V. Ramachandra Rao, Theodore Baskaran, S. Muthiah, and K. S. Subramanian. I am also grateful to Dr. M. Sundara Raj and Research Officer Hemalatha in the Tamil Nadu Archives. The late Bernard Bate offered hospitality in Chennai, companionship in the archives, and—as always—transformative conversation. He is deeply missed. I have also been fortunate that my research stints in Chennai overlapped with those of Ajantha Subramanian, Anand Pandian, and Geeta Patel, prompting the very rich conversations that one has when deep into research.

At Penn I have found a warm and supportive home. I have been grateful for my colleagues in the South Asia Studies Department: Daud Ali, the late Aditya Behl, Jamal Elias, Greg Goulding, Michael Meister, Afsar Mohammad, Deven Patel, Terenjit Sevea, Davesh Soneji, Ramya Sreenivasan, and Rupa Viswanath; and in the South Asia Graduate Group: Asif Agha, Nikhil Anand, Toorjo Ghose, Kathy Hall, Femida Handy, Devesh Kapur, Suvir Kaul, Ania Loomba, the late Anuradha Mathur, Justin McDaniel, Kathleen Morrison, Projit Mukharji, Rahul Mukherjee, Megan Robb, Rosane Rocher, Jim Sykes, and Tariq Thachil. Numerous other colleagues have made my time here rewarding, including Francesca Ammon, David Barnes, Eugénie Birch, David Brownlee, Andrew Carruthers, Paul Cobb, Karen Detlefsen, Mitch Fraas, Jeff Green, John Jackson, Mark Lycett, Ramah McKay, Jef Pierce, John Pollack, Karen Redrobe, Sophie Rosenfeld, Betsy Rymes, Pushkar Sohoni, Kok-chor Tan, Deborah Thomas, Greg Urban, and Dominic Vitiello. I am also indebted to Chip Bagnall, Amelia Carter, Jody Chavez, Juliana Di Giustini, Rachael Hickson, Zoe Katz, Diane Moderski, and many others who have offered other types of support.

I have also been fortunate to work with outstanding graduate students, from whom I am constantly learning. These include Tayeba Batool, Irteza Binte-Farid, Aliyah Bixby-Driesen, Brian Cannon, James Caron, Baishakh Chakrabarti, Michael Collins, Ananya Dasgupta, Ishani Dasgupta, Gabriel Dattatreyan, Melanie Dean, Kim Fernandes, Walt Hakala, Katy Hardy, Amber Henry, Amruta Inamdar, Indivar Jonnalagadda, Samira Junaid, Marc Kelley, Darakshan Khan, Sirus Libeiro, Michael Linderman, Leah Lowthorp, Aswin Mannepalli, Elliot Montpellier, Aaron Mulvany, Pooja Nayak, Kristina Nielsen, Kimberly Noronha, Samuel Ostroff, Purvi Parikh, Ryan Perkins, Josh Pien, Erica Redner, Xiao Schutte-Ke, Arjun Shankar, Sudev Sheth, Megan Stanton, Fatima Tassadiq, Sarah Pierce Taylor, Isa Thompson, Akhil Veetil, Praveen Vijayakumar, Steve Vose, and Rebecca Winkler, as well as Kripanand Komanapalli, Thomas Oomen, and Niharika Yadav who took advantage of Penn's reciprocal agreement with other universities to take classes with me. I particularly want to thank Indivar Jonnalagadda, Sirus Libeiro, and Fatima Tassadiq for the exceptional independent study reading group on the State, Sovereignty, and Political Anthropology of the City that they organized in spring 2017 while I was developing the most critical arguments of the book. I am also grateful to Sirus Libeiro for his research and transcription help, collation of a database of collective assemblies for chapter 4, and assistance with the index; Ashok Kumar Pindiga for his transcription and translation research assistance, as well as for his help in locating materials on dharnas in recent Indian history; and Indivar Jonnalagadda for compiling the bibliography and copyediting the endnotes.

Other friends and interlocutors who have enriched my intellectual life, offered support, or given feedback on specific portions of this book and its arguments include Ravi Ahuja, Jonathan Shapiro Anjaria, David Arnold, Jonathan Bach, Mukulika Banerjee, Bernard Bate, Debjani Bhattacharyya, Akeel Bilgrami, Susan Blum, the late Allison Busch, Dipesh Chakrabarty, Sanjoy Chakravorty, Uday Chandra, Ruth Chandy, Durba Chattaraj, Shahana Chattaraj, Indrani Chatterjee, Partha Chatterjee, Chris Chekuri, Hae Yeon Choo, Nusrat Chowdhury, Frank Cody, Benjamin Cohen, Lawrence Cohen, Leo Coleman, Janet Connor, James Costa, Whitney Cox, Jamie Cross, Dilip DaCunha, the late Kavita Datla, Don Davis, Rohit De, Prachi Deshpande, Kamaan Singh Dhami, Sascha Ebeling, Patrick Eisenlohr, Narges Erami, Joyce Flueckiger, Sandria Freitag, Michele Friedner, Curt Gambetta, Supriya Gandhi, Tejaswini Ganti, David Gellner, David Gilmartin, Will Glover, Sumit Guha, Akhil Gupta, Thomas Blom Hansen, Erik Harms, Barbara Harriss-White, Jack Hawley, Matthew Hull, Marilyn Ivy, Bharati Jagannathan, Chinnaiah Jangam, Bea Jauregui, Maya Joshi, Sunila Kale, Lipika Kamra, Sudipta Kaviraj, Tobias Kelly, Richard Kernaghan, Ian Kerr, Jon Keune, Razak Khan, Yukiko Koga, Mekhala Krishnamurthy, Sneha Krishnan, Kedar Kulkarni, Genevieve Lakier, Chaitanya Lakkimsetti, the late Paul Love, Ritty Lukose, Rochona Majumdar, Karuna Mantena, Rama Mantena, William Mazzarella, Pratap Bhanu Mehta, Dilip Menon, Farina Mir, Timothy Mitchell, Janaki Nair, the late R. P. Nair, Christian Novetzke, Philip Oldenburg, Francesca Orsini, Premila Paul, John Pemberton, Indira Viswanathan Peterson, Sheldon Pollock, Ritika Prasad, Ramanan Raghavendran, Velcheru Narayana Rao, Mridu Rai, Bhavani Raman, Anupama Rao, Gautham Reddy, Rachel Reynolds, Nate Roberts, Rashmi Sadana, Yasmin Saikia, Martha Selby, Juned Shaikh, David Shulman, K. Sivaramakrishnan, Ajay Skaria, Emilio Spadola, Jonathan Spencer, Howard Spodek, S. V. Srinivas, Nikita Sud, Nandini Sundar, Shabnum Tejani, Sharika Thiranagama, Sahana Udupa, Carol Upadhya, Arafaat Valiani,

Roxanne Varzi, Amanda Weideman, Andrea Wright, Anand Yang, Vazira Fazila-Yacoobali Zamindar, and Inez Zupanov.

I am also extremely grateful for the financial and institutional support that I have received for various stages of this project, as well as for the gift of time during sabbatical leaves from the University of Pennsylvania that have given me the space to research, think, and write. The initial archival, ethnographic, and oral history research on the political uses of railway spaces in India (on which the second half of this book is based) was made possible by an American Institute of Indian Studies Senior Research Fellowship in 2008–9, and its expansion to include the political uses of road and other public spaces was supported by grants from the National Endowment for the Humanities, the Trustees' Council of Penn Women, and Penn's Center for the Advanced Study of India.

My thinking has also been enriched by countless conversations, workshops, seminars, and invitations. Perhaps the first of these to have a direct impact on this project in its very earliest conceptualization was Partha Chatterjee's 2004 "Ethnographies of the Political" conference at Columbia University. His influence is apparent throughout this work, even when it may seem that I am pushing against it, and I would not be where I am today without him. Also formative following my first stint of fieldwork were a panel at the November 2012 Annual Meeting of the American Anthropological Association on "The Technologized Call," organized by Emilio Spadola, in which I first used the title "Hailing the State"; a workshop on "Extrapolitics" organized by Rupa Viswanath and Srirupa Roy at the University of Göttingen's Center for Modern Indian Studies in December 2012; and a conference on "Contested Spaces" organized in conjunction with two of my graduate students, Michael Collins and Sudev Sheth, in March 2013. I am also grateful to Sharika Thiranagama and Tobias Kelly for including me in their workshop, "Civility: Trust, Recognition and Co-Existence," in April 2015, which prompted an early draft of chapter 3; and to Amelie Blom and Stephanie Tawa Lama-Rewal for inviting me to give a keynote address at the Centre d'Études de l'Inde et de l'Asie du Sud conference, "Emotions and Political Mobilizations in the Indian Subcontinent" in February 2016.

Participation in the Humanities-Urbanism-Design initiative at Penn, funded by the Mellon Foundation, helped me think through my research materials in the company of historians, city planners, architects, art historians, and others with an interest in urban spaces over two and a half years of weekly faculty colloquia, as did the workshop, "Contemplating the Rise of Asian Cities," at Yale University, organized by Eric Harms, Helen Siu, and K. Sivaramakrishnan in 2016. Three workshops on "India's Politics in Its Vernaculars," co-organized with Anastasia Piliavsky in November 2016 and March 2018 at the University of Pennsylvania and in May 2018 at the University of Cambridge, further enriched my comparative thinking about India's politics across its linguistic regions and led to my participation in Anastasia's subsequent five-year European Research Council grant.

The actual writing of this book has taken place in fits and starts over the past decade but was especially supported by a Visiting Fellowship at Clare Hall, University of Cambridge, in 2014–15; a Mercator Visiting Fellowship in Global Intellectual History at the Freie Universität in Berlin in 2018; and the University of Pennsylvania's annual faculty writing retreats and their spin-offs throughout the year. In Cambridge, I want to thank Ed Anderson, Siva Arumugam, the late Chris Bayly, Susan Bayly, Joya Chatterjee, John Dunn, Kevin Greenbank, Binney Hare, Philippa Hird, David Ibbetson, Shruti Kapila, James Laidlaw, Annamaria Mostrescu-Mayes, Hugh Markus, Polly O'Hanlon, Nima Paidipaty, Norbert Peabody, Anastasia Piliavsky, Katherine Butler Schofield, Samita Sen, Ornit Shani, Charu Singh, and the late David Washbrook.

In Berlin, I owe a special debt to Margrit Pernau and Sebastian Conrad for their invitations to the Center for the History of Emotions at the Max Planck Institute for Human Development, and to the Global Intellectual History program at the Freie Universität, respectively. I have been grateful for feedback from and conversations with Anandita Bajpai, Sarah Bellows-Blakely, Stefan Binder, Oscar Broughton, Gautam Chakrabarti, Deepra Dandekar, Maria-Magdalena Fuchs, Lisa Hellman, Valeska Huber, Imke Rajamani, Susanne Schmidt, Benjamin Siegel, Yorim Spölder, Max Stille, Harry Stopes, Fidel Tavarez, Torsten Tschacher, Leonie Wolters, and Luc Wodzicki, as well as logistical support from Anja Berkes, Camilla Bertoni, and Sebastian Gottschalk.

To my co-conspirators in writing at Penn, including Julie Davis, Ann Norton Greene, Ayako Kano, Beth Linker, Jennifer Moore, Janine Remillard, Heather Sharkey, and others, this book goes on the list of what our faculty writing retreats have produced. I have also been prompted to turn my thoughts into coherent written arguments by numerous invitations to present portions of this work, including at the following universities: Wisconsin, Chicago, Pennsylvania, Rutgers, Yale, Columbia, Winston-Salem, Harvard, Stanford, and Texas at Austin in the United States; the Max Planck Institute for Human Development in Berlin, Cambridge University, the School of Oriental and African Studies of the University of London, Freie

Universität Berlin, and King's College London in Europe; and the English and Foreign Language University (Hyderabad), American College (Madurai), and University of Hyderabad in India.

An online reading group organized by Lisa Björkman throughout the COVID-19 pandemic lockdown provided much-needed connection during a time of isolation. I am extremely grateful to Srimati Basu, Tarini Bedi, Ravinder Kaur, Nikhil Rao, Ursula Rao, Llerena Searle, and Rachel Sturman for reading the entire manuscript and for their constructive feedback and editing suggestions. Lisa Björkman discussed nearly every part of this book with me, helped shape my ideas about collective assembly and political performance, and pushed me to clarify and defend my arguments. I am also grateful to the participants in the 2020–21 Wolf Humanities Forum on "Choice" colloquium—especially Karen Redrobe, Sophie Rosenfeld, Jonny Thakkar, and Tali Ziv—for feedback on the introduction and to two anonymous reviewers whose constructive feedback on the manuscript made this a much better book. Thanks are due also to my editor at Duke, Miriam Angress, for her patient shepherding of this project to completion.

The final revision and editing stage, co-terminus with the initial writing of a new project on translations of transnationally circulating political concepts into Telugu, was supported by a Senior Visiting Fellowship at the Max Planck Institute (MPI) of Social Anthropology in Halle (Saale), Germany. I am grateful to Ursula Rao for the invitation to the MPI; to Jutta Turner for producing the beautiful maps for this book and for her outstanding German lessons; to Jannik Bender, Viktoria Giehler-Zeng, Manuela Pusch, Viola Stanisch, and Nadine Wagenbrett for their administrative support; and to Michiel Baas, Srimati Basu, Samiksha Bhan, Siddharth Chadha, Anindita Chakrabarti, Jason Cons, Kavita Dasgupta, Carlo Diesterbeck-Roll, Pierre Druart, Marie-Claire Foblets, Arne Harms, Andrew Haxby, David Kananizadeh, Claudia Lang, Annika Lems, Rom Lewkowicz, Lukas Ley, Bettina Mann, Jovan Maud, Brenna Murphy, Hanna Nieber, Maria Nikolova, Dhananjay Ravat, Julia Vorhölter, Iain Walker, Biao Xiang, Jakub Zahora, and the members of the Political Assembly Working Group—Lisa Björkman, Mascha Schulz, Michael Vine, and Tyler Zoanni—for including me in their discussions and creating such a productive environment for writing.

An earlier version of chapter 5 first appeared in the *Indian Economic and Social History Review* 48, no. 4 (2011): 469–95. Portions of chapter 1 originally appeared as "Spaces of Collective Representation: Urban Growth, Democracy, and Political Inclusion," White Paper Series for World Urban Forum, University of Pennsylvania, 2018. Other portions of the book appeared in

*South Asia: Journal of South Asian Studies* 37, no. 3 (2014): 515–40; *Anthropological Theory* 18, no. 2–3 (2018): 217–47; Amelie Blom and Stephanie Tawa Lama-Rewal, eds., *Emotions, Mobilisations, and South Asian Politics* (London: Routledge India, 2019), pp. 46–67; and *Language and Communication* 66 (2019): 41–54.

I am also grateful to the Department of South Asia Studies at the University of Pennsylvania; the Max Planck Institute for Social Anthropology; and the European Union's Horizon 2020 research and innovation programme under grant agreement number 853051, for providing funding to enable this book to be made freely available through Duke University's Open Access program.

My in-laws—Ved, Seema, Akshay, Divyanshi, Yogesh, Pooja, Anoushka, and Anshika—are always ready with a warm welcome in Delhi, as are the extended clan in Dehra Dun, especially Rashmi, Mohan, Onima, and Shri. My father-in-law Shiv Narayan Singh Rawat (November 4, 1934–October 1, 2015) and my mother Sara Ann Mitchell (March 6, 1941–January 30, 2022) did not live to see this book in print. As always, I am grateful to my parents, Sara and Larry Mitchell, for exposing me to the world and for teaching me the importance of a good story and how to read, write, and think carefully. My father's daily questions at our dinner table (in an era before Google) had us running to the encyclopedia, dictionary, or other reference books at almost every meal and undoubtedly had a significant influence on my decision to become a researcher. To Ram, Leela, and Rohan, I owe my greatest debts. Watching Leela and Rohan learn about the world reminds me why our research is important. Ram Rawat has lived with these words the longest, and the intersections of our research questions and efforts to grapple with their answers have made our lives together my greatest pleasure.

March 2022<br>Halle, Germany

Collective Assembly, Democracy, and Representation

A people who can do this, and do it soberly and intelligently, may be weak and unresistful individually, but as a mass they cannot be dealt with too carefully. —LORD CANNING, governor general of India, to Sir Charles Wood, secretary of state for India, October 30, 1860

Democracy doesn't just mean elections. Elections are only one part of democracy. The real essence of a truly democratic system is that people must be able to continuously voice their problems and their turmoil, and democracy must provide a wide range of opportunities for people to communicate their concerns every day. The difference between a democracy and a dictatorship is that in a democracy, the people speak, and the rulers listen. In a dictatorship, the rulers speak, and the people obey. —G. HARAGOPAL, Hyderabad, May 15, 2018

On December 16, 2010, in what has been described by the *Economic Times* as one of the "largest political rallies across the world," well over a million people gathered in the city of Warangal, ninety miles northeast of the south Indian city of Hyderabad, to join in a Maha Jana Garjana (lit., "great roar of the people").[1] Hundreds of thousands of additional supporters were stranded along the highways leading to Warangal, blocking roads outside the city as they struggled to reach the assembly grounds.[2] The Jana Garjana followed repeated efforts to hold elected officials accountable for unfulfilled campaign promises pledging the bifurcation of the existing Indian state of Andhra Pradesh and sought to make advocates of a new Telangana state more visible.[3]

Nine months later, on September 12, 2011, in the wake of continued administrative stalling on the promised bifurcation of the state of Andhra Pradesh, more than a million people again assembled with growing frustration in the town of Karimnagar, one hundred miles north of Hyderabad, for another Jana Garjana in preparation for the next day's initiation of what was to become a forty-two-day Sakala Janula Samme (general strike; lit., "All People's Strike").[4] Those participating in the 2011 general strike included lawyers, coal miners, schoolteachers, state road transport corporation and electricity board employees, movie theater owners, auto rickshaw drivers, and members of other public and private sector unions, among many others. Together, their efforts effectively closed offices and schools, halted traffic, and brought everyday life in the districts of Telangana to a standstill.[5]

The massive Warangal and Karimnagar assemblies and the subsequent forty-two-day general strike were just three events in a much longer series of collective actions that intensified efforts to hold elected officials accountable to their repeatedly broken campaign promises and sought to represent the widespread support for the formation of a separate administrative state of Telangana within the Indian nation.[6] Although these events in southern India in 2010–11 occurred simultaneously with actions elsewhere in the world that came to be known as the Arab Spring and Occupy Movements, they garnered virtually no international news coverage.[7] This is perhaps because unlike the Arab Spring and Occupy events—consistently portrayed as both spontaneous and exceptional, and understood as rejecting the existing state and advocating alternative sovereignties—the Telangana movement's *garjanas* and strikes were understood in India as neither spontaneous nor exceptional in form. Instead, they were seen as tried-and-true methods of appealing to elected officials between elections and holding them to their electoral commitments, and therefore as working very much *within* accepted political structures and processes of engagement with the state and its elected representatives.

A wide range of organizations both old and new were involved in mobilizing people to participate in this long series of collective assemblies, including the Telangana Rashtra Samithi, a political party founded in 2001 with the sole agenda of creating a separate Telangana state, and the Telangana Joint Action Committee, an umbrella organization established in 2009 that successfully brought together a wide range of older and more recently established social, political, and cultural organizations. Although collective mobilizations of people in public spaces in India are most often mediated through organizations, unions, political parties, or neighborhood leaders, the Telangana movement also attracted individuals who were not already affiliated with specific organizations or political networks. A rally on March 10, 2011, for example—dubbed the "Million March" to evoke the February 1, 2011, Egyptian "Million Man March," which had received extensive international coverage—was regarded as exceptional for the way it attracted people independently of any organization affiliations. One feminist activist remarked,

Individuals don't come. Only organizations, they'll come. That kind of common sense, it's not there in the people. But the Telangana Million March? There, people, voluntarily they participated in the March, without the organizational membership. First time in my life I saw that! Individuals also, whoever was born in Telangana region, they participated in the rallies and meetings. Every Telanganite, they identified with the movement, so they owned up. . . . every individual, every person from rickshaw puller to even an industrialist or any politician, they owned up the movement.

She concluded by emphasizing that everyone felt that "it is my movement, it is our movement, it is for our people, it is for my children. That kind of understanding was there in the people."[8]

Despite this, the Warangal and Karimnagar collective assemblies in 2010 and 2011 were not only understood as building on existing organizational foundations and practices whose use had intensified since the late 1990s, but were also framed in relation to sixty years of earlier efforts by Telangana residents for political recognition (see figure I.1). Other actions included rallies, processions, long-distance pilgrimages to the site of a seat of power (*yātra*, journey or pilgrimage; *padayātra*, journey by foot), roadblocks (*saḍak bandh* or *rāstā roko*), rail blockades (*rail roko [āndōlan]*), walkouts

FIGURE I.1. "Praja Garjana" (People's Roar) public meeting organized by the Telangana Rashtra Samithi, Hyderabad, December 11, 2004 (photo: H. Satish/*The Hindu*).

of government employees, mass resignations of elected officials, the "Million March," and a "Chalo Assembly" (Let's Go to the Legislative Assembly) mobilization, as well as similar counteractions carried out by those opposed to the formation of the new state. These became increasingly frequent as both Telangana supporters and opposition groups sought to publicly communicate their opinions on the proposed administrative reorganization, and political parties vied to get in front of, define, and represent the various positions.[9]

The Telangana movement culminated on June 2, 2014, with the creation of India's twenty-ninth state, which bifurcated the existing Indian state of Andhra Pradesh (see Maps I.1 and I.2).[10] The new state of Telangana not only contains some of the region's poorest and most arid districts but also includes India's fourth largest and fourth wealthiest city, Hyderabad, home to special economic zones and knowledge parks like HITEC City, the Financial District, and Genome Valley. These new urban spaces host divisions of major multinational corporations such as Microsoft, Amazon, Bank of America, and Facebook, as well as biotech research centers for companies like Dupont, Monsanto, and Bayer.[11] The rapid growth of Hyderabad—a city dominated economically and politically by migrants from well-irrigated and prosperous districts of coastal Andhra—has further exacerbated long-standing feelings of exclusion among residents of Telangana and prompted the renewal of demands for greater inclusion in administrative state structures and more equitable approaches to economic growth.[12]

Although the questions this book seeks to answer were prompted by repeated periods of residence in both Telangana and Andhra Pradesh over the past three decades and by my close observation of the political practices described earlier, this is not a book about Telangana or the Telangana movement. Instead, it uses observations in Telangana as a starting point for interrogating understandings of the practice of democracy in India more generally and challenging the dominant historical and sociological categories used to theorize democracy. Although some may perceive the Telangana region (particularly outside Hyderabad) as marginal to India, the practices used within it are not marginal to Indian democracy. The many collective assemblies that sought to hold elected officials accountable to their promises to create the new state of Telangana are just one set of examples of the many similar practices that animate India's wider political terrain. Collective assemblies range from small local actions to large transregional and national mobilizations. Whether a crowd of schoolgirls staging a sit-down strike in front of the district collector's office to draw his attention to the lack of text-

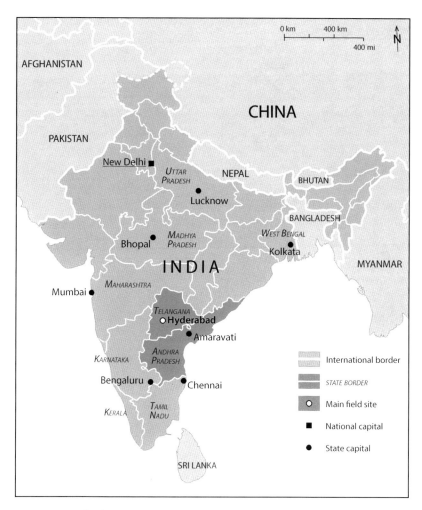

MAP I.1. Map of India. Jutta Turner/©*Max Planck Institute for Social Anthropology* (courtesy of the Max Planck Institute for Social Anthropology, Halle/Saale, Germany).

books in government schools (see figure I.2), or a few dozen slum dwellers sitting in the middle of a key intersection during rush hour to hold representatives of the state accountable to their promise of cyclone relief (see chapter 6), collective assemblies are widely seen in India as everyday communicative methods for gaining the attention of officials, making sure that election promises are implemented, and ensuring the equitable enforcement of existing laws and policies.

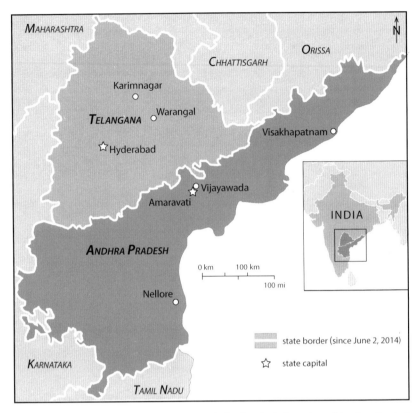

MAP I.2. Map of Telangana and Andhra Pradesh after the bifurcation of Andhra Pradesh on June 2, 2014. Jutta Turner/©*Max Planck Institute for Social Anthropology* (courtesy of the Max Planck Institute for Social Anthropology, Halle/Saale, Germany).

Such assemblies also serve as checks and balances in the face of hastily implemented laws that have not been adequately vetted through public discussion and debate. In the farmers' agitations of 2020–21, large and small farmers converged on the national capital of Delhi to demand inclusion in a dialogue with government leaders regarding a series of three farm acts introduced in September 2020 that deregulated the wholesale trading of agricultural commodities. The acts raised fears of the eventual removal of existing protections and systems of price supports that, when introduced decades ago, helped end widespread famine and ensure the survival of small farmers.[13] Following a rail blockade on September 24, 2020, an all-India *bandh* (shutdown strike) on September 25, scattered bullock-cart rallies, and another nationwide general strike on November 26, which trade union

FIGURE I.2. Students staging a dharna in front of the collector's office in Khammam to draw attention to the inadequate supply of textbooks, July 3, 2010 (photo: G. N. Rao/ *The Hindu*).

leaders claimed involved 250 million people, farmers marched toward the nation's capital in a Dilli Chalo ("Let's Go to Delhi") movement. The rail blockades, strikes, and marches to the capital were followed by blockades of major roads into the nation's capital by hundreds of thousands of farmers (November 28–December 3), a major procession on January 26, 2021, and roadblocks on state and national highways throughout the country on February 6, 2021, reflecting the long history of the effective use of many of these communicative techniques.[14] This series of collective assemblies resulted in the passage of the Farm Laws Repeal Bill on November 19, 2021, although many farmer unions continued to remind the government of earlier commitments to guarantee minimum support prices and double farmers' incomes by 2022.[15]

The collective emptying and filling of public spaces for these purposes— gaining recognition, encouraging dialogue, making representational claims, amplifying unheard voices, gauging public support for substantive agendas, vying to shape political decision making, defining and strengthening identity, performing power, and holding elected officials accountable to their campaign commitments—are not only widespread but also form a fundamental feature of the way that democracy works in India between elections. Practices such as *dharṇā* (hereafter, *dharna*, a sit-in, often in front of a government office or other seat of power); *nirāhāra dīkṣa* or *niraśana vratam* (a fasting vow or hunger strike); *garjana* (a mass outdoor public meeting, lit., "roar"; also *bhērī*, "kettledrum" in Telugu, or *murasu*, "drum" or "voice" in Tamil); neighborhood political meetings held on platforms erected in the middle of public roads; rāstā or rail roko [āndōlan], *saḍak bandh*, or *chakka jām* (a road or rail blockade); *samme*, *bandh*, or *hartāl* (a strike or work stoppage); *gherao* (the surrounding of a government official or administrator); *ūrēgimpu* or *pōru yātra* (a rally or procession, also *julūs* in Hindi/Urdu); padayātra (a pilgrimage on foot to a seat of political power); mass ticketless travel to attend meetings and participate in rallies; and *mānavahāram* (a human chain) all involve the coordination and movement of large numbers of people into and out of spaces claimed as public. These spaces include not only parks and open grounds but also streets, highways, intersections, railway stations, rail lines, and junctions.[16] The routine visibility of such collective assemblies within everyday contemporary Indian politics suggests the importance of understanding the specific social, economic, political, and legal genealogies that have established the local knowledge of how one "does" democracy. It also offers a challenge to more "modular" understandings of democracy as a fixed or homogeneous set of ideas or practices.[17]

Hailing the State: Beyond Althusser and Foucault

This book takes seriously acts of what I call "hailing the state," a wide range of practices that can be grouped together around their common aims to actively seek, maintain, or expand state recognition and establish or enhance channels of connection to facilitate ongoing access to authorities and elected officials.[18] Typically, such acts entail various types of public collective representation and performance. Interrogating the role of these forms within local understandings of democracy, I offer a counter and complement to existing Foucauldian analytic frameworks that prioritize attention to the expanding panoptic aspirations of states, which are sometimes implicitly assumed to be historically unidirectional. In doing so, the argument of this book inverts the Althusserian perspective upon which Michel Foucault built, in which representatives of the state are the sole active agents of the act of "hailing" and, by extension, of the act of surveillance.[19] In Louis Althusser's famous illustration of how ideology works, those on the street—the "subjects" of ideological state apparatuses—are significant only as passive recipients of the action and initiative of representatives of the state. In his most well-known illustration, that representative is a police officer.[20] Althusser refines the "categorical" Marxist understanding of the state as "a repressive 'machine' that enables the dominant classes to ensure their domination" by attributing the constitution of subjects to the institutions that recognize them: "I shall then suggest that ideology 'acts' or 'functions' in such a way that it 'recruits' subjects among the individuals (it recruits them all), or 'transforms' the individuals into subjects (it transforms them all) by that very precise operation which I have called *interpellation* or hailing, and which can be imagined along the lines of the most commonplace form of police (or other) hailing: 'Hey, you there!'"[21] Such an approach treats ideological state apparatuses as always already constituted, even static, and focuses on the process of interpellation as unidirectional.

Althusser's attention to this process raises several questions. First, how do institutions and their representatives themselves come to be recognizable and recognized? Might acts of hailing not also be seen as playing a significant role in constructing, reifying, and continually reshaping and repopulating ideological state apparatuses? Second, how can we understand processes of subject formation and subjectification when institutions and state apparatuses *refuse* to recognize potential subjects? This book addresses the first set of questions by attending to the ways that collective acts of hailing effectively create, alter, and reshape not only the composition of the state but also its existence, structures, practices, and ideologies. It answers the second question by considering ethnographic and archival examples of such refusals of recognition within the contexts of much longer chains of efforts to produce and sustain recognition and then tracing the impact of these chains on the production of populations and collective identities.

Althusser's analysis also assumes that ideological state apparatuses are always fully successful in recruiting their intended subjects.[22] But as Asif Agha argues, Althusser invests "magical efficacy in the act of initiation," portraying the receiver of the act of interpellation as powerless.[23] Althusser shows no interest in the processes through which individuals may interpret or attribute meaning to the act of hailing or to the impact of hailing on the representatives of the state who are enacting it. Agha suggests that for Althusser, "the act of hailing is presumed to identify addressees in such a way that 'identification creates identity.'" This collapses "the notion of 'subject-position' [which] identifies the one addressed . . . with the generic *subject-of* the State who is also the one normatively *subject-to* political control." Agha notes,

"The conflation achieves too much all at once: To experience the hail is to be shaped by it. Yet to hail someone is simply to draw their attention to a social role. Any such attempt may succeed or fail."[24] This critique can similarly be extended to Foucault's analysis of governmentality, by which he means "the ensemble formed by the institutions, procedures, analyses and reflections, the calculations and tactics that allow the exercise of this very specific albeit complex form of power, which has as its target *population*" and that constitutes "the 'governmentalization' of the state."[25] Populations are targets and objects of the "tactics and techniques" that bring them into being; analysis is unidirectional.[26]

In contrast, this book seeks to better understand the interactions between those "on the street" and authorities such as elected officials and bureaucrats, analyzing not just acts of hailing but also the responses to those efforts and the relationships that are created as a result. In addition to ignoring the possibility that ideological state apparatuses might fail to fully interpellate their intended addressees, Althusser also overlooks the fact that representatives of ideological state apparatuses sometimes misrecognize, ignore, or *refuse* to recognize potential subjects. In examining processes of subject formation under such conditions, this book responds to the state's refusal of recognition in two ways: by challenging existing scholarship that sees collective action only as resistance to state authority or ideology and by offering a framework that acknowledges desires for public recognition and voice. It is no coincidence that Althusser chose to locate his primary illustration of the practice of hailing in the street, rather than in a private home, government office, or an institutional site. Like Althusser, the following chapters demonstrate that the street is one of the most significant sites through which ideological formations are negotiated. They furthermore argue that collective performances of representation are an essential element of this process. However, unlike Althusser, the evidence offered in this book portrays the multidirectionality of practices of hailing, while also recognizing the conditions that enable some efforts at hailing to be more successful than others.

Not all collective acts are acts of hailing the state, however. This book advocates for the recognition of distinctions among collective actions despite their superficial resemblances. More specifically, it attends to differences between collective mobilizations that appeal to authorities and seek their recognition and response, and collective actions that explicitly reject the authority of the state. In the former instance, collective actions acknowledge and, in the process, reify state authority. In the latter, they resist, ignore, or challenge the sovereignty of the state and seek through their actions to establish an alternate sovereignty. The most extreme versions of resistance to the state and rejection of its sovereignty include armed revolutionary movements, such as the Maoist-inspired Naxalite movement or People's War Group in India or the Shining Path in Peru.[27] Because collectives massed in public often address multiple audiences simultaneously—recruiting both participants and witnesses in an effort to influence popular opinion, increase surveillance of the state, and exert pressure—these distinctions between hailing the state and rejecting its sovereignty function more like poles than absolute differences. Nevertheless, I lay out the contrast to encourage closer attention to the various audiences that collective actions address. Asking to whom a collective action is addressed, what its participants are seeking, what constitutes success, and what conditions determine whether it is successful or not, can help to accomplish this.[28]

In attending to state-hailing practices specifically, rather than to all forms of collective action, I am therefore prioritizing actions that seek—through collective forms of public assembly that explicitly address the state or its representatives—to expand inclusion and incorporation within state processes of decision making and the distribution of attention and resources. These practices may seek audience and greater dialogue with representatives of the state, they may demand political recognition and more rigorous or equitable enforcement of existing laws or administrative policies, or they may advocate for structural changes that promote broader inclusion such as smaller subnational administrative units (as in the Telangana movement) or expanded affirmative action initiatives.[29]

Many of my empirical examples therefore focus on collective assemblies organized by coalitions of members of minority or historically marginalized groups, rather than those carried out by majoritarian movements. Of course, majoritarian movements also make use of collective assemblies but often to assert sovereignty or domination, sometimes by displaying their ability to engage with impunity in unchecked violence against stigmatized minorities.[30] Padayātras, rallies, riots, and pogroms organized by the Rashtriya Swayamsevak Sangh, Shiv Sena, and Bharatiya Janata Party have, for example, been used to target and instill fear within minority groups, and as such have not always been addressed to the state as their primary audience.[31] Other examples of majoritarian assemblies, however, such as the rallies and road blockades used to express objections to the Mandal Commission's expansion of affirmative action quotas to include additional historically disadvantaged groups (from which historically dominant caste groups were excluded) can be seen as addressing the state.[32] As Tarini Bedi and Christophe Jaffrelot argue, people become involved in majoritarian movements for a wide variety of reasons, suggesting that in each case finer-grained analyses of the conditions through which individuals become involved in collective actions and the audiences they see themselves as addressing can better help map the distinctions I am proposing.[33] For now, it is enough to reiterate that not all collective assemblies are efforts to hail the state.

There is a growing literature on the politics of recognition, most of it generated in relationship to discussions of cultural difference and multiculturalism.[34] Central to these discussions, as Charles Taylor argues, is the problem of how to resolve the tension between individual rights, on the one hand, and collective goals, on the other.[35] In *Hailing the State*, however, I argue that this distinction between individual claims and collective claims may in many cases be a false one. By situating the emergence of collective claims within longer genealogies of state-hailing practices and efforts to achieve individual recognition, I demonstrate the relationship between individual and collective efforts to engage in communicative action. When individuals fail to gain recognition in response to their own communicative efforts, they begin to seek out others with similar concerns. Together, each hopes to improve his or her chances of being heard or acknowledged, recognizing that it is easier to garner attention collectively than individually.

Thus, my intervention is, at its most basic level, a temporal one that places synchronic snapshots of particular collective actions into much longer diachronic frames. Rather than understanding collective actions as demands for recognition by those with preformed social, political, or cultural identities, attention to the much longer trajectories of efforts to gain a hearing can help challenge understandings of identity as a preexisting foundation on which claims can be collectively amplified. Representations of identities, such as Telangana or Dalit identities, thus appear in my analysis as the eventual outcomes of the joining together of many separate individuals into collective mobilizations, rather than as preexisting foundations that precede political engagement.[36] Such an approach also makes visible the fact that not everyone within a movement shares identical interests and objectives, but that participants do feel that their own particular concerns have a better chance of being addressed when joined with the concerns of others.

There is no doubt that some collective identities have at various moments been more easily recognizable (and willingly recognized) by representatives of the state than others.[37] Yet even recognizable identities are not static, and much of the work involved in movements centers around changing the state's ability or willingness to recognize efforts to communicate as *political* acts (rather than as private or criminal acts, or as invisible) by making collectives more visible and therefore recognizable, a process I label "political arrival" (see chapter 7).[38] The Telangana identity, once widely presumed by many to be a natural part of a broader "Telugu" linguistic identity in southern India, offers an ideal context for tracing the shifting foundations for identities that have been constructed out of collective action and been made to appear in retrospect as natural platforms for that collective mobilization. Language, which reached its pinnacle as a foundation for regional political recognition in India in the second half of the twentieth century, has given way to the construction of new foundations for minority political recognition in the twenty-first century, exemplified by the creation of the new states of Chhattisgarh, Uttaranchal, and Jharkhand in November 2000 and Telangana in June 2014.[39]

Given these understandings of collective actions as performances of "state hailing" that produce and enable subject and identity formation, I ask why collective forms of assembly are so often assumed only to be protest against, opposition or resistance to, or rejections of authority, rather than also being understood as desires to contribute to or participate in policy making, or as appeals to elected officials or policy makers and efforts to hold officials accountable to their promises and to equitable implementation of existing legal and constitutional provisions. In answering this question, I place specific contemporary political practices—and their theorizations in relation to democracy—within longer histories of collective engagements with forms of authority in South Asia and within the colonial, historical, and social science literatures that have sought to understand them or contain and limit their impacts.

Theoretical Limits to "Resistance"

As the following chapters illustrate, despite frequently being described as "protests," many collective actions are efforts to seek recognition and inclusion. Yet, it is often in the interests of those in positions of authority to frame collective actions as rejections of (their) authority and as disrespect for existing institutions. These are framing mechanisms that function as methods for refusing recognition, silencing dissent, and denying expanded inclusion. The chapters that follow map this distinction by illustrating and exploring examples of efforts to seek political recognition and expand inclusion, attempts to establish and strengthen connections with or incorporation into networks of the state, and tactics for cultivating relationships with or collective influence over its representatives. They also track the varied government responses to these efforts. In approaching collective forms of action historically, the book takes seriously their roles not only in influencing the specific ways that democracy has come to be understood and practiced in India but also in continuing to shape the contours, meanings, and practices of engaged citizenship in India today.

Current scholarship encourages us to read collective action only as resistance, rejection, or rebellion, reflecting academic trends that Sherry Ortner characterizes as "dark theory." Ortner defines "dark anthropology" as "anthropology that emphasizes the harsh and brutal dimensions of human experience, and the structural and historical conditions that produce them," tracing its origins to the rise of "dark theory" more generally, defined as "theory that asks us to see the world almost entirely in terms of power, exploitation, and chronic pervasive inequality."[40] She identifies the writings of Karl Marx and Michel Foucault as exemplifying, as well as having shaped and perpetuated, this shift to dark theory. Writes Ortner, "Some of Foucault's work is an almost perfect exemplar of this concept, a virtually totalizing theory of a world in which power is in every crevice of life, and in which there is no outside to power."[41] Although acknowledging that Foucault's thinking shifted over the course of his career, Ortner maintains, "It is fair to say that it is the dark Foucault—the Foucault of the Panopticon, of *Discipline and Punish* (1977), of capillary power, and of multiple forms of governmentality—who has been having the greatest influence on sociocultural anthropological theory."[42] Actors who seek recognition, connections with, or incorporation into structures of state power—especially those from working-class, impoverished, peasant, or other marginalized origins—are thus regarded as suffering from "false consciousness" (Engels); as co-opted by bourgeois ideology (Marx), hegemonic consciousness (Gramsci), or ideological state apparatuses (Althusser); or as subjects of successful disciplinary discourses or practices (Foucault). In each case, the active desire for recognition and incorporation into state networks is regarded as passive ideological co-optation of the subject in question, ignoring other possible meanings of that goal.

Ortner contrasts dark theory with what Joel Robbins calls an "anthropology of the good," ending her analysis (which is particularly directed toward American anthropology) with a discussion of what she calls new forms of "anthropology of the good: the anthropology of critique, resistance, and activism."[43] In contrast to Ortner's turn, this book neither embraces dark theory nor offers an anthropology of the good. Instead, the book shifts attention to the many ways that people in India actively and self-consciously *seek* to be seen, heard, and recognized by the state. It focuses not only on the obstacles they encounter in attempting to gain such recognition but also on the ways that these efforts can and do alter the state. It also traces the resort to ever greater—and usually increasingly collective—efforts to actively achieve recognition and create connections (however heavily mediated) with the state, often leading to the escalation of efforts over weeks, months, years, or even decades, as in the case of the Telangana movement.[44] The result of this book's interventions is therefore a portrait of the Indian state that attends not simply to its ever-expanding powers and its increasingly micropolitical techniques of governance but also to the various forms of practice that seek—sometimes successfully—to surveil and place limits on the state and the forms of violence it condones, while also simultaneously seeking expansions of its interventions within the social and economic status quos.[45]

In approaching collective action in this way, I point to the widespread suspicion and cynicism directed toward the state within academic literature, suspicion ironically shared by those at opposite ends of the political spectrum—from anarchists on the Left (represented by prominent scholars such as James C. Scott and David Graeber) to libertarians and "limited-state" conservatives on the Right who seek to roll back government employment opportunities, state regulations, and the government administrative and regulatory bodies that generate them.[46] And yet, in the regions of South India where I have been living and doing research on and off for more than thirty years, many of my interlocutors continue to believe the state to be capable of providing individual opportunities and possibilities for social mobility, as well as catalyzing broader societal transformation. This belief is held by interlocutors I have spoken with on both the Right and the Left. People believe that the state has the capacity to act in ways that are socially and personally transformative, and they therefore believe in the utility of trying to persuade the state to act accordingly. In both the Telangana movement and the 2020–21 farmers' protests, the demands made were not for the overthrow of the state, but rather for dialogues with representatives of the state, for inclusion within the processes that would determine state policies, and for the fulfillment of earlier political promises that had not yet been realized.

Participants in the Telangana movement fervently believed that the new state would offer long-term benefits for them and their children. As Laxman, an auto-rickshaw driver who lived up the street from me, said on the evening of July 30, 2013, the day that the new state was approved by the United Progressive Alliance coalition government, amidst much jubilation in Hyderabad, "Now my children will have a future." Laxman is not alone in India in his belief in the power of the state to achieve social transformations. We can see this in the continued investment in India today in the affirmative action–style reservation quota system that governs public sector employment and admissions into government-aided educational institutions.[47] From 22.5 percent in 1950, the proportion of positions it governs has grown to nearly 60 percent in 2019.[48] Although this system was originally intended to be temporary, more and more groups have appealed to the state for recognition as historically marginalized communities.

Rather than disappearing, then, belief in government social engineering through the reservation quota system and in the power of the state to transform lives and the structure of society more generally has instead grown. This is true despite corruption, despite inequality, and despite neoliberalism and the growth of the informal sector. A long history of government employment offering one of the few routes for social mobility under British colonial rule no doubt plays a significant role in cultivating this view. Its legacy lives on in contemporary India, as new groups seek the mobility and security of the government employment that they saw previous generations experience. One Indian colleague, for example, told me about his father's reaction when he announced that he wanted to go to college to study history. His father, a government clerk, replied, "Why do you want to go to college? Only rich people go to college. You should get a government job, and then you'll be set for life." Although private sector employment since the liberalization of India's economy in the 1990s has offered significantly higher salaries, many in India still seek the stability and long-term security of public sector employment. Contestations over who should be eligible for reserved quotas for this employment, as well as for educational opportunities, remain one of the biggest fault lines of conflict in contemporary India.


Rethinking the Public Sphere: Collective Assembly
and the "Conditions of Listening"

Despite the ubiquity and long history of the wide range of forms of collective assembly in India and elsewhere, there has been surprisingly little effort to theorize their histories and significance in shaping the development, understanding, and practice of democracy today. Jürgen Habermas offered an early and remarkably influential history of the importance of coffeehouses within the development of democracy, arguing for their critical role in encouraging public debate and opinion making.[49] Yet the popularity of his work illustrates the fact that some practices—especially those that have been associated with bourgeois or mercantile engagements with the public sphere in placing limits on the aristocracy—have been authorized as more relevant to our understandings of the development and spread of democracy than others. Worldwide, there are many everyday practices and sites of communication and opinion making that have failed to be taken up for similar analysis. Habermas has rightly been critiqued for his exclusive interest in an idealized *bourgeois* public sphere and for his role in solidifying hegemonic liberal understandings of acceptable forms of participatory democratic practice.[50] Nancy Fraser, for example, demonstrates that competing "subaltern counterpublics" have always contested the norms of the bourgeois public sphere.[51]

Rather than seeing the public sphere as a space defined by the norms of the dominant masculine bourgeois society and reading the entrance of new and conflicting groups and interests as its decline (a common refrain among some historically dominant groups in contemporary India), Fraser suggests that we may be better served by attending to the sites where interactions not only of competing interests but also of competing *styles* of political participation occur. "Virtually from the beginning," she writes, "counterpublics contested the exclusionary norms of the bourgeois public, elaborating alternative *styles* of political behavior and alternative norms of public speech."[52] As a historian and anthropologist, I read this to mean that more careful genealogical tracing of the everyday practices and spaces used by various publics can help disrupt the ideological domination perpetuated by those segments of society that have traditionally held the reins of power even under the sign of "democracy." This means expanding our focus beyond the deliberative forms of speech action privileged by Habermas or those styles of communication that represent themselves as "rational" and portray their claims as free of emotion and directed toward the "common interest" or "universal" goals.

However, rather than attributing all differences of style to distinct "cultures," which the category of subaltern counterpublics implies, I depart from Fraser by arguing that some of the "differences" that have been assumed to be differences of *style* have instead been produced through failures of recognition.[53] When individuals and groups find that their speech actions and efforts to articulate their concerns are mocked, dismissed, or ignored, they are forced to find ways to amplify their voices to enable them to be heard by bureaucratic administrators, political leaders, and the general public or, to put it another way, to make it more difficult for their voices to continue to be ignored, as chapters 2 and 3 illustrate.

Similarly, Habermas's explicit interest in the bourgeois public sphere makes it clear that he recognizes the existence of other kinds of public spheres, most notably a "plebian" public sphere that he originally considered "a variant [of the bourgeois public sphere] that in a sense was suppressed in the historical process."[54] He suggests, however, that the relevance of these other publics to the history, practice, and theorization of democracy is both relatively recent and a product of technological transformations, arguing that it is only television that enabled these other publics to become significant factors worth examining. He writes, "The physical presence of the masses demonstrating in the squares and streets was able to generate revolutionary power only to the degree to which television made its presence ubiquitous."[55] In part, Habermas's downplaying of the relationship between corporeal mass assemblies in public space and the history of democracy comes from his privileging of speech action over all other forms of communication, and in part it emerges out of his understanding of the differences in the historical visibility of bourgeois and plebian public spheres. Either way, it ignores the many pre-televisual historical examples of the revolutionary power of collective assemblies in public space, including the American and French Revolutions, and the influence of coal miners, dockworkers, and railway employees' strikes on the expansion of democratic participation to include the working classes in Europe and the United States.[56] Characterizing these as separate "spheres," however, runs the risk of implying that mass demonstrations are a direct function of one's class status (plebian vs. bourgeois), rather than a result of the reception one's voice and interests receive.

In contrast to both Fraser's emphasis on differences of *style* and Habermas's association of specific communicative methods with particular *spheres*, I problematize the implied temporality of subject formation within liberalism. When one's interests are already well represented and one can be certain that one's voice will be heard, there is little need to mobilize collectively in the streets. However, when one's voice and interests repeatedly fail to find recognition, an alternative is to make one's articulations more difficult to ignore by joining together in collective communicative action. My ethnographic and archival examples take seriously the words and actions of my interlocutors in Telangana and elsewhere by giving primary attention to the rallies, processions, collective seeking of audiences with government officials, occupations of road spaces, halting of trains, and massing of bodies in public spaces that they see as fundamental to democracy. Close attention to the histories of these practices also suggests that Habermas makes a too hasty dismissal of pre-televised forms of mass political practice and their representations, however much television may indeed have produced qualitative changes in those representations.

The examples offered in this book prompt us to recognize ways in which other forms of communication—like the movement of people and vehicles or the prevention of their movement—have been used to broadcast political messages, hold officials accountable, compel dialogue, and recalibrate relations of power, even prior to the emergence of televisual forms. They make clear that as effective mediums of political communication, techniques such as mass processions and road or rail blockades function in India both via their performative effects and through their temporary control of communicative channels—telegraphing political messages over long distances by preventing and regulating the smooth flow of traffic and providing opportunities to cultivate, test, and make visible the effectiveness of collective networks and relationships. Attention to these less-privileged forms of practice takes seriously Partha Chatterjee's argument that we need to give equal attention to the forms of popular political practice that make up what he calls "the politics of the governed."[57] However, in placing particular practices within longer historical genealogies, it also disrupts the easy distinctions that have been made between the *practices* of "civil society" and those of "political society," making it more difficult to draw clear lines between the two. Chatterjee characterizes the practices of civil society as those stemming from "the closed association of modern elite groups, sequestered from the wider popular life of the communities, walled up within enclaves of civic freedom and rational law."[58] Members of civil society, writes Chatterjee, frame their demands in terms of *universal* claims and create hegemonic understandings of acceptable norms of participatory democratic practice. Members of political society, in contrast, "transgress the strict lines of legality in struggling to live and work" and use their positions within specific populations subject to governance to make *particular* demands of the state and ask for exceptions to existing laws.[59]

Close analysis of the historical trajectory of specific political practices like alarm chain pulling (chapter 5); road and rail blockades (chapter 6); processions, rallies, and the ticketless travel that supports them (chapter 7) shows that, although many commentators today would consider such forms of action to be characteristic of political society, their roots as forms of political practice often lie squarely within the Indian civil society of the early twentieth century. These historically informed analytic methods illustrate the fact that such practices are usually employed only after recourse to the types of practices typically associated with civil society have been unsuccessful—practices such as efforts to participate within public debates and deliberations and sending letters, petitions, and memoranda. Rather than being used only to demand exceptions to existing legal structures, there is evidence that collective assemblies are often organized to ensure that members of marginalized groups receive the *same* recognition within existing legal structures as is accorded to those in more privileged positions.[60] Bringing Chatterjee into conversation with Nancy Fraser, I interpret Chatterjee's interventions to mean that many of the limitations of both historical and contemporary analyses of democracy stem from the specific sites and channels of communication that are privileged for study at the expense of others.[61] The ethnographic and historical examples offered in this book expand our understandings of the sites and practices of political communication to illustrate both the politics spawned by governmentality and the forms of governmentality spawned by politics.

## Genealogies of Democracy in India

In contrast to the heavily ideological approaches to the history of democracy that have foregrounded liberalism, Timothy Mitchell offers a materialist genealogy for democracy that does not rely primarily on a history of ideas.[62] He introduces new methods for approaching the study of democracy by attending to the processes and material conditions that enabled various individuals and groups to come together collectively to help shape more inclusive structures of rule.[63] Mitchell focuses on the ways that coal miners, railwaymen, and dockworkers were able to demand recognition and inclusion within political decision making from the 1880s onward through their ability to restrict the movement of coal—a crucial commodity on which urban centers were fundamentally dependent. He argues that it was their particular connections and alliances that enabled the workers to control the movement of this essential commodity. Their ability to prevent coal from reaching its destination through strikes and work stoppages, thereby paralyzing urban centers, brought about the advent of both universal suffrage and the modern welfare state.[64] In *Hailing the State*, I extend Mitchell's method by approaching democracy not as a fixed and modular set of institutions put into place in *response* to such demands for inclusion, but rather as the various forms of practice through which actors establish connections and build alliances to produce greater inclusion within ongoing processes of collective decision making.

In embracing Mitchell's materialist analytic framework, I am following my Telangana informants in regarding democracy as something one *does* and in regarding access to spaces of participation and inclusion therefore as a fundamental part of what democracy means. As G. Haragopal emphasizes, "Democracy doesn't just mean elections. Elections are only one part of democracy. The real essence of a truly democratic system is that people must be able to continuously voice their problems and their turmoil, and democracy must provide a wide range of opportunities for people to communicate their concerns every day."[65] This approach sees democracy's history not simply as the introduction of electoral institutions that were earlier absent, but rather as a dynamic and ongoing set of contestations over recognition, inclusion, and voice within structures of decision making and economic transformation and over the spaces, mechanisms, and institutions that extend opportunities for participation.[66] In the Indian context, most existing histories of Indian democracy begin with Indian independence from Britain in 1947, or with the adoption of the Indian Constitution in 1950 or the first parliamentary elections in 1951–52, with very limited attention to earlier periods. As Atul Kohli observes, "India's 'transition' to democracy in the 1940s is understudied and ought to be further researched."[67] He points out that "historians have often left such issues to political scientists," and political scientists (and, I would add, many sociologists and anthropologists) "often do not concern themselves with the 'past,' the domain of historians."[68] There has therefore been little effort to connect post-1947 political practices with their pre-independence precursors. The little attention that has been paid to pre-independence democratic practices has focused almost exclusively on representative electoral institutions introduced under British colonial rule, understood to "prefigure" the "age of democracy in India."[69] These included the appointment (and eventually election) of Indian representatives to municipal boards and provincial councils in British India in the latter half of the nineteenth century and eventually the establishment of a Legislative Assembly, for which elections were first held in 1920.[70]

The methods offered by anthropology, however, offer promising opportunities for rewriting existing analyses and theories of the everyday practices of democracy by including corporeal communicative practices like garjanas, dharnas, yātras, and rāstā and rail roko actions. In bringing ethnographic approaches to bear on the study of democracy, Julia Paley and her collaborators demonstrate how anthropological methods can advance our theories of democracy by forcing us to account for practices as they happen on the ground, placing together subjects of analysis that are otherwise typically kept apart and thereby bringing them into a single framework. By situating "powerful and non-powerful actors within the same frame" and "examining how they selectively choose and resignify elements of a globally circulating discourse," we are forced to question the dominant representations of how democracy works worldwide.[71] Thomas Blom Hansen similarly emphasizes the importance of starting with practices on the ground when he writes, "Performances and spectacles in public spaces—from the central squares to the street corner in the slum, from speeches to images—must move to the center of our attention."[72]

## "Combinations" and Law: Genealogies of Collective Political Practice

The existing repertoires of political action routinely employed in the world's largest democracy are practices drawn from a long—but largely unrecognized and certainly undertheorized—history of practices in the South Asian subcontinent. This makes not just the region's political history but also its long history of intellectual thought and scholarship particularly rich contexts for examining the encounter of such practices with the new ideological, legal, and policing mechanisms introduced in the nineteenth century to curb the power of what the British routinely characterized as "combinations." Work stoppages, mass migrations, and collective strikes to shut down commerce and transportation are evident in South Asian archival sources from at least the seventeenth century, perhaps even earlier, and were clearly used to make representations to state authorities at the highest levels (see chapter 4). My growing awareness of the influences of earlier practices on the ways that people understand, talk about, and "do" or "perform" democracy in contemporary India, even in the face of the many shifts brought about by colonial and postcolonial political reconfigurations, has propelled me to rely centrally on historical methodologies in this book. This not only enables me to place contemporary practices into broader historical perspective but also facilitates an examination of the ways that scholarly writing is complicit in the framing of collective action almost exclusively as resistance.

Collective public performances of local opinions in response to East India Company (EIC) policies and procedures continue to be evident throughout the eighteenth and early nineteenth centuries. Local merchants and artisans routinely sought to negotiate with the East India Company-State and influence its decisions.[73] They did so by implementing a wide range of collective forms of communication in response to pricing, type, and timing of payments (e.g., payments for woven goods in overpriced grain rather than in cash); procurement systems; corrupt intermediaries; and overly invasive control of types and quality of goods, particularly in the wake of the EIC's establishment of a monopoly over trade by the end of the eighteenth century. These methods included petitions to the Board of Trade, British residents, and district collectors, as well as collective deputations and oral testimonies. When these petitions, deputations, and testimonies failed to be acknowledged, artisans and others subject to the EIC's administration used a variety of means to amplify their messages and make them more likely to be received. Well-organized processions from village to village were used to gather together larger groups that would then travel to meet with a higher authority to convey concerns in person and lobby to have them acknowledged and addressed.[74] Collective abandonment of homes or workplaces; collective relocation to an open space or temple outside an urban center; migration to neighboring territories; prevention of the movement of commodities through boycotts organized among porters, boatmen, palanquin bearers and others; and the stationing of those with grievances outside the office or residence of a person in authority in hopes of compelling a face-to-face meeting are all examples of historical strategies that have left substantial imprints, both in existing archival records and on contemporary repertoires, as part I demonstrates. By the nineteenth century, Indians also began to use newly available technologies, particularly the railway system, as communicative networks to amplify their voices and opinions. Part II illustrates the ways that practices such as alarm chain pulling, rail blockades, and ticketless travel that were initially regarded as criminal eventually came to be redefined by the government as political, providing officials with new strategies for confronting them and historians like myself with opportunities for tracking changes in the political.

East India Company officials—and later, Government of India administrators—referred to these collective actions as "combinations" or, less generously, as "insurgencies," "mutinies," "insurrections," "revolts," or "rebellions," even when their participants sought only to gain an audience with officials in circumstances in which earlier communicative efforts were ignored or refused. Because administrators saw such actions as challenges to their own authority and sovereignty, their first recourse was usually to seek methods of breaking or delegitimizing the ability of Indians to act collectively. Indeed,

British administrators often refused to acknowledge collective forms of representation or were quick to send in military troops, frequently insisting that Indians with grievances should represent only themselves as individuals, rather than cooperating collectively (see chapter 3). This state response suggests that the colonial invocation of liberalism, with its emphasis on the autonomous individual as the only legitimate subject of both legal and political action, offered a convenient mechanism for British authorities seeking to derail the surprisingly effective collective forms of representation that they encountered in British India. When they did acknowledge collective representations, they often misread or intentionally construed such group actions as "communal" in nature. Although studies have questioned colonial constructions of communalism, some scholars are still quick to associate (often dismissively) collective actions in India with caste or religious-based identitarian politics even when this may not be the case.[75] Although not denying that caste or religious connections can play a role by intersecting with substantive claims, this book approaches collective claims as not always premised on already reified prepolitical identities, but as emerging in relation to processes of alliance-building and the establishment of new connections, often involving substantive claims (see chapter 4). The book therefore seeks to identify the concerns that preceded and precipitated collective action, rather than assuming a communal or identitarian motivation post facto.

## Democracy and the Representation of Collective Assembly

The World Trade Organization protests in 1999, Arab Spring (2010–12), Occupy Movement (2011–12), Black Lives Matter mobilizations (2013–present), and Umbrella Revolution in Hong Kong (2014) are just a few of the collective mobilizations that have stimulated renewed interest in understanding the political significance of bodies massed in public.[76] They have encouraged a return to scholarship on crowds, as well as new inquiries into the relationship of public space to democracy and representation.[77] William Mazzarella's critical overview of crowd scholarship, for example, challenges our inheritance of the nineteenth century's scholarly legacy that saw crowds as subject to primal—even pathological—emotions and therefore as the antithesis of reason.[78] The history he offers suggests that crowds and their strong associations with "emergent energies [that] threaten the strenuously achieved autonomous liberal subject," play a key role within a "story about changing forms of political representation" and help shore up "an underlying narrative about an epochal shift in the deployment of modern power" that centers on the autonomy of the individual.[79]

What reading Mazzarella together with Timothy Mitchell brings into relief, however, is the fact that the advent of the celebration of the modern autonomous individual occurs at the same moment as the appearance of the successful political demands by large groups of workers on whom urban life crucially depended. Mazzarella points to recent liberal and postliberal desires to rehabilitate "the political possibilities of the masses" toward democratic ends, the former by turning them into "autonomous enlightened citizens . . . nurtured in the bosom of reasonable civic assemblies," and the latter, exemplified for Mazzarella by Michael Hardt and Antonio Negri's writings on the "multitude," through an investment in a sort of pure politics "imagined as an absence of mediation."[80] This book offers a third possibility. What Hardt, Negri, and Mazzarella share is an investment in imagining new possibilities for political configurations. These new possibilities appear in Hardt and Negri's writings as hopeful investments in "revolutionary politics . . . that can create a new world" in the future,[81] and in Mazzarella as an ethics that is situated in relation to an abstracted "moment of generative possibility in all social relations"—one that is "not external to the mediations of structured relations" but rather is "a moment in their enactment."[82] I take this to mean that social theorists play an important role in articulating the thinkable and therefore the realm of the possible and that, together with anthropologists' and historians' careful attentions to configurations of possibilities in other places and other times, they can offer new models of practice for the future. Before we give up on the present in favor of a future that has yet to be imagined and can only be grasped in the most abstract terms, however, this book argues that we still have substantially more work to do in concretely recognizing and understanding the ways in which social relations and forms of mediation within democratic polities actually do work in practice today. We also need to acknowledge the specific ways in which our theories and descriptions of democracy perpetuate particular ideologies of the unmediated autonomous individual in their failure to capture these social relations and forms of mediation.

Despite the renewed interest in collective forms of assembly and the widespread recognition of their historical roles in bringing democracies into being, collective corporeal forms of assembly and communication are still rarely theorized as playing a significant role within the *ongoing* routine processes and *internal* institutions of democracies. An important question is why we assume that collective assemblies are oppositional movements against the state, rather than efforts to reach out to the state's representatives and be recognized or heard by them. As the French democratic theorist and historian of political thought Bernard Manin writes in *The Principles of Representative Government*, the fact that representative democracy today gives no institutional role to the assembly of people, is "what most obviously distinguishes it from the democracy of the ancient city-states."[83] But we have yet to account for why and how this significant shift in the meaning and practice of democracy occurred. Manin's project involves tracing how elected representative forms of government, recognized by their founders as inegalitarian and elitist and therefore as the antithesis to democracy, have today come to be understood as both egalitarian and as one form (or even the only viable form) of democracy.[84] An equally important parallel project, and one that this book initiates, is tracing the changing concepts of the political that have pushed popular collective assemblies out of our understandings of the theory and practice of democracy.[85]

In continuing to be misunderstood and ignored as playing a significant role within "actually existing" ongoing routine processes of contemporary democracies, collective forms of political assembly are too often seen, as William Mazzarella argues, as belonging to an "earlier sepia-tinted version of industrial modernity," growing out of a bygone era.[86] At best, forms of collective assembly are today recognized as *external forces on* democracy or as playing a role in the *transition to* democracy. Jeffrey Schnapp and Matthew Tiews capture this widely accepted view when they write that historical shifts in the role of "mass assembly and collective social action" and the representation of "the equation between crowds and modernity" today "assign to large-scale mass political actions a fallback function restricted to times of exception (war, acute social conflicts, and the like)."[87] Judith Butler, writing in the wake of the Tahrir Square demonstrations in Egypt in 2011, likewise defines bodies massed in public as efforts to "redeploy the space of appearance in order to contest and negate the existing forms of political legitimacy"—rather than as a reification of state sovereignty or a desire to be recognized by the existing state and be actively (willingly, even eagerly) interpellated into its networks and included within its legal structures and ongoing processes of decision making.[88] Dipesh Chakrabarty—who has done much to model the value of tracing historical genealogies of contemporary forms of political practice into the pre-independence period—nevertheless similarly regards the escalation of collective strategies to gain recognition and inclusion as "techniques of challenging the sovereignty" of those in power.[89] Dario Azzellini and Marina Sitrin argue that slogans like "They don't represent us!" have been embraced "in mobilizations all over the world" and that these "are not phrased as rejections of specific political representatives, but as expressions of a general rejection of the logic of representation."[90] More recently, Jason Frank argues that "the resonant claim—sometimes implicit, at other times explicit—made by popular assemblies across an entire history of democratic enactments, from the storming of the Bastille to today's popular insurgencies, is: 'you do not represent us!'"[91] These assertions ignore the many examples—including those offered throughout this book—of people massing in public to express the idea that *because* you represent us, you must hear us or give us audience. This book argues not only that these claims are not the same but also that it is much easier for bureaucrats, elected representatives, and even elites more generally to dismiss or ignore the communicative efforts of those who are seen as rejecting their authority than it is to dismiss those who are recognized as embracing the legitimacy and responsibilities of those who formally represent them. In this sense, social scientists and historians must be careful not to frame collective assemblies in ways that align with the interests of those who do not wish to acknowledge or hear the communicative efforts of those they ostensibly represent.

Given the absence of formally acknowledged institutional roles for collective assembly within contemporary democratic processes, our historical memory of its earlier significance as a form of representative practice within democracy has also largely disappeared. Paul Gilje, for example, shows that in the decades leading up to American independence and continuing into the first five or six decades of the newly independent American republic, the belief was widespread that popular collective assemblies and street politics, even riots, were essential to preventing tyranny and maintaining a check on the excesses of the state.[92] In the wake of the American farmers' protests of 1786 and 1787 that came to be known as Shay's Rebellion, Thomas Jefferson wrote to James Madison that "a little rebellion now and then is a good thing, and as necessary in the political world as storms in the physical."[93] Although not everyone shared his view, Jefferson was certainly not alone in his suggestion that collective expressions of popular opinion in the street played a regular and routine role within a healthy republic. His belief that "the people are the only censors of their governors" and that "even their errors will tend to keep these to the true principles of their institutions" was widespread enough to sanction public crowd actions and even riots in the eyes of both elite and plebian community members.[94] Gilje suggests that this acceptance of the "politicization of the common man, clearly linked to the heavy dependence on crowd activity from 1765 to 1776," played a crucial role in compelling early American political leaders to "reformulate their own conception of good government" and expand decision-making processes to become even more inclusive. "By 1774," he continues, "laborers, seamen, and mechanics assumed that they had a voice in the affairs of the province, and the local congresses, committees, and conventions could do little without gaining the assent of the newly sovereign people." In short, he argues, "it was the persistent use of mobs and street politics that propelled the common man into the political arena."[95] His analysis shows that outdoor forms of street politics were not only essential to the politics of the American revolution but also the *only* means through which common folk were able to make their voices heard.

Bernard Manin demonstrates that thinkers as varied as Jean-Jacques Rousseau (1712–78); the American founding father, James Madison (1751–1836); and the leading political theorist of the French Revolution, Emmanuel Siéyès (1748–1836), all viewed systems of elected representation as quite radically opposed to what was understood as democracy in the late eighteenth century.[96] Madison, for example, characterized this difference as resting on "the total exclusion of the people in their collective capacity" from participation in the modern republic he was helping form.[97] And Siéyès, writes Manin, "persistently stressed the 'huge difference' between democracy, in which the citizens make the laws themselves, and the representative system of government, in which they entrust the exercise of their power to elected representatives."[98] Manin concludes by observing, "What is today referred to as a crisis of political representation appears in a different light if we remember that representative government was conceived in explicit opposition to government by the people, and that its central institutions have remained unchanged."[99] By taking us back to the contrasts made in the eighteenth century between indirect representative and direct democratic forms of governance, Manin is able to capture earlier understandings of democracy as "government by the people" and to show that the elected forms of representation that emerged in the wake of the English, American, and French Revolutions and that are today seen as "indirect government by the people" were once understood in radically different terms.

Today, in the United States and much of Europe, the term *democracy* has gradually come to be associated almost exclusively with electoral processes of determining representative government. Yet in South Asia, despite widespread investment in electoral processes and participation in voting at far higher rates than in the United States, elections are not the only or even the primary way in which many Indians conceptualize democracy. This suggests that the frameworks through which democracy is understood in India, shaped by the particularities of India's unique history, differ from understandings that have come to dominate contemporary Euro-American theoretical writings and practice. Indeed, ethnographic engagements with those from a wide range of economic and social backgrounds—along with archival research into the longer histories of many of the practices outlined in this book—have challenged my own understanding of what democracy means and pushed my inquiries beyond the study of elections to gain a better understanding of how people practice democracy in India *between* elections.

## Democracy and Public Space

Krishnamurthy, a teacher I have known since the mid-1990s, made this clear to me one afternoon in 2012 as we sat talking over a cup of tea. "Democratic spaces in Hyderabad have become more and more limited since 1987, and even more restricted since 1997," he declared.[100] Recalling an earlier era in which public space was more freely available to be used for everyday forms of political expression, he narrated the recent emergence of more restrictive government attitudes toward processions. "On earlier occasions people were permitted to go up to the Assembly, that was in the 70s and early 80s," he explained. Now, in contrast, he continued, "there are court orders which do not allow any processions at all. In Hyderabad, in fact, in the entire Telangana, the democratic activity had come to a standstill, after '87 all over northern Telangana. And the situation has worsened after '97, further deteriorated." Even in the increasingly rare instances when permission was granted, he lamented that the spaces in which political activity was allowed had dramatically contracted. "Now," continued Krishnamurthy, "if you want to take out a procession . . . only one route is permitted: Lower Tank Bund Road via Dhobi Ghat to Indira Park."[101]

In his view, however, the resurgence of the Telangana movement from 2009 has reinvigorated democracy. "With great difficulty during the Telangana movement we could create small spaces, and therefore people could come, meet, organize dharnas, hold discussions, it has become a little easier," he maintained. His comments are illustrative of an emphasis on space and the collecting together of people in urban public space as fundamental features of democracy. Venkat, a middle-aged human rights activist in

Hyderabad, echoed this emphasis when he told me, "Aspirations of Telangana people, that we want separate state, is conveyed democratically in diverse forums, not just elections. People, in their own way, they conveyed it through their festivals, in their rituals. In a very democratic way they are holding dharna. There was no violence anywhere. [Once] all people came out into the street one day [to perform a roadblock] and they cooked their food [there]. I always say that [Telangana] is one of the greatest democratic movements in the world so far that I have ever witnessed. Not even in the China revolution did this take place."[102] Startling to those for whom China and its revolution represent the antithesis of democracy, rather than a pinnacle, Venkat's comments reinforce the idea that democracy is understood not simply in "local" terms but also in transnational terms that differ quite dramatically from understandings in those parts of the world that have historically laid claim to the founders, promoters, and protectors of democracy.[103]

In an era in which much attention to the political has shifted to the virtual worlds of social media activism, the democratic theorist John Parkinson argues that democracy still "depends to a surprising extent on the availability of physical, public space, even in our allegedly digital world," and demonstrates that this physical space is currently under threat.[104] Using data from eleven capital cities across six continents, he traces increased restrictions on the uses of public space, suggesting that many of these restrictions apply only "when we act as politically engaged citizens, not when we act as shoppers or employees on a lunch break."[105] As more and more elected officials and city planners envision transformations of their urban settlements into "world-class" cities like Hyderabad, he predicts that such restrictions are likely to increase. Of particular concern to Parkinson is the growing inaccessibility of public buildings, and the importance of public spaces that are adjacent to political buildings.[106] He emphasizes the importance to democracy of not only prioritizing public spaces for political uses by engaged citizens but also ensuring their visibility and proximity to decision makers.[107]

Railways, Roads, and the Indian Political

In focusing on methods used to amplify voices and telegraph political messages across both distances and social worlds, this book is also concerned with the ways that political practices create, engage, and materialize larger networks of circulation and communication to enable marginalized individuals to gain audiences with elected representatives and other government officials. The methods explored throughout the book convey political messages through communicative circuits that connect towns and cities to one another and to their respective hinterlands and also make visible powerful networks and relationships. Rather than focusing exclusively on the more conventional communicative channels of print, audio, cinematic, televisual, and social media, sites that privilege speech action and images and that have generated entire departments and schools of scholarship, I turn my focus to the less thoroughly studied domains of road and railway networks as forms of public space. In doing so, I focus on these domains not in their capacities as networks of transport but rather to show the various ways that these spaces have been used as powerful mediums for the performance of political communication.

The significance for politics of the spaces of transportation networks was first made clear to me as I completed research for an earlier book on the formation of the first Telugu linguistic state in 1953.[108] The death of Andhra State activist Potti Sreeramulu in Madras (now Chennai) on December 15, 1952, was the culmination of a well-publicized fifty-eight-day fast, and as news of its fatal conclusion began to spread, enormous assemblies of people began to gather in towns throughout coastal Andhra as far as 700 kilometers to the north of Madras. In four of those towns, dozens of people were killed or injured by police bullets as authorities struggled to maintain order. Yet almost all of the assemblies, injuries, and police violence occurred *in and around railway stations* on the main east coast Madras–Calcutta railway line. Police fired on assembled crowds at the railway stations in Nellore, Anakapalle, Waltair (Visakhapatnam), and Srikakulam, all important stations along the main railway line, resulting in deaths in each location and pointing to the centrality of transport networks within the history of the political in India.[109] As I learned more, I realized that in 1952, the railway station served as the most important communicative node connecting towns to the wider world. Newspapers, mail, and examination results arrived by train, and news stories and headlines were often posted on a board in the station. News obtained firsthand from someone who had just arrived from a place where something had happened was considered much more trustworthy than the news printed in newspapers (seen as linked to specific political factions) or broadcast on the radio (seen as controlled by the government). Men often came to the station daily to meet their friends for a cup of tea or coffee, read the paper, and discuss the day's news, making the station a kind of coffee-house and center for the circulation of news and political views.

The Indian Railways offer a particularly important set of sites for tracing the genealogies of everyday forms of political practice. First and foremost, the vast size of the Indian Railways has given them a central role within everyday life in India. Not only do the Indian Railways carry more than seventeen million passengers per day but they have also been recognized as the largest employer in the world.[110] Historically, the Indian railway system was one of the very first direct interactions that many people had with the British colonial state. Railway stations—and the platforms, tea shops, bookstalls, and surrounding businesses through which they were integrated into local contexts—quickly became important new sites of public space in India as they spread during the second half of the nineteenth century. Later, during the first half of the twentieth century, railway stations provided a crucial forum for Gandhi and other nationalist leaders to arouse popular support for the anticolonial movement. Leaders traveled from station to station, giving public addresses from the backs of trains. Indian railway stations have been imagined as social spaces that extend people's domestic contexts; as intra-national "in-between" sites that bring individuals of all languages, classes, castes, and ethnicities together as members of a single Indian nation; and as one of the most important historical locations for integrating the larger world into local contexts via the newspapers, mail service, telegraphs, goods, passengers, and ideas conveyed by the railways. Under British rule, the railways were also a primary site for the inscription of what have been described as new structures of identity, including the "castefication of wage labor," racially based strategies of employment, and new class divisions shaped by the establishment of separate refreshment rooms, water fountains, and train compartments.[111] As the most essential form of transportation in India, the railways and the stations that connect them to local communities have provided a new communicative context for the circulation and transmission of news and rumor, for everyday routine social and economic exchange, and for unprecedented displays of collective political activity.

As the railways began to spread in the second half of the nineteenth century, their significance not only for transportation but also, even more importantly, for bringing remote locations "into . . . communication" was widely recognized, "opening up the country by means of extensions into hitherto isolated places."[112] It is therefore not surprising that railways should also have been early sites of political engagement. The Disorders Inquiry Committee of 1919–1920 reported,

Attacks on communications were in many cases motivated by sheer *anti-Government* feeling. The railway is considered, quite rightly, a Government institution and railway damage is in these cases simply a part of the destruction of Government property. . . . In the country districts the railway afforded almost the only opportunity for destruction of property other than Indian-owned private property, and the easiest and most tempting opportunity for loot. At night it was also the most difficult, of all the forms of violence, to discover or prevent; at the approach of an armoured train, the mobs could hide in the crops and return when the train had left.[113]

Today the Indian Railways continue to be seen by many as a key site for political communication. The chief minister of Bengal and two-time railway minister, Mamata Banerjee, noted in 2010, "Railways is a soft target as it is very visible. We lose substantial revenue due to frequent rail-rokos (stop the trains) on various issues where there is no connection with the railways. If any local issue happens, grievances find their outlet on railways."[114] Indeed, in its reach and penetration into India's hinterlands, the great visibility of the Indian Railways as a representative of the central government has made it one of the most convenient political targets from its very earliest days. Ranajit Guha shows this to be true almost immediately after construction of the very first railway line in India in 1853, even among those who directly benefited from its presence:

There can be no doubt about the fact that the introduction of railways added considerably to income and employment in the Santal country. . . . For the Santals this provided an opportunity to extricate themselves from the state of landlessness, low wages and bonded labour into which they had fallen. . . . Yet when violence [during the Santal rebellion] actually broke out in July 1855 the beneficiaries seem to have had no hesitation about slaying the goose that laid the golden eggs for them. . . . Railway works were among the very first and most frequently destroyed objects mentioned in the reports received from the disturbed areas within the first week of the uprising.[115]

This targeting of the railways—and, more recently, roads—as a form of communication with the state continues today. Recent actions by Telangana state advocates and opponents in south India, migrant laborers in Bihar, minority groups in Rajasthan, and farmers across India illustrate the ongoing importance of these networks of transportation as widely used mechanisms for political communication.[116]

The railways as sites for political practice also function in another spatially significant way. Using Henri Lefebvre's "conception of the state as a 'spatial framework' of power," Manu Goswami writes about how the railways helped consolidate the Indian state as a single conceptual and material space while at the same time reconfiguring it within "a Britain-centered global economy," producing and reinforcing "internal differentiation and fragmentation," and "spawn[ing] a new uneven economic geography."[117] Precisely because railways were "crucial instruments for the consolidation of political and military domination within colonial India,"[118] they quickly became media for the expression of political opinions and targets for political resistance and protest. By linking regions throughout India to a single network of communication, the railways also made themselves available for the rapid communication of political messages. Halting a train in one location enabled the broadcast of a message up and down the entire length of a railway line and forced those from other regions of India to pay attention to the cause of a delay. Grievances from one locality could be rapidly broadcast and transmitted to new audiences and locations across a mobile landscape. Such actions affected passengers from different regions who were on the train and those living in far distant locations. They also generalized concerns that might otherwise have remained locally contained. From localized immediate concerns over overcrowding in third-class railway carriages, alarm chain pulling, for example, was eventually popularized in ways that linked local concerns with more generalized translocal politics, such as the anticolonial movement and later regional movements, as chapter 5 demonstrates.

Although the use of rail lines for political communication has a history in India nearly as long as the railways themselves, with the increase in road travel, roads, too, became media for transmitting political messages.[119] Streets and intersections have become sites for rallies, processions, and roadblocks, with buses and cars targeted rather than trains to telegraph political messages by blocking and delaying passengers. The practice of letting air out of bus tires, known locally in Telugu as gāli tīyaḍam (lit., "taking out air"), is frequently used to create a rapid roadblock (chapter 6). Buses—run by state bus companies—are typically targeted for state-level concerns, whereas the centrally run railways are reserved for national-level central government issues. During the Telangana movement, mahā rāstā roko actions (great road blockades) blocked not just single intersections but entire lengths of national highways, ranging from 115 to 250 kilometers (chapter 6), and political pilgrimages (yātras and padayātras) often use both roads and mass ticketless rail travel to enable participants from distant cities to join rallies elsewhere (chapter 7).[120]

Although much work still needs to be done to expand the ways in which we approach the study of political communication between elections to capture the many practices used to attract the attention of state representatives and establish connections with them, I am fortunately not alone in these efforts. Jonathan Shapiro Anjaria, for example, has shown that "the street is not only a product of the disciplinary techniques of rational governance" but also "an outcome of a negotiated process."[121] His intimate ethnographic work among street hawkers in Mumbai points to the very incomplete execution, and even failure, of projects of governmentality, suggesting that the hegemony that scholars attribute to ideological state apparatuses or to middle-class visions of urban governance are not always victorious. Careful ethnographic and historical engagements of this sort offer dramatic revisions to dominant understandings of citizenship and governmentality.[122] Some may see the failure of political leaders and members of entitled classes to control and shape cities to match their visions of global centers of capital as a sign of the failure of Indian governance, but the careful treatment of the claims made by a wide range of actors seeking recognition from state officials and inclusion in state processes and decision making instead suggests that we can also read this as a kind of success of a more inclusive type of governance when viewed through other eyes. This is the perspective I bring to the analysis of the success of those who have felt excluded from government spaces, universities, and the rapid urban economic growth that has occurred in cities like Hyderabad across India. In helping expand participation within existing structures of governance, state-hailing practices can be understood along with other forms of democratic participation as referendums on how such growth is distributed.[123]

## Organization of the Book

The evidence offered in the chapters that follow suggest that it often takes much greater effort on the part of marginalized groups to make their voices heard and their concerns considered. Escalating strategies to amplify communicative efforts can help create conditions and spaces where marginalized interests can be heard, recognized, and brought into public discussion. This process of recognition, which I refer to as "political arrival," can take months, years, or even decades to achieve. Using historical and ethnographic examples drawn from the world's largest democracy, I argue that to understand and theorize democracy—in India and elsewhere—we must move beyond a focus on elections and forms of "indoor" deliberative and associational politics. These academic foci have pushed outdoor corporeal collective assembly out of our understandings of the history and theory of democracy, though not out of its practice.

This book therefore views collective forms of assembly that seek state recognition not as the antithesis to a healthy democracy, or as external signs of ill health that threaten liberal democratic sovereignty from the outside, but rather as fundamental and ongoing mechanisms for political representation and inclusion and for the shaping and reshaping of the state. I argue that efforts to theorize democracy must take into account not just what happens during elections but also that which occurs *between* elections. The book is therefore organized around seven sets of practices: (1) sit-ins (dharna) and hunger strikes (nirāhāra dīkṣa); (2) efforts to meet or gain audience (*samāvēśam*) with or present a petition or representation (*vinatipatram, vijñapti,* or *vijñāpana[m]*) to someone in a position of authority; (3) mass open-air public meetings (garjana); (4) strikes (samme, bandh, hartāl); (5) alarm chain pulling in the Indian railways; (6) road and rail blockades (rāstā and rail roko agitations); and (7) rallies, processions, and pilgrimages to sites of power (yātra, padayātra), along with the mass ticketless travel that often enables these gatherings. I trace genealogies of each of these forms of contemporary practice, mapping shifts in each over time, to make a series of interventions that explore the influences of these practices on the ways that democracy has come to be understood and practiced in India today. Particular attention is given to moments in which the meanings of practices are altered by shifting understandings of the criminal and the political.

Research for this book was conducted over the academic year 2008–9 and during the summers of 2007, 2012, 2013, and 2017, building on earlier fieldwork in 1995–97, 1999–2000, 2002, and 2004. Research in Telangana, Andhra Pradesh, Tamil Nadu, Uttar Pradesh, and Delhi was supplemented by archival research in the British Library in London. Archival collections in the National Archives of India (Railway, Public Works Department, and Home Political series), the Nehru Memorial Museum and Library (All India Congress Committee collection), the Indian Railway Museum in New Delhi, and Government Railway Police and private archival collections in Nellore, Secunderabad, Hyderabad, and Lucknow provided the foundation for extensive ethnographic and oral history interviews with Government Railway Police, Railway Protection Force officers and administrators, and Indian Railway officials in Secunderabad, Nellore, Lucknow, and Delhi, as well as with social and political activists, party leaders, and members and former members of human rights and student political groups in Hyderabad, Warangal,

Nellore, Lucknow, and Delhi. Although many of the questions in the chapters that follow emerged from my ethnographic encounters, historical and textual methods have played a significant role in developing the answers.

In chapter 1, "Sit-In Demonstrations and Hunger Strikes: From *Dharna* as Door-Sitting to Dharna Chowk," I argue that access to public spaces gives disenfranchised groups power and that the banning of access to such spaces—or, as is common today, the preventive arrest of activists—narrows communicative possibilities. Building the argument that collective actions may not always be acts of opposition, protest, or resistance, this chapter illustrates how such actions can be understood as efforts to use public opinion to create spaces in which authorities can be encouraged or even compelled to hear marginalized voices. Dharna can prompt those in asymmetrically more powerful positions to give audience to those in less powerful positions. Such sit-ins and hunger strikes are often used to hold officials accountable to their campaign promises or to ensure that existing laws are equitably enforced across social difference. What is often elided from efforts to represent the forms of political work that scholars have labeled as "peasant insurgency," "subaltern politics," or the actions of "political society" is the fact that collective actions, street politics, and even violence generally occur only *after* other efforts to make voices heard have failed. They are almost never embraced as options of first recourse.

Chapter 2, "Seeking Audience: Refusals to Listen, 'Style,' and the Politics of Recognition," argues that rather than focusing on speakers' failures to communicate, we should instead attend more closely to the other, less theorized end of the communicative chain, what Richard Burghart characterizes as "the conditions of listening."[124] Doing so enables us to better recognize the ways in which those in positions of dominance attempt to avoid hearing and refuse to acknowledge some efforts to communicate while acknowledging others. Offering evidence for why we should not immediately assume that all collective assemblies are rejections of state sovereignty, chapter 2 advocates for an openness to the possibility that such efforts may reify existing forms of sovereignty and embody the desires of citizens to be recognized, included, and heard by the state—either directly or through ongoing and dynamic networks and collectives that actively connect them with electoral representatives and government officials. The chapter also uses efforts to gain audience with authorities as a way of setting up the theoretical framework through which subsequent chapters historicize specific forms of practice.

Chapter 3, "Collective Assembly and the 'Roar of the People': Corporeal Forms of 'Making Known' and the Deliberative Turn," asks what deliberative democracy means in a context in which the majority do not speak in the dominant medium or dialect of communication and explores the responses of those who are ignored, mocked, or dismissed when they do speak. Illustrating conditions that make it nearly impossible to receive any sort of hearing, this chapter builds on chapter 2 to outline the options that are available when one's articulations are not able to be heard.

Chapter 4, "The General Strike: Collective Assembly at the Other End of the Commodity Chain," offers a preliminary example of the larger ramifications of this book's argument. Revisiting older scholarship to reflect on the ways that histories of the political have been written, this chapter uses comparative historiography of the general strike in Britain and India to argue for a new approach to the history of collective action. Despite evidence of long histories of collective negotiations with authorities in India that predate the European encounter, historians have persisted in attributing the rise of collective assembly within the Indian political to European origins.[125] Chapter 4 asks how these narratives of European origins came to be constructed and offers other frameworks for thinking about historical changes in the political within both Indian and transnational contexts.

Chapter 5, "Alarm Chain Pulling: The Criminal and the Political in the Writing of History," builds on the methodological interventions of earlier chapters by exploring the ways in which those in power play with the categories of the criminal and the political as tactics for managing (and limiting the impact of) demands for recognition and inclusion. The chapter also dismantles the binary distinctions made between civil society and political society, and between the political styles of elite and subaltern actors, by focusing on the distinctions made by representatives of the Indian state and their role in abstracting certain collective actions and removing them from their longer genealogies of efforts to communicate with state representatives.

Chapter 6, "Rail and Road Blockades: Illiberal or Participatory Democracy?" offers tools for distinguishing between participatory and adversarial forms of collective assembly, arguing that these tools enable more sensitive distinctions to be made among practices that too often get lumped together as the same. The ongoing interactions between the relationship- and network-building capacity of behind-the-scenes actors and the public performances, affirmations, and material manifestations of these relationships and networks offer opportunities for everyday public referenda that occur far more frequently than formal electoral decision making. This is not the Habermasian ideal of a public sphere in which all participants debate and deliberate equally in an open forum until the best solution is reached, nor is it one in which everyone votes every few years but goes about their private business in between elections. Rather it is one in which opportunities for creating and maintaining active and ongoing channels of representation are constantly being engaged and evaluated, and efforts are made to hold elected official accountable to their promises and to equitable enforcement of existing laws.

Chapter 7, "Rallies, Processions, and *Yātras*: Ticketless Travel and the Journey to 'Political Arrival'" explores methods of "making known" (Telugu, *āvēdana*) that move beyond the deliberative forms of speech communication that asymmetries so often preclude. These alternative mediums of "making known" illustrate how participation in larger networks functions to provide connections to various "axes of access" to representatives of the state and other authorities. Extending the focus on the always shifting line between the criminal and the political, chapter 7 demonstrates the ways that individuals coalesce into groups to eventually achieve what I characterize as "political arrival." It focuses on moments in which the state offers support to actions that are technically illegal—for example, by adding extra carriages or even full trains to accommodate ticketless travel to political rallies—thereby redefining practices viewed as criminal and transforming them into political acts. Arguing that these moments constitute a form of political recognition on the part of the state in which people simultaneously also recognize themselves, the chapter illustrates what successful "hailing" of the state can look like.

Tracing the continued use of colonial-era legal codes in postcolonial India to silence dissent, limit collective action, and prevent participation, the conclusion offers a cautionary warning for the future of democracy, both in India and elsewhere. Today's forms of electoral representation include both democratic and undemocratic features. Bernard Manin reminds us that "the absence of imperative mandates, legally binding pledges, and discretionary recall, gives representatives a degree of independence from their electors. That independence separates representation from popular rule, however indirect."[126] At the same time, he continues, "The people are at any time able to remind representatives of their presence; the chambers of government are not insulated from their clamor. Freedom of public opinion thus provides a democratic counterweight to the undemocratic independence of representatives."[127] It is these reminders—the "clamor" of the people that occurs between elections and that seeks to hold elected representatives accountable, along with the specific sites in which this takes place and their vulnerabilities—to which this book attends.

# PART I. SEEKING AUDIENCE

# ONE. SIT-IN DEMONSTRATIONS AND HUNGER STRIKES

## From *Dharna* as Door-Sitting to Dharna Chowk

Dharna means sitting in one place until some official, from government, has to come and take your representation. Up to that time we sit there. —Interview with activist in Hyderabad, August 15, 2012

I first visited Dharna Chowk, Hyderabad's designated assembly space or, more literally, "demonstration junction," in February 2002 to meet members of the Ambedkar Students' Association from the University of Hyderabad. The students were staging a *rilē nirāhāra dīkṣa*—literally a "relay fasting vow" or, more colloquially, a relay hunger strike—to publicize and seek the overturning of the expulsion from the university the previous month of ten Dalit students. In this type of hunger strike, participants take turns fasting in a visible location, in this case at Hyderabad's Dharna Chowk.

A relay hunger strike is a contemporary collective variation of individual hunger strikes, which were historically carried out in proximity to a seat of power or in front of the home or office of an individual with whom an audience was sought. Gandhi fasted numerous times to draw attention to a range of concerns and to urge not only the colonial state but also his followers to take specific courses of action. His hunger strikes drew the nation's attention to the condition of striking mill workers in Ahmedabad (1918), discouraged public violence leading up to and during the Non-Cooperation Movement (1919–22), advocated against untouchability (1932–33), objected to his detention by the British (1934), and promoted Hindi–Muslim unity (1924, 1947, and 1948).[1] Although Gandhi's hunger strikes are perhaps the most famous examples of individual hunger strikes, there exists a much longer history of political methods that influenced Gandhi's tactics of intervention.[2]

The rise of mass media has enabled hunger strikes to be staged and publicized from anywhere. The fifty-eight-day fast-unto-death in 1952 of the Telugu linguistic state advocate Potti Sreeramulu, for example, took place in a private home in the city of Chennai (then Madras) but was closely followed by the newspapers of the day.[3] As the critical event that finally forced Prime Minister Jawaharlal Nehru to declare the creation of the new Andhra state, Sreeramulu's hunger strike was tracked by daily detailed news reports of his wasting body. Readers could follow precise measurements of everything that went into and came out of his body, including the number of ounces of saliva he produced and the color, size, and odor of each bowel movement.[4] Before this final deadly fast, Potti Sreeramulu—an avid Gandhian who emulated Gandhi's practices—had fasted on multiple occasions, including twice in 1946 to demand the right to temple entry for Dalits and twice (in 1948 and 1949) to advocate for a monthly "day of service" to benefit the social uplift of Dalits.[5]

Hyderabad's Dharna Chowk, located two kilometers from the State Secretariat and tucked away on a quiet street behind Hyderabad's Indira Park, has been the site of thousands of political assemblies—including sit-in demonstrations, public meetings, and hunger strikes—since its creation in the 1990s. In 2016 alone, police records show that the site hosted an average of more than five assemblies per day addressing a wide range of issues.[6] Over the years Dharna Chowk has been used by citizens seeking to make heard a broad spectrum of concerns: students objecting to tuition hikes, home guards asking for pay scales on par with police constables, those with disabilities seeking government certificates, government contract health workers desiring the benefits of permanent employment, transgender people seeking equal rights, *anganwadi* (rural childcare center) workers demanding salaries and pensions comparable to full-time government employees, farmers drawing attention to their increasingly precarious economic conditions, and broader coalitions seeking to hold elected officials to their campaign promises or expressing their opinions on new legislation.[7] Of particular note is the increasing frequency of dharnas and hunger strikes carried out by those demanding that the state fill existing affirmative action quotas (figure 1.1), expand these quotas to include new groups, or provide benefits to casualized (nonpermanent) employees or government contract workers (figure 1.2), reflecting the increasing informalization of labor in India.

FIGURE 1.1. Relay hunger strike (rilē nirāhāra dīkṣalu) held by candidates who wrote the 2008 District Selection Committee (DSC) exams, demanding the filling of 31,000 vacant secondary-grade teacher (SGT) posts in government schools across the state, at Dharna Chowk, Hyderabad, June 8, 2010 (photo: G. Krishnaswamy/*The Hindu*).

Sometimes glossed as "protest," I have chosen to translate *dharna* as demonstration, sit-in, or assembly rather than protest to emphasize the fact that not all dharnas are protests *against* something. Instead, Dharna Chowk is widely understood as a space in which voices have the potential to be amplified. As argued in greater detail in chapter 2, this space is commonly used by those with "grievances [that] stem from the failure of government administrators to carry out the law" or by those seeking an audience with someone in a position of authority.[8] This chapter's epigraph frames dharna as a practice that uses enhanced visibility to compel an official from the government "to come and take your representation."[9] Many see dharna as being most important to "people who do not have any voice" or who are disadvantaged and "seek to have their small wishes heard and fulfilled by the government."[10] Dictionaries in various South Asian languages define the practice as "fasting on someone's doorstep in order to induce him to comply with a demand," "a sit-down strike," "picketing," or "sitting doggedly to enforce compliance of a demand."[11]

Although the practice of dharna in India can be traced back at least several centuries, the creation of designated public assembly sites like Dharna Chowk is a much more recent phenomenon. Established in the 1990s by

FIGURE 1.2. The forty-first day of a relay hunger strike (rilē nirāhāra dīkṣalu) organized by the Andhra Pradesh Contract Health Assistants Coordination Committee at
Dharna Chowk, Hyderabad, August 21, 2012 (photo: author).

Nara Chandrababu Naidu—then the chief minister of the united state of Andhra Pradesh—Dharna Chowk became the officially condoned site of collective political activity, replacing the more informal use of the corner of Lumbini Park, directly opposite the entrance to the State Secretariat. The ostensible reason given for this shift in location was the construction of an elevated flyover over the intersection in front of the government building—the first of seven to be built in Hyderabad at the time. Yet the establishment of Dharna Chowk was also widely regarded as reflecting Naidu's aspirations to create a "world-class" city by moving political activity to a less visible and less disruptive location (figure 1.3) where it would not impede the smooth flow of traffic, commerce, and government activity.[12] Despite initially meeting with strident opposition, Dharna Chowk quickly became an established feature of political life in Hyderabad, with residents of nearby cities even demanding similar spaces in subsequent years.[13]

The site again became a center of controversy in the wake of the announcement by Telangana chief minister Kalvakuntla Chandrashekar Rao in February 2017 that Dharna Chowk itself would be relocated to the outskirts of the city. Four locations were proposed, ranging in distance from twenty to twenty-seven kilometers from the State Secretariat, with the closest site adjacent to the municipal garbage dump.[14] Rao's decision was particularly surprising, given that his own election had depended on precisely the type of visible political activity that he was now seeking to move to the

FIGURE 1.3. Empty road in front of Dharna Chowk, Hyderabad, April 29, 2009 (photo: G. Krishnaswamy/*The Hindu*).

margins. Many thus saw the relocation as an authoritarian effort to silence dissent and limit political opposition or as a means to repurpose the land in question.[15] This time, the controversy did not die out quite so quickly. A year later, activists were still lobbying for Dharna Chowk's reestablishment in its previous location behind Indira Park. On May 15, 2018, members of the Dharnā Chowk Parirakṣaṇa Kamiṭi (Committee to Save Dharna Chowk) held a book release event for a collection of essays commemorating the first anniversary of the site's closing and arguing for its reopening.

Both the speeches and published essays emphasize that Dharna Chowk represents the *prajā gontuka* or "people's voice."[16] "It seems that if dharnas and meetings are held in the city, traffic will be obstructed," writes the political leader Chada Venkatreddy, in an essay titled "Are You Tying a Noose around the Voice of Dissent (Dharna Chowk)?" Pinpointing the central contradictions in the chief minister's decision to move the site to the margins of the city, he continues,

> What's more, with the coming of technology why does it matter where you hold dharnas? KCR has put forward a new logic that with the advent of live TV, one can broadcast to people from anywhere. So if that's the case, why was it necessary to organize a TRS [Telangana Rashtra Samiti, party of the chief minister] meeting in Warangal with fifteen lakh [1.5 million] people? If you just sit in Telangana Bhavan and speak won't all the TV stations broadcast it live? Not only TRS activists, but people everywhere will see it, won't they?[17]

His critique points to the fact that so often the subjects of news reports *are* mass gatherings and that the location at which large assemblies are organized matters—to those gatherings' ability to attract participants, to how visible they are, and to how likely they are to appear on the news.

The perseverance of the committee paid off. On September 18, 2018, the Hyderabad High Court challenged the chief minister's refusal to grant permission for collective assembly within the city limits, requesting additional information from the administration clarifying their policy. Chief Justice Thottathil B. Radhakrishnan and Justice V. Ramasubramanian responded to the public interest litigation challenging the state government's refusal to grant permission for assemblies within the city's limits in their opinion: "The protests have to be held in the people's presence. Indira Park is in existence for the past several decades and residences have came [*sic*] up later and this is India; you cannot curtail the protest voices of people. What is the use if people protest in remote places? What is the use in installing cell towers in forests when animals do not use the cell phones?"[18] The justices further noted, "This is India. The Constitution has guaranteed right to speech to the citizens of this country. The government cannot curb it. If inconvenience is caused to others because of such protests, then the government can impose reasonable restrictions as per the law." They added that it was unreasonable to "expect the people to hold dharnas at places which are 50 kilometers away."[19]

On November 13, 2018, the Hyderabad High Court issued a ruling directing the Telangana state government to reopen the Indira Park site, and it immediately began to be put to active use again (figure 1.4).[20] Calling the right to assemble and express opinions "the safety valve for democracy," Chief Justice T. B. Radhakrishnan and Justice S. V. Bhatt went on to declare that access to such a place "is a process through which democracy survives." The Chief Justice elaborated, "You cannot ask people to protest in forests so that your development in the city can go on. Development means not just the development of private institutions. Development of democracy is also a good development. In fact, it is better than the development of private

FIGURE 1.4. Dharna condemning the illegal arrest of Varavara Rao, at Dharna Chowk, Hyderabad, November 25, 2018 (photo: Abhishek Bhattacharyya/originally published by *Ground Xero*).

sector which is crushing the people's rights."[21] Although cautioning that the state can still "impose reasonable restrictions before permitting the protests at Dharna Chowk," including the requirement to obtain police permission, the High Court stressed that it cannot deny access for those who abide by reasonable restrictions.[22]

Despite India's long history of collective assemblies for political purposes, efforts to contain public political activities within circumscribed spaces have intensified throughout urban areas in the wake of the liberalization of the country's economy in the early 1990s.[23] As in Hyderabad, authorities in New Delhi stopped granting permits for political gatherings and demonstrations at sites like the Boat Club and India Gate, which were in direct view of Parliament and in close proximity to the seats of political power. By the early 1990s, the government began selectively granting permission for political activities on a quiet street just behind the eighteenth-century astronomical observatory (and current tourist attraction), Jantar Mantar, located slightly less than two kilometers (a twenty-minute walk) from the Parliament (figure 1.5).[24] As with Dharna Chowk, the initial resistance to this relocation of collective activity gradually gave way to the embrace of Jantar Mantar as a popular site for political assemblies. Also, as with Dharna Chowk, the government attempted to ban assemblies at this site in October 2017; this ban was similarly lifted in July 2018 in response to a Supreme Court injunction. Supreme Court Justice A. K. Sikri, in a lengthy judgment, cited several legal precedents for the injunction:

> The right to protest is, thus, recognised as a fundamental right under the Constitution. This right is crucial in a democracy which rests on participation of an informed citizenry in governance. This right is also crucial since it strengthens representative democracy by enabling direct participation in public affairs where individuals and groups are able to *express dissent and grievances, expose the flaws in governance and demand accountability from State authorities as well [as] powerful entities*. This right is crucial in a vibrant democracy like India but more so in the Indian context to aid in the assertion of the rights of the marginalised and poorly represented minorities.[25]

Despite this injunction, in November 2018, police issued a new standing order severely limiting assemblies at Jantar Mantar and redirecting large political gatherings to the Ram Lila Maidan, four kilometers away.[26] That citizens have had to fight for continued access to public spaces like these across multiple cities in India marks an important shift as city and state officials seek to

FIGURE 1.5. Advertisement for Jantar Mantar published in the *Indian Express* (Delhi edition), February 6, 2014.

remake their cities in ways that are attractive to capital investors and foreign corporations, valuing the minimization of disruptions and the preservation of public order over what the court justices have defined as continued democratic engagement.

Even though collective forms of assembly were very effective during the Indian nationalist struggle, there were debates over whether they were still needed in the early years after independence. Many leaders of the new nation suggested they were outdated, whereas others continued to model their political engagements on these earlier examples of successful public space activism.[27] Yet despite these debates and subsequent administrative efforts to place limits on such practices, the prevalence of collective political activity in urban public space has actually grown since independence, becoming a visible feature of the world's largest democracy. Administrative efforts to reduce or restrict political activity have not been entirely effective but have succeeded in criminalizing practices that were previously considered everyday forms of political participation. Assemblies in many Indian cities now require permits and are subject to restrictions that limit their location, size, and duration. This has had the effect of converting assemblies without permits and those in nonapproved locations into illegal acts.

Although this trend toward establishing designated urban spaces for political assembly is a recent shift, restrictions were placed on collective forms of action as early as the eighteenth century. The practice of dharna—for which Dharna Chowk was named—was first prohibited by the Court of Justice at Benares in 1793, then made a punishable offense by Bengal Regulation VII in 1820, and eventually incorporated into Section 508 of the Indian Penal Code of 1860.[28] Sections 141–60 of the Indian Penal Code were drafted in 1860 to address "Offences against the Public Tranquility," including assemblies and rioting, whose descriptions in official reports were often blurred together such that even nonviolent collective assemblies were sometimes characterized as riots. These sections are still present in the postcolonial Indian Penal Code and continue to be invoked today to disband, censure, or prosecute assemblies of five or more persons.[29] Section 144 of the Indian Criminal Procedure Code, first introduced by the British in 1861 but also not abolished after independence, allows police to issue a preventive prohibitory order that can remain in place for up to two months, defining in advance any assembly held in the locations covered by the order as unlawful.[30] These laws have not prevented a wide range of public assemblies from taking place, either under the British or today, but they have made it easier for authorities to selectively criminalize some instances of collective assembly (see part II).

As an up-and-coming contender for "most dynamic global city" and as a site of some of the most active ongoing public political engagement in the world, Hyderabad offers an ideal context for exploring the relationships between rapid urban growth, the political uses of public space, and efforts to create "world-class" cities.[31] Globally, the uses of public space have become increasingly contested as city planners, administrators, and elected officials seek to attract new types of foreign and domestic investment. Debates over these issues raise important new questions, including concerns about the inclusivity of efforts to create "world-class" cities. Who benefits from efforts to remake cities as sites attractive to foreign direct investment, and who is excluded from these processes? Do street protests, processions, open-air meetings, and other political forms that use public space mar the attractiveness of urban centers as sites of investment or, as some have suggested, mark the "incompleteness" of India's implementation of democracy?[32] Do they represent a failure of democracy or a stage "on the way to" full democracy? Or do they represent a more intensified version of democracy, one that extends democracy beyond the ritual of the ballot box and offers deeper, more inclusive, and more frequent opportunities for representation that encompass a wide range of participatory practices both *between* and during elections?

This chapter argues that struggles over space in Hyderabad are themselves part of the process of democracy and that a close examination of dharna and its spatial history can help us better understand relationships between public space and democracy. A history of dharna also suggests that access to the use of public space for political purposes is an important feature of a healthy democracy and is not incidental to it. Furthermore, the location of this public space matters. Just as the space in front of Hyderabad's Legislative Assembly or State Secretariat was seen as more valuable and effective for communication with elected officials, so, too, the centrally located Dharna Chowk is currently considered much more valuable and effective than a similarly sized or even larger space on the outskirts of the city. Particularly when attempting to undertake development in ways that expand rather than narrow inclusion in decision-making processes, it is crucial to recognize localized histories of political participation that deploy public space in particular ways.

In what follows, I use Hyderabad's recent rapid growth and the resurgence of the Telangana movement to demonstrate how public spaces can expand participation, give audience to more voices, and make planning and political decision making more inclusive. I argue that ensuring the availability and accessibility of public space—not just as green or open spaces providing access to fresh air or as locations for shopping and commodity consumption but also as sites for nonviolent political performance and representation— deepens democracy by holding lawmakers and elected officials more accountable to electoral promises and encouraging them to pay attention to voices that they might otherwise ignore. By way of illustration, I trace the changing meaning of dharna—for which Hyderabad's designated assembly space is named—and situate its practice within discourses of the right to the city in the face of the growing power of global capital. I use this to argue that the Euro-American normative understandings of democracy that dominate our frames of reference for analysis have impoverished our tools for interpreting the recent waves of occupation of public space that have swept much of the world and for understanding histories of collective action more generally.

In tracing the changing meaning of the practice of dharna, I also locate the shifting spaces in which it has been practiced. In doing so, I model a method for approaching the study of democracy, urban growth, and public space—taking into account the multiple histories of the meanings and practices that have shaped the specific experiences of the political within which urban residents reside. Such attention to local meanings enables the revision of implicit normative assumptions of what the role of public space is or should be, particularly in relation to political decision making. In Justice Sikri's words, "Citizens are guaranteed [the] fundamental right of speech, right to assemble . . . [and] the right to protest."[33] He makes clear that this set of rights "strengthens representative democracy by enabling direct participation in public affairs where individuals and groups are able to express dissent and grievances, expose the flaws in governance and demand accountability from State authorities as well as powerful entities."[34]

From Dharna as Door-Sitting to Dharna Chowk:
Public Assemblies in India

Situating the concept of dharna amidst a larger field of political, legal, and social categories can help emphasize changes in the visibility of new forms of media and urban spatial arrangements. Dharna—like other practices discussed in this book—uses public opinion to help gain an audience with someone in a position of power. In carrying out a public appeal, it seeks to position an authority, leader, or official such that they can be encouraged to act more inclusively, more ethically, or more in line with an existing moral economy or their own campaign promises. Rather than opposing or rejecting the power and authority of the person or institution with which an audience is sought, such appeals celebrate and further reify the ability of someone in a position of power to bring about an action or change. Yet this is not always how dharna has been understood, particularly by the British through the legal and administrative structures and forms of policing and dispute resolution they introduced during the eighteenth and nineteenth centuries. Because the British saw dharna as a challenge to their own authority, the first recourse of British administrators was usually to seek methods to block or delegitimize the ability of Indians to act collectively.

John Shore, also known as Lord Teignmouth, governor-general of British India from 1793 to 1797, offers one of the earliest published efforts to translate the concept of dharna as a generalized practice into English. Shore was the translator of a number of Persian works written by Hindus, and he played a significant role in the British reform of the Indian land revenue system. This reform, known as the Permanent Settlement, had far-reaching consequences for economic, political, and legal practices in India. He was also a close friend of the philologist William Jones, founder of the Asiatic Society of Bengal, and succeeded him as the group's president. In the fourth volume of the Asiatic Society's periodical, *Asiatic Researches*, published in

1798, Shore offers a description of the Indian practice of "sitting dharna" or "watching constantly at the door":

> The inviolability of a *Brahmen* is a fixed principle of the *Hindus*; and to deprive him of life, either by direct violence, or by causing his death in any mode, is a crime which admits of no expiation. To this principle may be traced the practice called *Dherna*, which was formerly familiar at *Benares*, and which may be translated *Caption* or *Arrest*. It is used by the *Brahmens* in that city, to gain a point which cannot be accomplished by any other means; and the process is as follows: The *Brahmen* who adopts this expedient for the purpose mentioned, proceeds to the door or house of the person against whom it is directed, or wherever he may most conveniently intercept him: he there sets down in *Dherna*, with poison, or a poignard or some other instrument of suicide, in his hand, and threatening to use it if his adversary should attempt to molest or pass him, he thus completely arrests him. In this situation the *Brahmen* fasts, and by the rigor of the etiquette, which is rarely infringed, the unfortunate object of his arrest ought also to fast; and thus they both remain till the institutor of the *Dherna* obtains satisfaction. In this, as he seldom makes the attempt without resolution to persevere, he rarely fails; for if the party thus arrested were to suffer the *Brahmen* sitting in *Dherna* to perish by hunger, the sin would forever lie upon his head.[35]

For Shore, the two keys to dharna's effectiveness were (1) the intensity of resolve of the party who enacted the practice to persevere until death and (2) the fear on the part of "the object of arrest" of being held responsible for another's death, particularly that of a Brahmin.

Although he offers no citation, Shore's source of information on dharna was almost certainly Jonathan Duncan, the British resident at Benares from 1787 to 1794. In a series of reports submitted to the governor-general between 1792 and 1794, Duncan describes the practice of dharna as "one of the superstitious prejudices, which have so long and so generally been cherished here."[36] The historian Radhika Singha interprets Duncan's accounts as defining dharna of that era as a way to defend a claim in which a person "'cast himself' at the threshold of a person against whom he had a grievance to be redressed, or a debt or claim to be satisfied. He would refuse to get up or eat, and would obstruct the movement of the household till the offending party negotiated terms."[37] She notes that practices such as dharna were used to contest issues or seek redress by "exposing the issue to the opinion of the neighborhood."[38] However, British administrators characterized these practices as "products of a barbaric state of civilization" and targeted them for reform as part of a larger process of constructing the colonial legal subject and reordering civil and criminal legal authority.[39] Singha observes that these "reforms" first required wrenching practices like dharna "out of the codes of meaning and the structures of authority in which they were embedded," often by redefining them as criminal acts.[40]

Sanskrit dictionaries offer a range of meanings for the cognate term, *dhāraṇa*, including "holding, possessing, suffering, enduring" and "immovable concentration of the mind," enabling its derivatives to be used in a range of ways.[41] As applied to a set of practices in Indian history, the earliest citations of the term *dharna* associate it with those efforts, often individual ones, that prevent movement and make known a hardship, thereby compelling the target of the action to recognize the hardship and agree to enter into negotiations. The Yale professor Washburn Hopkins notes in 1900 that dharna, "literally 'holding up' a defaulting debtor by preparing to commit suicide at his door," had come by the turn of the twentieth century to mean "not only 'door-sitting' but also any form of obstruction, for example, obstructing a water-course" and that "fasting is not, therefore, a necessary concomitant of dharṇa."[42] In elaborating, he classifies such forms of obstruction with other modes of exacting payment, including seizing a debtor's wife, son, or cattle, and other means of "moral suasion"—a category that also includes advice, remonstrance, and "following about" (*anugama*).[43]

Rochisha Narayan's exploration of the colonial archive suggests that it was not simply the prevention of movement and the fear of responsibility for another's death that made the practice of dharna so effective. The public aspect of the performance of dharna was also critical to its power. She mentions a crucial but often overlooked detail of a much-cited case of a dharna carried out by a Brahmin widow named Bina Bai over her right to inherit her father-in-law's property after his death in 1791. She conducted her dharna not in front of her brother-in-law's house, the party against whom she had the grievance, but rather in a temple, thereby illustrating the importance of local visibility. Conducting a dharna in full view of an audience enabled her to seek public support for her position in what we might otherwise view as a domestic familial dispute.[44] By staging a performance that effectively functioned as a referendum in the face of public opinion, the widow's thirteen-day dharna was successful in compelling her brother-in-law to negotiate with her. This suggests that dharna was often a last resort for those in structurally less powerful positions, used when other avenues failed to garner recognition or a response.

Narayan's research on colonial law in eighteenth- and nineteenth-century Banaras has shown that poor Brahmins, including on occasion Brahmin widows, were sometimes employed by others to sit in dharna, often in groups.[45] Yet we also have evidence that the practice of dharna was one that a much broader segment of the population, including bankers, merchants, and other non-Brahmins, saw as a method to obtain recourse. On the basis of her archival research in Banaras, Sandria Freitag concludes that sitting dharna was typically used by merchants seeking to collect monies owed to them, rather than by Brahmins.[46] Hopkins, too, observes that, although earlier European commentators had interpreted the practice of door-sitting as being limited to Brahmins, nothing explicit is said to support this in any of the textual sources cited.[47]

Examples from the colonial archive also suggest that it was a practice that was engaged in both individually and collectively. An anonymous author in 1835 described a famous house tax strike in Varanasi in 1810–11 as a dharna:

> Government having imposed a house tax of considerable amount, the natives, startled by the innovation were immediately in a ferment. . . . The whole population of the city and its neighbourhood determined to sit in dharna until their grievances should be redressed. . . . Before Government were in the least apprized of the plan above three hundred thousand persons as it was said deserted their houses, shut up their shops, suspended the labour of their farms, forebore to light fires, dress victuals, many of them even to eat, and sat down with folded arms and drooping heads like so many sheep on the plain which surrounds Benares.[48]

This definition suggests that any effort to unionize, strike, or join together to collectively gain recognition or audience from someone more powerful would have, at least by 1835, been categorized as dharna.[49] Many other references to dharna and to the threat of self-harm or suicide in colonial-era sources suggest their widespread use to resist the imposition of new colonial taxes.[50]

These examples of using public opinion to create opportunities for negotiation with authorities point to a growing relationship between dharna and the state. Radhika Singha suggests not only that the colonial state found such practices threatening precisely because they were evidence of preexisting "codes of meaning" and "structures of authority" over which the British had no control but also that these preexisting codes and structures can help us better situate the history of such practices in relationship to existing forms of the political.[51] Henry Maine in his *Lectures on the Early History of Institutions*, published in 1875 as a sequel to *Ancient Law*, uses John Shore's descriptions as part of a larger argument that characterizes dharna as an illustration of an early evolutionary stage of redressing a grievance and obtaining justice—a stage just beyond "*sudden plunder or slaughter.*"[52] Strikingly, he recognizes dharna as existing in both the Indian and Irish contexts, both sites of British colonial occupation. In contrast to his understanding of dharna as representative of an early evolutionary stage, Maine locates those forms in which the state is directly involved in resolving grievances as the most highly developed form of legal redress.[53] Any other type of arbitration through which justice could be sought at a local level was seen as a threat to British authority.

Most of the available examples of dharna drawn from the eighteenth century involve family members in conflict with one another or private parties with grievances over business or economic arrangements with other private parties. Yet from the early nineteenth century onward, the state increasingly becomes the primary target of dharna, simultaneously with the growth in power of the East India Company (eic). Despite the eic's efforts to prohibit dharna, Shore notes that the practice was so widely accepted that "the interference of that Court and even of the Resident has occasionally proved insufficient to check it."[54]

The varied historical descriptions of dharna share two features: its use by those in structurally less powerful positions to gain an audience with those more powerful and the reliance on public opinion to compel negotiation. By drawing wider attention to what might have begun as an interpersonal or interfamilial dispute, practitioners sought to bring the weight of collective moral norms to bear on the person or institution with which they wanted to negotiate. This end could often only be accomplished by taking the dispute into the public domain and broadcasting it to gauge the likelihood of wider support and, if successful, using that wider support to force parties to enter into negotiations to reach an equitable resolution. In effect, dharna can be seen as a way of making injustice (or perceived injustice) more visible to a wider social community and of redefining the constitution of public and private domains. Resort to dharna is likeliest when practitioners feel they will have widespread popular support for their side of a dispute.

This does not always mean that popular opinion will side with the person performing dharna. One of the earliest representations of a hunger strike in the Indian context appears in the Hindu epic, *The Ramayana*. When the hero Rama is exiled to the forest for fourteen years, his half-brother Bharata, who is to replace Ram as king of Ayodhya, appeals to Rama to remain and assume his rightful role as king. When Rama refuses, Bharata makes this request of his father's second wife: "Spread darbha grass on the ground for me, Sumantra. Until my brother agrees to come back to Ayodhya and be crowned, I will fast—to death, if need be!"[55] When Rama still refuses, Bharata appeals to the people of the kingdom of Ayodhya, asking, "Why do you stand so quietly? Why don't you force him to return?" But the people respond with "an uneasy silence," supporting Rama's decision. Realizing the lack of support for his fast, Bharata ultimately concedes.[56]

Before the advent of mass media, a dharna was only visible locally, and its success depended on the moral norms of the immediate community in which a dispute was aired. Under British colonial rule, expanding state control of practices like dharna was intertwined with efforts to codify and standardize legal frameworks that would facilitate and centralize the project of political and economic administration. The widespread moral support for existing practices, however, often made new laws difficult to enforce, something that continues to be the case. Although the state tried to respond forcefully to the Varanasi sit-down strike of 1810–11, it eventually gave up and rescinded the unpopular house tax. Today, hunger strikes and sit-down demonstrations are frequently mass mediated to reach larger audiences; however, even when technically still defined as illegal, actions with widespread popular support are not always prosecuted and sometimes even garner official sanction and protection.[57]

Dharna in Contemporary India

Today, what gets labeled as a dharna is most commonly an action that targets the state or its representatives. District collectors, chief ministers, and members of Parliament are all frequent targets for complaints as varied as substandard schools and textbook shortages, inclusion in affirmative action quotas, increases in university tuition, falling commodity prices, or the rising cost of gasoline. Mallikarjuna, a resident of Warangal, described to me his very first participation in a dharna, as a tenth-grade student, over a government hike in college fees: "In the first phase, we took out a rally. More than one thousand people participated. We went from college to the authorities. Then we submitted a memorandum. After one week there was no response, then we started agitation. We started a relay hunger strike. For one month daily some twenty-five to thirty people sat there. Then afterward we went to an indefinite fast—one dozen people. Then the authorities came, and they agreed with our demands. So, no fee hike."[58]

Mallikarjuna is not exceptional in placing dharna agitations within an escalating series of strategies for being heard, obtaining recognition, or opening negotiations. Dharna is rarely the option of first resort. Instead, it tends to be used only when actors have been unsuccessful in obtaining recognition of their concerns and other available options have been exhausted. Prakash, the local leader of the Dalit wing of a major political party, shared with me his earliest experience of a dharna.[59] In 1985, a brutal attack on Dalits in the village of Karamchedu led by close relatives of the chief minister's son-in-law—members of the dominant land-owning caste community in the village—left six Dalit young men dead, three Dalit girls raped, and an additional twenty severely injured. For fifteen days, Prakash participated in a dharna in front of the State Secretariat demanding that justice be carried out for the Karamchedu victims.[60] More specifically, the dharna drew attention to the following demands: that the police arrest and prosecute the perpetrators in accordance with the law, that judiciary procedures be followed, that rehabilitation services be provided to the victims at government expense, and that existing rules regarding minimum wages and working conditions for agricultural laborers (the primary occupation of the victims) "be strictly implemented throughout the state."[61] Prakash went on to explain that the Karamchedu massacre was an important moment that mobilized many Dalits across the state and led to the formation of new organizations for the representation of Dalit agendas, including the Dalit Mahasabha.[62] As with so many other examples (see figure 1.6), the goal of the dharna was to produce action on the part of the state and hold government officials accountable for implementing existing laws fairly.

Probably the most famous exemplar of hunger strikes and sit-in demonstrations in India is Gandhi.[63] Yet placing Gandhi's tactics within their longer genealogies also demonstrates the rich set of practices from which he drew and shows that, even though he was brilliantly adept at using and popularizing such practices, he did not invent them.[64] His original contributions included bringing existing nonviolent forms of making distress known to an international audience that was unfamiliar with such practices and coining a new term, *satyagraha*, often translated as "truth-force."[65] Satyagraha called upon the moral authority evoked in face-to-face encounters and, like the practices on which it drew, used public opinion to encourage

FIGURE 1.6. Flyer announcing a dharna to demand a judicial inquiry into the massacre of twenty Adivasi (Indigenous) villagers, July 31, 2012 (source: author's collection).

authorities to participate in negotiations. Rather than rejecting the sovereignty of the authorities against whom satyagraha was practiced, Gandhi called for mutual recognition within an ongoing relationship in contexts in which such recognition did not happen naturally. He also was one of the first to recognize mass media's power to extend the audience (and therefore the potential moral judges) for performative acts of self-deprivation and potential self-harm.

In the wake of Gandhi's popularization of hunger and sit-down strikes as satyagraha, the willingness to engage in such practices began to be taken as a mark of leadership and the ability to mediate on behalf of others within the newly emerging political landscape. Telugu autobiographies of anticolonial "freedom fighters" and other political leaders often position their early participation in such actions close to the beginning of their narratives, framing political commitments as having begun in late childhood or early student days and thus highlighting their credentials for their roles as political mediators/leaders from an early age. The Indian nationalist and Telangana struggle leader Arutla Ramachandra Reddy, for example, in his *Telangāṇā Pōrāṭa Smṛtulu* (Memories of the Telangana Struggle), offers two such examples in the opening pages of his first chapter. When he discovered in 1930 that some of the students in Nampalli High School where he was studying were being allowed to take the final examination while he was not, he responded by "doing satyagraha"—here a sit-down strike—in front of the headmaster's car.[66] He then writes about Gandhi's salt march in April of that same year and goes on to describe a hunger strike that he carried out against his father-in-law shortly after his marriage. Its purpose was to persuade his new wife's parents to allow her to come to Hyderabad to be educated. His father-in-law, seeing the strength of Reddy's commitment to his wife's education, relented and allowed his daughter to be educated.[67] Coming as they do in the opening pages of Reddy's autobiography, these examples serve to strengthen the claims he later makes to be a leader of the people and a mediator of their representations to authorities.

Dharna has been significantly transformed by mass media. With the advent of widespread televised coverage of dharna agitations, physical blockages and the prevention of movement—once central to dharna—became less important than publicity gained through enhanced visibility. This can help explain why Chandrababu Naidu's creation of a new designated protest space in Hyderabad in the 1990s was met with such short-lived protest. Although processions and dharnas might take place anywhere in the city of

Hyderabad, they had previously been particularly popular at sites of political power, including the Legislative Assembly (where the state's elected representatives meet), the State Secretariat (administrative offices of state government employees), Raj Bhavan (the official residence of the governor of the state, who acts as the local representative of the president of India), and the Hyderabad district collector's office (the Indian Administrative Service appointee who serves as head of the district).

When civil society groups in the 1990s began to realize that no police permits would be granted for processions or dharnas at any locations except the newly established Dharna Chowk, there were initially some attempts to protest this change. Krishnamurthy, the teacher we met in the introduction, recalled to me the earlier era in which there existed greater access to what he characterized as "democratic spaces in Hyderabad." In the 1970s and 1980s, he told me, "Dharnas were permitted in front of the [State] Secretariat. Permissions we had to get, but they were never denied. It was a kind of routine affair," he said. "I don't even remember even one instance where it was rejected [by the police]."[68] But by 1987, and increasingly into the 1990s, he continued, the government began to restrict access to public spaces through a series of court orders. "And the situation has worsened after '97, further deteriorated. You can't go, you can't organize a dharna, and even your meeting could be disturbed."[69] The most significant indication of the dramatic contraction of access to political spaces for democratic purposes, however, was the fact that the government "stopped permission for dharna at the Secretariat. It shifted to Indira Park, and they named it Dharna Chowk [assembly space]. It's a place that no one ever goes. It's a godforsaken place, no one will see you at all."[70] Dharna Chowk's location on a quiet back street behind Indira Park (figure 1.3)—a thoroughfare to nowhere and a road on which almost no one ever goes—means that its occupation blocks nothing and faces no one, a dramatic contrast with what dharna had earlier been.

Yet despite this out-of-the-way location, it was not long before Dharna Chowk was embraced as a critical site for "making known" grievances and concerns, with reporters assigned to cover it on regular beats. With the growing importance of televisual media, the goal of many dharnas shifted from appealing to local public opinion through a public display in front of a site of power or through the prevention of movement of a representative of the state, to appealing to a much broader public by appearing on that day's news. Even rail blockades—a closely related form used for drawing public attention to a *federal*-level grievance, which typically target the most popular express train to Delhi—shifted from sending their message to the national capital by inconveniencing travelers headed there to sending their message via televised media. Although in the past they might delay a train for hours or even days, many activists agree that today it is enough to halt a train for fifteen to twenty minutes, just long enough for photographers and television cameras to capture the banners and chants, before releasing the train, often with the full cooperation of railway officials.[71] In the creation of designated protest spaces off the beaten track and at arm's length from sites of power, dharna has shifted from a practice characterized by the focused concentration of a single person to prevent the movement of the object of protest and compel someone in a structurally more powerful position to come to the negotiating table, to a more symbolic performance of collective assembly in a fixed and designated space that blocks no one and prevents nothing. This does not mean that the location of dharnas no longer matters—as the opposition to moving Dharna Chowk to the city's outskirts illustrates—but it does mean that media coverage has become an additional essential factor.

A final and surprising recent development in relation to dharna is its use by state officials against other state officials. In January 2014, members and supporters of the recently elected Aam Aadmi Party (Common Man's Party), the democratically elected ruling party of the Indian union territory that makes up the capital region of Delhi, staged a sit-down protest in front of the Home Minister's office in Delhi to demand greater control over the city's police force, which falls under the control of the central government rather than the state government. The action prompted accusations of "vigilantism" and "anarchy," as well as widespread surprise that a successfully elected political party in power should engage in a form of political action more typically led by opposition parties or by those in structurally marginal positions. The *Los Angeles Times* called it "the most unpredictable Indian political development in a generation."[72] Indeed, for a ruling party to stage a demonstration against the state might initially appear to be the most dramatic of contradictions. Yet it might be explained by the recent dramatic increase in the number of elected officials nationwide. Amendments 73 and 74, introduced in 1992, created a third tier of local-level elected offices, resulting in three million new locally elected offices in addition to up to 795 members of Parliament at the national level and more than 4,000 members of the various state-level Legislative Assemblies.[73] Many who used to negotiate with or struggle against the state on a regular basis now literally *are* the state and serve as elected officials.[74]

If, as Henri Lefebvre has argued, the state provides the template on which the abstract space of the city is today produced, "created by the imperatives of a capitalist economy and the state's involvement in the management and domination of space," what does it mean when sit-in demonstrations and hunger strikes themselves enter the very practices of the state?[75] One way to begin to answer this question is to recognize the changes in meaning that dharna and related practices have undergone historically and to trace the shifts in how dharna has been understood, both by those addressing the state and by those who occupy positions within the state. The analysis of public space in Hyderabad outlined in this chapter offers insights relevant for those interested in the workings of democracy. For practitioners of dharna, the location of public space matters. In particular, as John Parkinson has argued, public space located in proximity to public buildings and sites of decision making and that are visible to lawmakers and elected officials are more valuable to democracy than spaces at a distance.[76] As Hyderabad illustrates, an open space at the center of the city in close proximity to seats of power is quite different from a space on the urban outskirts near the municipal garbage dump and miles from political offices.

In a 2012 judgment, Indian Supreme Court Justice Swatanter Kumar emphasized the importance of the practice of dharna to Indian democracy:

> Freedom of speech, right to assemble and demonstrate by holding dharnas and peaceful agitations are the basic features of a democratic system. The people of a democratic country like ours have a right to raise their voice against the decisions and actions of the Government or even to express their resentment over the actions of the Government on any subject of social or national importance. The Government has to respect and, in fact, encourage exercise of such rights. It is the abundant duty of the State to aid the exercise of the right to freedom of speech as understood in its comprehensive sense and not to throttle or frustrate exercise of such rights by exercising its executive or legislative powers and passing orders or taking action in that direction in the name of reasonable restrictions. The preventive steps should be founded on actual and prominent threat endangering public order and tranquility, as it may disturb the social order. This delegate power vested in the State has to be exercised with great caution and free from arbitrariness. It must serve the ends of the constitutional rights rather than to subvert them.[77]

For Justice Kumar and his colleague, Supreme Court Justice Dr. B. S. Chauhan, the "right to assemble and demonstrate by holding dharnas and peaceful agitations" is not something simply to be tolerated but rather to be actively encouraged as "the basic features of a democratic system."[78] In the next chapter, I elaborate distinctions between practices that protest against authority and those that seek inclusion and participation within formal processes of decision making by examining the conditions that enable individuals to be heard by representatives of the state.

# TWO. SEEKING AUDIENCE

Refusals to Listen, "Style," and the Politics of Recognition

If there is someone you do not wish to recognize as a political being, you begin by not seeing them as the bearers of politicalness, by not understanding what they say, by not hearing that it is an utterance coming out of their mouths. . . . In order to refuse the title of political subjects to a category—workers, women, etc . . . it has traditionally been sufficient to assert that they belong . . . to a space separated from public life. . . . And the politics of these categories has always consisted in re-qualifying these places . . . in making what was unseen visible; in getting what was only audible as noise to be heard as speech. —JACQUES RANCIÈRE, "Ten Theses on Politics," 2001

Podile asked us to come back the next day. He had staff, wardens and security personnel when we came back. Podile told us, "I do not need to answer you, I have full powers given by the VC [vice chancellor]." He then asked the security guards to throw us out. A scuffle broke out and some glass got shattered. Podile then said we assaulted him and got ten of us rusticated [suspended] on January 10. —Student suspended from the University of Hyderabad in 2002 after repeated efforts to present a memorandum to the chief warden of hostels, quoted by Sandhya Ravishankar, "No University for Dalits," 2016

On January 10, 2002, ten students from the University of Hyderabad—a Government of India centrally administered university—were suspended after repeated efforts by a group of more than one hundred students to collectively present a list of concerns to the university's chief warden of hostels.[1] The students were members of the Ambedkar Students' Association (ASA), an organization founded in 1993 by a small group of Dalits studying at the University of Hyderabad.[2] Established to respond to various forms of discrimination and to advocate for the rights of Dalit students, the ASA has subsequently expanded to other university campuses, including Hyderabad's Osmania University, the Tata Institute of Social Sciences in Mumbai, Pondicherry University, University of Mumbai, Central University of Gujarat, Central University of Kerala, and Panjab University in Chandigarh.

Although a propensity for violence was the reason cited by university officials for suspending the ten students, the members of the ASA were attempting to raise several issues with the chief warden during the encounter that precipitated their expulsions.[3] Their chief concern was the dramatic increase in hostel mess fees by nearly 60 percent over the previous six months, brought on by the chief warden's decision to centralize purchasing.[4] The move toward centralization, widely seen as a step toward privatization, increased the financial strain on those students who were dependent on university fellowships and whose stipends were insufficient to cover the raised catering fees. Many interpreted the fee increase as an attempt to push such students out of the university and as "a slur on the integrity of mess secretaries," many of whom were Dalits who lacked familial financial support and sought to defray expenses by working in the hostel mess in exchange for reduced meal fees.[5] An additional concern was the recent demotion of a Dalit warden—who had opposed the centralization of the mess catering service and acted as an advocate for many Dalit students—from his overall administrative and financial responsibility for the hostel to taking care of "sanitation and gardening." This was seen as a deeply demeaning move by members of the communities that had historically been relegated to such tasks. Together, this fee increase and the demotion must be read within a context in which many upper-caste Hindus—both students and faculty—have felt resentment at the increased numbers of students from historically marginalized backgrounds, both those admitted via government-mandated affirmative action policies and through general quotas.

This was not the first time the students had attempted to voice their concerns to university authorities. Their collective efforts to speak with the chief warden in January 2002 followed a series of attempts to communicate with university authorities, including participating in meetings in the hostel and a general student body meeting, sending a petition to the vice chancellor, and attempting to meet with and present a memorandum to the chief warden. They had also submitted a formal written complaint to university authorities in November 2001 in response to posters that were hung in the hostel calling Dalit students "pigs and uncivilised, violent brutes," and describing them as "corrupt" and "shameless."[6] No action was taken in response to their repeated efforts to raise these concerns or in response to the offensive posters. Nor did university officials ever acknowledge their formal complaint or their petition to the vice chancellor, and their memorandum to the chief warden and efforts to meet with him were refused. Yet, in the wake of the students' suspensions, rather than addressing how university administrators had failed to acknowledge the escalating series of concerns raised by the Dalit students, *The Hindu* newspaper quoted the vice chancellor as asking, "What makes the Dalit students so angry?"[7]

The discursive representation of emotion has been used to include and incorporate others into a social body, but it can also exclude, mark out as different, silence, and prevent active participation. In an earlier book, I explored ways of representing emotion to incorporate and suggest inclusion in a social body, focusing on new recognitions of emotion in the late nineteenth and early twentieth centuries.[8] In this chapter, I argue that emotion and emotionally charged violence have been portrayed as reflecting a particular "style" of political communication and that this attribution of political style can be used to silence marginalized voices, mark difference, and prevent and counteract formal inclusion. I illustrate this argument by identifying the representation of emotion in refusals to recognize and give audience to speaking subjects.

## Seeking Audience in South Asia

The formal role of holding audiences has a long history in India. Ethical rulers or leaders are expected to offer their constituents, followers, or subjects regular opportunities for communication. The classical Indian text on the science of statecraft and politics, the *Arthaśāstra*, is perhaps the earliest work to capture this ideal.[9] A section on administrative organization recommends that rulers divide each of their days and nights into eight equal (ninety-minute) portions. The second ninety-minute portion of the day is explicitly designated for public audiences; it is a time to hear and consider "the prayers and petitions of the subjects."[10] Regardless of whether rulers actually followed the *Arthaśāstra*'s template, the fact that giving audience to subjects was considered important enough to occupy daily attention suggests its centrality in theory. The Telugu language similarly offers glimpses into an understanding of a concept of audience that does not easily translate into English. The Telugu noun *koluvu*, for example, has a complex meaning that encompasses references to both the physical *space* in which an audience takes place ("a hall of audience" or "court") and to a *relationship* ("service" or "employment").[11] The English term *service* itself is widely used in India to refer to government or public sector employment, thus the "government servant." The combination of both meanings in the same word suggests a conceptual history that points to the importance of the government job in Indian history, as discussed in the introduction. Government employment has long been seen as one of the most effective routes to social mobility in South Asia, distinct from agriculture or mercantile occupations, and continues to be privileged in the context of the affirmative action reservations that are expanding in India today. Koluvu evokes some of this history while also placing the giving of an audience within a privileged position.

Although the form and organization of power have obviously changed in an era of electoral politics, many politicians and elected officials today still hold public audience sessions with their constituents on a regular basis, often in the form of regular reception hours or a weekly "Grievance Day," *vijñaptula dinam* or *darakhāstula dinam* in Telugu (see figures 2.1 and 2.2).[12] Jennifer Bussell, for example, found that between two-thirds and three-quarters of the visitors received by elected officials in India are constituents seeking services or assistance and that elected officials spend between one-quarter and one-third of their time receiving constituents and addressing their petitions and needs.[13] The architectural and spatial arrangements of the offices of elected officials and higher-level bureaucrats in India reflect the expectation that they will spend time entertaining petitioners, with a reception area or audience hall integrated into the design. When meeting a senior official or elected representative, it is not uncommon to be ushered into a room in which rows of seats are arranged facing the official's desk, enabling multiple petitioners to be present simultaneously. Officials skillfully manage their various appeals while also performing their power by hearing and settling cases in front of an audience of other petitioners (see figure 2.3). When the Mahbubnagar district collector T. K. Sreedevi discontinued the Collectorate's traditional weekly Grievance Day in February 2015 after launching a website for receiving online petitions, the move was met with great protest. Feeling excluded from direct access to the collector, many requested that the weekly audiences at the Revenue Bhavan be reinstated.[14]

Anastasia Piliavsky describes another example of the spatial arrangements that enable face-to-face communication with those in power in the context of the north Indian state of Rajasthan:

FIGURE 2.1. People waiting to meet with the collector on Grievance Day, Thoothukudi Collectorate, July 24, 2006 (photo: N. Rajesh/*The Hindu*).

FIGURE 2.2. Farmers attending a Grievance Day meeting with Revenue Divisional Officer P. Murugesh, Tirupur, December 12, 2008 (photo: M. Balaji/*The Hindu*).

FIGURE 2.3. Superintendent of Police Labhu Ram listening to grievances raised by members of Scheduled Caste and Scheduled Tribe groups in Mangalore, November 6, 2011 (photo: R. Eswarraj/*The Hindu*).

In the *darbar*, or the royal assembly, the king receives his visitors in two separate halls: the commoners in the *diwaan-e-aam* (the common assembly) and special visitors in the *diwaan-e-khaas* (the special assembly). The *diwaan-e-aam* occupies a green, spacious courtyard, which fills every morning with petitioners seeking an audience with the king. The courtyard leads, through a screened door, into the inner chamber where the king receives envoys, aristocrats and notable visitors from abroad. The commoners come separately or in groups and the king, when he does appear, dispenses various "gifts" and he adjudicates.[15]

Yet, the king in question, she goes on to tell us, "is not an erstwhile Rajput, Mughal or Maratha sovereign, but a current Member of the Rajasthan Legislative Assembly."[16] Her contemporary portrait, based on fieldwork conducted in the first two decades of the twenty-first century, emphasizes the ongoing relevance in India of seeking audience with a government official (see figure 2.4). Even when arrangements for audiences are not formally instituted by government administrators themselves, citizen groups or intermediaries like journalists often stage them. The Hindi-language newspaper *Hindustan* in conjunction with its English-language counterpart *Hindustan Times*, for example, organizes a

FIGURE 2.4. Cartoon illustrating the desire of citizens to be heard by government officials (here Prime Minister Narendra Modi), published in the wake of the Pegasus spy scandal revelations that dozens of Indian politicians, activists, journalists, and government critics were potential targets of snooping by Israeli-made spyware, July 21, 2021 (courtesy of cartoonist Satish Acharya).

biannual program, "At Your Doorstep," to facilitate opportunities for "resource-poor" people to gain audiences with administrators.[17] Such events not only offer opportunities to share grievances and suggestions but also position members of the press as key brokers between the state and its citizens.

But what happens when an elected or appointed official, such as the chief warden of hostels at a central government-administered university, refuses to give an audience and hear a petitioner? In this chapter I argue that throughout Indian history there has been a direct relationship between the refusal on the part of officials to entertain petitioners and the subsequent emergence of collective action. Indeed, one way of approaching the history of collective action in India is to view it as the holding of an audience in reverse. Instead of a leader extending an audience to petitioners to enable grievances or concerns to be heard and addressed, forms of collective assembly are frequently used in India to compel an audience with someone in power under conditions in which recognition may not otherwise be forthcoming. Many collective assemblies—in both designated assembly spaces and other public spaces—are staged specifically with the aim of gaining an audience with someone in the government.

The 2020–21 farmers' agitation discussed in the introduction is a case in point. An explicit goal of the farmers' occupation of public spaces at various entry points into Delhi was to gain an audience with government officials, reflecting their frustration that they had been given no opportunity to provide input about the new agricultural policies. Komal Mohite's ethnography of the 2017 Tamil Nadu farmers' dharna in Delhi's designated assembly space at Jantar Mantar similarly illustrates this desire for an audience. One farmer explained to her that their "spectacular protests are done with the precise aim of getting the attention of the Prime Minister Narendra Modi and that the farmers want Modi to come and meet with them and accept their demands."[18] Although the Tamil Nadu farmers did not succeed in meeting with the prime minister, their media-savvy strategies to gain attention—which included shaving half their beards and hair, displaying skulls and femur bones purported to be from farmers who had committed suicide, eating rats and snakes, marching in the nude to the prime minister's office, and vowing to drink their own urine and eat their own feces—did motivate the Madras High Court to direct the Tamil Nadu government to waive the cooperative bank loans of *all* farmers on the twenty-second day of their action, temporarily halting their protests.[19] The decision was later stayed by the Supreme Court, however, and the farmers returned to Jantar Mantar.[20] As we saw in chapter 1, such collective assemblies—in full public view—are seen by marginalized actors as particularly effective in mobilizing public opinion in ways that encourage a leader to give a hearing to, and enter into discussion or negotiations with, those in structurally less powerful positions, particularly after earlier efforts to seek audience were refused or ignored. Yet this is not always how such actions are understood or portrayed, especially by those in more dominant positions. Instead, those in positions of authority use a range of strategies to avoid hearing the voices of those in marginalized positions.

Emotion and Collective Action

The question of why Dalits are so angry is one that has been voiced repeatedly by non-Dalits in India in recent years, particularly as Dalit political mobilization has become more visible since the 1980s and 1990s.[21] Newspaper headlines and academic paper titles alike suggest that we are witnessing, in the words of Nicolas Jaoul, a shift from "meek Harijans" (Gandhi's somewhat patronizing term for Dalits) to "angry Dalits."[22] But rather than endeavoring to explain "why Dalits are so angry," I argue in this chapter that we instead need to ask how and why efforts to make voices heard are so often framed as something *other* than acts of communication or constructive participation in the public sphere. Particularly for members of already marginalized groups, the reduction of their political articulations to emotional outbursts, or their representations as noise, violence, or excess, can silence the *illocutionary* dimensions of their communicative acts. Making only the form or rhetorical style of a communicative act visible and audible, such representations elide the specific intended meaning that an intersubjective performative act seeks to make understood. The intended meanings often remain unheard and unacknowledged.[23] An exclusive focus on form or style of communication allows potential listeners—in this case, authorities at a government-administered university—to convince themselves and others that they need not recognize an act as communicative and therefore can avoid hearing or acknowledging it. In these acts of communication that are specifically addressed to authorities, I analyze the complicity of social theory and historiography within the conceptualization of communicative acts in ways that license a refusal to hear. In doing so, I argue that, by situating each collective act of mobilization within a longer temporal frame, we can identify the role that earlier refusals of recognition have played in shaping the forms or "styles" of later actions. Paying attention to emotions in the absence of such larger contextualization can further disempower those already on the margins.

## Participatory and Adversarial Politics: Beyond European Historical Genealogies

Daniel Cefaï defines mobilization as "any collective action oriented by a concern for promoting a public good or for repealing a public evil, that gives itself adversaries to fight against."[24] He is not alone in associating collective actions with an adversarial stance. Scholars of the political in South Asia have inherited analytical tools from European and colonial political projects, making it more challenging to move beyond an understanding of collective mobilization as contention, resistance, insurgency, or opposition to or rejection of the state. As the introduction argues, social theorists are quick to assume that people mobilizing in the streets are resisting and questioning the legitimacy of the state or seeking to subvert and negate its authority.[25] Attending to the histories of those who engage in collective action and to the official reactions to their communicative efforts allows us to contextualize their desires for recognition from the existing state, for interpellation within its networks, and for inclusion within its ongoing processes of decision making.

Ideas of negation and adversarial opposition loom large in discussions of collective forms of state-directed assembly in both European and South Asian scholarship. Ranajit Guha's *Elementary Aspects of Peasant Insurgency*, for example, does much to reclaim peasants as political actors, particularly in his critique of Eric Hobsbawm's notion of the "pre-political."[26] However, by focusing only on the stages of protest in which actors had already become what he identifies as "rebels" and by framing his analysis as an examination of peasant *insurgencies*, Guha elides the earlier nonviolent actions that peasants took to appeal to the state. This has had the effect of inscribing a deep separation between the actions and ideologies of the peasant actors who form the object of his analysis and the forms of practice engaged in by elites. This bifurcation lives on, for example, in Partha Chatterjee's more contemporary distinction between *political society*—those who act collectively as objects of governmentality—and *civil society*, or the bourgeois minority who function as individual "rights-bearing citizens in the sense imagined by the constitution" and who interact with "organs of the state" either "in their individual capacities or as members of associations."[27] The intention of these analytic interventions has been to develop tools that take "subaltern" forms of claim-making seriously. Yet the acceptance of categorizations such as insurgency, rebellion, riot, and revolt—even for the many nonviolent actions and efforts to communicate with state officials that preceded uprisings—has had the effect of collapsing both violent and nonviolent forms of collective assembly under the sign of opposition, inscribing a sharp contrast between collective forms of action and individual forms.

The specific attention to the emotional states of peasant and other "subaltern" actors has played a significant role in constructing this binary. James Scott's foreword to the 1999 edition of Ranajit Guha's classic text makes this clear: "What Guha does is to restore the passion, anger, and indignation to popular movements. . . . The presumed cultural, economic, and social inferiority of the tribal, the peasant, the outcast(e) in a complex indigenous and colonial order—their subaltern status—is precisely the relationship that forms the basis for all acts of insubordination, resistance, refusal, and self-assertion."[28] In this way, the emotions of subaltern actors are frequently made central within the analyses of collective action. It is far less common for this same attention to be devoted to the emotions of those in positions of authority, even when there is archival evidence of their anxiety, anger, or fear.

What is crucial to recognize, then, is not a distinction between elite and nonelite cultural *forms* or *ideologies*, as Ranajit Guha implies in his use of terms like *rebel consciousness*, his understanding of society as shaped by "class antagonisms," and his adoption of the Gramscian perspective that the peasant "learnt to recognize himself not by the properties and attributes of his own social being but by a diminution, if not negation, of those of his superiors."[29] Instead, I argue for attending to distinctions in the level of responsiveness by authorities to various individuals and groups. Rapid and positive responses have empowered some voices to be easily heard politically *as* individuals, whereas others who find themselves repeatedly silenced or ignored have no hope of being heard unless they come together to act collectively—and even then they still may not be heard. Nonviolent efforts to communicate with the colonial state—using conventionally recognizable civil society tactics like letters, petitions, and delegations, as well as other nonviolent forms of what we today recognize as civil disobedience or noncooperation—often grew violent only after being repeatedly ignored or in response to violent efforts of the British to quell them.[30] Guha acknowledges the widespread use of civil society and nonviolent civil disobedience tactics by subaltern groups in a single sentence in passing when he writes, "In many instances [peasants] tried at first to obtain justice from the authorities by deputation (e.g., Titu's bidroha, 1831), petition (e.g., Khandesh riots, 1852), and peaceful demonstration (e.g., Indigo rebellion, 1860) and took up arms only as a last resort when all other means had failed."[31] With the exception of this single sentence, however, these various deputations, petitions, strikes, peaceful assemblies, and other nonviolent efforts in which Guha's various "rebels" engaged before resorting to violence disappear from the text, turning a continuum of practices shaped by the responsiveness of authorities into a binary between elite and subaltern "cultural" worlds. Nor are we offered insights into the emotions of the district collectors, police superintendents, army officers, and other colonial administrators or authority figures who issued orders to fire on collective assemblies or advocated the use of force to disperse the gathered crowds.

Similarly, the appeals made by members of the Ambedkar Students' Association also turned violent only after repeated unsuccessful efforts to gain an audience with authorities and be heard by them. Although it is unclear exactly how the encounter turned violent, we do know that the chief warden refused to meet with a smaller group of students the first time they sought an audience with him and that when they returned the next day at the appointed time, they found that he was not alone but had gathered reinforcements—including security personnel. One student suspected that the warden's derogatory attitude toward the Dalit students might have reflected "a deliberate campaign" to get them expelled: "Podile asked us to come back the next day. . . . He had staff, wardens and security personnel when we came back. Podile told us, 'I do not need to answer you; I have full powers given by the vc.'" He then asked the security guards to throw us out. A scuffle broke out and some glass got shattered. Podile then said we assaulted him and got ten of us rusticated."[32] It was clear to the students not only that the chief warden was not interested in hearing their concerns but also that he found them out of line for even daring to raise them, regarding their desire to be heard as itself insubordinate.

## Anger, Violence, and the Representation of Rational Speech Action

Mary Holmes has written of "the threat that anger poses for political order," suggesting that it has given rise to "strong cultural and political norms that seek to suppress the expression of anger."[33] Although she acknowledges that "anger bears no 'natural' allegiance to the downtrodden," any anger that challenges the status quo appears more marked and visible to those in power who enjoy the benefits of the current situation. Holmes therefore advocates for the importance of analyzing "anger as embedded within situated power relations."[34] She draws on the work of Elizabeth Spelman, who shows that the expression of anger by subordinate groups is not well tolerated by those in dominant positions. It is therefore much more likely to provoke both comment and retaliation than anger expressed by members of dominant groups.[35] As in the case of the university authorities' reaction to the members of the ASA, the expression of anger on the part of those in historically marginalized positions is often interpreted by those in power as itself "an act of insubordination."[36] All this suggests that, when it comes to the expression of anger, what matters is who is doing the expressing. Laura Ring's study of everyday life in a Karachi apartment building in Pakistan demonstrates how anger can be cultivated as "a hallmark . . . of masculine efficacy and power." It is not only permitted but also encouraged in boys—but not in girls—from a very young age, functioning as "a powerful lexicon of difference" that is "deeply imbricated in the specific symbolic content of ethnic enmity."[37] Ring's deep ethnography supports the argument that anger expressed by anyone in a historically subordinate position is much more likely to encounter negative comments and censure than anger expressed by those in dominant positions.

Thus, when Peter Lyman identifies anger as "an indispensable political emotion," writing that "without angry speech the body politic would lack the voice of the powerless questioning the justice of the dominant order," he is careful to demonstrate that "the expression of anger is [also] a resource for the dominant."[38] Why, then, is it the anger of the powerless that so often becomes the focus of attention? And why do we not interrogate the feelings experienced by those like Podile who appear to resent the presence within the university of members of historically marginalized groups? Daniel Cefaï argues, "There is no collective action without perceiving, communicating, dramatizing and legitimizing an experience of indignation."[39] Amelie Blom and Nicolas Jaoul, building on Cefaï, argue that "public responses to illegitimate orders and perceived injustices are rarely devoid of anger."[40] Yet how much of our understanding of the role of anger within collective mobilizations of the powerless is shaped by existing social theory? And what of the anger or other emotions experienced by those in historically privileged positions when they feel their privilege to be in jeopardy? Lyman, for example, reminds us that the dominant representation within social theory of anger as a "subordination injury" emerges out of a very particular European historical genealogy shaped by European class and status anxieties.[41]

Drawing on Max Weber's analysis of Protestant asceticism and the rise of professional knowledge workers and bureaucratic knowledge techniques, as well as Svend Ranulf's study of middle-class indignation at the arbitrary power of the European aristocracy, Lyman demonstrates how the claim that "reason should be in control of the emotions" functioned as a form of ideology specifically intended "to silence angry speech" and prevent the lower orders from sharing in the new redistributions of power within modern liberal societies.[42] In short, he locates "the social construction of order as the *opposite* of anger" as one of the most fundamental contradictions of European liberalism.[43]

The context of opposition to an entrenched and arbitrary European aristocracy by a newly emerging and status-anxious European mercantile middle class was quite different from that experienced by various populations in South Asia as they engaged with this very same European middle class of professionals—a class that eventually came to rule them. European commodity traders and administrators brought with them a version of the new impersonal legal and bureaucratic structures that were emerging in Europe and that helped secure their own political authority. However, the receptions and meanings attributed locally to these new legal and bureaucratic techniques by those who had little ideological investment in them meant that law and bureaucracy were understood much differently by residents of South Asia. Many simply took the legal and bureaucratic realms as yet another domain for playing out local competitions for power, status, and economic gain.[44] European discourses of liberalism—with their constructions of the autonomous individual as the ideal political subject, as well as the oppositions between rationality and emotion and between order and anger used to keep the lower orders at bay—spread through colonial encounters, but they never entered into a vacuum. Instead, these new discourses intersected with preexisting practices, ideas, and representations wherever they were introduced, leading to very different histories of the relationship between emotion and politics in, for example, South Asia or Latin America, when compared with Europe.[45] These historical differences must be taken into account as we approach the representation of emotion within politics, recognizing that practices that appear similar may not mean the same thing in different parts of the world. Indeed, the history of collective action in South Asia demonstrates that collective forms of mobilization and communication need not necessarily be premised on anger.

Take, for example, the contrast offered by Ramachandra Guha in his analysis of the reactions of the native rulers of the hill province of Tehri Garhwal versus those of the British colonial administrators who controlled the adjacent territory of Kumaun in response to nearly identical forms of practice. Analyzing a series of collective appeals in both locations during the early twentieth century, he demonstrates a marked difference in understandings of what he calls "rebellion as custom" and "rebellion as confrontation."[46] Although his use of the term *rebellion* here already reflects the dominant ideology that assumes all collective action to be rebellious rather than participatory, his close readings of concrete examples suggest something else. Guha focuses on the nonviolent form of collective communication known locally as *dhandak*, writing that "there existed in the moral order of society mechanisms whereby the peasantry could draw the attention of the monarch to the wrongdoings of officials."[47] He explains,

In the dhandak the absence of physical violence, barring isolated attacks on officials, was marked. The moral and cultural idiom of the dhandak was predicated firstly on the traditional relationship between raja [king] and praja [people], and secondly on the democratic character of these peasant communities. The rebels did not mean any harm to the king, whom they regarded as the embodiment of Badrinath [a manifestation of the deity Vishnu]. *In fact they actually believed they were helping the king restore justice.*[48]

Guha contrasts this understanding with that of British officials, "particularly those deputed from British India, who were often the targets of such revolts." He argues that the British officials "were unable to comprehend the social context of the dhandak" and therefore "invariably took *any* large demonstration to be an act of hostile rebellion."[49] Guha's description suggests that the dhandak was a communicative act rather than an act of rebellion or anger.

As K. M. Panikkar and Upendra Nath Ghoshal show, such actions were sanctioned by Hindu scripture in circumstances where the king had failed to protect his people.[50] Dhandak—along with *dum* or *dujam*, describing very similar forms of protest practiced in nearby Simla—sought to "draw the king's attention to some specific grievance" by "abandon[ing] work in the fields and march[ing] to the capital or to other prominent places."[51] Given that revenue collection would decrease when agricultural labor was suspended, Guha tells us that "the king would usually concede the demands of the striking farmers."[52] Guha interprets the marked "absence of physical violence" in such actions as evidence that local rulers were usually quite responsive in promising redress to such appeals, at which point "the crowd would disperse" and return to work.[53] In contrast, the British had much different understandings of the meanings of such collective appeals to authority, perceiving the massing of bodies in public space as itself a potential crime and typically responding with immediate punitive action rather than entertaining collective requests for audience.[54] Guha's extended analysis of a mass dhandak that emerged in 1930 in Tehri Garhwal reveals that there was no violence at all until the army was brought in to disperse the *dhandakis*.[55]

Although British officials clearly interpreted large demonstrations as angry and aggressive, it is not clear that either anger or rebelliousness defined such events. Instead, Guha portrays the dhandak as a socially condoned mechanism for communicating with authority and securing recognition as members of a larger social body. This example opens new possibilities for better conceptualizing how people in India have understood their relationships with state officials—not always in adversarial terms but also in relation to historical forms that enabled recognition, inclusion, and ongoing relationships between sovereign and subjects.

## Violence and Collective Action

As with the representation of anger in contexts where efforts to be recognized and heard had failed or were repeatedly ignored, violence is most obvious in the historical record in cases where the state sought to silence or disband an assembled group. Guha writes that, although the peasants of Kumaun offered a direct challenge to state authority, "physical violence was very rarely resorted to."[56] Archival evidence shows that, despite their frustrations with what they saw as insubordination and disorder, even British administrators recognized the absence of violence during collective actions in India. In response to the large collective action in Banaras in 1810–11, in which much of the population vacated the city to protest the imposition of a house tax, the collector himself acknowledged the peaceful nature of their action. Writing to the Revenue Department secretary at Fort William, he remarked, "Open violence does not seem their aim, they seem rather to vaunt their security in being unarmed in that a military force would not use deadly weapons against such inoffensive foes. And in this confidence they collect and increase, knowing that the civil power cannot disperse them, and thinking that the military will not."[57]

When collective actions did become violent, it was often in response to authorities firing on crowds to silence and disperse them.[58] The Indian historian Dharampal reinforces this view when he writes, "On the occasions when the people actually resorted to violence it was mostly a reaction to governmental terror, as in the cases of the various 'Bunds' in Maharashtra during the 1820–40s," a point that he connects with Tilly's observation of a similar phenomenon in the context of Europe.[59] Writes Tilly, "A large proportion of the European disturbances we have been surveying turned violent at exactly the moment when the authorities intervened to stop an illegal but nonviolent action. This is typical of violent strikes and demonstrations. Furthermore, the great bulk of the killing and wounding in those same disturbances was done by troops or police rather than by insurgents or demonstrators."[60] David Hardiman similarly recognizes a relationship between a nonresponsive state and the likelihood of violence, writing that "in situations in which the ruling classes were closed to any dialogue with the people and in which they enforced their will by brute force, action by insurgents was likely to involve counter-violence."[61] But, he continues, "in situations in which channels were kept open for dialogue, protests might be almost entirely non-violent."[62]

The completely nonviolent 1810–11 Banaras collective action, which culminated in the British revocation of their proposed house tax, stands in sharp contrast with a very similar collective action in Bareilly just six years later in 1816, when the East India Company (EIC) revived efforts to implement a house tax. Unlike the Banaras protest, however, British authorities responded to the Bareilly "disturbances" by slaughtering some three to four hundred protesters, and no concessions were ultimately made to protesters' concerns. Although the Bareilly events have been widely historicized as an uprising of communal violence, with the EIC justifying its violent actions as a necessary response to the threat of Muslim radicalism, Waleed Ziad argues that the protest was "a coordinated cross-class mode of collective action aimed at repealing the tax, rather than a pre-meditated revolt to overthrow the local political structure."[63] As in Banaras, the Bareilly events began with nonviolent efforts to raise concerns about assessment of the tax, which was intended to support the establishment of a centralized municipal police force. Opposition came from a wide range of communities within Bareilly—Hindus and Muslims, landed gentry, religious leaders, "Buneyahs [traders], cloth merchants, and brokers," as well as "weavers, shoemakers, bricklayers and all lower orders," led by a "popularly chosen" local religious leader, Mufti Mohammad 'Iwāz.[64] When the mufti submitted a petition to the British magistrate asking that the tax be repealed, the magistrate not only disregarded it but also reportedly had stocks and fetters prepared for the tax evaders.[65] The magistrate of Bareilly noted that "two proclamations were put up inviting people to resistance," "combinations were formed," and "on the 28th [of March] the shops in the town were shut, and an immense multitude of [unclear] and shopkeepers of every description assembled in a tumultuous manner near my Cutcherry [government office]" in a strike that continued for several weeks.[66] Following a skirmish with company soldiers after the second week, the strikers moved to a Sufi shrine on the outskirts of town, where they were joined by "considerable numbers" of supporters from neighboring towns in the region.[67] Company troops followed them there and finally ended the strike on April 21 by firing directly on the crowd, killing between three and four hundred protesters.[68]

In analyzing the events at Bareilly, Ziad observes that colonial commentators attributed the violence to the "natural temperament" of local residents, thereby identifying violence as an attribute of a particular type or class of individual.[69] British colonial officials described the initially peaceful protest as a "clash with an unruly mob" and as an "act of aggression upon 'the whole small European population, cooped up in the cantonment with only a handful of sepoys to protect them.'"[70] Ziad observes that even otherwise careful historians like Chris Bayly and Azra Alavi characterize these events as "premeditated uprisings promoted mainly by displaced Afghan nobility and an antagonistic religious official" and suggest that they typified "Muslim 'oppositional' attitudes" of the time.[71] Bayly, for example, calls the event a "savage urban riot that centered on a Muslim holy man" and "one of the most spectacular armed outbreaks against British rule."[72] What he fails to point out, however, is that the majority of the fatalities were among those opposed to the house tax. Strikers were killed at a rate more than ten times that of British soldiers, and it was the British who initiated the violence.[73]

### Collective Assembly: A Matter of "Style" and "Subculture"?

Because of the increased British documentation of any event that became violent, mass claim-making efforts before Gandhi's entrance into the nationalist movement in India were frequently historicized only under the sign of violence. Nonviolent collective actions that were resolved peaceably were less often documented. Nonviolent efforts to communicate with authorities that later turned violent, usually in response to British attacks, therefore typically entered historical archives as violent confrontations. One of the earliest objectives of the Subaltern Studies project, for example, was to make sense of the "logic and consistency" of "peasant violence," about which colonial counterinsurgency operations had amassed such rich archives.[74] In *Elementary Aspects of Peasant Insurgency*, for example, violence was the criterion that determined which events were chosen for analysis, lending the impression that subaltern actors were more prone to violence than elites. Yet as Charles Tilly reminds us, "Instead of constituting a sharp break from 'normal' political life, violent protests tend to accompany, complement, and extend organized, peaceful attempts by the same people to accomplish their objectives."[75]

Even more importantly, as Parthasarathi Muthukkaruppan argues, the violence perpetuated against marginalized groups—not only by the state but also by dominant groups fearful of losing their privileged positions—too often remains ignored.[76] He shows that violence is at the heart of persistent unequal social relationships like caste. Offering a close analysis not only of "visible and large-scale mass killings and mundane forms of corporeal violence meted out to Dalits" in India today but also structural and symbolic forms of violence, he points to the complicity of social science and other scholarship in actively eliding the central role of violence perpetuated against socially marginalized groups in constructing and maintaining discriminatory social structures.[77] "As long as the hierarchy is in place in all spheres of life for men and women," writes Muthukkaruppan, "it is misleading to characterise the relationship as though it is based on 'cultural' difference and not on inequality or hierarchy."[78]

Similarly, the examples cited in the previous section suggest that it is when authorities take steps to actively *silence* grievances that violence is most likely to occur. This observation should prompt us, as Muthukkaruppan suggests, to pay closer attention to the practices and violence of those in structural positions of power. Being wary of binary oppositions that represent marginalized subcultural groups as more prone to engage in violent or excessively emotional "styles" of political engagement can help us recognize the broader structural effects of repeatedly not being heard.

Subculturalist approaches have characterized not only violence but also collective assembly itself as a "style" of politics associated with certain groups. In critiquing these approaches, I demonstrate that collective assembly is a communicative medium available to all but typically used only when more cost-effective (in terms of time, labor, and energy) methods of communication like petitions, letter writing, deputation, and individual face-to-face forms of communication have proven ineffective. Framing forms of collective assembly along a continuum, rather than as a distinct "style," allows us to better see the ways in which "impolite," aggressive, or violent encounters may themselves be produced by authorities seeking to silence competing opinions rather than being an intentional style of political intervention of members of an underclass or marginalized group. However, once a political encounter has turned violent, regardless of who initiated it, it becomes substantially easier for those in positions of power or authority to dismiss the content of what a group was attempting to communicate and make heard.

The historical construction of a dichotomy between order and anger and between civility and violence has been so successful that social theorists and authorities alike frequently assume that anger and potential violence play a constitutive role in virtually *any* large collective effort to approach or meet with those in positions of power.[79] This assumption is not made in response to individual efforts to meet with authorities, even when the motivating concern is the same. A sharp distinction between rationality and emotion also continues to inform both theories of the political and theories of communication in ways that aspire to be universal. Jürgen Habermas's *Theory of Communicative Action* is one of the more influential examples of how this dichotomy continues to pervade social theory, and it is to this theory and its influences as a representative example that I now turn.[80]

## Civility, Speech Action, and Collective Assembly

Representations of civil society—and indeed, of civility more generally— have privileged a form of restrained and unemotional speech action as an essential feature of the public sphere, often portraying such speech as offering protection and enabling more equal access for all. Consider, for example, the role that forms of speech action associated with the English coffeehouses, French *salons*, and German *Tischgesellschaften* (table societies) of eighteenth-century bourgeois social life played in the development of Jürgen Habermas's theory of communicative action. Despite variations "in the size and composition of their publics," writes Habermas, these various spaces "had a number of institutional criteria in common." First and foremost, "they preserved a kind of social intercourse that, far from presupposing the equality of status, disregarded status altogether. The tendency replaced the celebration of rank with a tact befitting equals. The parity on whose basis alone the authority of the better argument could assert itself against that of social hierarchy and in the end can carry the day meant, in the thought of the day, the parity of 'common humanity.'"[81]

Although the extent of the recognition and inclusiveness of a "common humanity" was likely quite limited in the early eighteenth century, Habermas suggests that

> the same process that converted culture into a commodity . . . established the public as in principle inclusive. However exclusive the public might be in any given instance, it could never close itself off entirely and become consolidated as a clique; for it always understood and found itself immersed within a more inclusive public of all private people, persons who—insofar as they were propertied and educated—as readers, listeners, and spectators could avail themselves via the market of the objects that were subject to discussion. The issues discussed became "general" not merely in their significance, but also in their accessibility: everyone had to *be able* to participate.[82]

This, then, was seen by Habermas to constitute "a sphere in which state authority was publicly monitored through informed and critical discourse *by* the people."[83] As a result, "control over the public sphere by public authority was contested and finally wrested away by the critical reasoning of private persons on political issues."[84]

In his examination of why Habermas's concept of the public sphere has had such widespread and lasting appeal, the historian of England's coffeehouses, Brian Cowan, suggests, "For Habermas, the eighteenth-century public sphere was important in world-historical terms because it seems to offer the closest thing to an actually-existing example of what he would later develop into the notion of an 'ideal speech situation,' that is, the conditions in which *individuals* may freely engage in rational and critical debate about the political and ethical issues of the day and come to a universally agreed-upon conclusion."[85] A broadsheet of 1674 offered the following "Rules and Orders of the Coffee House" that, even if written as a parody as some suggest, mark the representation of the newly emerging set of values:

*Enter sirs freely, But first if you please, Peruse our Civil-Orders, which are these.*

First, Gentry, Tradesmen, all are welcome hither, and may without affront sit down together: Pre-eminence of place; none here should mind, But take the next fit seat that he can find: Nor need any, if Finer Persons come, Rise up to assigne to them his room.

He that shall any Quarrel here begin, Shall give each man a Dish t'atone the sin; And so shall he, whose Complements extend So far to drink in COFFEE to his friend; Let Noise of loud disputes be quite forborn, No Maudlin Lovers here in Corners mourn, But all be brisk, and talk, but not too much.[86]

By privileging restrained speech action, limiting loud and angry voices, and curtailing sentimentality and other strong emotions within an idealized public sphere as the keys to maintaining civility, attention has been directed away from the other end of the communicative process: the act of hearing or listening. Analytic attention to speech action perpetuates the hegemony of this idea of civility and frames the reception of speech acts and the act of recognition as playing no role in the maintenance of civility or, indeed, in the smooth workings of the public sphere.

A number of scholars, however, have challenged the presence of the ideal of formal universal equality that dominates theories of the public sphere and of democracy. Nancy Fraser, for example, questions the Habermasian claim that differences can be bracketed to enable interlocutors "to deliberate 'as if' they were social equals."[87] In critiquing the contributions of Habermas's foundational account of an idealized and exclusively *bourgeois* public sphere to the formation of normative discourses of the public sphere, she seeks to challenge the hegemonic representations of the public sphere that support liberal understandings of acceptable forms of participatory democratic practice. Fraser argues instead that competing publics have always contested the norms of the bourgeois public sphere. "Subaltern counterpublics," she writes, "function as bases and training grounds for agitational activities directed toward wider publics."[88] As discussed in the introduction, rather than seeing the public sphere as a space defined by the norms of masculine bourgeois society and reading the entrance of new and conflicting groups and interests as causing its decline, Fraser's argument suggests that we may be better served by attending to the sites where interactions occur not only of competing interests but also of competing *styles* of political participation. She writes, "Virtually from the beginning, counterpublics contested the exclusionary norms of the bourgeois public, elaborating alternative *styles* of political behavior and alternative norms of public speech."[89] Michael Warner similarly suggests that the competing styles of counterpublics, particularly those that employ the body in a "creative-expressive function," may help us imagine public agency—including agency in relation to the state—in new ways:

> It might be that embodied sociability is too important to them; they might not be organized by the hierarchy of faculties that elevates rational-critical reflection as the self-image of humanity; they might depend more heavily on performance spaces than on print.... To take such attributions of public agency seriously, however, we would need to inhabit *a culture with a different language ideology, a different social imaginary*. It is difficult to say what such a world would be like. It might need to be one with a different role for state-based thinking.[90]

In drawing attention to bodily challenges to hegemonic norms, Warner advocates broadening our understanding of what constitutes communicative acts beyond the speech actions of a masculine, heteronormative public sphere.

Despite the importance of these interventions, these approaches share with the critics of the ASA's actions a preoccupation with the styles and forms of communication rather than with their content and reception. Popular views mirror these academic approaches in associating particular styles of intervention with specific countercultures that seek to challenge bourgeois norms. Although it is certainly important to broaden the recognition of specific forms of communication, such arguments contribute to and exacerbate two persistent problems. First, tying particular *political* behaviors to specific groups through the attribution of culturally (or subculturally) framed political "styles" implies the existence of substantively unique cultures that in turn produce distinct styles of communication. And second, this ignores the ways that structural inequalities and repeated refusals of recognition push individuals toward the adoption of collective communicative methods that are both more labor intensive and better able to be heard.

In Britain, for example, unrest erupted across England in the wake of the August 2011 shooting death by white police of Mark Duggan, a twenty-nine-year-old man of mixed British and West Indian descent. In Tottenham, the London neighborhood where Duggan was shot and where the rioting began, a young Black man explained the need for escalation in public spaces in order to be heard. "Two months ago we marched to Scotland Yard," he told reporters, "more than 2,000 of us, all blacks, and it was peaceful and calm, and you know what? Not a word in the press. Last night a bit of rioting and looting and look around you." The reporter in turn reflects, "Eavesdropping from among the onlookers, I looked around. A dozen TV crews and newspaper reporters interviewing the young men everywhere."[91]

Yet most commentators portrayed the unrest as resulting from a cultural style of behavior that encourages rioting, reflecting a "street code of vengeance,"[92] a "culture of violence" and a "pernicious culture of hatred,"[93] or a "particular sort of violent, destructive, nihilistic gangster culture,"[94] rather than recognizing the events as the escalation of increasingly frustrated efforts to be heard.[95] In 2014, during collective assemblies in the United States protesting police brutality against Black Americans in the wake of the wrongful death of Eric Garner, protesters took pains to communicate that their demonstrations were not riots but rather attempts to communicate with police, policy makers, and members of the judiciary.[96] Daniel J. Watt, in a political performance outside Manhattan's Times Square police station on July 29, 2014, made clear that he and his collaborators aspired "to provoke, not riots, but conversation."[97] Watt's song lyrics illustrate that concerns over racial disparities in policing in the United States have been both misunderstood and gone unheard, and that when repeated efforts to engage in conversation go unheard, there is little choice but to find ways to amplify one's communicative efforts. At the same time, these examples also illustrate the structural disparities that exist in policing, with members of groups marginalized along racial and caste lines far more likely to be the victims of violence than the perpetrators, despite being more quickly associated with "cultures" of violence.

Labeling collective assemblies—both nonviolent ones and those that for whatever reason do turn violent—as political "styles" or as reflecting a unique political "culture" obscures the repeated efforts to be heard made by members of marginalized groups that are often identical to the forms of political communication used by members of dominant groups. These include (but are not limited to) writing letters, signing and circulating petitions, investing in efforts to hold face-to-face meetings with political leaders and representatives of the state, and engaging in restrained, rational, and polite speech actions. As the efforts made by members of the ASA at the University of Hyderabad demonstrate, even when forms of political communication used by members of marginalized groups do conform to what are seen as mainstream norms of civility, they may still continue to go unheard, unrecognized, and ignored. And, as argued in the introduction, the goal of these communicative acts is often simply to ensure equal and uniform enforcement of existing laws and constitutional provisions or to hold state representatives and officials accountable to their promises.[98]

## Speech Acts, Validity Claims, and Recognition

Let us return to the situation with which this chapter opened. Members of the ASA repeatedly raised what Habermas would call a validity claim: "The speech act of one person succeeds only if the other accepts the offer contained in it by taking (however implicitly) a 'yes' or 'no' position on a validity claim that is in principle criticizable. Both ego, who raises a validity claim with his utterance, and alter, who recognizes or rejects it, base their decisions on potential grounds or reasons."[99]

Yet rather than receiving either a "yes" or a "no"—agreement or rejection of the specific validity claim in question based on "potential grounds or reasons"—members of the ASA instead received silence (from the authorities whom they addressed), retribution (in the removal of the Dalit hostel warden who had supported them), and scorn and degradation (from others in the hostel dining room who objected to their very presence and participation in the university public sphere and who expressed this by hanging up hostile posters). What the members of the ASA did *not* receive were arguments countering their claims. By Habermas's definition, theirs was a failed speech act. But why did it fail? To answer this, we must look beyond the purely linguistic features of the communicative acts engaged in by members of the ASA to examine the conditions of recognition.

Expressing frustration with Habermas's efforts to "theorize modes of rational discourse purified of rhetoric," Iris Young argues that he builds on "a strain of Western philosophy" that claims that "allegedly purely rational discourse abstracts from or transcends the situatedness of desire, interest, or historical specificity, and can be uttered and criticized solely in terms of its claims to truth."[100] She advocates instead for "an expanded conception of political communication" by drawing on Emmanuel Levinas's conception of the "Saying" (the aspect of communication that involves "subject-to-subject recognition") as a supplement to Habermas's attention to what Levinas calls the "Said" (the "aspect of expressing content between the subjects").[101] Young extends Levinas's focus on the role played by forms of public recognition within political interactions by identifying greetings as a fundamental part of inclusive communication.[102] This "public acknowledgement," she writes, "names communicative political gestures through which those who have conflicts . . . *recognize* others as included in the discussion, especially those with whom they differ in opinion, interest, or social location."[103] Unlike Charles Taylor's attention to a politics of recognition as a political end, however, Young sees recognition "as a condition rather than a goal of political communication that aims to solve problems justly."[104] Locating her intervention within "a theory of democratic inclusion" that, she argues, "requires an expanded conception of political communication," she suggests that "the political functions of such moments of greeting are to assert discursive equality and establish or re-establish the trust necessary for discussion to proceed in good faith."[105] As such, Young argues that they represent a moment "prior to and a condition for making assertions and giving reasons for them."[106] As a precondition, they are as essential to inclusive political communication as the actual assertions and reasons.

Such an analysis prioritizes attention to efforts that expand or reduce opportunities for recognition and face-to-face communication. In India, earlier ideals of socially embedded relationships with those in authority now intersect in complex ways with discourses of ideal speech action drawn from liberal frameworks that celebrate individual autonomy, disinterestedness, and impersonal technique. As we have seen, practices such as holding regular audiences to which constituents may bring concerns, formally acknowledging collective appeals, and permitting spaces in front of government offices to be used for assembly are still regarded by many as essential parts of how democracy works in South Asia. At the same time, however, these features of democracy have been threatened not only by a history of efforts to limit political access to public spaces but also by attempts to reduce or restrict opportunities for recognition and face-to-face communication. New innovations that have sought to individualize and depersonalize administrative processes, including moves toward "e-governance" and personal identity numbers, have similarly made processes of collective recognition more challenging.[107]

In the case of the ASA, rather than branding their "style" of communication as more emotional or violent than that of other students, such an expanded conception of political communication would focus not simply on its members' communicative acts but also on the conditions that have enabled or prevented them from being heard. It also would encourage attention to the very conditions of presence, noticing, for example, that efforts to raise the cost of the hostel mess fees well above the level of university fellowships have challenged the very presence of economically marginalized students within the space of the university.

## Analyzing Communicative "Style," Emotion, and Politics

When writing about the "style" of political engagement, therefore, it is important to ask at every stage (1) whose "style" we are attending to; (2) where these individuals are located socially and politically; (3) at what point in a longer progression of efforts to communicate is "style" (including emotional states, anger, or violence) first marked; (4) who first marks communicative "styles"; and (5) what their relationship is with those whose "style" is marked. By recognizing the conditions that enable those already empowered to expect that their voices will be heard and acknowledged even when they speak softly, in moderate tones or as individuals, we can approach the history of the autonomous speaking subject from an alternate perspective. Those who stake exclusive claims to rationality and civility are too often those with existing access to established networks of power. Their attempts to frame their audibility simply as the product of the reasonableness of their arguments stem from the same conditions of privilege that also enable them to ignore, refuse to acknowledge, and silence communicative efforts with which they do not wish to engage. This suggests that we must be particularly attentive to all such markings of difference and must ask what work is being accomplished when collective actions are labeled as angry, emotional, disruptive, uncivil, or irrational.

In addition, we must not attend only to the anger, emotion, or emotional styles of those in structurally less powerful positions, effectively treating the communicative actions of those with access to networks of power as though they do not also experience emotion. In the case of the expulsion of the ten Dalit students from the University of Hyderabad in 2002, we should be equally interested in the emotions of the chief warden and of the students from dominant caste communities responsible for the derogatory posters. Asking about the role that anger and resentment play among caste Hindus who fear their own loss of privilege in the face of the expanded inclusion of historically marginalized groups can help redistribute our attention to emotion. As Iris Young observes, "The only remedy for the dismissiveness with which some political expressions are treated on grounds that they are too dramatic, emotional, or figurative is to notice that any discursive content and argument is embodied in situated style and rhetoric. . . . No discourse lacks emotional tone; 'dispassionate' discourses carry an emotional tone of calm and distance."[108] Attending to the ways that proximity to institutional authority shapes the freedom to play with various styles of communication can help avoid reinforcing the idea that rationality is the absence of emotion.

Rather than strengthening existing hierarchies by assuming that anger is the standard *choice* of the marginalized and that calm speech is the *choice* of those in positions of power, we can work to recognize the work that goes into *not* hearing, as well as the ways in which depersonalized bureaucratic structures can function to relieve those in authority from the obligation to listen or to recognize collective communicative acts as political participation.[109] Tracking historically, ethnographically, and textually the construction and maintenance of powerful distinctions in the representation and marking of different political and communicative styles; interrogating the "styles" and emotions of structurally empowered speakers as often as we do the styles of those already marginalized; and asking what those in power stand to gain from dissecting the communicative styles of those on the margins can go a long way toward these goals. In the next chapter, I explore the longer history of representations of the autonomous individual speaking subject and collective forms of communication in the wake of the deliberative turn in the study of democracy.

# THREE. COLLECTIVE ASSEMBLY AND THE "ROAR OF THE PEOPLE"

Corporeal Forms of "Making Known" and the Deliberative Turn

As certain of these persons have persisted in attending daily at the Board of Trade office, the Board here explain that, under the existing Regulations each *Individual* weaver, if aggrieved, has the means of laying his Complaint before the Commercial Resident, or as the case may be of proceeding by an action in the Zillah Court, and with this protection held out to the weavers of Vizagapatam *Individually*, The Board cannot sanction Combinations of weavers for the purpose of Making General Complaints nor acknowledge persons stating themselves to be agents of such Combinations. The Board cannot dismiss this Petition without noticing the disrespectful *style* thereof to the authorities of Government. —J. GWATKIN, Secretary, Board of Trade, Madras, March 1, 1817

Why is it that we have students here forming action committees? When they came to me, I told them clearly that I was prepared to meet students but not an Action Committee. I do not accept action committees of students or workers or anyone else. —JAWAHARLAL NEHRU, prime minister of India, "Students and Discipline," Patna, August 30, 1955

"This is an atrocity," Kaloji Narayana Rao exclaimed, banging his hand on the table for emphasis. "This is an atrocity and exploitation. The Telangana person will never be in advantage in any field, spoken language or written language. Neither he can become a storywriter, nor a writer, nor a poet, nor an essayist. Nothing. In everything he will fail." Five years before his death in 2002, I sat with the octogenarian activist in his front room one humid April afternoon. A long-standing advocate of the creation of a separate regional state of Telangana within the Indian nation as a response to economic and cultural domination by migrants from coastal regions of Telugu-speaking southern India, Kaloji emphasized the great harm caused by the Telugu Spoken Language Movement (Vyavahārika Bhāṣa Udyamam) of the early twentieth century. The movement, which sought to make written Telugu more closely resemble ordinary educated speech, has been widely historicized as a liberal effort to modernize the Telugu language and make literacy in Telugu (the most widely spoken language in southern India) easier to acquire, extending the written language to a broader population.[1] But Kaloji argued that the movement had instead perpetuated a widespread "atrocity" and "exploitation" of the residents of the more economically marginalized Telugu-speaking regions, particularly in the wake of the linguistic reorganization of India in 1956.[2] By defining the speech of dominant groups within the most agriculturally prosperous and economically powerful districts of Telugu-speaking south India as the new "standard Telugu," advocates of the Spoken Language Movement effectively placed those from the remaining regions under linguistic domination.

Kaloji was not alone in experiencing linguistic domination. During my fieldwork numerous residents of Telangana reported having their speech ignored or mocked by migrants from coastal Andhra. Sridevi, who grew up in the Telangana district of Mahbubnagar, described her experience in a botany class at Osmania University in Hyderabad. Even though Osmania University and the city of Hyderabad both lie within Telangana and she correctly identified a groundnut plant by using the term commonly used for the plant in Telangana, her answer was greeted with laughter from the professor and the rest of the class, most of whom were from coastal Andhra.

The experience of domination and humiliation described by Kaloji, Sridevi, and many others—not only linguistic but also economic and political—fueled the widespread assemblies, strikes, and other public performances that culminated in the creation of India's twenty-ninth state on June 2, 2014. Organized by the Telangana Joint Action Committee, the umbrella organization formed in 2009 to coordinate the efforts of a wide range of existing organizations, the Jana Garjana (People's Roar) assemblies and Sakala Janula Samme (All People's Strike) described in the introduction sought to hold elected officials to their campaign promises to bifurcate the existing regional state of Andhra Pradesh and create the new state of Telangana. These promises had been made and broken several times by different political parties.[3] The massive 2010 and 2011 public meetings—each involving more than a million participants—were just two representational performances in a long series of rallies, processions, long-distance pilgrimages to the site of a seat of power, road and rail blockades, walkouts of hundreds of thousands of government employees, mass resignations of elected officials, and a "Million March," all of which were framed in relation to six decades of earlier efforts by Telangana residents to seek recognition.

The imposition of an alien communicative standard on residents of the more economically disadvantaged Telugu-speaking regions of Telangana might not have been as devastating if it had not occurred along with another, even more significant, shift in communicative regimes. In the nineteenth and twentieth centuries, individual speech action, the voice of the autonomous individual, and new forms of deliberation and debate—both oral and printed—began to be valorized in ways that reframed the meanings of collective, corporeal forms of representation, communication, and mediation. This chapter examines the relationship between individual speech action and large-scale collective actions like the Jana Garjana assemblies and the Sakala Janula Samme and their respective roles within the world's largest democracy. It uses scholarship from South Asia along with analyses of everyday practice to argue that such collective performances are neither antithetical nor incidental to the functioning of India's democracy but rather play an essential role in how representation works in India today.

To build this argument, the chapter analyzes two of the most dominant Euro-American frameworks used today for understanding democratic politics: deliberative democracy and agonistic pluralism. Using the concept of "civility" as an entry point, I demonstrate that both theoretical approaches fail to account for the larger processes that, over time, have encouraged participation in collective actions—both in India and arguably elsewhere as well. The chapter argues that these frameworks ignore the very conditions that make individual speech audible and legible in the first place: political recognition and the responsiveness of authorities. As Sharika Thiranagama, Tobias Kelly, and Carlos Forment argue in their introduction to a special issue of *Anthropological Theory* on "Civility: Global Perspectives," liberal theoretical approaches emerging from the "development of bourgeois urban cultures of post-Enlightenment Europe" have dominated scholarship not only on democratic participation but also on civility.[4] Querying approaches to civility that explore "how people relate to each other where they would appear to have profound differences," Thiranagama and her coeditors show how these dominant accounts focus primarily on individual comportment in the face of difference: "the public citizen, willing and able to contribute to the wider good" or "free individuals" who "come together in a space of equality."[5] In using the work of Norbert Elias to trace the ways that this civility of the individual emerges not in the face of the disappearance of violence but rather in conjunction with its reorganization, they point to the importance of attending to the state's role in creating conditions of political recognition. They conclude by bringing histories of recent struggles for dignity and self-respect in the context of deeply embedded social hierarchies— including Dalit struggles and the south Indian Self-Respect Movement—into conversation with Étienne Balibar's reflections on the role of civility in confronting dominating forms of violence.[6] Responding to their call to provincialize civility, this chapter places ethnographic analysis of collective action in the context of postcolonial India into dialogue with both the redirection of attention toward the role of the state in creating conditions for civility and Balibar's privileging of collective political action over the comportment of individuals in his conceptualization of civility.[7]

The events that led to the formation of the new Indian state of Telangana in 2014 are just one example of how collective corporeal action has been used in India. Work stoppages and the collective emptying and filling of public spaces occur in India at rates much higher than in many other parts of the world. As fundamental features of everyday political practice in India, they offer a productive context for challenging understandings of collective action, civility, and incivility generated in Euro-American contexts (see figure 3.1).[8] Police records collected over one eleven-month period in 2011 from the ten districts of the Telangana region, for example, document 1,847 separate collective assemblies using public space in which criminal charges were filed—an average of five to six per day. This figure does not include legal assemblies for which permits were obtained or unofficial assemblies in which the police did not intervene, either out of sympathy or indifference.[9] More generally, the combined region of Telangana and Andhra Pradesh saw a dramatic increase from only four agitations in 2007 to 9,882 in 2015 (956 in Andhra Pradesh, and 8,926 in the new state of Telangana).[10] By comparison, the number of agitations in the north Indian state of Uttar Pradesh—the most populous state in India with a population more than five and a half times that of Telangana—increased from 1,156 in 2006 to 5,758 in 2015.[11]

And yet, despite extensive attention to Gandhi's use of civil disobedience in Indian nationalist confrontations of British colonial rule,[12] the tools and frameworks for thinking about political action within India's contemporary democracy continue to be heavily influenced by Western political theory's attention to individuals as the operative political unit, either as voters or

FIGURE 3.1. Thousands of *anganwadi* (rural government childcare) contract workers from throughout the state of Karnataka participate in a "Bangalore Chalo" (Let's Go to Bangalore) procession "to draw the government's attention to their long-pending demands," Bangalore, February 12, 2015 (photo: V. J. K. Nair/All India Federation of Anganwadi Workers and Helpers).

as individual contributors to deliberative processes.[13] Shaped by the specific historical genealogies and definitions that influenced the development of democratic forms in European and North American contexts, scholars continue to identify civil disobedience, general strikes, and other forms of collective political engagement in India as derivative imitations of collective forms that originated in the West only in the wake of industrialization (see chapter 4) or as ancillary to what is perceived to be the real stuff of democracy—elections.[14] Even scholars who have done the most to encourage serious attention to everyday forms of collective corporeal political engagement in India frequently historicize such actions under the signs of insurgency and violence, arguing that they belong to a domain separate from "civil society" or framing them as "rituals of humiliating the officialdom" that are "not oriented to a future"—thereby offering little purchase for considering them as fundamental parts of representational democratic practices or in relation to the concept of civility.[15]

It is for these reasons that closer attention to the everyday practices of India's "actually existing democracy" can help us generate new tools for analyzing collective action and its relationship to civility.[16] In what follows, I outline the frameworks offered by advocates of deliberative democratic models and proponents of agonistic pluralism, before analyzing ethnographic examples from southern India to identify and clear a productive space between the deliberative and agonistic models. As I demonstrate, both approaches see collective corporeal forms of action—both violent and nonviolent—as inherently adversarial in nature while not making similar assumptions about individual speech action. If individual speech action is portrayed as ranging from polite and constructive participation in deliberation to antagonistic incivility, collective action, as I show, is seen as running a narrower gamut beginning with agonistic intervention, which frames others as adversaries, and extending to antagonistic refusals that frame others as enemies.[17] Chantal Mouffe, for example, in her advocacy of a model of agonistic pluralism that can channel "*collective* passions . . . that can [otherwise] tear up the very basis of civility," writes, "*Antagonism* is a struggle between enemies, while *agonism* is struggle between adversaries."[18] There appears to be no space within either deliberative or agonistic frameworks to consider *collective* action as nonadversarial participation on a par with individual contributions to deliberation. Even representations of civil resistance or civil disobedience frame "civil" forms of collective action as adversarial, defined by opposition, rejection, or resistance to existing structures of authority and hegemony. Although not disavowing the important contribution made by agonistic pluralist approaches to the acknowledgment of conflict in the public sphere, I argue that together these two frameworks fail to capture a variety of practices and understandings that operate in India and elsewhere today. The relative density and routine nature of participatory collective practices in the former British colony of India, however, help make clearer the distinction I am drawing between hailing representatives of the state and rejecting them, enabling the wider application of this argument to other contexts in the world.

In framing collective political action as naturally contentious and adversarial, both deliberative and agonistic frameworks fail to account for examples of collective corporeal action that seek to "hail the state" as a way to be heard, recognized, and included—even peripherally—in processes of decision making. The examples that follow build on the argument in chapter 2 that positions collective forms of political action in relation to longer trajectories of efforts to be included within deliberative political processes. Understanding collective political action as a form of amplification and desire for inclusion moves it from its default positioning in opposition to individual speech action, situating it instead along a continuum of participatory forms of action. Without political recognition, I argue, it is difficult for civility to be legible. Approaches to the analysis of collective communicative action, then, need to be able to account for efforts to create the conditions necessary for civility to exist and thrive.

Deliberative Democratic Approaches to Civility:
Individual "Soft Speech" as the Foundation
of "Civil" Society

John Dryzek argues that "the essence of democracy itself is now widely taken to be deliberation, as opposed to voting, interest aggregation, constitutional rights, or even self-government," marking what he calls "the deliberative turn in democratic theory."[19] But he also observes that this has meant that "deliberative democracy's welcome for forms of communication is conditional."[20] This turn to a Habermasian emphasis on individual speech action and rational debate and deliberation as the most important site of political subjectivity has made civility a crucial foundation for deliberative encounters.[21] Colin Farrelly, for example, defines civility as "a willingness to listen to others, a commitment to resolve our disagreements via deliberation and a democratic process rather than through deception, manipulation or the appeal to violence." Characterizing civility as "a prerequisite for achieving a reasoned, negotiated compromise on how we are to live together as a society," he contrasts what he calls "civic liberalism" with current practices that "pit factions of society against one another in a struggle to win or retain political power."[22]

The definition of civility as something on which deliberative democracy and a functioning civil society depend locates it firmly within the autonomous individual as a set of practices or style of comportment to be affirmed and cultivated as preparation for participation as an individual within deliberative processes. Edward Shils, for example, makes a distinction in his definition of civility between "the civility of good manners" and "the civility of civil society." The former, he writes, has been understood to mean "courtesy, well-spokenness, moderation, respect for others, self-restraint, gentlemanliness, urbanity, refinement, good manners, politeness . . . the description of the conduct of individuals in the immediate presence of each other." The latter "considers others as fellow-citizens of equal dignity in their rights and obligations as members of civil society; it means regarding other persons, including one's adversaries, as members of the same inclusive collectivity, i.e., as members of the same society, even though they belong to different parties or to different religious communities or to different ethnic groups."[23] Clarifying that the "civility of good manners" is included in the "civility of civil society," Shils characterizes civility as "a mode of political action which postulates that antagonists are also members of the same society, that they participate in the same collective self-consciousness. The individual who acts with civility regards the individuals who are its objects as being one with himself and each other, as being parts of a single entity."[24] Shils invokes Carl Schmitt's characterization of the political activity of a society "organized around the poles of friends and enemies" as the "antithesis of civil society" and as an accurate description only of "societies which are on the verge of or are already engaged in civil war."[25] He then uses this opposition to argue that "the effectiveness of the laws both in the state and in civil society—and the family—depends in part on the civility of individuals."[26] "Softly spoken, respectful speech is more pleasing to listen to than harsh, contemptuous speech," he asserts. "Civility in manners holds anger and resentment in check; it has a calming, pacifying effect on the sentiment. It might make for less excitability. Civil manners are aesthetically pleasing and morally right. Civil manners redound to the benefit of political activity."[27] Thus, it is soft speech, expressed by individuals, that best characterizes civility for Shils.

Richard Boyd also offers two versions of the definition of civility, distinguishing between the "formal" meaning of civility, or "the manners, politeness, courtesies or other formalities of face-to-face interactions in everyday life," and the "substantive" meaning, "the condition of being a member of a political community."[28] The former implies that "to be 'civil' is to speak or interact with others in ways that are mannerly, respectful or sociable," whereas the latter brings into focus the "attendant rights and responsibility" linked to membership in "the same political community, interacting on grounds of civic equality."[29] The analyses offered by Shils and Boyd are representative of liberal understandings of civility more generally in their emphasis on the individual as the site of civility—whether focusing on individual comportment, the rights and responsibilities of the individual as a member of a political community, or the regard that individuals hold for others. Viewed in this way, civility is recognizable in the behavior, comportment, and, most of all, the speech of individuals. "Respect for others" (including one's adversaries), "softly spoken, respectful speech," the holding of "anger and resentment [and other strong emotion] in check"—these are the marks of civility on which civil society is thought to be built. In this chapter, however, I demonstrate that placing attention on the speech and comportment of individuals ignores the very conditions that enable soft speech to be audible in the first place: recognition and responsiveness.

Rather than approaching civility as a quality of comportment or manners locatable within autonomous individuals and forming a precondition for democracy, as advocates of deliberative democracy do, I argue that we can approach civility as a condition created through recognition and the existence of a responsive state—one whose representatives entertain and give audience to the concerns and grievances of the governed and recognize them as political subjects. Viewing civility as an effect rather than a cause or precondition enables us to highlight both the discontinuities and the continuities of the relationship between state representatives and those who seek to interact with and be recognized by them. I define a responsive state, then, as one in which representatives recognize their authority as contingent on their ongoing relationship with and responsiveness to those whom they govern. Viewed in this way, some forms of apparent incivility—ranging from acts interpreted as disrespect to varieties of violence and disruptive behavior—appear structurally as the product of unresponsive, repressive, or inflexible authorities. In other words, only in a context in which authorities recognize and are responsive to the concerns, grievances, and conditions of life of its citizens, and offer structures through which these considerations can not only be expressed but also heard, can civility thrive. A goal of this book is to shift our analytic attention away from the comportment surrounding individual communicative actions to that surrounding the other end of the communicative chain: what Richard Burghart calls "the conditions of listening."[30] Although many proponents of deliberative democracy would agree in theory that "a willingness to listen to others"[31] is as important as "softly spoken, respectful speech,"[32] in practice, it is not at all uncommon for some people to find that their soft speech is more easily heard than the soft speech of others, usually for reasons that have little to do with the rationality of their arguments, as this chapter's examples illustrate.[33]

## "The Conditions of Listening"

In his analysis of forms of political communication in Nepal, Burghart challenges from a different angle the assumptions behind an ideal of communicative speech action premised on equality. Burghart suggests that, in the context of South Asia, "the voice of authority . . . is a deliberately curtailed speech in which the words used are few, the amplitude in low." He combines this with the observations that agency in South Asia is often "expressed by manual passivity and self-restraint" and that these features are imitated "in 'big caste' speakers, leaving rustic speakers to express through their vociferousness the necessity of their domination."[34] There is substantial evidence that sovereigns and high-status speakers in South Asia traditionally did not speak in public and, indeed, did not need to do so to have their desires met and their concerns addressed quickly and efficiently. They might receive subjects and listen to the oration of supplicants, but it was a sign of their power that they did not need to speak. Bernard Bate demonstrates persuasively that political oratory—the speaking of higher-status individuals in public—emerged only in the early decades of the twentieth century:[35]

> This period also saw the transformation of practices among higher-status people who, in previous generations, had left loud, audience-directed utterances (in particular, drumming) to lower classes. The drum, a leather-bound object wielded by the lowest classes and castes, appears as the very paradigm of generalized interpellation in Tamil India, for millennia perhaps, a calling out to a social universe regardless of status or distinction. Its voice or "roar" [*murasu*] spoke to all without distinction, a feature that led *murasu* to become the name of some early Tamil newspapers, texts printed to be broadcast into the world. To be a leader, on the other hand, such as a king or even a district or village-level official, was to be relatively taciturn in speech, even silent; it certainly did not involve anything as vulgar as directly addressing a crowd.[36]

Political leaders, government bureaucrats, chief hostel wardens, and others of status inherited from these earlier sovereigns the power to receive supplicants and offer them an audience, but it continues to be a sign of their status that they do not need to speak in public, and when they do, it is more likely to be a public performance of their power than an effort to persuade an audience or contribute as equals to a shared dialogue and open debate.

Ethnographic evidence further substantiates this inheritance. Anastasia Piliavsky's research in small-town Rajasthan illustrates that, far from promoting free and equal participation in dialogue and debate, public spaces are morally ambivalent spaces of potential exposure in which people from "reputable families" take pains to be extra vigilant about their words, actions, and appearances to tightly protect the images they project. Piliavsky writes,

"The general rule for respectable people is that in the bazaar all personal expression must be subdued: one must not speak too much, gesticulate wildly, laugh loudly, or even smile broadly enough to show teeth."[37] Indeed, she observes, "Only 'bazaar people' loaf about in the streets—uncouth youths, rickshaw drivers, beggars, and other riffraff. Respectable people move quickly and cautiously across roads from one familiar place to the next."[38] This does not mean that political leaders and other high-status individuals never speak in public, but when they do, their speeches are sermons rather than "invitations to dialogue or contributions to debate."[39]

But when speaking in public can itself be seen as a sign of low status, this presents a significant problem for those without status who want to intervene in the political sphere. Or, perhaps more accurately, it presents a significant problem for existing theories of speech action and the public sphere. Burghart writes that if "the king or highest authority in the land has the voice of authority and is also the listener, then how is it for others who may wish to speak up? They cannot speak with authority. They cannot speak from a platform upon which they will be listened to." The dilemma for those from historically marginalized backgrounds is that, if they want to speak so they can be heard, they must do so in ways that mark their hierarchically low position—loudly, repeatedly, emotionally, even angrily—or they must find other ways to make known their grievances and achieve recognition. Burghart provides evidence of long-standing collective corporeal strategies for exerting power within asymmetrical relationships in South Asia, suggesting that in a political structure that reflects embedded social hierarchies, power can move in two directions: the person at the top depends on the cooperation and functioning of those below to be able to claim the right to rule. Those who are in distress or have a grievance alert the more powerful party to this fact by "making known" their distress, but not necessarily via speech. Burghart offers an illustration from his work in Nepal, in which engaging in a symbolic or token strike (*sanketi hartāl*) can make a grievance noticeable enough to attract the attention of the person at the top but not noticeable enough to draw public attention. By drawing the attention of their superiors to the fact "that there is some *taklīf* [problem]" and symbolically demonstrating that "the body politic no longer functions," participants create an opportunity for resolution or negotiation.[40] If those in authority do not respond, then they are failing in their obligations, and a moral space has been created for public criticism. This allows dependents to escalate their protest, air their grievance in front of a broader—now public—authority (the authority of public opinion), and pose themselves as obstacles to their superior's freedom of movement. This escalation is more easily achieved collectively, however, as petitioners in Telangana and generations of petitioners in structurally less powerful positions before them have recognized.

As Burghart concludes, "The very act of constructing a moral space for criticism . . . involves an attempt to communicate with the king, rather than simply an act of negation or rebellion. Therefore, as a form of consciousness it is rather more theatrical than critical."[41] This also helps explain why—despite the rise of democratic electoral politics in South Asia with its ideology of one person, one vote—efforts to reify authorities and their relationships with particular social bodies have been a common precondition for political action, offering a dramatic contrast to theories of collective mobilization as a rejection of or resistance to authority. The examples of collective assembly offered throughout this book illustrate the wide range of ways of "making known" in Indian history and support the argument for a theoretical and historiographic framework that recognizes not only speech actions but also the "conditions of listening" within the public sphere and the forms of communicative action that make hearing and recognition possible.

Repeated refusals of recognition can push those who are ignored or silenced toward forms of amplification that enable them to be heard more effectively. Scholars have pointed to the constitutive role of the state in mobilizing collective action. This happens, for example, when the state refuses to recognize caste violence or extend equal legal protections to socially marginalized groups. K. Satyanarayana observes that Dalit collective political mobilization in independent India was spurred by the failures of the state to prosecute upper-caste groups who carried out brutal mass killings of Dalits, including in "Kilvenmani (1968) in Tamil Nadu, Belchi (1977) in Bihar and Karamchedu (1985) in Andhra Pradesh." He argues that "a direct consequence of this modern violence in post-independence India is the emergence of dalit movements."[42] The failures of both the police and the court system to arrest and convict the perpetrators of this violence, as well as the perception that police have sided with them, have played particularly significant roles in mobilizing Dalit collective political organization.[43]

This parallels the pain, frustration, and exhaustion experienced by Black citizens in the United Kingdom and the United States in the face of unequal policing that have led to movements such as Black Lives Matter.[44] A corollary of my argument, then, is that violence need not necessarily be seen as the product or outcome of incivility. Instead, when violence emerges in the context of collective forms of hailing, my proposed shift in analytic attention can reveal it to be the direct result of unresponsive authorities who fail to recognize the concerns of particular segments of citizens or who criminalize or aggressively silence communication through their own initiation of violence.[45]

## Agonistic Approaches to Civility and Collective Action: Collectives Pitted in Struggle

Although Farrelly does not explicitly label the model against which he defines civic liberalism—a model in which factions of society are pitted in struggle against one another—his description corresponds with what other scholars have characterized as agonistic pluralism.[46] On the surface, agonistic pluralism appears better suited than models of deliberative democracy for theorizing the widespread use of collective political practices, not only in India but also in other democratic contexts worldwide. Chantal Mouffe, for example, who focuses on "the creation of collective political identities," argues persuasively that "political identities are not pre-given but constituted and reconstituted through debate in the public sphere."[47] And yet, although advocates of deliberative and agonistic models of democracy disagree over which model offers a more "adequate understanding of the main task of democracy,"[48] which can most effectively "process the toughest issues concerning mutually contradictory assertions of identity,"[49] and how best we might "deepen or extend democracy,"[50] they also share a set of unspoken assumptions about the nature of individual and collective forms of communicative action. In the face of what both models recognize as a "rampant crisis of legitimacy affecting western democracies"[51] and "ever more prominent identity politics, sometimes in murderous form in deeply divided societies,"[52] both readily and quickly associate collective action—but not necessarily individual action—with strong passion and emotion, with identity politics, and with conflict and adversarial positions. For both models, collective assertions are inherently adversarial, if not also violent, passionate, and "murderous."

In agonistic models, Thomas Fossen writes, "Political action is conceived as contestation, and requires tension as a precondition."[53] Mouffe characterizes "a well-functioning democracy" in terms of its "vibrant clash of democratic political positions"—not individuals but positions—and "its recognition and legitimation of conflict."[54] "Political identities, which are always collective identities," writes Mouffe, "entail the creation of an 'Us' that only exists by distinguishing itself from a 'Them.'"[55] Approaching political subjects as inherently representing adversarial collective identities and as inherently engaged in struggle leads her to reframe the problem as one that "requires providing channels through which collective passions will be given ways to express themselves over issues."[56] In both her advocacy for an agonistic approach and in her critiques of deliberative democrats, then, she views "the field of politics" as the place not where individuals come together but rather where groups clash as adversaries.[57]

Although civility does not play a large role within the arguments of agonistic pluralists, it is not absent from their discussions. Robin Lakoff defines agonism as "the unwillingness to acknowledge a middle ground in debate—what Tannen calls The Argument Culture."[58] Tannen describes a culture that "urges us to approach the world—and the people in it—in an adversarial frame of mind."[59] Lakoff's invocation of Tannen points to her understanding of argument culture in opposition to civility, writing, "This is not another book about civility. 'Civility' suggests a superficial, pinky-in-the-air veneer of politeness spread thin over human relations like a layer of marmalade over toast."[60] Instead, she continues, "This book is about a pervasive warlike atmosphere that makes us approach public dialogue, and just about anything we need to accomplish, as if it were a fight." Such a culture, she argues, "rests on the assumption that opposition is the best way to get anything done" and produces conditions in which the goal "is not to listen and understand. Instead, you use every tactic you can think of—including distorting what your opponent just said—in order to win the argument."[61]

Mouffe, however, positions civility slightly differently, using it as a kind of limit-foundation essential to distinguishing adversarial (agonistic) politics from antagonism, in which opponents are regarded as enemies. In the former, opponents "share a common allegiance to the democratic principle of 'liberty and equality for all' while disagreeing about its interpretation," whereas in the latter, this common allegiance is not shared.[62] Invoking the concept of civility without explicitly defining it, she writes that in the absence of "a vibrant clash of democratic political positions," we must be cognizant of the risk "that this democratic confrontation will be replaced by a confrontation among other forms of collective identification, as is the case with identity politics. Too much emphasis on consensus and the refusal of confrontation lead to apathy and disaffection with political participation. Worse still, the result can be the crystallization of collective passions around issues, which cannot be managed by the democratic process and an explosion of antagonisms that can tear up the very basis of civility."[63] This emphasis on "positions," however, makes no distinctions between collective mobilizations that stem from a desire to advance *different interests* and those that simply seek *equal* treatment in the eyes of the law, as made clear by the examples of Dalit victims of caste massacres in India and Black victims of police violence in the United Kingdom and the United States.

## "The Conditions of Listening" in Telangana

Kaloji Narayana Rao, with whom I opened this chapter, clearly recognized that only some people were entitled to "soft speech" that could be heard and recognized as speech within the public sphere. To illustrate the ways that this linguistic domination was accomplished, he described a child from Telangana who was asked to read from a Telugu primer. The child began reading and then abruptly stopped. Kaloji continued his story:

> Again he repeats, "*Rōzū kāki mētaku . . . Rōzū kāki mētaku . . .* [Every day the crow to the grazing pasture . . . Every day the crow to the grazing pasture . . .]." And then stops. I say, "Why is it like that you are not finishing the sentence? And what is that?" . . . I took away the book from him. It is written there, "*Rōzū kāki mētaku vellēdi* [Every day the crow went to the grazing pasture]." And no person, except for those educated classes of the two or three communities [from Coastal Andhra]—no child speaks as 'vellēdi'. Different. Usage is different in different places. "*Poyēdi*." "*Pottadi*." The person from Warangal, or Telangana, will say *pottadi. Rōzū kāki mētaku pottadi.* He will never say "*vellēdi*." It is very difficult for him to say *vellēdi*, and write *vellēdi*. And when he writes in his examination, *pottadi*, the persons who are at the helm of affairs, and the teachers and the examiners, they say this is wrong. Principally, the child is correct when he writes *pottadi*.

But it is not simply that the language of the majority of the state began to be regarded as substandard and erroneous. Kaloji also pointed out the ways in which speakers from his region of the state had effectively been silenced, their voices made inaudible through their eradication from the public sphere:

> There is "Balanandam" [a children's program] on the radio.[64] "Balanandam"—in every week three, four, five times, and in every "Balanandam" session, twenty, thirty, twenty-five children partake. . . . But the person who is at the desk, who is in charge of the "Balanandam," lady or gentleman, they are from the coastal districts. So again, during these

forty years, at least twenty to thirty lakhs of children [two to three million] were involved in, were a part of "Balanandam." And I tell you, a challenge, that not a single child, girl or boy, from these twenty-two districts, oh except those two or three communities from Krishna and Guntur [districts] has ever been heard on the program.

So they have an advantage. For the last forty years they have led. . . . Of all the disadvantages created in the linguistic grouping . . . this is the greatest disadvantage. We have been thrown back hundreds of years. So for every radio program . . . in all those stations, any story recited, any poem recited, any essay, broadcast, any program, a drama, anything . . . is in the spoken language of the educated classes of the two districts [in Coastal Andhra]. . . . That, too, not the entire population of the two districts is represented. So this is the two or three communities, educated classes, groups against the entire population of the state.

Pausing for emphasis and looking at me to make certain I was following, he continued, "When the *grānthika bhāṣa* [classical Telugu language] was the standard for writing, there was no question of advantage for one group. The difficulty came when a standard spoken language that is *linked to a particular community* became the written language."[65]

It is perhaps not surprising, then, given the overwhelming feeling that their speech fails to be audible within the public sphere, that hundreds of thousands of residents of Telangana have taken to the streets to participate in the large collective assemblies known as jana garjanas to gain recognition and voice. As a result of former chief minister Chandrababu Naidu's efforts to transform Hyderabad into a "world-class" city in the 1990s, the city experienced rapid growth and multinational corporations established offices in its new knowledge parks and special economic zones. Yet the benefits of Hyderabad's rapid growth have been widely seen as flowing primarily to the migrants from the well-irrigated and prosperous districts of coastal Andhra who have dominated the city both economically and politically. This disparity has exacerbated long-standing feelings of exclusion and neglect among residents of Telangana and prompted the renewal of demands for the creation of a separate administrative state structure and more inclusive approaches to economic growth.[66] Thus, efforts to transform Hyderabad into a "world-class" city have been widely perceived as coming at the expense of the many for the benefit of a few. The "people's roars," strikes, and other collective actions of recent years have effectively functioned as referenda on the way that rapid economic growth was implemented in this region of southern India.

This uneven economic development illustrates one of the key limitations of the deliberative model of democracy: its inability to account for historical conditions that render some voices inaudible while proclaiming formal equality of access to the public sphere for all.[67] At the same time, however, it is difficult to argue that an agonistic model captures the meanings of the types of collective assembly that have emerged to amplify previously ignored or silenced communicative efforts, including deliberative contributions and decisions clearly articulated via the ballot box. Collective assemblies were ultimately prompted not by antagonism toward migrants from coastal Andhra, but by the repeated refusals of political parties to implement their clear promises and electoral mandates to create the new state of Telangana. Rather than pitting themselves against residents of coastal Andhra as adversaries, residents of Telangana saw themselves as seeking inclusion within the larger body politic dominated by migrants from coastal Andhra and as holding their elected representatives to their electoral promises. A series of formal policies designed to more fully integrate and incorporate residents of Telangana into the urban economic growth might have begun to address these concerns had they been implemented, but educational and employment opportunities created under the banner of affirmative action for natives of Telangana in 1975 routinely went unfilled. The failure of more recent efforts to compel their implementation further reinforced a feeling of being left out of the state's rapid economic growth.[68] Yet even when residents of Telangana took to the streets, their corporeal communicative actions were not addressed toward the migrants from coastal Andhra at large—those whom they perceived to have benefited most from the region's economic development. Instead, their collective assemblies were addressed toward the state—to their elected officials—not as adversaries but as authorities capable of carrying out their campaign promises to implement more equitable structures of representation, education, and state employment. Whether the creation of the new state in 2014 has, in fact, led to greater inclusion within the public sphere and to more equitable distribution of resources remains to be seen, but clearly, those who took to the streets in support of its formation believed it would.[69]

In contrast to the residents of Telangana who did not perceive the authorities as adversaries, there are forms of collective action and movements that *do* reject the sovereignty of the state. The People's War Group and other Maoist movements in India, as well as the Shining Path in Peru, are examples of groups that have rejected existing forms of authority and sought to set themselves up as alternative sovereigns, adjudicating disputes and dispensing justice independently of existing state structures.[70] Although these examples are beyond the scope of the current book, they enable us to see more clearly the civility of communicative action as an effect of being recognized and heard. Those who find that they are recognized and know they will be heard have the luxury of *appearing* to be more civil. They are enabled to speak softly, secure in the knowledge that their voices will still be heard, making them appear more rational and less emotional. Those whose voices are routinely ignored, however, find that they must exert increased effort to repeat themselves or engineer amplifications of their voices, making speakers appear louder, more aggressive, and less civil.

## Turning Up the Volume

I turn now to a second set of examples involving efforts to implement more inclusive political structures in India and expand affirmative action policies for those from marginalized backgrounds. These examples link the argument of this chapter with that of the preceding chapter on seeking audience. Many in India today resent the entrance of formerly marginalized groups into public, political, and academic spaces. The growing visibility of Dalits, Indigenous peoples, and members of other lower-caste and minority religious communities has been experienced by some as a threat to their existing privilege. Tensions have repeatedly emerged in public settings when some from communities that have historically held positions of authority or privilege have sought to maintain their status and have displayed reluctance to acknowledge other voices. Members of dominant caste groups sometimes attempt to mark those from historically marginalized backgrounds as angry, uncivil, excessive, or otherwise inappropriate in their speech and actions while simultaneously claiming that their own position stems only from reasoned speech, hard work, and natural merit rather than from historically privileged access to land, wealth, education, and employment opportunities.[71]

As the above examples illustrate, those securely embedded within networks of power are able to engage in individual communicative actions, speaking softly or writing in moderate tones with the expectation that their voices will be heard and acknowledged. They can also use this ability to be heard as autonomous individuals to stake claims to rationality and civility, enabling those with access to networks of power to frame their power as the product of their individual style and form of communication, rather than as a function of their existing positions and social relations. This portrayal of their own communicative acts as reflecting a distinct "style" enables them to refuse to acknowledge those efforts to communicate that appear to reflect a different form or style. Marking such differences enables those with access to power to discredit communicative actions that are loud, collective, or repetitive; to dismiss them as emotional, excessive, disruptive, irrational, or uncivil; or to treat them as noise or noncommunication.

Rupa Viswanath, for example, writes about the first generation of formally appointed political representatives from the "Depressed Classes" (the term then used by the government for those historically treated as untouchable by orthodox Hindus) to the newly reformed Madras Legislative Council in 1919.[72] She illustrates the types of misrecognitions and failures to be heard that these historically marginalized speakers experienced, even in the Legislative Council. A. Veerian, one of the first representatives of the Depressed Classes, saw himself as responsible for representing the concerns of his constituents as he sought to ensure that existing legal reforms on paper were fully implemented in practice. When an employee of the Pachayappan Motor Service Company refused to allow two of his Depressed Classes constituents to ride on one of its buses, even though both had purchased tickets and the refusal clearly violated the Motor Vehicle Amendment Act, Veerian raised the issue in the Legislative Council. His efforts to draw the Legislative Assembly's attention to the company's violation, however, were met by willful misunderstandings of his words that both mocked and ignored the substance of what he was trying to communicate. When he persisted by sending letters to each and every person in the chain of command responsible for enforcing the law in question, rather than receiving administrative support, he received this reprimand from the district magistrate:

> Mr. Veerian wrote letters to Government, to the Labour Commissioner and to me, as well as to the Sub Inspector of Police on the same day (30th May 1925.) In his letter to the Sub Inspector he wrote, "Please let me know whether you have reported the matter to the District Superintendent of Police as well as to the District Collector and the President, District Board for cancellation of the license . . ." I think this opportunity might be taken to tell Mr. Veerian that he might restrict the scope of his epistolary exuberance . . . he surely need not write to the whole hierarchy of officials at the same time.[73]

Viswanath points out that the magistrate's response highlights excess—Veerian's "epistolary exuberance"—rather than the point Veerian is trying to convey and fails to take seriously his concerns and, by extension, those of the larger community. She observes,

> The bus incident was but one of roughly a hundred similar incidents that Veerian brought to the attention of the Council in the period between 1924 and 1926, each recorded in huge bundles of documents, most of which are in Veerian's own hand, and all displaying the same concern for the workings of the local state, and the same commitment to the duty of representatives to represent the specific interests, even of single aggrieved individuals, among the represented.[74]

But recognition of the legitimacy of Veerian's claim to speak for his constituents was slow to materialize; he was instead discredited and chastised for his representational efforts.

In chapter 2, I analyzed the mainstream representations of Dalit students at Hyderabad University as angry and emotional, but here I highlight both their use of collective action to amplify their efforts to communicate with those in positions of authority and the repeated refusals of those authorities to listen to or acknowledge these efforts. When their individual efforts to speak in hostel and student body meetings went unheard, the students resorted to collective petitioning and presentation of memoranda. When these too failed to elicit any recognition, they went en masse to seek a personal audience with the chief warden. Despite the refusal of the chief warden (and the university administration more generally) to recognize their communicative actions, it was the Dalit students who were marked as "uncivil."[75] When their soft speech failed to be heard, the students used their collective presence to attempt to compel the chief warden to grant them an audience. This effort was ultimately unsuccessful but nevertheless resulted in their being labeled uncivil, angry, emotional, and violent.

The negative framing of such communicative amplifications has a long history in conjunction with refusals to hear and acts of silencing. Those who are already marginalized are less likely not only to be heard when using ordinary "soft speech" but also to be granted permission to communicate collectively. The visible entrance of new groups into shared public spheres and their increased efforts to create and maintain visibility as political actors make some in positions of power feel uncomfortable.[76] For many of the descendants of the early postcolonial governing class in which English-educated elites and upper-caste Hindus were disproportionately represented, the rise of vernacular political movements and the active mobilization in shared public spaces of Scheduled Caste (sc) or Other Backward Class (obc) groups have been disconcerting and have prompted resistance.

On March 26, 1999, for example, the Madiga Reservation Porata Samithi, a Dalit association in Andhra Pradesh, submitted an application to the Hyderabad commissioner of police requesting permission to hold a procession from Baghlingampally to the Dr. B. R. Ambedkar statue in celebration of Ambedkar's birthday on April 14. They assured the authorities that the procession would be carried out "with most discipline and very peacefully" and asked to be "permitted Mic[rophone] facilities to pass message[s] and drinking water points." The response from the commissioner of police, dated April 10, 1999, stated, "Your request . . . has been duly considered and rejected from the point of view of public order." The Madiga Reservation Porata Samithi responded by submitting a writ petition to the Andhra Pradesh High Court, arguing "that the right to assemble peacefully is [a] Constitutionally protected right under Article 19(1)(b) of the Constitution of India and also the right to freedom of speech and expression as well as the right to freely move throughout the territory of India are Constitutionally guaranteed rights." The lawyer for the Madiga association went on to argue that processions had been permitted for other groups, and so this one should be permitted as well:

> To a pointed question whether any such procession consisting of about 3 lakhs of people, was ever permitted or took place in the City of Hyderabad, the learned Advocate-General fairly answered saying that earlier on several occasions, such processions did take place and permissions were accorded and such processions were organised by various political parties and some social and religious organisations like Ganesh Utsavam [Festival] Committee of Hyderabad etc. As a matter of fact such processions took place earlier and the State permitted such processions.[77]

In the end, the High Court judge ruled, "The Commissioner of Police is not justified in issuing the impugned order," and he directed him to allow the procession to take place. Such a protracted debate simply to enable entrance into the visible public sphere is in marked contrast to the responses to other organizations, such as the Ganesh Utsavan Committee.

Such efforts to impede political action by marginalized groups have not been restricted to Telugu-speaking southern India, but are common throughout the country, as an example from neighboring Tamil Nadu illustrates. Writes S. Viswanathan, "On 6 August [1998] in Chennai, what was perhaps the largest ever mobilisation effort by dalit organisations in Tamil Nadu was severely curtailed by state action. . . . The severe restrictions placed on the dalit rally were in marked contrast to the attitude of the authorities towards the several caste-based processions and rallies that have taken place in the last few years in Tamil Nadu."[78]

Such restrictions on the efforts of marginalized groups to organize collective forms of representation and political mobilization are also portrayed in Indian fiction. In his short story "Bhūmi" (Land), first published in 1978, Telugu writer Allam Rajayya narrates efforts to organize a poor people's association (garībōlla sangam) or agricultural laborers' association (raitukūli sangam).[79] The landless laborers in the story explicitly model their association (sangam, also sangham) on the many civil society organizations already in place for doras (landlords, members of the owning classes, or members of dominant caste groups). The story identifies by name these various associations established by members of the dominant owning classes (dora sanghālu): an Association for Palm Sap Tappers, Association for Contractors, Association for Manufacturers of Clay Tiles, Association for Rice Millers, Association for Motor Drivers/Transporters, Association for Rent Collectors/Village Officers, Association for Village Council Presidents, and even, in cities, an Association for Lions (the Lions Club).[80]

Yet, in response to the formation of an Association for Agricultural Laborers (raitukūli sangam), the members of the village's dominant caste go on a rampage, beating up those who have joined the new organization, capturing four laborers, and imprisoning them in the village landlord's compound. When the landless villagers gather and approach the compound to inquire after the four imprisoned laborers, the landlord opens fire on the crowd. The police arrive, and at first, the villagers are relieved, thinking that the police have come to bring about justice. They quickly realize, however, that the police have instead come to defend the landlord. The gathered petitioners are thus characterized by the landlord and the police as a violent mob seeking to attack the dora. The narrator of the incident, an old man from the village, comments, "All guns are of the same caste [kulam], the same community [jāti]. I think perhaps the gun was born only to use on people like us!"[81]

The type of upper-caste opposition to lower-caste political organization and the formation of associations by nondominant groups captured by Allam Rajayya continues to be of concern to human rights advocates. A 1992 report describes numerous incidents of violence committed by landlords to discourage the formation of collective associations of landless agricultural laborers (raitukūli sanghams) that seek to advocate for minimum wages and labor rights.[82] The report also documents police assassinations of sangham leaders.[83] What appears as legitimate political organization or as the adoption of collective political strategies that are widely available to dominant groups—such as the formation of associations—seems threatening when adopted by marginalized individuals who have begun to come together into organized groups. One common defense mechanism adopted by those in dominant positions has been to reframe such actions as criminal. This porosity between representations of the "criminal" and the "political" and their relationship to political recognition are discussed in greater detail in part II.

## Colonial and Postcolonial Continuities: Framing Individual Civility and Collective Incivility

British colonial administrators responded to the forms of public assembly they encountered in India by trying to define collective communicative efforts as "illegal assemblies," "mutinies," "sedition," or "conspiracies," even when acknowledging that they were often orderly, peaceful, and disciplined, at least until British troops were sent in to disperse them. In Bengal, for example, the refusals of peasant cultivators to continue planting indigo led to widespread "disturbances" from 1859 to 1862, which were characterized by the British as another "mutiny," occurring soon after the uprisings of 1857–58.[84] Toward the end of August 1860, in the midst of the growing controversy over indigo cultivation, John Peter Grant, the lieutenant governor of Bengal, traveled by boat from Calcutta to conduct an inspection tour of the Dacca Railway. While traveling up the Koomar and Kalligunga Rivers, he writes, "Numerous crowds of Ryots [peasants or tenant farmers] appeared at various places, whose whole prayer was for an order of Government, that they should not cultivate indigo."[85] According to a newspaper report, as Grant's boat "was passing the Salgamudia factory of Thomas Kenny, two hundred [indigo cultivators] assembled on either side of the river, joined hands and called out for justice with a loud lamentable groan. Grant directed his steamer to anchor, and some headmen were taken on board. All the petitions taken were referred to the local authorities, but many ryots were not satisfied and followed his ship to Pabna."[86] On Grant's return along the same two rivers a few days later, he was astonished that "from dawn to dusk . . .

for some sixty or seventy miles, both banks were literally lined with crowds of Villagers, claiming justice in this matter."[87] He writes that they "must have collected from all the Villages at a great distance on either side" and clearly interprets their collective presence as an effort to attract the attention of the government and express "their feelings and their determination in language not to be mistaken."[88]

As their foothold in the subcontinent grew by the early decades of the nineteenth century, the East India Company (EIC) struggled to establish legal, ideological, and policing structures that could keep at bay the influence of collective forms of assembly. This process may have contributed to what appears to be our collective amnesia regarding the scope and effectiveness of earlier forms of what the British identified as "combinations." Leaders of the newly independent India in 1947 largely inherited both the ideological perspective on collective assembly and the legal and policing systems established by the British, with many of the laws established during the nineteenth century still in effect today.[89] The success of the collective methods mobilized by Gandhi and other nationalist leaders created a dilemma for postcolonial leaders like Nehru, independent India's first prime minister, however, since he regarded collective actions in ways reminiscent of the attitudes of colonial officials. He described those who take part in demonstrations "in the name of politics," for example, as "immature," "childish," and inappropriate for "an adult, mature, independent nation."[90] But the memory of the effectiveness of these collective methods helped keep alive practices that may have had antecedents in earlier understandings of the responsibilities of those in positions of authority.

Yet, the continuities between colonial and postcolonial administrative attitudes toward collective assembly further contribute to our historical amnesia, so that even historians of India suggest that mass civil resistance emerges "in Europe in the ferment of the post-French revolutionary period" from "the sphere of civil society—the site of a free association of individuals in public bodies, associations and the like—which were valorized in the political thought of the Enlightenment as providing a means for checking and correcting the excesses of state power and governmental authority."[91] But at the same time, this history of collective assembly has also been placed firmly in the past, positioning it as premodern in opposition to individual speech action. For example, Nehru rejected collective "action committees" in the early postcolonial period, contrasting them with "modern" individual students (who represent only themselves), with whom he was willing to meet, as illustrated in this chapter's epigraph.[92]

His refusal to recognize representatives of collectives sounds much like the colonial insistence on entertaining "individual" petitioners rather than representatives of "combinations." J. Gwatkin, secretary of the EIC Board of Trade, for example, refused to recognize those who claimed to be agents of "combinations" of petitioners, writing the following in 1817:

> As certain of these persons have persisted in attending daily at the Board of Trade office, the Board here explain that, under the existing Regulations each *Individual* weaver, if aggrieved, has the means of laying his Complaint before the Commercial Resident, or as the case may be of proceeding by an action in the Zillah Court, and with this protection held out to the weavers of Vizagapatam *Individually*, The Board cannot sanction Combinations of weavers for the purpose of Making General Complaints nor acknowledge persons stating themselves to be agents of such Combinations. The Board cannot dismiss this Petition without noticing the disrespectful *style* thereof to the authorities of Government.[93]

Not only were such efforts at collective representations deemed inappropriate but they were also regarded as disrespectful and as reflecting a distinct "style" of representation.

Nehru, similarly, equated the formation of "action committees" with "hooliganism":

> The United States, the UK, the Soviet Union, China, Japan and Germany are all part of the international system. But I would like to ask if you have heard of the people or students of any of these countries, whether they are capitalist, communist, or socialist countries, behaving in this hooligan-like fashion? Have you heard of action committees being appointed? I would like to have one example of such things happening anywhere else in the world, in Asia, Africa, America or Europe. Then why is it that we have students here forming action committees? When they came to me, I told them clearly that I was prepared to meet students but not an Action Committee. I do not accept action committees of students or workers or anyone else.[94]

In this statement, Nehru also reinforces the belief that collective action is an expression of anger and antisocial "hooliganism" and that processions and the shouting of slogans represent a style that is the opposite of self-control and discipline and that belongs firmly in the past. "We learned to control our passions and convert them into a great organized strength instead of frittering it away in useless ways," he wrote of India's progress, which was acquired "step by step" as "we learnt to be organized and patient and to put a brake on ourselves at full speed."[95] "Gone are the days when we expressed our anger by shouting slogans and taking out processions," he proclaimed. "We are on the threshold of the nuclear age in which terrible forces of destruction are being amassed. India is not lagging behind in the field of atomic energy. It is next only to a few countries like the United States, the UK, France, Canada who are leading. India has made great progress in this field. But we cannot go very far unless the people learn to exercise self-control and discipline."[96]

Like the colonial rulers who preceded him, Nehru placed individual speech action within a temporal trajectory that framed it as representing modern political behavior, using it to signal India's arrival in the fraternity of modern nations. "It is all very well for you to shout slogans. But you must think how it affects India's reputation and stature in the world," he proclaimed.[97] "The days when revolutions like the French Revolution were wrought on the streets are gone. Nowadays, revolutions are of other kinds."[98] His comments relegated public collective assemblies and processions through the street firmly to the past. At the same time, despite widespread efforts to marginalize and delegitimize forms of collective corporeal communication—both in India and more globally and fueled by new legal, ideological, and policing regimes—they were never entirely successful in eliminating the collective practices that offered time-tested models for effectively engaging and communicating with officials, authority figures, and others in positions of power.

Collective Assembly as Amplification
and the Politics of Recognition

In exploring the possibilities of a civility defined by its capacity to set limits on extreme violence, incivility, and humiliation, Étienne Balibar coined the term *antiviolence*, which he conceptualizes as "a politics that is neither an *abstraction* from violence ('nonviolence') nor an *inversion* of it ('counterviolence'—especially in its repressive forms, state forms, but also in its revolutionary forms, which assume that they must reduplicate it if they are to 'monopolize' it) but an internal response to, or displacement of, it."[99] He goes on to ask, "How well does the word *civility* designate the political action that specifically pursues such 'antiviolence'?"[100] In answering this question, he points toward *collective* rather than individual action, invoking the Hegelian conception of *Sittlichkeit*—the third of Hegel's three spheres of right—as the best equivalent of "civility" and describing *Sittlichkeit* as "a profoundly political concept that encompasses the 'state' and 'nonstate' spheres of *collective action*."[101]

There is substantial evidence that many in southern India (and elsewhere) see collective assembly even today not as the opposite of individual speech action or as resistance or adversarial conflict, but rather as a mechanism for turning up the volume and intensifying the effect of individual communicative action, particularly in contexts where participants have not gained recognition as political subjects. The Telugu terms that are most often used to describe outdoor political meetings are the nouns *garjana(m)*, literally a "roar," and *bhērī*, also the word for "kettledrum," used especially for making public announcements.[102] In neighboring Tamil Nadu, a common Tamil term is *murasu*, also meaning "drum" or "tabour" and also used in the sense of a "roar," or of voicing or broadcasting. *Murasu* also appears in the names of Tamil newspapers and television stations.[103] As Laura Kunreuther suggests in her analysis of a related South Asian concept, *āwāj* (voice), such terms point to "aspects of democracy that are often disavowed or aggressively disparaged in mainstream discussions of a rational public sphere and the political ethics of communication." They reveal categories of meaning "which cannot be fully understood within the classic frames of the [deliberative, rational] voice of publics or the unruly [irrational] noise of crowds."[104] These terms emphasize the idea that a collective public meeting can be a method to amplify individual voices, making a "message heard within the polyphony of perspectives that can constitute ongoing, collaborative deliberation . . . in a transmission of sound that is at once mass-mediated and acutely embodied."[105] Although it may be easy to ignore a single voice, it is much more difficult to ignore the sound made by thousands of voices together. Indeed, authorities could not ignore the growing collective embodiment of support for the creation of the separate state of Telangana.

Recognizing the ways in which collective embodiment can be continuous with efforts to make individual speech actions heard within the public sphere can help us reframe debates on how to "deepen or extend democracy" most effectively, thereby resolving some of the stalemates confronted by discussions of deliberative and agonistic abstractions of democracy and clearing space for a new analytic frame.[106] Acknowledging efforts to "hail the state" and finding ways to give audience to and amplify these efforts can lead to strategies for more effectively incorporating marginalized voices into democratic processes, both individually and collectively. In contrast to the deliberative and agonistic models of democracy, this chapter demonstrates the importance of recognizing civility not as a feature of individual comportment and as a precondition for democratic participation, but rather as a product of structures of authority that facilitate the recognition of political subjects and give audience to their voices.[107] Those who find that they are recognized then have the luxury of *appearing* to be more civil. They can speak more calmly and quietly, secure in the knowledge that their voices will still be heard, thereby making them appear more rational and less emotional. Those whose voices are routinely ignored, however, find that they must exert increased effort to repeat themselves or engineer amplifications of their voice, making speakers appear louder, more aggressive, and less civil. Rather than assuming that speakers are active and listeners are passive, we would do well to follow Richard Burghart's recommendation that we instead investigate "how a people who are listened to gain a voice."[108] Whether documenting a "loud lamentable groan" or a "great roar of the people," theories of idealized Habermasian communicative action premised on the individual speaking subject, as well as agonistic approaches that see all collective action as oppositional or as a rejection of sovereignty, have clouded our ability to recognize efforts of the already marginalized to participate within democratic processes. Our existing theories contribute to their silencing, converting their communicative acts into passion, anger, or noise or simply making them unrecognizable. In the next chapter, I review the much longer history that connects colonial and postcolonial efforts to frame collective political action as disrespectful, uncivil, and the opposite of individual speech action.

# FOUR. THE GENERAL STRIKE

## Collective Assembly at the Other End of the Commodity Chain

The fact is that, in India, the nation at large has generally used passive resistance in all departments of life. We cease to cooperate with our rulers when they displease us.
—MOHANDAS KARAMCHAND GANDHI, *Hind Swaraj*, 1946

Colonial India's high strike frequency is hard to account for in terms of current theories of strikes and collective action in general. —SUSAN WOLCOTT, "Strikes in Colonial India," 2008

As we have seen, the Telangana forty-two-day Sakala Janula Samme, or "All People's Strike," that began on September 13, 2011, was just one in an escalating series of events intended to hold elected officials accountable to their promises and communicate widespread support for the formation of a separate administrative state of Telangana within the Indian nation.[1] General strikes such as this one have played a significant role within everyday politics in India, past and present. Yet, most histories of general strikes and of their role, as part of civil society, in checking state power place their origins—and the origins, more generally, of civil society—firmly in Europe. Such historiographic narratives do little to help us better understand sociopolitical phenomena in India. This chapter challenges the role of historical and social science literatures in constructing and placing boundaries on the political. I use a comparative history of general strikes in India and England to trouble received history and to enrich and strengthen our analysis of the historiography of civil society, democracy, and democracy's relationship with civility and its opposites—incivility, disorder, and violence. Sharika Thiranagama and Tobias Kelly observe that this historiography has been geographically limited: "The discussion of civility and civic-ness as a normative value has been primarily focused on the formal squares of liberal democracy, especially in the west. In contrast, debates around violence, heterogeneity and conflict have been equally marked by their focus on the global south." They go on to suggest "a more fruitful mingling," arguing that "while the notion of civility may have its origins in a very particular history of liberal democracy, civility can be understood as a term with global salience and multiple local histories."[2]

To carry out just such a fruitful mingling, this chapter contextualizes ethnographic research on contemporary general strikes in the Telugu-speaking region of southern India by focusing on a larger corpus of historical primary source materials documenting a wide range of general strikes in Indian history between 1669 and the present. I also analyze secondary scholarship and historiographic writing theorizing these actions and compare them with writings on general strikes in Europe, with particular attention to literature on England. I use these examples of general strikes in India's past and present to (1) reframe our understandings of the relationships between collective action, civility, and democracy; (2) decenter England (and Europe more generally) as the "precocious" and normative site for historical innovation in collective forms of contentious political action, particularly as these innovations have been linked to the growth of democratic structures and the ability to check state power; and (3) reconsider theoretical and historiographic approaches to the relationship between civil society and the state. More specifically, I compare three features of mass strikes in India and England to build on chapter 3's argument that, rather than being a precondition for democracy or a quality of individual comportment or manners, civility can be understood as the product of a responsive state.

## The General Strike

European historians appear to have reached a consensus that the idea of the modern general strike was born in the 1830s, originating in England in conjunction with the industrial revolution and its new industrial labor forces before spreading elsewhere in Europe and only then to the rest of the world. Charles Tilly, for example, has been widely cited (and has gone virtually unchallenged) in locating a significant transformation in forms of collective contentious behavior in England between 1758 and 1833. He writes, "Among the world's states, Britain was precocious. Other countries were moving in the same general direction, but in most of them public meetings, demonstrations, special-interest associations, and related forms of interaction became standard instruments of popular politics only considerably later in the century."[3] Among these various new shifts in practices, says Tilly, "the most visible alteration of the working-class repertoire of collective action in western countries has been the rise of the strike," which, according to him, emerges as a *regular* feature of contentious practice only during the nineteenth century: "Strikes were rare events at the beginning of the nineteenth century. By 1900, they were routine facts of working-class life."[4] As his collaboration with Edward Shorter on strikes in France makes clear, Tilly sees the strike as a product of industrialization, defined as "any net movement of production . . . (a) away from agriculture toward manufactured goods and services, (b) away from households, kin groups, communities or individual entrepreneurs, toward specialized formal organizations."[5] Tilly's identification of Britain as the precocious origin of the development of new forms of contentious collective behavior like the strike and his focus on the early nineteenth century as the pivotal period of transformation in collective practices have been shared and reinforced by numerous other scholars over the last century, writing both before and after Tilly.[6] European scholars—most recently Sidney Tarrow in 2011—are, in fact, joined by scholars of South Asia, from R. R. Diwakar in 1969 to David Hardiman more recently, in reinforcing the view that South Asians draw their engagements with strike-like practices from European models.[7]

The history of strikes in the South Asian context, however, troubles this origin story, as the historian Dharampal first suggested in 1971 before his untimely death.[8] I highlight three features that emerge from a comparison of data on Indian strikes with those in England that challenge these received chronologies and thus have the potential to dramatically alter existing understandings of the relationships between civility, contentious collective action, and the state. Evidence from Indian primary source materials indicates the widespread existence of mass strikes in India well before the 1830s that were (1) orderly to an extent that surprised and confused British authorities; (2) translocal (incorporating multiple and diverse groups unrelated by kinship over a large geographic area); and (3) state-directed during a period in history when European contentious gatherings were being used to enforce very local social norms rather than to communicate with representatives of the state. The careful comparison of the rise of translocal mass strikes in England and India suggests that the position of strikers within global commodity chains—and the specific economic, social, political, and legal structures that connected local contexts to global economies—were ultimately more significant than the abstract role of the Enlightenment or industrialization in enabling the expansion and contraction of conditions for democratic participation. This comparison also reinforces the argument that civility is a by-product of more inclusive political structures, rather than their precondition. The remainder of this chapter offers a brief overview of the history of strikes in England and in India, and then addresses each of the three features of Indian strike events in turn.

*General Strikes in England*

In analyzing more than eight thousand examples of contentious collective action in Britain between 1758 and 1833, Charles Tilly identifies three key shifts in the nature of the repertoires used for collective claim-making in Britain. His data suggest that in eighteenth-century Britain, available repertoires of action were *parochial* ("interests and interaction involved were concentrated in a single community"), *bifurcated* (taking direct action to address local issues but using intermediaries like patrons or local authorities for representation beyond the local), and *particular* ("varying considerably in detail from one locality to another and transferring only with difficulty").[9] By the nineteenth century, however, new collective forms of contention could increasingly be seen as *cosmopolitan* or *national* ("referring to interests and issues that spanned many localities or affected centers of power whose actions touched many localities"), *modular* ("easily transferable from one setting or circumstance to another"), and *autonomous* ("beginning on the claimants' own initiative and establishing direct communication between claimants and nationally significant centers of power," rather than "taking advantage of authorized assemblies or routine confluences of people").[10] And it is in Britain, he argues, that this transition to cosmopolitan, modular, and autonomous forms of contention occurs first.

More recently, Sidney Tarrow leaves these assumptions unchallenged in his study of social movements and contentious politics, building on Tilly's analysis of how repertoires of collective contention changed between the eighteenth and nineteenth centuries and similarly privileging early modern Europe as the initial site of innovation. In the 1780s, Tarrow writes, "People certainly knew how to seize shipments of grain, attack tax gatherers, burn tax registers, and take revenge on wrongdoers and people who had violated community norms," but "they were not yet familiar with modular forms of contention such as the mass demonstration, the strike, or the urban insurrection." Yet by 1848, he continues, "Performances such as the petition, the public meeting, the demonstration, and the barricade were well-known routines of contention, which were used for a variety of purposes and by different combinations of social actors."[11] Collective enforcement of social norms of the late eighteenth century could include attacks on particular local middlemen or "petty culprits" blamed for adulterating foodstuffs or hoarding grain during times of shortage.[12] There also were disciplinary actions and forms of public shaming like rough music, charivari, or skimmington—forms of loud, public, mocking processions or demonstrations of protest outside someone's home famously analyzed by E. P. Thompson—used against those seen to be engaging in inappropriate coupling, such as remarriage of a man to a much younger woman, "conjugal infidelity," or "women at odds with the values of a patriarchal society: the scold, the husband-beater, the shrew."[13] Strikingly, in England and in Europe, more generally, these earlier forms of enforcing collective norms were rarely addressed toward representatives of the state but instead targeted individuals seen to be acting in violation of the local moral economy. Like Tilly, Tarrow insists that the shift toward a new, increasingly state-directed repertoire of contention developed first "in early modern Europe" and only later "spread around the world."[14]

The birth of the *general* strike, which differs from ordinary strikes both in size and scope, is similarly attributed to an English origin.[15] A strike may target a single workplace or be carried out by a single group or community, whereas a general strike typically incorporates participants from a range of different occupations or includes many locations within a single coordinated action. The English printer, preacher, and political reformer William Benbow is often regarded as the originator of the idea of a mass general strike. In 1832, he published a pamphlet titled "Grand National Holiday, and Congress of the Productive Classes, &c.," in which he argued the following:

> Our lords and masters, by their unity of thought and action, by their consultations, deliberations, discussion, holidays, and congresses, have up to this time succeeded in bringing about the happiness of the *few*. Can this be denied? We shall then by our consultations, deliberations, discussions, holiday and congress, endeavour to establish

the happiness of the *immense majority* of the human race, of that far *largest portion* called the *working classes.* What the few have done for themselves cannot the many do for themselves? Unquestionably.[16]

He goes on to assert the power of the people united in congress: "We have shown that the parish authorities are entirely dependent on the people, and that without the consent of the people they can raise no rate, nor dispose of any fund already accumulated."[17]

His ideas were taken up by the Chartist movement and used in the 1842 General Strike (also known as the "Plug Riots") that began among coal miners in Staffordshire and then spread to factory and mill workers in Lancashire and Yorkshire and coal miners throughout Britain. Benbow's emphasis on the strike as a tool of the working classes continued in later writings on general strikes. Socialist and anarchist thinkers viewed the general strike as a means of overthrowing the capitalist government, but many were conflicted about how effective it might be in practice.[18] In contrast, in India, the goal of mass strikes was less likely to be the overthrow of the government; they instead functioned more often as an appeal to authorities for recognition or redress.

Although Benbow was not opposed to the use of violence, later theorists sought to clearly distinguish collective actions like strikes from violent methods, labeling nonviolent actions as "civil" resistance. European theorists have argued that the industrial revolution and European capitalist innovations are responsible for the birth not only of the strike but also of nonviolent civil resistance more generally. Michael Randle, for example, identifies civil resistance as a by-product of the industrial capitalism, urbanism, and factory system that emerged in Europe in the nineteenth century with new forms of trade unions, labor movements, and radical parties.[19] After arguing that the 1819 Peterloo Massacre in Manchester played a significant role in establishing the right to hold public demonstrations in England, he writes, "In the economic and social struggle, too, the strike more and more replaced machine-breaking, rick-burning and similar actions as the chief weapon of the working-class protest and resistance. The timing of this shift in organization and methods of action varies from one country to another, starting earlier in those countries such as Britain and France where capitalist industrialization first took root."[20] Paralleling Tilly's and Tarrow's studies of the shifts in repertoires of contention, Randle's research similarly locates the emergence of civil resistance in the wake of capitalist industrialization in Europe.

South Asian historians, too, have largely supported a European-centered chronology when attributing M. K. Gandhi's political innovations of the early twentieth century to his exposure to postindustrial European influences. In 1969, R. R. Diwakar argued, "There are no recorded instances in Indian history of long-drawn strikes of the nature of the modern 'general strike.'"[21] David Hardiman's 2003 book on Gandhi continues to reinforce this general trend. "Mass civil resistance," writes Hardiman, "emerged in Europe in the ferment of the post-French revolutionary period. It came from the sphere of civil society—the site of a free association of individuals in public bodies, associations and the like—which were valorised in the political thought of the Enlightenment as providing a means for checking and correcting the excesses of state power and governmental authority."[22] Although he acknowledges that "these forms of struggle developed in embryonic form in India long before Gandhi emerged as a leader," he limits his recognition of direct influences to those Indian movements in the latter half of the nineteenth century whose elite leadership was made up of those who had been exposed to the new European forms of industrial protest.[23] These movements included the 1859–62 indigo revolt, the anti-landlord movement in Bengal in the 1870s, and the 1872–73 no-tax campaign in Maharashtra— all identified as "mass movements in which peasant protest was supported by fractions of the elite, such as English-educated, middle class and generally high-caste Indians, certain paternalistic colonial officials, and socially concerned missionaries."[24] For Hardiman, as for historians of Europe, post-Enlightenment European civil society was the site of the key changes in repertoires of practice that influenced the development of democracy, first in Europe and then elsewhere.

Given the almost universal agreement that civil disobedience, strikes, and other nonviolent forms of collective action emerged in Europe within the sphere of a new post-Enlightenment civil society, what are we to make of the mass strikes that occurred in India as early as the seventeenth century? There is evidence that these strikes were used to draw the attention of the Mughal emperor to grievances in the seventeenth century, and the English East India Company (EIC), chartered in 1600, found its methods of restructuring the procurement of Indian textiles increasingly challenged by collective forms of assembly in India, with examples going back at least to the second half of the 1600s.[25] Mass strikes continued to regularly challenge EIC administrative decisions during the eighteenth and early nineteenth centuries, particularly when these were taken without first seeking local input. The frequency of strikes appears to have diminished somewhat in nineteenth-century India in the wake of the EIC's introduction of new legal structures, centralization of policing, and efforts to inculcate an ideology prizing the individual over the collective, but then they reemerged strongly in the twentieth century. Between 1921 and 1938, for example, the rate of strikes in India's textile industry was ten times that in Britain and the United States during a similar stage in the development of their textile industries.[26] In examining three specific features of early Indian general strikes, this chapter challenges existing genealogies of strike actions, particularly the role of European industrialization, associations, and formal unions in developing innovations in the collective forms of contention that produced strike actions. It suggests the need to reconsider historiography's characterizations of a specifically European civil societal role in innovating methods of placing checks on authorities and in paving the way for greater democratization. Excerpts from EIC administrative records and other Indian primary source materials, as well as secondary sources, are used to situate the historical appearance of mass strikes in India and to compare three key features— orderliness, cosmopolitanism, and engagement with the state—with those of mass strikes in England.

Archival evidence from India suggests that forms of what David Hardiman usefully identifies as "dialogic resistance"—work stoppages, strikes, mass migrations, and other ways of redressing grievances—were widespread in India well before the colonial period.[27] One feature that seems to have escaped the notice of historians, however, is their use in addressing state authorities as their primary audience far earlier in South Asia than in Europe, emerging at least as early as the second half of the seventeenth century. On September 23, 1669, in what Gulammohammed Zainulaeedin Refai characterizes as "the first successful strike in Mughal history," some eight thousand members of Surat's Hindu and Jain mercantile communities "left their families under the care of their relatives, and quitted Surat," located on the western coast of India, in protest against the policies of Emperor Aurangzeb's newly appointed Qazi (local administrator).[28] By the end of the seventeenth century, Surat was one of the most important and most cosmopolitan trading ports in the world and the home of several of the world's wealthiest merchant-traders, bankers, and shipping magnates.[29] The city's large population included not only Hindus, Jains, Muslims (Sunni and Shia), and Parsis but also merchants from Armenia, Arabia, Turkey, Portugal, Holland, France, and England and was the site of an EIC factory (a trading station for storing goods for export) from the second decade of the seventeenth century.[30] In 1669, despite threats of dire consequences from the Qazi, the Jain and Hindu traders refused to return, stating that they would appeal to the emperor for justice. They remained for the time being at the neighboring port of Bharuch, some seventy kilometers to the north. After lengthy correspondence with Emperor Aurangzeb, they finally received "a letter promising security and greater religious freedom."[31] The Qazi was recalled, and "the merchants, satisfied with these arrangements, returned from Broach [Bharuch]."[32]

EIC administrators were similarly confronted by quiet but determined objections to their attempts to conduct trade exchanges on terms disadvantageous to local artisans and merchants and later to their efforts to assess municipal taxes and make administrative changes to existing political, economic, and policing structures. The Indian historian Dharampal argues that the mass strikes, work stoppages, and migrations (both temporary and permanent) that resulted should be recognized as types of civil disobedience and noncooperation well before the actions of Gandhi.[33] Just a decade after the Surat strike, in 1680, the EIC's *Records of Fort St. George* reveal complaints regarding the settlement of accounts in the wake of the death of one of the chief native merchants and key EIC agent in Madras, Kasi Viranna (identified as Cassa Verona in the *Records*).[34] This dispute resulted first in the departure from the town of many of the city's remaining important merchants as well as "the Chief Painter with the other Painte[rs], the Muckwa's [boatmen], Cattamaran Men and Cooleys" who "had left the Towne privately the last night and yesterday upon a Combination."[35] When this action failed to force the British to settle the outstanding accounts, the merchants began to boycott trade with the EIC, which eventually escalated into an embargo. EIC accounts report,

> The Painters [cloth painters] and others gathered together at St. Thoma having sent severall letters to the severall Casts of Gentues in Towne, and to severall in the Companys service as Dubasses, Cherucons or Chief Peons, Marchants Washers and others, . . . stopt goods and provisions comeing to towne throwing the Cloth off of the Oxen and laying their Dury, and in all the Townes about us . . . the Drum has beaten forbiding all People to carry any Provisions or wood to Chenapatnam alias Madrasspatnam, and the Mens houses that burnt Chenam for us are tyed up and they forbid to burne any more, or to gather more shells for that purpose.[36]

The EIC, viewing the striking merchants, artisans, and laborers as "Mutineers" and characterizing them as an "evill combination," refused to acknowledge any responsibility for the grievances raised and instead sent out soldiers to imprison several key leaders and take into custody the wives and children of the various fishermen, boatmen, and coolies to compel the men to return.[37] When this failed, they then published a list of the names of key "Mutineers," as they were characterized, accused them of having "gathered many People together to make head against this government," and threatened the confiscation of their "houses, goods and Estate" and their permanent banishment from Madras if they failed to immediately come forward.[38] Despite their attempts to resolve the issue solely through force, the EIC eventually acknowledged corruption within their own ranks and mediated a resolution to facilitate continued trading, suggesting that such methods were effective.[39]

During the next century, there was a high demand for skilled artisans, particularly for those connected with the weaving industry, and such forms of making grievances known continued.[40] EIC administrators frequently complained about the migration of disgruntled weavers to neighboring territories outside their jurisdiction, sometimes making appeals to Indian rulers for assistance in forcibly compelling their return.[41] Toward the end of the eighteenth century, as the EIC began to assume the right to collect land revenue, its officials became increasingly concerned with preventing the migration of laborers to ensure the regular cultivation of land under their jurisdiction, thus maximizing their revenue.[42]

The 1680 Madras strike and embargo illustrate each of the three points that the remainder of this chapter elaborates. First, the emptying of Madras and the widespread work stoppage that ensued displayed evidence of remarkable organization. Although references to the operation of "caste" in India abound, we know very little about how the structure of social organization in India made possible such extended and effective mobilizations. EIC administrators suspected that at least some of those who left the city and participated in the subsequent embargo were compelled to do so. Even if this were true, it still tells us very little about the interests and relationships at stake or the social mechanisms through which such a feat could be accomplished so easily. Second, those who participated reflected a wide spectrum of mercantile, artisan, and laboring groups. The strike and embargo were not the actions of a single occupational or interest group. As the strike continued, neighboring towns and villages were also recruited to participate. Third, EIC officials, in their capacity as creators and arbiters of administrative policy in the settlement, were the target of this action. This was not a disciplinary action against a community member in violation of local social norms, but rather an act on the part of members of a civil society to place a check on the excesses of what Philip Stern characterizes as the "Company-State."[43] In addition, the action appears to have been nonviolent, at least on the part of the strikers. Although the EIC resorted to the use of soldiers, there is no evidence that the merchants, artisans, and laborers engaged in violence. The next three sections offer additional examples to illustrate each of these three features of Indian strikes in greater detail.

## Civility and Order

As we saw in chapter 3, the concept of civility has most often been associated with individually cultivated "behavior or speech appropriate to civil interactions" and with "politeness, courtesy, consideration."[44] But it is also invoked in the context of efforts to maintain "civil order; orderliness in a state or region" or the "absence of anarchy and disorder."[45] This definition tells us little, however, about the means and mechanisms through which order is produced or maintained. From its very earliest days of trading, the EIC found collective forms of assembly in India to be breathtakingly well organized and powerful—a far cry from the narratives of riots, disorderly mobs, and violent insurgency that dominate the accounts of even many of the most critical historians of British India.[46]

Indeed, the writings of British administrators in India display a sense of surprise and bewilderment at how well organized such actions were. Their surprise suggests that the Indian actions differed significantly from the methods of social organization with which the British were familiar at home. Prasannan Parthasarathi goes so far as to suggest that in India there was a very different understanding of sovereignty that may have encouraged or, at the least, freely permitted and given audience to such collective appeals.[47] He further observes that scholarly attention to such well-organized assemblies in pre-1850 Indian history has been sorely inadequate and that much remains to be known about "the nature and forms of resistance and protest" in earlier eras of Indian political practice.[48] I would take his observations one step further and argue that much of what we have recognized as "forms of resistance and protest" may actually have been something else. EIC administrators and later colonial officials did not see themselves as engaged in embedded social relationships of mutual obligations with those they ruled. Instead, they viewed efforts to communicate grievances to representatives of the government as forms of disrespect and insubordination, characterizing as forms of corruption any efforts on the part of those they ruled to maintain and use social networks. Even so, they could not help but be impressed by the capacity for order and level of organization displayed in local efforts to communicate with the state.

In 1798, in a series of actions that were described in EIC records as a "revolt," "tumultuous assemblies," and "insurrection," weavers in Godavari District on the Coromandel Coast resisted new textile procurement and contracting policies by refusing to undertake work for the EIC.[49] When their concerns continued to be ignored, they began to march toward the city of Masulipatnam (today Machilipatnam), nearly 100 kilometers away, gathering with them the weavers in each village they passed through on their way.[50] A number of scholars have documented this and other weaver protests on the Coromandel Coast, but what has not been widely recognized is how surprised officials were by the level of organization of these actions.[51] EIC officials responded with confusion and a sense of disbelief at the organizational capacity of the weavers, asking "by what means people so miserably poor as weavers are generally known to be, could now contrive to keep so long together" and prompting the creation of new legal mechanisms intended to prevent what the British persisted in characterizing as "sudden" protests and insurgencies, a narrative of spontaneity that is sometimes sustained by postcolonial historians.[52]

Similar examples of orderliness and discipline displayed in mass strikes and work stoppages drew colonial attention in other parts of India. In the Banaras house tax strike of 1810–11, mentioned in chapter 2, local residents are described as closing their shops, abandoning their occupations and livelihoods, and leaving their homes to collectively assemble in an open field on the outskirts of the city, where they established a camp and were prepared to stay for as long as necessary to communicate their dissatisfaction with the tax. Commerce, transportation, and virtually all aspects of everyday life in the city—including the disposal of dead bodies—came to an almost complete standstill. The mass work stoppage continued for well over a month, with other members of protesters' households providing maintenance for those camped in the field.[53]

Although colonial administrators described the Banaras protest as an "illegal assembly" and "conspiracy," what comes through quite clearly in EIC administrative reports of the event was the British perception of the assembly as orderly, peaceful, and disciplined. "Instead of appearing like a tumultuous and disorderly mob," wrote J. D. Erskine, acting third judge of the Court of Appeal and Circuit for the Division of Banaras, "the vast multitudes came forth in a state of perfect organization." This "state of things continued for more than a month," yet was organized in such a way that "was sufficient to maintain the greatest order and tranquility."[54] Even James Mill, in his famous history of India, observed, "Their conduct was uniformly peaceable; passive resistance was the only weapon to which they trusted." He described the event as involving "all ranks and description of the inhabitants of Benares" and that "meetings of the different castes and trades were held to determine upon the course to be pursued."[55] He also noted that "a solemn engagement was taken by all the inhabitants to carry on no manner of work or business until the tax was repealed" and that in the end the action succeeded.[56]

Their Indian subjects' exceptional levels of order and organizational ability continued to be recognized by colonial administrators even after the implementation of direct crown rule displaced the EIC's administration in 1858, following the widespread uprisings of 1857–58 that came to be understood as the "Great Indian Mutiny" by the British and the "First War of Indian Independence" by other commentators.[57] Despite being unsettled by "the display on the part of tens of thousands of people, men, women, and children" seeking "an order of Government" that might bring them "justice," as he returned from his inspection tour in August 1860, John Peter Grant—the lieutenant governor of Bengal whom we met in chapter 3—was nevertheless deeply impressed. He reflected, "I do not know that it ever fell to the lot of any Indian Officer to steam for fourteen hours through a continued double street of Suppliants for justice. All were most respectful and orderly; but all were plainly in earnest. . . . The organization and capacity for combined and simultaneous action, in the cause, which this remarkable demonstration over so large an extent of country proved, are subjects worthy of much consideration."[58] Governor General Lord Canning similarly wrote of the many thousands of people who participated in this demonstration, "A people who can do this, and do it soberly and intelligently, may be weak and unresistful individually, but as a mass they cannot be dealt with too carefully."[59] The capacity for order and the level of organizational ability displayed in these public displays were deeply unsettling to British officials, offering a markedly different sociological object than the nineteenth-century European crowds and mobs bequeathed to us in scholarly literature as disorderly, emotional, and irrational.[60]

Although the Indian historian Dharampal made an effort in the 1970s to link all these various types of protests and construct an argument offering a longer history of noncooperation and civil disobedience in India that pre-dated Gandhi, most scholars have regarded such events as local phenomena. Sandria Freitag's important efforts to consider both violent and nonviolent forms of public assembly within the same analytic framework offers a close analysis of the Banaras House Tax protest but characterizes it as reflecting a unique local Banarsi style of protest.[61] She explains the protest as stem-ming from the fact that Banaras "reflected a society more culturally inte-grated than that of any other urban center in U.P. [the United Provinces]."[62] However, identical house tax protests were occurring simultaneously in other towns, including Patna, Saran, Murshidabad, and Bhagalpur, and in subse-quent years in other towns like Bareilly, suggesting that this was not simply a local phenomenon.[63] Similarly, Howard Spodek argues that the influences on Gandhi of practices like fasting, *traga* (the infliction of self-harm to place pressure on someone else), *risāmanu* (the temporary severing of personal re-lationships), and other forms of passive resistance can be attributed to the unique political heritage of the Kathiawad region of the Gujarat peninsula.[64] Yet, the many examples from throughout the subcontinent—not only the United Provinces and Kathiawad but also Surat, Madras, coastal Andhra, Kannada-speaking districts of the south, Bengal, Maharashtra, Garhwal, and Kumaon—suggest that these practices existed much more widely.

Exceptional levels of organization within work stoppages and strikes con-tinued into the twentieth century. As Susan Wolcott argues, "Unorganized Indian workers could initiate a very large strike in as orderly and complete a manner as the most organized examples in English and U.S. labor history."[65] Even in the face of what Susan Wolcott calls "an absence of formal union organization or state support for collective bargaining" in India, Indian tex-tile workers went on strike *ten times* as often as comparable workers in Brit-ain and the United States.[66] Wolcott's data show that the dramatically higher frequency of strikes in India is difficult to account for using existing theories of strikes and collective actions, suggesting that our analytic toolkit for un-derstanding collective organization is indeed inadequate.[67] Writing about the first Indian strike of the interwar period to involve more than 100,000 workers, Wolcott observes that this 1919 strike "predated any unionization" but developed first as a wage dispute in a single mill of 2,500 workers, who then marched to a second mill owned by the same family. In a process re-markably similar to that used by weavers in the Coromandel Coast, the workers then "proceed[ed] systematically through the textile mills of [the Bombay neighborhood of] Parel and other industrial districts, persuading the workers in each case to quit work and join their ranks. . . . Newspaper accounts described the procession as 'orderly and well behaved.'"[68] These twentieth-century descriptions echo those describing weavers' strikes of the previous century.

## Cosmopolitan Claim-Making

The second feature of Indian work stoppages and strikes is the translocal and transcommunal nature of collective claim-making occurring at the same time that English contentious actions were, in the words of Charles Tilly, *parochial, particular,* and *bifurcated.* Although the 1669 strike in Surat appears to have consisted primarily of prominent merchants, it also included both Hindus and Jains. The 1680 strike in Madras incorporated not only cloth painters, spinners, and weavers but also merchants, agents, boatmen, laborers, fisherman, wood sellers, lime manufacturers, and washermen, and it quickly spread to neighboring towns. By the eighteenth century, collective actions began to occur not just in individual cosmopolitan port cities but also across cities, towns, and villages to span entire regions, using remarkably similar methods across great distances.

Charles Tilly argues that the shift from *parochial* to *national* or *cosmopolitan* forms of collective claim-making began to be apparent in Britain only by the early decades of the nineteenth century.[69] Although he invokes the nation, a comparison of the distances across which mobilization occurs in India and in England suggests that the critical historical factor was the emergence of a centralized administrative body with which local actors had a relationship. On the Coromandel Coast, the distances across which collective claims were being made as early as the eighteenth century rival the size of the territories represented in nineteenth-century British collective assertions, even if they do not correspond to anything yet recognizable as a "nation." In 1766, the EIC gained political control of much of the Coromandel Coast and began to reorganize the procurement systems for textiles by bringing weaving villages throughout the region under a newly created structure known as the "mootah" system, in which groups of villages were assigned to distinct administrative units. These new units replaced earlier informal textile procurement methods with formal administrative mechanisms for distributing monetary advances, evaluating the quality of cloth pieces, and keeping track of the accounts of individual weavers. By 1774, these changes had eliminated opportunities for weavers to engage freely with Dutch and French traders in an open market, dramatically decreasing competition, lowering the earning potential of the various artisans involved in textile production, and restructuring the EIC's reliance on local merchants and middlemen. In response, cloth weavers within three factory jurisdictions— Visakhapatnam, Injeram, and Maddepollem—and under the control of twenty-seven mootah divisions came together to collectively express their grievances with the new system.

By way of comparison, the distance from Maddepollem to Visakhapatnam is 268 kilometers, or slightly longer than the distance from Manchester in northwest England to London in the southeast (262 kilometers). During a subsequent inquiry that was launched in response to continued unrest among weavers and others, witnesses were called from as far away as Cuddalore, some 976 kilometers to the south of Visakhapatnam, or slightly longer than the distance from London to Milan (952 kilometers). Thus, the distances across which weavers, merchants, transport workers, and other laborers came together in strikes and other collective actions were clearly comparable to the scope of collective assemblies in nineteenth-century Britain. The house tax protests that emerged in north India in 1810–11 also covered extensive distances. Banaras and Murshidabad, two of the cities involved, are approximately 652 kilometers apart or roughly comparable to the distance between London and Edinburgh (668 kilometers). Clearly, these were not parochial, localized phenomena.

Well-developed mechanisms existed through which news and information traveled across large distances even before the development of railways.[70] Messages were passed from village to village through letters, the beat of drums, and the movement of people, involving, at times, processions of protesters from village to village. In response to yet another tax protest in southern India, in January 1831, H. Dickinson, the collector of Canara in south India wrote,

> Things are here getting worse. The people were quiet till within a few days, but the assemblies have been daily increasing in number. Nearly 11,000 persons met yesterday at Yenoor. About an hour ago 300 ryots [peasant cultivators] came here, entered the Tahsildars Cutcherry [administrative office], and avowed their determination not to give a single pice [penny], and that they would be contented with nothing but a total remission. . . . The Tahsildar came to me to ask what answer he should give; I said that the best thing was to disperse them, if possible . . . [and] to issue instructions to all persons, &c, to prevent by all means in their power the assemblies which are taking place daily, and if possible to intercept the inflammatory letters which are

at present being despatched to the different Talooks [administrative subdivisions]. . . . The ferment has got as far as Barcoor and will soon reach Cundapoor . . . the dissatisfaction seems to be against the Government generally.

It was also clear that protesters knew what they were doing. Dickinson, in response to the rapidly spreading agitation (Cundapoor is more than 100 kilometers from Yenoor), also wrote, "The ryots say that they can not all be 'punished,'" indicating that they knew well the power and effectiveness of collective action.[71]

## Strikes and the State

The third and perhaps most distinctive feature of collective actions in India is that, well before the 1830s, representatives of the state were much more likely to be the primary target than in Europe. While a wide range of weavers, spinners, cloth painters and printers, boatmen, transport workers, merchants, and agents in seventeenth- and eighteenth-century southern India were engaging in various forms of nonviolent and orderly collective actions to appeal to EIC representatives, silk weavers in London's Spitalfields were using violence not to lodge their complaints with the state but to protest against the competition posed by imports of Asian textiles and against the consumers who purchased these imported goods.[72] Silk weavers in England also took the law into their own hands. Between the 1690s and the passage of the 1721 Calico Act, their collective actions frequently took the form of direct attacks on women who were wearing gowns made of imported calico.[73] On June 13, 1719, for example, "a mob of about 4,000 Spitalfields weavers paraded the streets of the City attacking all females whom they could find wearing Indian calicoes or linens, and sousing them with ink, aqua fortis, and other fluids." Efforts were made to control the rioters, but as soon as they were released, "the mob re-assembled, the weavers tearing all the calico gowns they could meet with."[74] As the eighteenth century progressed and the Spitalfields silk weavers found it more and more difficult to earn a living, they began attacking fellow weavers who were willing to work for lower pay, often breaking into houses or shops to slash an offending weaver's work or cut it from the loom. In 1765, when the king was attending Parliament, weavers did hold a procession in protest against the importation of French silks, but this seems to have been an exception to their more common attacks on consumers or fellow weavers. It was these attacks targeting the looms of weavers willing to work for lower wages that caused riotous Spitalfields silk weavers to be popularly known by the name "cutters."[75]

In contrast, in the growing port cities of India like Surat, Machilipatnam, and Madras as early as the late seventeenth century, the targets of the collective actions of merchants and artisans were almost exclusively representatives of the state. The eight thousand Jain and Hindu merchants in Surat, who left the city in protest against the appointment of a new local administrator, appealed for redress to the Mughal emperor Aurangzeb and received it. Eleven years later, merchants and artisans in Madras engaged in a very similar action—vacating the city and relocating to St. Thomas, fifteen kilometers south of the EIC's Fort St. George, to hold the company-state accountable for the debts of its chief agent, who died owing large amounts to local Indian merchants. As the EIC's administrative authority expanded along the Coromandel Coast in the eighteenth century, particularly from the 1760s onward, its representatives were confronted by a growing number of appeals to their authority. Grievances included the EIC's economic reorganization of mechanisms for procuring woven textiles, which sought to limit investment risk for the British by eliminating competition and undermining the market power of weavers under its jurisdiction, but which also reduced the earnings of local artisans and merchants.

As Parthasarathi notes, scholarly attention to these well-organized protests has been quite inadequate, and much therefore remains to be known about "the nature and forms of resistance and protest in eighteenth-century South India, or South Asia for that matter."[76] He goes on to argue that although the Subaltern Studies Collective has been particularly attentive to the period after 1850, they have left "largely unexplored, an earlier tradition of resistance [that] haunts [their] writings, as it is often invoked to explain the peculiarities, and especially the failures, of protest in the colonial period."[77] Despite the "frequent reference to the persistence of pre-colonial, semi-feudal or pre-capitalist traditions or modes of behavior and to the 'primordialism' of subaltern groups, be they peasants, workers or tribals," Parthasarathi argues that it is plasticity rather than rigidity that characterizes the social world of India's weavers, with ties of solidarity "not fixed, but continually made and remade.... Weavers did not take social relations or solidarities as given and ties of caste, kinship or other 'primordialisms' did not in some simple or automatic way determine or limit their actions. In fact ... the act of protest itself and the demands of mobilizing for protest led weavers to explore and create new forms of solidarity."[78]

A sample of south Indian weaver protests discussed by Parthasarathi and others illustrates clear differences from the forms of collective action used by English weavers. In 1768, weavers in the Northern Circars tied up their own looms and declared a work stoppage in protest against the EIC reforms.[79] Although the formation of associations has been widely characterized as a European innovation central to the emergence of a civil society capable of maintaining checks on the state, it is clear that this was not a foreign notion in south India during this period. In 1775, to communicate their concerns to the EIC, four of the main weaving communities came together to organize what they called a *samayam*, or "a Company of people gathered to enforce the execution of some business."[80] Support for the cause was not limited to weavers alone; instead, they actively sought to enlarge their membership by appealing to neighboring peasants and others for assistance. Agriculturalists in Jagganadaporam sent a letter to the residents of Mundapettah, some seventy kilometers away, appealing to them to support the cause of the weavers. Parthasarathi shares a translation of their letter preserved in the EIC records:

> As the four different casts of the weavers namely Salavar, Davanguloo, Carnevar and Kackullavar have formed a Samayem . . . it becomes you to cause one man out of each house of the weavers to join the said Samayem, you will therefore advise the weavers to do so. We must remark that ever since the Samayem hath been formed at Golconda we both (meaning our people and those of the weavers) lived in perfect union as the milk and water wherefore you will exert yourself at this time to support the said Samayam by all means which will gain us a good name and reputation. This is not to be regarded like other Business.[81]

Such samayams appear to have been common in the Telugu-speaking regions of southern India.

Although evidence attesting to the organizational structures of samayams is only fragmentary, there is enough to show that a wide range of strategies were used to gain the attention of the state. Weavers, for example, sent both petitions and delegations of various sizes to meet with government officials, as Swarnalatha demonstrates. They also engaged in collective marches from village to village, gaining additional numbers at each stop in an effort to enhance their collective power.[82] At one point the EIC's commercial resident in Injeram refused to accept the submission of a samayam petition, stating that the weavers had not signed it. The weavers responded by writing, "The names of all the weavers as far as Rajahmundry and Ellore, you have note [*sic*] down in your book. You may be induced to think that this Samium is made by one man—by one it cannot be done." At another point in the same year, four thousand samayam members "assembled and prepared to go to Injeram to express their grievances" but were attacked by EIC peons and prevented from reaching the government officials they wished to meet.[83] Far from recognizing these actions as evidence of the associational politics of an active "civil society," the EIC dubbed them a "sudden action" and "insurrection" by "fugitive" weavers. The collector saw them as a form of "extortion," expressing the hope that the weavers "would yield to reason" and insisting that they "represent their story in a quiet submissive manner," for which their collective appearance apparently did not qualify.[84] Even though petitions addressed to authorities often stated explicitly that their goal was to "attract . . . the notice of the Resident, and other civil officers of the Honorable Company's Government" or "to make known their very deplorable case to Government," EIC representatives often willfully ignored the weavers' desires to gain an audience and be recognized by them.[85]

Such evidence suggests that state-directed collective actions were expanding in India at a time when collective actions in Europe were still being used primarily to enforce local social norms. Practices like charivari, rough music, and skimmington, as well as various forms of violence and rioting, were used as forms of social discipline against those seen to violate local social norms or negatively affect others' abilities to earn a livelihood.[86] Targets of such actions included women wearing imported calicoes, hoarding millers during times when prices for grain were rising, adulterous spouses, those seen to be engaging in unnatural or inappropriate coupling, or workers willing to work for lower wages than was customary.

The contrast between the violent repertoires of contention used by the Spitalfields weavers against consumers and the orderly and nonviolent mass strikes organized by the weavers of southern India to communicate with company-state administrators makes it difficult to argue that strike actions and practices of collective assembly in South Asia are derivative of postindustrial European forms of the political. Petitions and other records of mass efforts to appeal to the government in India, including evidence of the formation of associations and large-scale pilgrimages to appeal to government officials in person, make clear that government representatives were the primary objects of collective actions. Paying careful attention to the ways in which forms of collective political action are directly linked to global commodity chains, however, enables us to trace longer genealogies for the contemporary South Asian forms of political practice discussed through-out this book—forms that first attracted global attention only during the anticolonial nationalist mobilizations of the early twentieth century. This approach also challenges existing histories of civility, associational politics, and civil society as uniquely European foundations of democracy.

## Collective Action at the Other End of the Commodity Chain

Mass strikes emerged most visibly in contexts that formed key nodes within modern global trade in commodities. In South Asia, we see this occur most dramatically in relation to cotton textiles. Woodruff Smith's research on the history of consumption reminds us that these are the very same cotton tex-tiles that enabled the public demonstration of the new forms of gentility and virtue that were so critical to the establishment of respectability and status within the newly emerging public spheres of Europe. "*Calico* even-tually came to mean any of a wide range of cotton textiles, but before the eighteenth century the term usually referred to a particular kind of heavy cotton fabric, usually printed or painted with distinctive designs," explains Woodruff. "Calicoes were used primarily for tablecloths, wall hangings, and window treatments throughout Europe until about the middle of the seven-teenth century. Then something happened."[87]

What exactly happened seems to have been linked, Smith continues, to two key factors that dramatically expanded the use of calicoes after the 1660s. The first was the "increased availability of calicoes due to the im-ports of the English East India Company," and the second concerned "the dynamics of fashion in the French capital, which was just in the process of assuming its role as the source of fashions in dress for the rest of Europe."[88] It was in Paris, Smith tells us, that new institutions were developing "outside and *parallel to the royal court*, that created venues for individual competi-tion in display of talent, taste, and gentility. These were the famous Parisian salons."[89] These are, of course, the same salons that Jürgen Habermas argues were central to the forms of civility emerging within the new bourgeois pub-lic sphere at this time.[90]

In a carefully traced argument, Smith demonstrates that "it was the con-nection between the networks of fashion centering around the salons and the commercial capabilities of the East Indies companies (especially the En-glish EIC) that made the [calico] craze and its extension possible." Of key importance, argues Smith, "was the *meaning* of printed cottons in a changing context of gentility that made them an element of eighteenth-century culture strong enough to defend itself against the full brunt of mercantilism, and to emerge as a vital stimulant to the Industrial Revolution."[91] He goes on to explain,

> Many eighteenth-century commentators noted with great disapproval the fact that people at middling levels of income and status had taken to wearing printed Asian fabrics, and that even people of conventionally low status (especially servants) had done so as well. The fact that wearing calicoes was a statement of participation in gentility, to some degree at least, was well understood and was often presented as a danger to the social order. The crux of the matter was that the traditional foundation of gentility was birth. . . . But the combination of a fashion item that met all the requirements for status and that could be supplied in large quantities, in ever changing varieties, and at prices that were neither prohibitively high nor unfashionable low, with a desire for signification of status by many people who could not readily claim gentle birth, could be taken as a threat to the notion of inherited gentility as the framework of meaning for social hierarchy.[92]

Even though the 1701 and 1721 Calico Acts imposed severe restrictions on the import of Indian calicoes, there was continued demand for the cloth fueled by the "purchases by people of a widening variety of social backgrounds who wanted to take part in the culture of gentility."[93] It was precisely this demand for a good that could not be obtained anywhere else but India that gave artisans, merchants, and laborers in its growing urban trade centers such new political possibilities.

Although the widespread efforts of the EIC (and later the British crown) to limit the influence of contentious collective assemblies on the state were not entirely successful in eliminating those collective practices from political repertoires, they were effective in erasing them from global historical narratives of the political. The fact that by 1837 the *Asiatic Journal and Monthly Register* wrote, in a report on the "Disturbances at Bareilli," that "the resistance to the tax was one of those movements not altogether unknown in more western countries, but little expected in the East," in which "a common spirit pervaded the whole people,"[94] suggests that many of the earlier effective forms of collective assembly in India were already beginning to be erased from historical memory. This erasure has made it much easier to write histories of general strikes and other forms of *cosmopolitan, modular,* and *autonomous* collective claim-making as though these forms of practice were invented in a "precocious" postindustrial Europe, further reinforcing a historical framing that positions non-European forms of practice as always a few steps behind Europe.

The EIC and later the colonial state used a range of strategies for diffusing the power of collective assembly, strategies that, as I have argued, influenced our collective amnesia regarding the scope and effectiveness of earlier forms of Indian "combinations." We can identify at least three such strategies. The first established new legal structures for the resolution of conflicts and banned—as early as 1793 (with limited success)—existing local conflict-resolution practices, such as door-sitting to collect a debt, which offered competition to British forms of dispute resolution. As we saw in chapter 1, dharna was first prohibited by the Court of Justice at Benares, then made a punishable offense by Bengal Regulation VII in 1820, and eventually incorporated into Section 508 of the Indian Penal Code of 1860. Sections 141–60 of the Indian Penal Code were drafted in 1860 to address "Offences against the Public Tranquility," including assemblies and rioting, and can still be used today to disband, censure, or prosecute assemblies of five or more persons. Section 144 of the Indian Criminal Procedure Code, first introduced to India by the British in 1861 but never abolished after independence, allows police to this day to issue a preventive order that can remain in place for up to two months, defining in advance any assembly held in the locations covered by the order as an unlawful assembly. These laws have not prevented a wide range of public assemblies and forms of protest from continuing to take place, either under the British or today, but they *have* succeeded in making it possible to selectively criminalize them if authorities so desire.

The second method of diffusing the power of collective assemblies was to create an increasingly centralized system of policing. This strategy often involved levying additional taxes to pay for new urban police forces, displacing locally controlled neighborhood watchmen, and diminishing the power of local neighborhoods. Although resistance was strong to these early British efforts to establish centralized policing, by the end of the second decade of the nineteenth century the British had largely been successful in replacing local forms of policing with their own security forces. We see this especially clearly in the contrast between the conciliatory EIC reaction to the House Tax protest in Banaras in 1810–11 and their much more violent response in Bareilly just five years later.

The third strategy was to delegitimize collective political efforts and refuse to recognize those who claimed to act as representatives of collectives.

Instead, EIC administrators began to insist on only recognizing individuals acting on their own behalf. In 1816 and 1817, the weaving communities in the coastal south Indian city of Visakhapatnam submitted a series of petitions to EIC administrators objecting to its new mechanisms for obtaining and paying for woven goods, which had become increasingly disadvantageous to weavers. When their petitions were rejected—for reasons as varied as using disrespectful language to not being written on stamp paper—twenty thousand residents of the city, in violation of new laws prohibiting public congregations, vacated their homes and workplaces and relocated to the temple at Simhachalam atop a hill outside the city, and a delegation traveled to Madras to petition the Board of Trade directly.[95] But, as detailed in chapter 3, the response of the Board of Trade's secretary was that "*each Individual weaver*, if aggrieved, has the means of laying his Complaint before the Commercial Resident, or as the case may be of proceeding by an action in the Zillah Court . . . *The Board cannot sanction Combinations of weavers* for the purpose of Making General Complaints *nor acknowledge persons stating themselves to be agents of such Combinations.*"[96] In effect, the Board of Trade sought to invalidate all efforts to represent grievances collectively, instructing those with grievances to present their complaints individually in accordance with new regulations established the previous decade.

Far from being sudden, spontaneous, or the product of emotional contagion, such protests clearly reflected well-developed and well-organized structures of social communication and coordination, and they show little evidence of stemming from European influence. The effectiveness of such well-organized collective efforts was not lost on the British, who continued to seek new strategies to limit their power throughout the nineteenth century. Nonetheless, these strategies were never completely successful. Where these new disciplinary regimes were effective, however, was in reframing the meaning of collective corporeal action as the opposite of individual speech action, diminishing our understanding of it as amplification. One of the most successful strategies was linking narratives of the development of democracy (and of the "political" more generally) to narratives of industrialization and economic development, making it difficult to recognize other genealogies for the contemporary practices of Indian democracy and for non-Western democratic forms of practice, more generally.

Based on his comparison of data on strikes in coal mining and other industries, Timothy Mitchell argues that democracy expanded in response to the labor activism and political mobilization from the 1880s onward in which coal miners played the most prominent role, showing that they went on strike at a higher rate than workers in other industries and that their strikes typically lasted much longer.[97] The position of coal miners and railway and dock workers who transported coal to the concentrated populations within urban centers "gave them, at certain moments, a new kind of political power ... derived not just from the organizations they formed, the ideas they began to share or the political alliances they built, but from the extraordinary concentrations of carbon energy whose flow they could now slow, disrupt or cut off."[98] Mitchell is not suggesting that we substitute a materialist account for the "idealist schemes of the democracy experts." Instead, he argues,

> Understanding the relations between fossil fuels and democracy requires tracing how these connections are built, the vulnerabilities and opportunities they create and the narrow points of passage where control is particularly effective. Political possibilities were opened up or narrowed down by different ways of organizing the flow and concentration of energy, and these possibilities were enhanced or limited by arrangements of people, finance, expertise and violence that were assembled in relationship to the distribution and control of energy.[99]

Mitchell's method suggests the importance of looking more carefully at sites where new concentrations of people have controlled narrow flows of commodities on which consumers depend.

Archival evidence from early modern India suggests that the flow of cotton textiles from India and the dependence on these textiles that quickly developed among those who sought to participate in the growing European public spheres opened up similar kinds of new political possibilities. European ports in India grew rapidly by attracting artisans, merchants, laborers, and others engaged in the textile industry, creating concentrated urban populations on which the EIC was heavily dependent. This, at least for a time, enhanced the political power of these concentrated populations and encouraged new forms of social organization that could make use of this power. That this power began to diminish somewhat as Europeans developed their own means of producing the textiles and other consumer goods that continued to fuel rapidly expanding practices of consumption should not blind us to the importance of recognizing and understanding the ways that contemporary democratic practices have built on and reshaped these earlier forms of social organization. Understanding the impact of these earlier structures of social organization is at least as important as understanding the impact of imported ideological writings on democracy and structures of electoral practice. Yet social scientists have long dismissed political practices, forms of collective mobilization, and voting behaviors in India that are perceived to be tainted by caste, communalism, ethnic loyalties, patronage, and other supposedly premodern forms of power, without fully understanding how such forms of social organization actually work in practice.

Fortunately, exciting new work on contemporary politics in India is beginning to recognize how little we understand the forms of social organization through which democracy functions in India, not just at the time of elections but also between them, as citizens seek to gain access to the state, hold elected officials accountable, and attain recognition. New questions and areas of inquiry that promise to disrupt unitary narratives of European origins and diffusion are being opened up by efforts to understand the "vernacularisation" of Indian politics and by the use of ethnographic tools to examine the patterns of communication and mutual obligation that circulate within asymmetrical relationships between elected officials and voters, patrons and their followers.[100] Thachil and Teitelbaum, for example, have shown that ethnic parties, once widely dismissed as holdovers of a premodern era that reduce voter autonomy by delivering votes as a bloc, can, in fact, have the effect of expanding the autonomy of marginalized voters by disrupting "the prior encapsulation of these voters by traditional political elites" and raising incentives "for politicians to spend on public goods."[101] And Lisa Björkman's political ethnography has persuasively argued that political behaviors that political scientists have so quickly dismissed as "cash for votes," or read as insincere participation in staged and manipulated processions and rallies, can be understood as much more complex negotiations whose outcomes are never known in advance.[102] These new directions demonstrate that, rather than being archaic holdovers of a premodern era that are holding back the development of an authentic democracy in India, the various forms of social organization that appear to shape Indian politics today—caste, religion, region, language, patronage—are "deeply modern" in the ways that they "produce, perform, and display public authority and powers of mediation," as Björkman argues.[103] Ultimately, a better understanding of the processes and forms of social organization that function within India's vibrant "actually existing democracy" can offer new narratives for how political representation works, how citizens can and do access channels of representation through which they endeavor to make their voices heard, and ultimately how state recognition (or lack of recognition) of collective voices shapes civility.[104]

# PART II. THE CRIMINAL AND THE POLITICAL

# FIVE. ALARM CHAIN PULLING

## The Criminal and the Political in the Writing of History

Democracy always develops around the chief means of communication. —Indian Railway Traffic Service officer, Lucknow, March 26, 2009

On December 23, 1916, Mr. D. V. Panvalkar, of Dhulia in northwestern Maharashtra, addressed the following letter to the secretary of the Railway Board, Simla:

> Sir, I remember to have read some time ago in newspapers that if any railway compartment be overcrowded and the railway servant do not help to bring down the number to the proscribed limit, it is not improper use of the alarm-chain, if it be pulled under the above circumstances. It seems that there are decided judicial cases to that effect. Will you therefore kindly let me know whether my impression is right and oblige? I beg to remain, Sir, Your most obedient servant.[1]

Rail travelers in India are familiar with the ubiquitous alarm or emergency chain—the communication cord as the railways so aptly refer to it—that is present in each bogie (carriage) of an Indian train (figure 5.1). When pulled, the alarm chain creates a break that results in a loss of air pressure (or vacuum in the case of vacuum brakes) that causes the train's brakes to be applied immediately. Although fines of up to 1,000 rupees are currently levied for pulling alarm chains "without reasonable and sufficient cause," it is difficult for railway authorities to immediately locate the break and identify

FIGURE 5.1. Emergency chain (in front of door) in an Indian Railways compartment, December 28, 2006 (photo: Nichalp/Creative Commons Attribution-Share Alike 2.5 Generic License).

the person who pulled the chain. Once pulled, there is nothing that the driver of a train can do to prevent a train from stopping, making this emergency feature an ideal target for those seeking to halt a train for other reasons.[2]

Most people would likely consider Mr. Panvalkar's procedural query to the Railway Board as a constructive form of civic engagement. It involves no violence, addresses itself to the highest government authority with jurisdiction over the Indian railways, and engages in a form of polite written discourse. He writes as a private individual to clarify an interpretation of a point of law—a law to which he is subject as a resident within the British colonial state. But what if Panvalkar had taken the next logical step, as others later did, and pulled the alarm chain in an overcrowded third-class bogie in an effort to draw the attention of the railway authorities and compel them to relieve passengers in uncomfortable circumstances? Would that action also be easily classifiable as a form of constructive civic engagement? What if the alarm chain were pulled to draw the attention of authorities to a social injustice not directly related to the railways, as it began to be used by the 1930s and '40s during the height of the anticolonial nationalist movement?

And would pulling the chain still be considered constructive when done to compel officials to uphold campaign promises, constitutional provisions, or existing laws, as has become increasingly common in postcolonial India? At what point does the use of a particular form of political practice to draw the attention of authorities to injustice or failure of governance cease to be classifiable as a form of civic engagement and begin to be regarded as a form of disruption or extralegal violation? And what is the relationship of these various practices—treated not as homogeneous but as a set of related practices—to the history of Indian democracy?

I identify three distinct phases in the role of alarm chain pulling in relation to the development and emergence of new forms of political communication and democratic practice in India. The first phase involves experimentation with a new form of political practice. We see inquiries, tentative engagements in test cases, and extensive circulation of the results of these tests within the popular newspapers of the day. The overcrowding of third-class railway bogies was a widespread complaint among native subjects of colonial rule, and was taken up by Gandhi as an early symbol of the unfair treatment of Indians by their British rulers. Alarm chain pulling was eventually widely popularized as a method for persuading authorities to address this problem of overcrowding. During the second phase, the practice of alarm chain pulling in the context of railway-specific complaints began to be applied to other nonrailway concerns, becoming recognizable as a properly political tactic. In this stage it expanded from a mechanism directed at alleviating the specific problem of overcrowding to address wider nationalist agendas within the larger anticolonial program by halting trains and causing general inconvenience to the railways and therefore to the state. It is also during this phase that alarm chain pulling was reframed by the colonial state as a political rather than a criminal problem, a shift that was to have far-reaching consequences. In the third phase, despite the transfer of political rule from Britain to India in 1947, political activism continued to draw from existing repertoires of practice. Local political movements, particularly those that sought to communicate with central government authorities in Delhi, continued to target the railways by halting trains even after independence, a practice that continues to the present. In the last section of the chapter, I examine alarm chain pulling by marginalized groups and individuals to express more generalized discontent and resistance, arguing that the widespread availability and recognition of this specific form of practice allow it to be taken up by groups and individuals in ways that may exceed what we might see as the properly political.

Early Experimentation, 1915–1930

Let the Railway Agents beware. If the aggrieved passengers, taking their cue from this case, start pulling the chain, not only the trains but their administrations will be brought to a standstill. —*Tribune*, Lahore, August 9, 1929

Let us now return to Mr. D. V. Panvalkar, with whom the chapter opened, and his 1916 query to the Railway Board regarding the legitimate use of the alarm chain to draw the attention of railway authorities to the problem of overcrowding. After his letter was received on December 25, the archival record makes clear that the members of the Railway Board were reluctant to provide him with a definitive answer. One of their internal notes suggests, "It is very doubtful whether this office should be allowed to be treated as an enquiry office," and proposes instead that "he may be told that the Ry. Board regret that they cannot supply the information asked for and that he should himself arrange to obtain it from newspapers."[3] Indeed, in the end, the assistant secretary of the Railway Board approved this reply dated January 9, 1917: "Sir, With reference to your letter dated the 23rd/25th December 1916, enquiring whether any judicial decision has been given in regard to the right of passengers to resist overcrowding by resorting to the communication cord, I am directed to state that the Ry. Board regret that they are unable to supply you with the information asked for."[4]

But the matter did not end there. Mr. Panvalkar was not so easily put off by the nonreply he received from the Railway Board and wrote again to its secretary in Simla:

> Sir, I am in receipt of your letter No. 119-T-16, dated the 9th instt. and am thankful for the same. Under Sec. 93 of the Indian Railways Act, the Company is liable to a fine if it allows more than the prescribed number of passengers in a compartment. As such if a railway servant refuses to take out the excess number of passengers, he makes his master (the company) liable to the fine. Therefore if a passenger pulls the cord under the circumstances, I believe it will not be improper use of the cord. Please therefore let me know whether this belief is right or wrong. The Railway Guide or any other authoritative book does not exhaustively give a list of the circumstances under which the pulling will be the proper use, and hence as the highest authority, I am referring this matter to you. I, therefore, hope you will kindly satisfy my query and oblige. I beg to remain your most obedient servant, D. V. Panvalkar.[5]

In the Railway Notes and Orders appended in the archives to the original letter, a note reads, "The writer is evidently trying to inveigle the Board into giving a decision on a purely legal point. We may, perhaps, suggest his consulting legal opinion in the matter," which indeed is the response that was ultimately approved and sent back to Panvalkar: "Sir, With reference to your letter of the 26-1-1917, on the subject of the right of passengers to prevent overcrowding by resorting to the communication cord, I am directed to state that as the question put by you raises legal issues, the Ry. Bd. would suggest your consulting legal opinion in the matter."[6]

It is likely that Panvalkar's query was prompted by an article the previous year in the *Bombay Chronicle*, reprinted in a Pune newspaper, *Mahratta*. The newspaper report generated a flurry of correspondence as railway officials struggled to figure out whether and how to respond to this adverse publicity. Titled "The Right to Resist Overcrowding," the newspaper article described an unnamed pleader (lawyer) who was reported to have resisted the entry of additional passengers into the bogie in which he was traveling because their entry would have caused the compartment to exceed the number of passengers permitted by law. The news report goes on:

> An altercation ensued between him and the extra passengers who ultimately called the station-master. The latter forcibly thrust them into the compartment, despite the pleader's protests. No sooner had the train started than the pleader pulled the emergency chain, and brought the train to a dead stop. The guard and the station-master hastened up to the compartment whereupon the pleader told them that, unless the extra passengers were removed, he would not allow the train to proceed. The astonished railway officials asserted that as there was no room elsewhere, the overcrowding must continue and restarted the train. But the pleader knew his rights too well to allow himself to be bullied as the average third-class passenger does. He at once had another pull at the chain. For the second time the train stopped. . . . The officials' next move was to take the name and address of the pleader, and after threatening him with prosecution for delaying the train, once more gave the signal for starting. But the threat had no effect. Our worthy friend pulled the chain the third time before the train could clear the platform. This time the station-master and guard yielded to the inevitable. The extra passengers were removed and escorted to another compartment. Then the pleader allowed the train to proceed.[7]

Several features of this report are quite striking when compared with more recent reports of alarm chain pulling. First, a clear distinction is made between the class and the confidence of the unnamed pleader who had initiated the action and "the average third class passenger." In other words, the pleader's educational background and occupational position enabled an awareness of rights that ordinary colonial subjects did not possess.

Second, the news article presents the story as an instructional one, from which others may learn. The opening sentence reports that the incident "should prove highly instructive to persons interested in exercising their right to resist overcrowding."[8] The report then concludes with a more general piece of advice: "The moral is clear. Work the emergency chain when your attempt to resist overcrowding is not heeded. Work it again, if necessary. If the extra passengers are still not taken out, don't lose heart or get frightened by the threats of railway servants. Make a fresh dash at your emergency chain, and yet once more, if necessary. Remember the law is on your side and you *must* succeed."[9] The incident is presented as an experiment that succeeded and could now serve as a precedent for others to successfully engage in similar actions. It is clear from reading the internal railway notes (those stamped not to be sent out of office or printed) that the Railway Board's reluctance to give Mr. Panvalkar a straight answer, much less make any sort of public statement on this issue, stemmed precisely from their fear that such a practice could indeed be made into a precedent, which, in the words of another railway official, "might be very embarrassing for railways."[10]

So vexing was the problem that it was still unresolved almost a decade and a half later. On August 9, 1929, the *Tribune*, published in Lahore, reported a similar effort to test the legality of such an action:

> It is very rarely that men like Mr. Popatlal bring things to a head. He was travelling from Calcutta to Bombay. At Bhusawal he found that his compartment was congested. Failing all other methods, he pulled the chain five times to bring the scandal to the notice of the authorities. He was prosecuted for refusing to be suffocated. But the learned Magistrate held that Mr. Popatlal was within his rights in "pulling the chain to remove overcrowding." Let the Railway Agents beware. If the aggrieved passengers, taking their cue from this case, start pulling the chain, not only the trains but their administrations will be brought to a standstill.[11]

The widespread use of alarm chain pulling as a tactic for addressing the problem of overcrowding had by this time spread to all corners of the country.

We see the recognition of the widespread use and effectiveness of alarm chain pulling reflected in the following question put to the Legislative Assembly on September 24, 1929: "Are Government aware that the Railway authorities had not paid any attention to complaints regarding overcrowding till the passengers pulled the alarm chain?"[12]

On July 14, 1930, another question was raised in the Legislative Assembly regarding alarm chain incidents on the Madras and Southern Mahratta Railway. Mr. N. G. Ranga Nayakulu asked the following:

(a) Has the Honourable the Commerce Member come to know that one Mr. Srihari Rao was charged on a number of occasions at Rajahmundry under the Railway Companies Act by the Madras and Southern Mahratta Railway authorities for continuously pulling the alarm chain in the mail and other passenger trains to draw the attention of the Railway authorities to overcrowding in the third class carriages?

(b) Is the Honourable the Commerce Member aware of the fact that strong resentment prevails all along the Northern Circars against this action of the Railway authorities? Is it a fact they have not tried, in spite of the agitation carried on by Mr. Srihari Rao, to improve the conditions of the third class travelling?

(c) Is he also aware that if in case no satisfactory action is taken by the Railway authorities or by the Government of India to lessen the overcrowding in third class carriages, there is a great likelihood of there being many more Satyagraha demonstrations on the trains, imitating Mr. Sri Hari Rao? [This paragraph is crossed out and the following letter "(d)" is crossed out and renumbered "(c)."]

(d) Will the Honourable the Commerce Member be pleased to state what action he proposes to take to lessen the overcrowding in the third class carriages of the Madras and Southern Mahratta Railway Company?[13]

Thus, it should not come as a surprise that once the practice of alarm chain pulling was well established, people began to extend it to other causes and concerns. The Lahore *Tribune*'s report not only reflected its widespread use against overcrowding but also recognized that the communication cord could be used to bring the administration to its knees. This set the stage for the second moment I consider: acceptance of the more widespread use of chain pulling for raising and advancing nonrailway-related political concerns.

## Alarm Chain Pulling as *Satyagraha*, 1930–1947

Travelling without tickets and pulling railway chains should be popularised to the utmost. —Inaugural issue of *Free India*, August 10, 1942

By the 1930s, chain pulling had begun to be used for a variety of political purposes, and the number of incidents began to increase. What had largely been restricted to protests against overcrowding in third-class carriages began to be associated more broadly with a larger program of nationalist satyagraha. After his return from South Africa in 1915, Gandhi quickly became an advocate for the relief of the deplorable conditions in the rail carriages used by ordinary Indians. As early as September 1917, he published a short essay on third-class railway travel, announcing, "I think that the time has come when I should invite the press and the public to join in a crusade against a grievance which has too long remained unredressed."[14] Yet strikingly, the use of the alarm chain—either to relieve conditions of third-class rail travelers or as more generalized protest against British rule—was never on Gandhi's agenda. In 1945–47, he went so far as to explicitly condemn the practice of alarm chain pulling to halt trains:

> One vulgar and uncivilized practice must be given up. There is the chain on every train to be used strictly in times of danger or accidents. Any other use of it and the consequent stoppage of the train is not merely a punishable offence but it is a vulgar, thoughtless and even dangerous misuse of an instrument devised for great emergencies. Any such misuse is a social abuse which, if it becomes a custom, must result in a great public nuisance. It is up to every lover of his country to issue a stern warning against such wanton abuse of a humanitarian device intended for public safety.[15]

These objections were obviously voiced in response to the increasingly widespread and seemingly uncontrollable pulling of alarm chains as a tactic within the anticolonial nationalist movement.

As early as 1933, the Indian Railways had begun to view the practice as a serious enough problem that they proposed introducing stiffer penalties for pulling the chain in nonemergency situations.[16] They sought to add two years' imprisonment to the existing fine of 50 rupees for those who used the communication cord inappropriately. Although the bill failed to pass, it is clear from the Legislative Assembly debates that the stiffer penalties were being proposed to combat the growing use of alarm chain pulling as a form of civil disobedience. An amendment introduced by the Honorable Sir Brojendra Mitter captured the shift in the practice when he suggested that penalties should be applied "if a passenger intentionally stops a train by using any such means of communication, without reasonable and sufficient cause and without any cause in relation to which the railway servants in change of the train could properly afford assistance."[17] The debates were tinged with alarm that chain pulling was no longer simply being used to address railway-specific problems like overcrowding but had expanded to include "an intensive programme . . . of train stoppage as a variety of direct action" that had as its purpose the new goal "of paralysing the train services."[18] Another speaker summed up the problem when he stated that in these cases the only motive "was to stop the traffic and to cause inconvenience to the travelling public and dislocate the trains."[19] No longer was the simple relief of overcrowding the goal of alarm chain pulling. Nationalist activists were now using it to achieve the larger goal of freedom from British colonial rule.

It was the Indian Railways' inability to prevent this practice, along with ticketless travel and the removal of rails to halt trains, that made these tactics part of an easily available repertoire of effective political strategies. By the early 1940s, chain pulling was even more formally institutionalized as an important form of civil disobedience. A confidential letter sent by R. E. Marriott, of the East Indian Railways in Calcutta, to Sir Guthrie Russell, the chief commissioner of the Railways, reflects the privileged place of alarm chain pulling within anticolonial civil disobedience activities. Marriott, quoting from a report sent to him by the divisional superintendent of Dinapore, wrote on April 9, 1940, "The Superintendent, Railway Police, Patna, informed me that there is a likelihood of Civil Disobedience being started in the immediate future. Travelling without tickets and pulling of Alarm Chains will be in the Programme."[20]

During the height of the Quit India movement in 1942 and 1943 when Gandhi, Nehru, and most of the other leaders of the Indian National Congress were jailed, the railways became a key target of anticolonial protest. Virtually every major railway line in the country saw repeated roko agitations (blockages), sabotage, destruction, and shutdowns, with damage and delays on some lines so great that it took weeks or even months for service to restart. Indeed, the colonial archive of this period shows a preoccupation with the compromised state of railway communication. A confidential circular distributed by the Andhra Provincial Congress Committee on July 29, 1942, issued instructions to its District Congress Committees outlining six distinct stages of action to be implemented. The fifth stage included the following suggested activities:

(1) Stopping trains by pulling chains only.
(2) Travel without tickets.
(3) Cutting toddy yielding trees.
(4) Cutting telegraph and telephone wires.[21]

A translation of another cyclostyled Telugu version of these instructions, "Programme of Work for the Attainment of Complete Independence," included "travelling in trains without tickets and pulling the chains to stop trains" among a list of twenty-one suggested actions.[22]

The following month, in the wake of the passage of the Quit India Resolution at the Bombay session of the All India Congress Committee (AICC) on August 8, 1942, and the arrest the following day of Gandhi and much of the rest of the Congress's national leadership, a few senior Congress leaders who had escaped arrest quickly compiled and circulated a "12-Point Programme" for bringing a free India into being. The eleventh point stated, "The most important part of the programme is paralysis of the war effort, chiefly by paralysis of transport. This may be done by cutting telegraphic wires, by disturbing railway communications. Travelling without tickets and pulling railway chains of running trains should be popularised to the utmost. Strikes amongst railway employees should be organised on as large a scale as possible."[23]

Disruption of rail traffic reached such heights and became such a regular challenge to authorities that the Indian Railways again proposed heightened penalties for inappropriate use of the alarm chain. Although it had been unsuccessful a decade earlier in convincing the Legislative Assembly to approve stiffer penalties, the heightened wartime conditions provided a new opportunity for revisiting the possibility. In July 1942, with the Japanese approaching the Indo-Burmese border and the Indian National Congress debating a resolution to demand complete freedom from the British, a majority of the regional railway companies expressed their concern over an increase (observed or expected) in the number of alarm chain pulling incidents.[24] The Railway Board was convinced that something urgently needed to be done to curb this rampant practice.[25] Yet, given the long history of legal precedents establishing the rights of passengers in overcrowded bogies to use the alarm chain, it was clear to everyone involved that the ability to enforce stiffer penalties, assuming they could even be passed, was not strong.[26] Wartime conditions placed additional burdens on railway transport, increasing rather than alleviating the overcrowded conditions, particularly in third-class carriages, and making it even more difficult to enforce any legal recourse should a widespread alarm chain pulling campaign be initiated.

Finally, on August 10, 1942, in the wake of the Quit India Resolution on August 8, a new suggestion was introduced to the debate over alarm chain pulling circulating among the members of the Railway Board—a suggestion with dramatic and perhaps unanticipated consequences. It included the following proposal:

> In view of the present situation, it is for consideration whether this matter should not be treated entirely on different lines, i.e., to forestall as far as possible any organised attempts to dislocate traffic by a wide-spread campaign of interfering with the communication cords in passenger trains.
>
> Section 62 of the Railway Act requires us to provide and maintain in passenger trains such efficient means of communication between the passengers and the railway servants in charge of the train as the Safety Controlling Authority has approved. . . .
>
> I suggest, therefore, the issue of the Defence of India Ordinance exempting Railways from the provision of Section 62 of the Act for the period of the war or such lesser time as may be determined.
>
> It is a simple matter to render the communication chain inoperative on individual carriages. . . . The Board may, therefore, please consider the desirability of the issue of such an order which if it is to serve its purpose of preventing any large scale dislocation of traffic should issue at once.[27]

Interestingly, the proposal to disable the alarm chains was not to be applied universally but instead only to the lower-class carriages (those in which the majority of Indians traveled). The appended proposal suggested that alarm chains might be rendered inoperative either "on all 3rd and Inter carriages" or, alternately, "on all 3rd and inter carriages which do not include a women's compartment."[28] The final instructions did not, however, specify which compartments should be subject to the disabling of their alarm chains, preferring to leave this decision to the discretion of local authorities.

On August 26, 1942, all Class I and Class II Railways were issued the following instructions: "In order to prevent excessive delays on this account and to forestall, as far as possible, any organised attempts to dislocate traffic by a widespread campaign of alarm signal chain pulling in passenger trains, it has been decided to promulgate a notification giving railway administrations the power to disconnect, for the time being, the means of communication provided in all, or any of the passenger carriages in any train."[29] So powerful had organized alarm chain pulling campaigns become that the railways saw as their only recourse the disabling of the very safety mechanism that allowed the practice in the first place. But the implications of this decision are even more important than they might initially seem, because in shifting their focus from a legal solution to their problem to a technological one, the Railway Board was, in effect, conceding that their problem was one of a political nature, rather than a criminal one.

## Alarm Chain Pulling in Postcolonial India

It only took four people. With four of us we could stop a whole train! —Interview with former student activist, speaking about the 1950s, October 16, 2004

Once alarm chain pulling was established as a political rather than a criminal act during the Quit India movement, it became even easier to use it for a wide range of collective ends. Alarm chain pulling entered a repertoire of proven political actions that included hunger strikes, various forms of passive resistance, dharnas (demonstrations), hartāls and bandhs (general strikes involving the closure of businesses and stoppage of transport), yātras (processions or pilgrimages), roko agitations (road or rail blockades to prevent the movement of traffic), and rallies. Most of these practices were (re-) popularized during the anticolonial movement and, once firmly established (or reestablished), continued to be regarded as part of the repertoire of effective political tactics after independence. In the decades immediately following independence, many of those who were engaged in political movements of various sorts had firsthand experience of these tactics, having personally used them in the anticolonial struggle. It was natural then that they would draw from their existing knowledge base when the need arose.

We can see this, for example, in the movement for a separate Telugu linguistic province that culminated in the creation of Andhra State in 1953. Interviews conducted between 1998 and 2004 with individuals from coastal Andhra who participated in this movement in the early 1950s show that they explicitly invoked their experiences of the anticolonial Quit India movement in their conceptualizations of the Andhra movement. One participant in both movements found it difficult to even talk of the Andhra movement without comparing it with the Quit India movement (during which there was a warrant out for his arrest, he told me). With more than a little nostalgia, he said, "In 1952 everyone was reminded of the 1942 struggle. Nineteen fifty-two was a repetition on a small scale of 1942. Nineteen forty-two was a *real* mass movement."[30]

Many of the same tactics were used in both movements. One of the signs read by many as evidence of the significance of the Andhra movement was the halting of a very large number of trains, as was the case during the Quit India movement. "For three days after [Andhra State activist] Potti Sriramulu's death [by fasting] all trains were stopped," reported one activist, speaking of the culminating days of the Andhra movement that led to Prime Minister Jawaharlal Nehru's declaration of the new state.[31] He went on to explain that "buses were very few in 1952, so stopping trains was a big deal."[32] Another former student activist, now in his eighties, also recalled with great fondness one of his favorite methods of halting a train during the 1952 movement:

> With four of us we could stop a whole train! You see, if only one person pulled the alarm chain, the location would quickly be identified and the train would resume its journey. But with four people, you could spread out, with each person in a different bogie. This way, by the time the authorities located all of the bogies in which the alarm chain had been pulled, all of the passengers would have gotten off the train, making it much more difficult to resume the journey.[33]

Others explained that once a bus or train was halted, activists would circulate, passing out fliers, publicizing future meetings, and talking with members of the public.[34]

Yet, the continued use after 1947 of many of the political practices that had been most effective against the British was not without controversy. Dipesh Chakrabarty writes about the difficulties that this continuity of practice posed for leaders of the newly independent nation of India and the many questions it raised regarding the practices appropriate for its citizens.[35] He cites, for example, Jawaharlal Nehru's conclusion that certain forms of political practice were appropriate "only in countries under foreign rule" but could not be considered "the sign of a free nation."[36] Nehru conceded that some of the more nonviolent political tactics used against the British like hunger strikes and satyagraha "may be necessary sometimes," but he argued that to use them for what he called "day-to-day problems" only "weakens us politically."[37] There was a consensus among many of the leaders at the highest level of government that the types of civil disobedience and passive resistance that were so effective in the anticolonial struggle were no longer appropriate in postcolonial India. However, this feeling was obviously not shared by everyone, given that almost all the most popular and successful anticolonial tactics—processions, hunger strikes, rail blockades, alarm chain pulling, bandhs, hartāls, and dharnas—continued to be used by new and existing political parties and social movements in subsequent decades. Nehru's position continued to be held by members of dominant classes in India during subsequent generations, but it is worth asking whether the issues regarded by some as less significant "day-to-day" problems might be regarded by others as much more significant "life-and-death" problems. It would also be worthwhile exploring exactly who is included in the "us" that Nehru feared might be weakened politically by continuation of these political practices in independent India.

Many members of marginalized segments of the population have modeled their political engagements on the practices used by the movements that preceded them. In many cases this has meant that tactics that were previously under the control of educated and elite groups or restricted to certain types of uses began to be seen as more widely available to all. Some interpret this expansion of participation in political practices as a sign of the decline of Indian democracy, holding that these practices do not match their own ideals of civil society or images of the way that democracy is practiced in other parts of the world.[38] One railway official, for example, in talking about the different nature of political practice in colonial versus postcolonial India, explained to me, "Before 1947 it was linked to democracy, but today basically it is just demands, not major demands—local demands."[39] Yet one person's local demand may be another's major demand. Indeed, "major" and "local" are another way of articulating the distinctions (often hegemonic) between "universal" and "particular" demands or between "public" and "private" interests, categories that Chatterjee and Fraser urge us to examine more carefully. When members of elite groups dismiss particular forms of practice as illegitimate simply because they have been taken up by other groups to which they do not belong, that is yet another reason why our close attention to the longer genealogies of individual forms of political practice is so important. As with alarm chain pulling, genealogies of other popular forms of practice may similarly show that their origins lie in elite and educated political strategies of an earlier era.

The railway official's distinction between "local" and "major" demands also points to the ways in which alarm chain pulling and related practices such as rail and rasta roko actions challenge and reshape spatial relations of power, drawing attention to neighborhoods, regions, groups, and problems that were previously ignored. Nancy Fraser captures this when she writes, "What will count as a matter of common concern will be decided precisely through discursive contestation. It follows that no topics should be ruled off-limits in advance of such contestation. On the contrary, democratic publicity requires positive guarantees of opportunities for minorities to convince others that what in the past was not public in the sense of being a matter of common concern should now become so."[40] As we have seen in chapter 3, it often takes much greater effort on the part of marginalized groups for their voices and concerns to even be heard, much less considered. The use of escalating strategies is often required to create spaces of discursive contestation where marginalized interests can be raised and recognized enough to be brought into public discussion.

The railways as sites for political practice also function in another spatially significant way. Using Henri Lefebvre's "conception of the state as a 'spatial framework' of power," Manu Goswami writes about how the railways helped consolidate the Indian state as a single conceptual and material space while at the same time reconfiguring it within "a Britain-centered global economy," producing and reinforcing "internal differentiation and fragmentation" and "spawn[ing] a new uneven economic geography."[41] Precisely because railways were "crucial instruments for the consolidation of political and military domination within colonial India," they quickly became targets for political resistance and protest as well.[42] By linking regions throughout India to a single network of communication, the railways also became available for the rapid communication of political messages. Halting a train in one location enabled a message to be broadcast up and down the entire length of a railway line and forced those from other regions of India to pay attention to the cause of the delay. Grievances from one locality could be transmitted to new audiences and locations across a mobile landscape. Such actions affected passengers from different regions who were on the train, as well as those in far-off locations. Concerns that might otherwise have remained locally contained were communicated across the country and sometimes gained wider support across regions. From localized concerns over overcrowding in specific railway spaces, alarm chain pulling was eventually popularized in ways that linked many types of specific local concerns into more generalized political movements, such as the anticolonial movement and later regional movements for linguistic statehood.

Despite the apparent continuity of practices before and after 1947, we can also identify several significant shifts in the use and reception of alarm chain pulling in the postcolonial period. The first obvious transition, one apparent as early as 1942, was the shift from surreptitious to more open forms of activity. Anonymous halting of trains, either through chain pulling or through sabotage to the tracks—including the placement of foreign objects on the tracks or the removal of rails or sleepers (crossties that support the rails), often accompanied by the display of red flags to warn oncoming trains of the danger ahead and prevent them from proceeding—gradually gave way to the more open blocking of traffic in the form of rail roko actions. Roko actions, or blockades of a railway line or road, usually with human bodies, are now routinely conducted in open daylight and reflect the growing confidence that activists will not be prosecuted for what is increasingly accepted as a political rather than a criminal act. Rather than seeing this shift as evidence of the deterioration of democratic politics, however, we can read this as a sign of Indian democracy's success in recognizing and incorporating participation from a wider spectrum of the population beyond the bourgeois public sphere.

Second, not only did political groups draw from existing repertoires of practices but they also expanded them, using new forms of transport and communication and adapting existing practices to suit new media. We see, for example, the extension of blockades from the railways to important roadway intersections, particularly in areas where buses are more important than trains. Because the road transport corporations that run bus lines are often controlled by individual states, a bifurcation of political labor is also apparent, with railways targeted for central government issues and buses for state-level issues.[43] Many existing political practices have also taken on unique local forms. In Telangana, for example, the practice of gāli tīyadam, or the removal of air from bus tires to effectively block a major road intersection, has gained popularity as bus travel has grown more important with the expansion and improvement of roadways.[44]

A third significant feature of alarm chain pulling is its widespread use by students, often to create an unscheduled stop more convenient to their colleges. An assistant security commissioner for one of the branches of the Indian Railways explained, "Our biggest problems today with alarm chain pulling are places like Saket College near Ayodhya. Students want to get down [from the train] just in front of their college. When we try to take action, students do road rokos."[45] Although it may appear difficult to label as political such applications of alarm chain pulling, a number of scholars argue that we can read examples of collective youthful male assertion as "a form of empowerment which expresses 'the fact of powerlessness.'"[46] Craig Jeffrey's ethnographic research among university students in Meerut, for example, illustrates not only the ways in which colleges and universities today function as political training grounds but also how they provide a place and identity for those who have been unable to find employment and therefore a place of their own within the wider society.[47] Jeffrey offers numerous examples of individuals who have returned to universities to complete degree after degree in a perpetual state of waiting after being repeatedly unsuccessful in the competition for jobs. His ethnography of the politics of waiting in India today suggests that we may well want to read the defiant use of the alarm chain by college students within a much longer history of political practice in the face of exclusion.

## Democracy and Communicative Action

Successful political action works at several levels. In the words of one particularly astute railway official, "Democracy always develops around the chief means of communication. . . . The railways are a major form of communication and news creation, and also cadre development."[48] Alarm chain pulling has a long history of functioning as an effective medium of political communication, both through its control of communicative channels and its performative qualities. In concluding, I suggest that, in creating and sustaining democracy in India, such practices have also functioned to create, mobilize, and strengthen collective forms of identity—identities defined not necessarily or always in relation to ethnic, caste, or linguistic foundations but rather in relation to a wider sense of structural marginalization.[49] Emerging from bourgeois Indian civil society in an era when educated elite Indians felt marginalized by the British in their own country, the practice of alarm chain pulling has spread to a new set of individuals who continue to feel excluded or that their concerns and anxieties are not being heard or addressed. Is it any wonder, then, that a technological device designed to facilitate communication would get used for precisely that purpose?

# SIX. RAIL AND ROAD BLOCKADES

## Illiberal or Participatory Democracy?

If we only use memorandums, no one will respond to us. —Dalit activist's justification of rail roko actions, Warangal, April 22, 2009

In January 2009, when I was on my way to the Tamil Nadu Archives in the south Indian city of Chennai one morning around 8:00 a.m., my taxi became ensnared in a traffic jam at a major intersection in the upscale Besant Nagar neighborhood in the southern part of the city. After inching slowly forward, we finally discovered the cause of our inconvenience, only to be forced eventually to turn around and go back the way we had come, but not before investigating what was going on. Some twenty-five or thirty people—mostly women, with a sprinkling of men and children—were seated in the middle of the extremely busy intersection, unaffected by the pleas of parents unable to drop their children at one of the several schools surrounding the intersection and of officegoers trying to reach their workplaces (figure 6.1). When I inquired, one of the women seated in the intersection explained that their houses had been destroyed during Cyclone Nisha, about eight weeks earlier. The chief minister at the time, M. Karunanidhi, had designated 100 crore rupees (approximately USD 20,000,000 in 2009) in relief funds to aid the victims of the cyclone, promising each of the most vulnerable families 2,000 rupees (approximately USD 40) toward the costs of rebuilding their damaged or destroyed huts. The funds had not yet been distributed, however. Those seated in the intersection had repeatedly tried to collect the promised relief aid, appealing to various government representatives, only to be shuttled from one office to another with no clear process in sight to enable them to access the promised aid. The woman explained that they were sitting in the middle of one of the busiest intersections in Chennai at peak commuting time in hopes of gaining the attention of someone in the government who could carry out its promise.[1] Tired of being shunted from one government office to another, with no one willing to acknowledge their claims or even their efforts to communicate, these petitioners were attempting to create conditions that would compel someone in authority to give them an audience and listen to them. Their request—that the government make good on its promise—was only made audible by their occupation of the intersection, which elevated their concern to higher authorities and drew attention to the inaction of lower-level officials.

The use of human bodies to block a road (rasta roko) or railway line (rail roko) to prevent vehicles or trains from passing occurs almost daily in some parts of India. The word *roko*—an imperative form of the transitive Hindi verb *roknā*, "to stop or detain something or someone"—continues to be widely used as a verb in the Hindi-speaking belt of India. In addition, it has begun to be used in both English and regional languages, particularly in some southern regions, as a noun, usually in the noun phrases *rail roko* or *rasta* [road] *roko*. This usage suggests that the concept resonates widely because of its ability to capture and effectively label a nationwide practice. During the height of the Quit India movement in 1942 and 1943, when Gandhi, Nehru, and most of the other leaders of the Indian National Congress

FIGURE 6.1. Victims of Cyclone Nisha blocking traffic to hold the Tamil Nadu government accountable to its promise of relief aid, January 22, 2009 (photo: author).

were imprisoned, the railways became a key target of anticolonial protest, as discussed in chapter 5. Virtually every major railway line in the country saw repeated rail roko actions, and some lines took weeks or even months to reopen.[2] Indeed, the colonial archive reflects a preoccupation with the compromised state of railway communication and includes extensive debates on the enhancement of penalties for actions that compromised railway and telegraph lines.[3] Although some of the activity targeting the railways was nonviolent—in keeping with Gandhi's desire that violence not be used—some did turn violent, with trains and stations burned and looted, rails removed, signals and telegraph equipment damaged, and other forms of physical sabotage.[4] This was the period in which Gandhi famously gave his "Do or Die" speech and nationalist supporters were encouraged to think only of freedom from the British, even at the expense of their own lives. Gandhi and other nationalist leaders were in agreement that "British rule in India in any shape or form must end."[5] "Leave India to God. If that is too much, leave her to anarchy," wrote Gandhi in May 1942.[6] A "12-Point Programme," issued by the All India Congress Committee after Gandhi's arrest and discussed in chapter 5, stated, "Victory or death should be the motto of every son and daughter of India. If we live we live as free men, if we die we die as free men."[7] Rail roko actions in this context—like alarm chain pulling during the same period—were unquestionably a challenge to British sovereignty in India. But like alarm chain pulling, subsequent rail and road roko actions following India's independence in 1947 have more often been carried out to compel the Indian state to take action, intervene, or fulfill existing promises or legal provisions, thereby valorizing and reifying the state's power, rather than challenging its sovereignty.

Recent evidence suggests that the incidence of rail and road roko actions is on the rise. A senior Indian Police Service (IPS) officer formerly in charge of handling disturbances in Lucknow, the capital of the most populous state in India, told me in an interview in March 2009 that the number of road blockage disturbances in that city alone during the period she was posted in the city could easily reach a dozen in a single day: "Employees' unions are particularly strong and active, and also farmers [who protest] over prices or availability of inputs—and also political parties. They block roads in front of the Legislative Assembly, in front of the chief minister's house, in front of other ministers' houses—so many places."[8] Although the Bureau of Police Research and Development of the Indian Ministry of Home Affairs does not maintain separate data on road and rail blockages, they do tabulate annual statistics on "agitations," which they define as the "collective expression of dissatisfaction with the state authorities and others on a variety of issues like education, essential services, transport facilities, wages etc." Its annual report states,

> In a democratic system expression of protest by different groups/ sub groups of public is a common feature. Police personnel of both the States and CAPFs [Central Armed Police Forces] need to consciously strive for upgrading their professional and behavioral skills in order to manage crowds agitated over any perceived, real or imaginary, cause of injustice/dissatisfaction against the authorities or some other sections of the society without use of force as far as possible.[9]

Their data show that the incidence of agitations has more than tripled over the last decade.[10] But rather than being classified according to methods used, agitations are instead categorized according to the groups who initiate them—student, labor, communal, government employees, political parties, and others. Many of the rallies, processions, and roko agitations held in conjunction with the Telangana movement were called by the Telangana Joint Action Committee (TJAC), the umbrella organization that united students, employees' unions, political groups, and other organizations. Existing data do not clarify how the police bureau classifies events that cross organizations or identity groups.

Yet, roko agitations have also undergone changes in form with the dramatic transformations in dominant media. One shift in rail and road rokos' roles has been the relative decline in the importance of actual physical blockages as mass media coverage of political actions has increased since the early 1990s. This change has enabled groups to hold more symbolic blockage agitations that often—as in the case of numerous rail roko agitations reported by railway authorities at the Secunderabad station—last just a short time and cause little, if any, delay in departures. Both Railway Protection Force and Government Railway Police officials repeatedly told me of the arrangements they typically establish with the organizers and leaders of rallies, yātras, roko agitations, and other collective mobilizations. Mr. Mehta, one of many senior Government Railway Police officials I interviewed, explained that in most cases, the Railway Police will simply look on and make no arrests as long as the blockage of the train does not last too long—no more than about fifteen to twenty minutes, he said—and is not violent. "That gives them time to climb up on the engine, unfurl their banner, and pose for the media cameras," he told me (see figures 6.2 and 6.3).[11]

Current representations of roko actions—along with allied practices that prevent movement such as the *gherao* (surrounding a government official to impede their movement) and the samme, hartāl, or bandh (a strike or shutdown)—typically portray them in one of three ways. First, in their capacity to disrupt day-to-day life and the movement of people and goods, rail and road roko and related actions are often characterized as practices engaged in only by members of economically or socially marginalized groups for whom such disruptions are imagined to matter little. A second common framing of roko actions is as a law-and-order problem and a sign of failure, either of citizens to behave appropriately or of the state to function well enough to meet the needs of its citizens. A third portrayal of roko actions is as challenges to state sovereignty and rejections of its authority. I address each of these portrayals in turn. Using ethnographic interactions with political activists, railway employees, government officials, and Indian police, this chapter mobilizes Alexis de Tocqueville's distinction between a democratic government and a democratic society to argue that we need to approach democracy not as a static set of institutions and laws or as a *product* of history but rather as an ongoing *process* of engagement and communication that constantly expands recognition.[12]

## Roko Agitations as Practices of the Poor and Disenfranchised

Much existing scholarship offers theoretical frameworks supporting the idea that disruptions of everyday life are produced only by uneducated members of economically or socially marginalized groups. As we saw in the introduction, these approaches to Indian democracy frame and analyze separately those practices assumed to belong to or be characteristic of distinct demographic groups—marking, for example, distinctions between the practices of elites/middle classes and masses/subalterns, between legal and extralegal domains, or between civil society and political society.[13] Such approaches assume a direct—and sometimes exclusive—relationship between communities or demographic groups and their practices, making it difficult to recognize the ways in which particular everyday political activities may be part of a larger repertoire of practices that is shared (when needed) across a wide range of domains and demographic groups.[14]

Members of marginalized groups are sometimes regarded critically as engaging in such types of action because they have not (yet) adequately learned "critical-rational" forms of political communication, or they may be regarded more sympathetically as having no recourse to the methods of political participation used by better educated middle- and upper-class citizens. Javeed Alam, for example, illustrates the Indian middle class's anxieties regarding the expansion of political participation to historically marginalized groups when he suggests that recent trends in Indian democracy reflect an increasing gulf not only between the values held by well-educated Indians and the masses but also between the specific forms that their political practices take:

> There is a major difference in the manner in which democratic awareness emerges among the exploited and oppressed, in comparison with the elite. It is evident that the masses do not learn about democracy by making use of or working the institutions. They are not, in fact, adept at handling institutions. The practices involved and the negotiations required for the successful use of democratic institutions are unfamiliar to them. Their verbal skills are inadequate for the rules of the parliamentary game.[15]

He goes on to conclude that because "people of these vulnerable communities are ill-equipped to act in public as individuals, with their lack of confidence and inadequate verbal skills," they therefore "enter together in large numbers to make up for the lack of verbal skills."[16] This, he argues, causes the dialogical space for "rational-critical debate" to become more and more compressed, with Indian politics becoming increasingly "unruly" and "noisy."[17] He suggests that discretely identifiable groups participating in Indian democracy can be distinguished not only by their particular interests, which may be in competition with one another, but also by the nature of the specific practices in which they engage, a notion that appears to be widely held in India today.[18]

More sympathetic versions of this distinction between the "elite" and the "masses"—or those "adept at handling institutions" and those who are understood to be "verbally inadequate"—such as Partha Chatterjee's influential distinction between civil society and political society, reinforce the idea that specific demographic groups use identifiably different methods for engaging with the state.[19] In suggesting that the practices that today characterize political society may be laying "the foundations of a new democratic order," Chatterjee is arguing that there has been a fundamental qualitative change in the nature of the actual practices that make up Indian democracy, rather than simply a quantitative shift brought on by the expansion of participation. Is this, in fact, the case? How, for example, should we understand the exclamation of the very well-educated, elite, upper-caste Brahmin Indian intellectual we met in chapter 5, who by all accounts would be defined as a rights-bearing citizen and a member of bourgeois civil society, who proudly and excitedly explained to me, "It only took four people. With four of us we could stop a whole train!"[20] Examining the longer history of practices like alarm chain pulling and road and rail blockages enables us to identify the ways in which individuals from a broad range of demographic backgrounds—the middle classes, farmers' groups, students from prosperous elite, middle-class, and nonelite backgrounds, slum dwellers, squatters, and coalitions that include all of these—have all engaged in the shared repertoires of practice that have shaped ways of "doing democracy" in India today.

Different demographic groups do often find that they meet with quite dramatically different responses from authorities, however. Acknowledging this fact complicates our use of these categories and suggests that the shifts in Indian democracy may have less to do with the nature of specific political practices and more to do with the socioeconomic status and cultural capital of groups who have been able to successfully adopt and use them without having to contend with the discretionary power of the police and government officials. Keeping apart the analyses of the actual practices of these different demographic groups obscures the ways in which those who recently entered the political realm may have acquired their repertoires of politcal practice from those very same elites who now feel threatened by their shrinking political authority. At the same time, India has been confronted by new questions about majoritarian movements and their implication for democracy.

"Illiberal" Democracy? Roko Agitations as
a Problem of Law and Order or a Disregard for Existing
Legal Structures

A second common framing of rail and road roko actions is as a law-and-order problem and a sign of the failure of citizens to behave with appropriate respect for existing legal structures. V. N. Mathur, former member (Directorate of Traffic) of the Indian Railway Board—who frequently fielded railway-related questions raised in the Indian Parliament—explained in September 2008 that roko agitations were "a very serious problem for the railways. . . . In the past one year, incidents have been on a rise, affecting both passenger and freight services. This is a law-and-order problem, which comes under the state governments. However, during the Gujjar agitation [demanding an affirmative action quota], which has been the largest disruption in the recent past, no one was willing to help us. As a result, we had to divert trains through much longer routes."[21] Such perspectives place the blame on those who engage in road and rail blockages, regarding them as lacking in respect for existing legal structures and as impeding the freedom of those whose movements they are interrupting. This view sees roko actions as violating the tenets of constitutional liberalism because of the limits they place on the liberty of others.

Genevieve Lakier, writing about "street protests" in the context of Nepal, cautiously extends Fareed Zakaria's description of "illiberal democracy" to describe the ways that Nepali road block actions impede the freedom of movement of others.[22] Zakaria's definition of "illiberal democracy" focuses on "democratically elected regimes, often ones that have been reelected or reaffirmed through referenda, [that] are routinely ignoring constitutional limits on their power and depriving their citizens of basic rights and freedoms."[23] In offering this definition, he argues that democracy need not always be *liberal* democracy. Zakaria separates liberal democracy analytically into two parts to define it as "a political system marked not only by free and fair elections, but also by the rule of law, a separation of powers, and the protections of basic liberties of speech, assembly, religion, and property."[24] He argues that "this latter bundle of freedoms—what might be termed constitutional liberalism—is theoretically different and historically distinct from democracy."[25] Its absence constitutes illiberal democracy.

Lakier applies Zakaria's idea of "illiberal democracy" to civil society groups engaging in blockages through "protests such as the *gherao* (sit-in), *chakka-jam* (traffic blockage) and *bandh* [general strike]" as well:

By erecting blockades and shutting down traffic (in the case of a *chakka-jam*) or by impeding passage into or out of a public building (as in the case of a *gherao*) or by forcing the suspension of all transportation, production and commerce in a city, a district or even the entire country for a day or more (as in the case of a *bandh*), political groups exploit the extreme sensitivity of industrialized mass society to any kind of blockage in mobility and productivity. In so doing, they impede the individual autonomy of other citizens and transform the neutral space of the public into a politicized domain.[26]

In extending Zakaria's analysis, Lakier makes two sets of distinctions: one primary and one secondary. Her primary distinction (as indicated in the title of her article) is between "liberal" and "illiberal" forms of protest. Although she recognizes both as forms of "political speech," she contrasts "the rallies and public meetings that characterize normatively liberal public protest" with protests like general strikes and traffic blockades that "function not by simply expressing dissenting opinion, but by enforcing it."[27] Yet Lakier also recognizes another distinction, one that plays a more subsidiary role in her overall analysis, but that is even more important in relation to the argument of this book. This latter distinction is between "movements that used protest to demand *emancipation*—the recognition by the state of their political and social rights"—and those that were "organized in order to defend or demand institutional privileges and economic monopolies when these conflicted with liberalizing economic law."[28]

Lakier illustrates emancipatory movements with an analysis of "the freedom struggle of Kamaiyas—bonded labourers . . . officially 'liberated' by His Majesty's government in 2000," one group of whom failed to successfully lobby their landlord (a former government minister) to bring their wages in line with the new minimum wage law implemented by Parliament. After their efforts to enlist the local government for help in enforcing the law also failed, the Kamaiyas "went for assistance to a higher level of bureaucratic authority." When several efforts to escalate their concerns also failed to produce results, they turned at last to a sit-in demonstration in front of the office of the chief district officer. Lakier concludes, "The sit-in achieved, within a span of days, what other mechanisms . . . could not. The use of shaming and pressure tactics served not to convince but to *enforce* the demands of the Kamaiyas, which were nevertheless understood, in the end, by all the parties as their right." Later efforts that sought to expand the local success to a national level included a sit-in and eventually a road blockade in front of the Parliament. Lakier goes on to observe, "It was not that the Kamaiya organizations wanted to defy the government; they wanted, it seemed, nothing more than to be embedded within its legal order."[29]

Lakier contrasts the Kamiaya struggle for the full implementation of legal rights with another roadblock action organized by the Federation of Nepal Transport Entrepreneurs (FNTE) in 2003. The FNTE was established in 1978 as an umbrella organization to advocate for the interests of a wide range of local Transport Entrepreneurs Associations, made up of very small-scale owners of buses, trucks, jeeps, mini-buses, and other forms of transport. In 1992, under pressure from the International Monetary Fund and "in line with the rest of market liberalization," a new Transport Management Law "established absolute freedom in the running of buses" in an effort to restructure the existing transport system.[30] The new law sought to replace the existing system of "complementary" zonal authorities—which assigned routes, set fares, and regulated the terms of business—with complete free-market competition. When private companies began to enter the market, however, the existing transport organizations tried to resist and restrict their growth. This led to the passage of a new government act in 2001 that banned all existing transportation organizations. When a chief district officer tried to implement the new act and "gave the right to run minibuses to a jeep organization," thereby violating the long-standing understanding that "one sector was running buses, and the other sector was running jeeps," it prompted a local roadblock action that quickly spread throughout the country, stranding travelers and leading to food shortages.[31]

In contrast to the Kamaiya's struggle for what Lakier characterizes as "the expansion of liberal rights," she describes the FNTE's roadblock as a "defence of corporate privileges *against* the application of (liberal) law."[32] In other words, what sets this action apart from the Kamaiya action is that "the syndicate did not win by changing the law." Lakier writes, "What lay behind the conflict was not a question of the legal rules but of what we can call the syndicate's institutional privileges, privileges that indexed a balance of power in which the state did not enjoy ultimate control but instead shared sovereignty over the passage of vehicles on 'its' roads."[33] Yet Biswo Poudel suggests that such transport associations "were actually started to address the incomplete insurance market" and were "run by insecure individuals," many of whom "are formerly poor individuals who entered the industry as helpers."[34] As a result, those who owned a truck or other form of transport, often as their sole asset, "realized that they could form an association, pool the risk, and start their own insurance fund" and that "they could engage in collective bargaining with the government and victims."[35] He cites a 2015 study that found that, although "an average truck owner owned 2.4, the median owner owned only one," suggesting that the latter "were desperately trying to make a profit out of their sole significant asset" and that transport unions helped them protect this investment and pooled their risk.[36] He also suggests that the public may have viewed them negatively because "their average education level was low" and "they were not well connected with media."[37]

Even more than her distinction between liberal and illiberal forms of assembly, Lakier's subsidiary argument is useful for the distinction it makes between groups addressing themselves to the state and seeking recognition from it, like the Kamaiyas who sought "nothing more than to be embedded within its legal order," and those—like the road transport unions—seeking to establish their own sovereignty and legal structure parallel to that of the state. This suggests that not all "protests that take over public space and obstruct public passage" are the same, despite their shared categorization as "illiberal forms of political practice." Lakier's distinction offers further evidence that practices that may superficially appear similar or even identical may have very different goals and audiences, making them fundamentally different actions. A focus on "illiberal democracy" prioritizes the distinction between the legal and the illegal over this second distinction, in some cases completely effacing it. But as chapter 5 has demonstrated, the line between legal and illegal actions is often less clear than it might initially appear. It is open to interpretation by elected representatives, local administrative officials, and police superintendents and commissioners who are tasked with implementing the law. Representatives of the state often use on-the-spot interpretations of the law to make decisions about whose voices can be heard in the public sphere by granting or refusing permission for collective assemblies and turning otherwise legal collective efforts to communicate into illegal actions. Groups may also find that the only way to ensure the full implementation of an existing law is—as illustrated by the Kamaiyas—to engage in a collective public action like a sit-in in a location in which such a practice is technically illegal. In other cases, groups may find methods of "sharing" sovereignty more effective than efforts to repeal laws introduced in the face of new austerity and liberalization laws backed by powerful international organizations like the World Bank and the International Monetary Fund and only reluctantly accepted by local democratically elected leaders. Decisions to liberalize the economy are not always made democratically or with the participation of stakeholders, as the Indian farmers' protest discussed in the introduction illustrates.

Roko Agitations as Challenges to State Sovereignty

The third way in which roko actions are commonly represented is as challenges to state sovereignty. Dipesh Chakrabarty points out that, in the efforts to shape the political practices of a new Indian citizenry after independence, the first prime minister Jawaharlal Nehru could not help but recognize that the unruliness, violence, and indiscipline being displayed by students and other actors in various parts of the newly independent nation "were reminiscent of the anti-British nationalist movement of the pre-independence period."[38] Yet, even though Nehru conceded that such practices were "somehow acceptable when students of a country under foreign rule resorted to them," he ultimately did not believe that they were "suitable for an independent democratic country."[39] In exploring Nehru's question about whether one can "create postcolonial politics from the political repertoire and techniques of anticolonial movements," Chakrabarty's answer ultimately relies on his interpretation of the meanings and intentions that he feels are implied by particular *forms* of agitation and his assumption that these meanings are tied to specific political *practices*, rather than to the agendas and uses to which they are put.[40] There is a tension in both Nehru's and Chakrabarty's writings around whether it is the practices themselves that are producing the meanings we attribute to them or whether their meanings are being produced by the particular actors who engage in the practices or by the goals they are used to achieve. This tension stems from the assumption that the "forms of political agitation" that were effective against the British were all specific "techniques of challenging the sovereignty" of those in power, rather than more generally recognizable means of political communication that enable a much wider range of political messages.[41] These messages might include challenges to sovereignty (as in the case of Maoist actions in India or the Nepali Transport Entrepreneurs Associations discussed earlier), but they may also include appeals for recognition, connection to the state, inclusion within decision-making processes, and efforts to hold officials accountable to existing laws, policies, or campaign promises (as demonstrated by Telangana state activists or the Kamaiya actions in the previous section).

Chakrabarty offers two contemporary examples of continuations of colonial-era practices in postcolonial India, one a roko agitation that blocked traffic to demand a meeting with senior railway officials and one a gherao that encircled an official responsible for negligence at a state hospital.[42] He argues that, although such efforts to impede movement may have been appropriate for members of civil society to engage in during the anticolonial struggle, today these actions have been reduced to "rituals of humiliating the officialdom." He suggests that the faceless "multitude" in each of these cases has no real goal except to force senior officials (as elite members of society) to concede, if only for a moment, some of their power to the people by making them eat "humble pie."[43]

But strikingly, both of his examples have been removed from their original contexts and are offered as isolated incidents without discussion of the longer local histories in which they emerged. Although he acknowledges that "there are genuine grievances and particular histories at issue in both cases" and that both incidents "speak to continuing problems with public utilities in West Bengal—hospitals and transport—and particularly so in the context of the move to liberalize the economy and privatize some of these critical services," he also writes that these are "details I cannot go into." We know nothing of earlier efforts to hold local officials accountable or appeal to them for resolution of grievances, and instead are encouraged to understand these actions as rituals whose sole purpose is to give participants a momentary "pleasure and sense of authority in seeing the government lose face." This suggests that Chakrabarty not only equates particular types of action with the social position of the actors carrying out the actions, but that he also joins Nehru in considering the engagement in disruptive practices to have been appropriate as part of a "programmatic" vision "oriented to a future" during the anticolonial movement but not for seeking an audience with representatives of the state in postcolonial India, something Nehru regarded as "indiscipline in public life." Given his acknowledgment that these are "senior officers (who normally would not deal with members of the public)," it is not clear how else marginalized citizens may have been able to obtain a meeting with them and have their concerns heard.[44] And surely seeking to be heard is distinct from seeking to humiliate an official. That officials may have *felt* humiliated in having to speak to grieving or frustrated members of a disenfranchised and nonelite public is a different matter.

Chakrabarty's examples offer us an ideal opportunity to ask not just whether the medium is the message but also whether the medium can be used to positively identify the sender of the message. As we saw with alarm chain pulling in chapter 5, forms of political practice used in both colonial and postcolonial India as means of political communication were and continue to be effective in conveying a wide range of political messages by groups from an equally wide range of classes, political orientations, and educational backgrounds. Placing everyday practices into their larger historical and cultural contexts, I argue, also enables us to recognize the ways that members of civil and political society do, in fact, share a common political language and set of practices, albeit often with very different interests at stake. Using rail and road roko agitations to challenge state sovereignty is indeed one of the uses to which such actions continue to be put, but significantly, it is not the only use, and it is to these other uses of roko actions as forms of political communication that I now turn.

Although not all rail and road roko actions are successful, they do surprisingly often result in an audience with authorities and at least a formal acknowledgment of the concern, if not a complete resolution, as the examples above illustrate. Remarkably, many times this acknowledgment that comes with recognition appears to be enough. As with other practices explored in this book, in a large percentage of cases, roko actions rely centrally on an understanding of the state as the ultimate adjudicator of disputes and claims. Groups therefore use roko agitations as a way to draw attention to breaches in legal procedure, lapses or inequities in governance and policing, or failures to fulfill existing policy decisions. Because of their use to gain attention, roko actions and associated forms of political practice have taken on a level of legitimacy in contemporary India, even prompting administrators to alter their notions of legality informally, if not also formally. The state accommodation of roko actions can be understood alongside other discretionary decisions made by those in positions of authority. Preventing people from proceeding along a road or rail line may technically be illegal, but placing such practices in the same analytic frame as the failure of administrators or elected officials to implement existing policies, disburse funds to their legitimate designees, or prosecute perpetrators of violent crimes against members of marginalized groups repositions their meaning and offers a new perspective on the nature of political power and its everyday mediation in India today.

A genealogy of rail blockades is also connected to a longer history of train-wrecking and railway sabotage activities from the 1880s onward, the early stages of which Dipesh Chakrabarty has traced.[45] Train-wrecking and sabotage sought to physically damage railway lines by pulling up track or placing obstructions on the track before arrival of a train. Yet, unlike blockades, these actions were performed anonymously. In contrast, roko actions are now regarded with enough moral weight that those who participate today feel they can do so openly, appealing to authorities with limited fear of arrest or punishment. Publicly and collectively sitting or lying down on railroad tracks or in the middle of a busy intersection, those who participate in roko actions today share in the physical, bodily control of public space. While it is possible to draw a line between "legal" actions and those that are technically "illegal," there are also other important ways to distinguish between different types of political actions and their levels of acceptability. The next section explores "emic" meanings in southern India that have helped to shape understandings of the acceptability of various types of rail and road roko actions.

Mr. Kohli, a senior railway official in the South Central Railway, offered one set of contrasts that first led me to recognize the importance of identifying the different types of audiences being addressed by railway-related actions.[46] Over coffee at his office one brisk January morning, he divided roko actions into two categories, each with two subcategories, for a total of four distinct types. The first overarching category, he said, included all forms of peaceful, largely nonviolent demonstrations, and the second he characterized as "illegitimate, illegal, and disruptive activities." He further divided the "peaceful, largely nonviolent" category into two types—"preplanned and spontaneous"—saying that both types usually forwarded "legitimate demands." Finally, he subdivided his second overarching category of "illegitimate, illegal, and disruptive activities" into actions "with the intention to disrupt but not harm lives" and "targeted planned violent activity with the goal of maximum damage to human life and property."[47] Although this is just one of many ways of conceptualizing distinctions between different types of railway-directed actions, I explore his four categorizations to illustrate the point that not all roko actions target the same audiences or generate their meanings in the same way.

### "Preplanned Nonviolent Roko Actions"

"The goal," said Mr. Kohli, of preplanned rail roko actions "is to embarrass or criticize the political party in power, and also to influence public opinion. They usually last ten to fifteen minutes, in the morning, and usually are completely dispersed by 12:00 noon."[48] Most significantly, this type is also largely accepted, at least by railway officials. "We also come to an understanding with the opinion makers," he said. The fact that they are contrasted with "illegitimate, illegal activities" suggests that, although technically not legal, rail roko actions are seen as a largely legitimate form of political activity in contemporary India. Although the Railways sometimes took legal action and arrested leaders, usually when actions became violent, for the most part, Mr. Kohli's view was shared by many railway and police officials I interviewed. A senior railway administrator in Lucknow, Mr. Kapur, for example, explained to me that "as long as a group got in and out quickly and didn't delay the train by more than ten or fifteen minutes," the Railways largely turned a blind eye, "allow[ing] the leaders [to] climb up on the loco[motive], put up their banner, and pose for media cameras," thereby enabling the moment and their demands to be publicized before disbanding.[49] Mr. Chatterjee, another senior railway official with responsibility for security in one of the major Indian Railways divisions, said that typically the record would show that a preventive arrest was made, but in actual practice, the leaders would be set free. Although he claimed that more efforts were being made to book leaders of rail roko actions "in each and every case," he also said that only three cases had resulted in convictions since 2005, all of which are currently in the High Court on appeal.[50]

In Secunderabad, preplanned rail roko actions of this sort occur regularly, "once or twice in a month," said Mr. Kohli, and usually target the most popular trains bound for Delhi, the seat of the central government. Rail roko actions tend to be used to send messages to the central government, he said, whereas road roko actions are preferred for state-level or local issues, a distinction confirmed by political activists. In planning actions, activists recognize that the Railways are controlled by the center, while bus services are controlled at the state level. In Secunderabad, the train that has been subject to the most rail roko actions is the A.P. Express (now the Telangana Superfast Express) departing daily for Delhi in the early morning.[51] Mr. Kohli explained that "the participants are usually mostly from the lower strata," and their "leaders, mostly mid-level leaders, [are] usually from political parties."[52] Indeed, preplanned roko actions have come to take on an almost ritualized formula, with the various parties involved— including official representatives of the state in the form of railway officials or the police—carrying out very predictable roles. Newspaper photographs and YouTube footage of several rail roko actions orchestrated by members of the Telangana movement show numerous police personnel standing idly by, watching the proceedings as activists climb up on locomotives, unfurl their banners, and lie down on the tracks in front of the engine, shouting slogans all the while (figures 6.2 and 6.3). Images frequently show many more police looking on than the number of participants, suggesting that if the police wanted to prevent or shut down a roko action, they could very easily do so. This visual evidence also confirms Mr. Kohli's statement that authorities and demonstrators come to an understanding with one another that enables the latter to represent themselves and make their appeal for recognition. Indeed, the growth of the mass media in the wake of India's 1991 liberalization of the economy has shifted the focus of roko actions toward the publicity and photo opportunities they generate and away from their earlier goal of inconveniencing the public. In this we can see a significant historical shift in the nature of the channels available for communicative use.

FIGURE 6.2. Rail roko agitation in Vijayawada against the decision to create the new state of Telangana, December 17, 2009 (photo: Ch. Vijaya Bhaskar/*The Hindu*).

FIGURE 6.3. Rail roko agitation in Belgaum over the government's release of Cauvery water to Tamil Nadu, September 21, 2012 (photo: D. B. Patil/*The Hindu*).

Mr. Kohli offered his fourfold system of categorization primarily as a way of thinking about rail roko actions, but his categories can also be applied to actions targeting roads and intersections, or rasta roko events. There is a great deal of regional and even local variation in the implementation and practice of road blockades, with specific key intersections, particularly in administrative capitals, more likely to be targeted than others. In Hyderabad, for example, the president of a local women's organization described to me the practice of *gāli tīyaḍam*, or the method of removing air from bus tires to start a rasta roko action, narrating the typical routine:

> We choose some corners. We stop a bus by standing opposite [in front of] it. One or two [of us] would get in the bus. We'd have pamphlets or address the passengers to educate them. While this is happening someone would put the pin to the tire to take out the air. We do three, four buses and then they'd try to divert the buses. We've done this for so many issues—after the Basheerbagh police firings, against the electricity tariff hike during Chandrababu Naidu's time, so many other times, too.[53]

She went on to explain that because the pin is placed in the tire's valve, no permanent damage is typically done to the bus or its tires.

Many of the activists I met in India agreed that different forms of political practice typically represent distinct phases of intensification of political efforts. Like dharnas, roko actions were usually employed as one stage within a hierarchy of efforts to gain recognition and provoke a reaction from or meeting with officials. "It depends on the issue," explained a local leader of the Communist Party of India. "If it's a burning issue," he continued, "and we want to react quickly, then we go for rasta roko, like in the case of the price hike of petrol and diesel or other essential commodities." But other issues required more systemic approaches: "For something that's a longer process, we take a phase-wise plan. A total bandh [a complete strike shutting down everything] is the most effective, but we use it only when it is necessary [as the last phase]. Otherwise people will become upset with us. Rasta rokos are most effective during peak time, between 10:30 and 11:00, when employees are going to work."[54]

Preplanned roko actions target the busiest intersections at the peak of their usage to create maximum impact. Indeed, a certain amount of disruption of everyday life is seen as essential to being heard. Prakash, the local leader of the Dalit wing of a major political party, introduced in chapter 1, explained that road and rail blockades can be essential because "if people suffer in the train or in the bus, their awareness will also be raised about issues. If we only go for press, then only educated people or readers will know the issue. Even just a half hour late, then everyone, also the common man knows what the issue is."[55]

Yet, it is clear that roko actions are not typically the first activity undertaken by a group. They usually occur only after other channels have been exhausted. After the Union Carbide gas disaster in Bhopal in 1984, activists have continued to advocate for adequate compensation for the victims. A rail roko action was held on December 3, 2011 to amplify demands that victims should receive additional compensation (see figure 6.4). In elaborating and justifying the staging of the rail roko event, the International Campaign for Justice in Bhopal explained its rationale:

We are stopping trains to:

1.  Get adequate compensation from Union Carbide Corporation and The Dow Chemical Company.
2.  What we have got is too little and it has not had any deterrent impact on the corporation.
3.  This is because the government sold us out in 1989 and let the corporation walk away.
4.  Last year the government promised to make amends for its betrayal in 1989 by filing a Curative Petition.
5.  The Curative Petition massively downplays the number of deaths and the severity of injuries—even though the government's own figures show the true picture—and demonstrates that the government is keener to protect the interests of the American corporations than those of the victims.
6.  The government is going against its own data to let the corporations get away once again with paying a pittance.
7.  We have been trying to talk to the government about this issue for a year without any resolution.
8.  We have tried other forms of popular protest but they have not moved the government enough.
9.  That is why we are forced to take this step.
10. We hope you sympathise with our demand and appreciate that justice in Bhopal is a step towards toxic free future for all of us. You may not be a Bhopali survivor but you too have corporate toxins in your body. In that sense this is our common battle.[56]

The decision to perform a roko action was taken only after efforts to gain the government's attention through other means had failed. In contrast to earlier attempts, however, organizers of this rail roko deemed it successful in gaining the attention of the government. Reporting it as a "victory" on their website, the International Campaign for Justice in Bhopal announced that the chief minister of Madhya Pradesh had met personally with survivors of the tragedy, offered support to their demands, and forwarded them to the prime minister.[57] Other activists I spoke with also confirmed the decision to use roko actions only after other efforts to gain an audience with government officials had failed. Another Dalit leader explained, "If we only use memorandums, no one will respond to us," emphasizing the fact that some types of political communication are easier to ignore than others.[58]

There has also been a rise—especially in Telangana—in preplanned *mahā rāsta roko* actions (mega roadblocks) that block not just a single intersection but instead an entire length of national highway, sometimes as much as 250 kilometers.[59] Local groups set up tents, cook food, sleep in the middle of the highway, and park bullock carts and tractors to prevent traffic from moving along the road. These actions have been used to demand an increased power supply to farmers, to oppose the establishment of a toll plaza by the National Highways Authority of India, and to promote land redistribution and regularization of land titles.[60] A variation on this theme was the Telangana "Palle

FIGURE 6.4. Announcement for a "Rail Roko for Your Rights" event in Bhopal demanding compensation for victims of the Bhopal gas disaster, December 3, 2011.

FIGURE 6.5. "Separate Telangana" advocates having lunch on the railway tracks at Hasanparthy Railway Station in Warangal District during a "Palle Palle Paṭṭala Paiki" (Villages on the Rail Tracks) dawn-to-dusk maha rail roko agitation, March 1, 2011 (photo: V. Raju/*The Hindu*).

Palle Paṭṭala Paiki" (Villages on the Rail Tracks) on March 1, 2011—a day-long maha rail roko event in which people cooked, sat, slept, socialized, and carried out their everyday lives on the railway tracks. Its primary purpose was to hold elected officials accountable to their campaign promises to form a new Telangana state (see figure 6.5).[61] The one-day rail blockade, called by the TJAC, prevented all trains from entering or leaving the South Indian city of Hyderabad from 6:00 a.m. to 6:00 p.m.[62] This action was just one in a long series of roko events staged both by advocates and opponents of the new state between December 2009 and the new state's formation in 2014. In some cases, both sides held roko actions simultaneously.[63]

Elsewhere in India, we can see examples not only of the spatial extension of roko events but also of their temporal extension, spanning not just a single day or period of hours but weeks or even months. In the northwestern state of Rajasthan, hundreds of men and women of the Gujjar community sat, squatted, and laid down on the railway tracks for nearly two months, blocking railroad traffic with their bodies to send a message to New Delhi asking to be included within the government's affirmative action quota. From April through June 2008 their actions severely disrupted traffic on major railway routes, causing the cancellation of "some 381 trains," rerouting of other trains on lengthy detours, and the loss of more than 650 million rupees in passenger revenues, with additional roko actions staged by Gujjars in subsequent years.[64] Farmers in various parts of the country regularly sit on the railway tracks to draw the government's attention to shortages of fertilizers, water, or other inputs, or to express hardships caused by prices of agricultural commodities. Most recently, farmers have used this method to convey their opposition to the rapid implementation of new farms laws in which they had no input.[65]

So powerful are roko actions that even the state has been known to halt trains as a way of preventing other forms of political activity. Nine days after the "Palle Palle Paṭṭala Paiki" roko action, forty-three passenger trains, four express trains, and three of the four routes of the Multi-Modal Transport System (local commuter trains) connecting the Telangana districts and surrounding outlying areas to the twin cities of Hyderabad and Secunderabad were canceled by the government in an unsuccessful attempt to prevent the widely publicized "Million March" in the city of Hyderabad.[66]

Although the use of rail lines for political communication has a history in India nearly as long as the existence of the railways, with the increase in road travel and improvement of national highways, road blockages have become equally important ways to convey political messages. In July 2009, some five hundred students and parents of the New Era School in Mumbai blocked all six lanes of a major Mumbai arterial road for a full seven hours, drawing attention to the government's inaction in reopening the school, mired for the previous eight months in legal battles.[67] The parents in Mumbai succeeded not only in gaining an immediate meeting with the state education director that same day but also in getting the school reopened several days later.[68] Their action was widely criticized for the inconvenience it caused to commuters, but it is important to recognize that it occurred only *after* a range of other efforts had failed to successfully gain attention. Haresh, the father of one of the students, outlined the earlier efforts that parents had tried:

I am father of a nine-year-old daughter who is at home for last two months thinking why is she not going to school? Why is this injustice being meted out to her? A young mind today is talking about courts and street protests instead of learning history, science and maths, which will lead her to nation building. Does anyone even know that parents and students with sitting MLA had been on hunger strike for seven days, handing out roses to passer-byes and motorists on the same road for days to end? . . . When the state turns a blind eye to injustice, and greedy people with power and corruption turn predators, public will take the same course we took. Though the entire struggle has been peaceful, both us parents and students heartily apologise for even the smallest inconvenience to anyone. . . . Mumbai Police and the chief minister deserve a salute for their fairness and support.[69]

Only when other strategies failed to achieve a timely resolution did parents turn to a roko action.

As we can see from these various examples, roko actions are staged both by formal political organizations and coalitions with extensive experience in political activism, like the TJAC or its opposing coalition, the United Andhra Joint Action Committee, and by local or neighborhood groups with little or no formal political experience or prior association as a formal group. In addition, both middle-class Indians, such as the parents of children at the New Era School, and more marginalized socioeconomic groups, like the Chennai cyclone victims, participate in preplanned roko actions. Earlier examples of roko āndōlans from the 1980s and 1990s similarly offer evidence that individuals from a wide range of socioeconomic and caste backgrounds also participate in such actions. A major rasta roko event staged in the western Indian state of Maharashtra in November 1981, for example, was led by an organization made up primarily of the sons of "big farmers who dominate the villages and have become mainly a capitalist farmer class, working their lands through wage labourers and selling a major portion of their crops on the market."[70] In the early 1990s, faced with the prospect of expansion of India's system of affirmative action to make more equal the educational and employment opportunities available to marginalized groups, roko actions and other forms of political protest were led, in the words of one observer, by "the privileged upper caste pampered students and their parents who, having had it good all these years, fear that their empire is now being threatened."[71] In Chandigarh, one of many cities where anti–affirmative action agitations occurred, government employees joined students in filling the streets and blocking roads in protest.[72] Thus, roko actions are a form of political communication used not only by members of marginalized, lower-caste, or impoverished groups but also by wealthy farmers, university students from elite families, government employees, middle-class parents, and members of upper-caste groups. This troubles existing arguments that suggest that it is only slum dwellers, squatters, illiterate and uneducated laborers, and members of lower-caste and other populations defined as targets of governmentality who engage in such forms of political activity.[73]

### "Spontaneous Nonviolent Roko Actions"

The second subtype within the category of peaceful, nonviolent demonstrations offered by the senior railway official, Mr. Kohli, are spontaneous roko actions. These, too, Mr. Kohli said, were "also usually non-violent" and occurred in response to "a fairly legitimate complaint."[74] Spontaneous roko actions almost always occur in response to a very localized issue, usually a specific event, and they usually have "no clear leaders." This lack of clear leaders, he said, often made such actions more difficult for the Railways to deal with, because it was never clear exactly with whom officials should negotiate.

As an example of this second, more spontaneous type, Mr. Kohli offered the following: "We [the South Central Railways] have 38,000 unguarded level crossings. Once villagers sat on the tracks to protest the killing of an auto rickshaw driver by a train at an unmanned level crossing. The villagers refused to vacate, and eventually mild force was needed to break it up."[75]

Most of the examples he offered of this form were responses to very local, immediate concerns and therefore typically occurred in the absence of mediation by a formal organization or political party. This is in contrast to preplanned roko actions, most of which are organized by a party, coalition, neighborhood association, or other formal organization.

### "Illegitimate, Illegal, and Disruptive Activities with No Intention to Harm Lives"

Mr. Kohli went on to contrast preplanned and spontaneous "largely peaceful demonstrations" with his second overarching category of "illegitimate, illegal, and disruptive activities," which also has two subcategories: actions "with the intention to disrupt but not harm lives (except perhaps for enemies of the state)" and "targeted planned violent activity with the goal of maximum damage to human life and property." As an example of the first subcategory, he offered the Maoist-inspired Naxalite revolutionaries, referring to the underground rural movement prevalent in several parts of India—most notably, Bengal, Telangana, Andhra Pradesh, Jharkhand, and Chhattisgarh—that resorts to armed encounters with landlords and police. "Whenever Naxalites want to show their strength," Mr. Kohli said, "they capture a [railway] station, remove the people, and blast the communication and signaling systems. This can cause a one-month delay while it gets rebuilt, or a slowdown causing trains to run more slowly." Previously this type of action occurred once or twice a year; however, over the past decade it has become less common, he said.

What surprised me, however, was that Mr. Kohli and many others in the senior level of the railways were still willing to grant some legitimacy to these violent actions. Another senior security commissioner with the Northern Railways told me that, during the two years he was posted in Hyderabad, "the Naxalites would warn the railways in advance to clear a station, and as a result, not one railway person or passenger was ever hurt in their attacks."[76] He attributed the rise of this militancy to social disparities, saying, "The rich are getting richer and the poor are getting poorer," and added, "Tribal areas are the main places that this Naxalite problem exists. Tribals see it as their recourse. Industrialists, traders, businessmen come in. Profit is being extracted by outsiders and in return they're not getting anything and the government hasn't done much for these people. So they feel deprived of their legitimate dues. If their demands are met, maybe one day they will shun violence."[77] Thus, he acknowledged that this "illegitimate" activity was a result of the concerns of the disenfranchised continuing to go unheard, despite their efforts to communicate.

These observations of the "legitimacy" of militant action align with the ethnographic observations of Lipika Kamra and Uday Chandra, who argue that militant Maoist movements, despite their apparent antipathy to electoral politics and animosity toward the state, have actually deepened democracy rather than working against it.[78] They argue that "revolutionary praxis" is less "a vanguardist imposition on the masses than a site of ongoing negotiations."[79] They show the ongoing interaction between the domains of electoral politics and Maoist practice, as residents turn to both electoral representatives and Naxalite leaders for assistance in gaining recognition and getting their concerns addressed. "Yesterday's rebels may be tomorrow's legislators," they write, explaining that "'state' and 'society' are both transformed simultaneously" and that "ordinary villagers, far from being sandwiched between rival political authorities, have grown accustomed over time to approach each authority with a particular set of demands and expectations. . . . Far from being sandwiched between rival authorities or led by kinship relations to one side or another, subalterns committed themselves to multiple allegiances and hedged their bets to ensure their physical security."[80] Kamra and Chandra argue persuasively that

> the Maoist insurgency has brought a renewed focus on these margins of modern India [regions of central and eastern India in which Maoist activism is widespread], paradoxically deepening democracy even as it is contested from the "outside." Local, state and national elections are regularly held in insurgent areas. Despite its stated antipathy towards Indian democracy, the Maoist movement has not subverted or diminished it in any sense. . . . Insofar as modern "democracy" retains its original meaning as the rule of the demos, the antinomies of subaltern agency ought to be regarded [as] at the heart of popular democracy. Rather than destroying the so-called sham of mass democracy, Maoist revolutionary praxis may have, in fact, revitalized it.[81]

Nandini Sundar similarly asserts that local villagers "want both the Maoists and the state but for different reasons. They need open parliamentary parties and civil liberties groups who can help them when they get arrested, as well as a party like the Maoists who can help them keep their land."[82] Rather than showing revolutionary violence as the opposite of democracy then, Sundar, like Kamra and Chandra, concludes that Maoist practices have deepened democracy, a view reinforced by the research of other scholars as well.[83]


*"Targeted Planned Violent Activity*
*with the Goal of Maximum Damage"*

The final subtype described by Mr. Kohli was "targeted planned violent activity with the goal of maximum damage to human life and property." As an example, he offered the November 26, 2008, bomb blasts in Mumbai, which targeted Chhatrapati Shivaji Terminus (formerly the Victoria railway station) among other sites and resulted in more than 170 deaths and over 300 injured. A second example was the July 2006 series of seven bomb blasts on the Mumbai Suburban Railway, which killed 209 people and injured more than 700 others. One of the most striking features of Mr. Kohli's characterization of "illegitimate, illegal, and disruptive activities" is that most of the actions he described were not performed with the intent of advancing a specific demand of the state. Instead, they were more typically done to refuse the state's authority and to demonstrate the power of their own actors and leaders as an alternate body of authority.

### Participatory versus Adversarial Actions

Mr. Kohli's categories, although obviously not the only way we can distinguish among various types of action that may appear superficially the same, help confirm the simple fact that not all roko actions mean the same thing or address the same audiences. His latter scenarios—his third and fourth groups—may be ones that Chakrabarty and others imagine when they refer to roko actions as rejections of state sovereignty.[84] But it is important to recognize that these violent actions make up just one subset of a much wider variety of roko actions, many of which are not efforts to reject the state's sovereignty. Richard Kernaghan, in his ethnographic work on the Maoist-inspired Shining Path and its blockage and control of roads in the context of Peru, observes that these types of roadblocks generally have more to do with creating a sense of solidarity among followers through the successful assertion of power than with any attempt to negotiate or engage with the state or its representatives.[85] This is an important distinction to make in comparison with the earlier examples I offered, and we should be cautious about grouping together these very different kinds of political actions and dismissing them all as rejections of or challenges to the state's sovereignty.

What are most useful for the reconsideration of theoretical approaches to blockades are the actions that fall within the first two subcategories—those that Mr. Kohli regarded as more legitimate—and it is these actions that most clearly illustrate two of this book's arguments. First, these practices can be seen as forms of negotiation with and reification of the state rather than as a rejection of its sovereignty. Second, the widespread recognition of at least some legitimacy in these actions' demands has resulted in recognizable alterations in the authorities' everyday applications of legal systems. I offer Mr. Kohli's categorizations to show that breaking down such events into specific subcategories enables us to make important distinctions in the motives, goals, strategies, and contexts shaping each incident, rather than collapsing together all of these examples as a single undifferentiated form of political practice, as has been more common. It also enables us to recognize the ways in which members of different demographic groups participate in a shared repertoire of available political practices.

Moving from viewing roko actions only as "law-and-order" problems that require sending in the police, railway officials are increasingly taking the approach of granting audiences to those blocking railway traffic. Ashima Singh, the divisional railway manager for the Northeastern Railways, whom I met in 2009, has been recognized for pioneering a new method for responding to roko blockages and other political disruptions of rail traffic. She introduced face-to-face meetings in which senior railway officials talk directly with those preventing the movement of trains. The method has gained traction within the railway administration and is now being used to train railway officers in other divisions. And Ashima Singh herself was subsequently promoted to the position of director of the Indian Railway Institute of Transport Management. She described to me what she characterized as a typical situation:

> There's a river called the Saryu, between Barebanki and Gonda, near Saryu station. There was a *mela* [fair or festival] going on there. Some of the occupants of a train—on their way to the mela—pulled the communication chain while the train was on a bridge so that they could get down to get water from the [holy] river to take to the temple. It was a seven-span bridge, about 300 meters. A speeding train came from the other direction as they were walking on the tracks. Seventeen people were killed. A message came to us that some three thousand people were sitting on the track and not letting the train move further. We received this message at 8:30 p.m., but we immediately traveled 70 kilometers from Lucknow. I and another lady, just the two of us with no police, we went and sat on the tracks with them. Twenty-five thousand passengers were stranded. There were six trains waiting on either side. We went and sat on the track with them. We told them, "What you want to do, do it to us rather than to your own colleagues."[86]

A relief train was sent to take the bodies, and rail traffic resumed shortly thereafter. Singh attributed this quick resolution both to the railway officials' willingness to communicate directly with those blocking the tracks and to their refusal to call in the police, which would quickly have turned the problem into a law-and-order issue and likely resulted in violence. She understood that those sitting on the tracks wanted to be acknowledged and were seeking an audience with a representative of the state. Regardless of the legitimacy of their grievance, she argued that allowing them to air it and redirect it away from railway property toward specific government officials was more constructive than sending in military or police reinforcements. "You have to encourage them to target an individual person, not the railway as an institution or arm of government," she said.

Other examples have had similar outcomes, but what is most striking was the opposition she said she initially encountered from her superiors. "When we started this method when we were younger, our seniors also objected to this method," she said. "They feared that if anything happened to us, they would be held responsible." In another incident, a local group kidnapped an assistant engineer and blocked railway traffic after their earlier efforts to get the railways to make urgent repairs had failed. Singh again went out to speak personally with the villagers involved. In this case, those blocking railway traffic wanted the railways to repair a railway embankment that was in imminent danger of giving way and flooding the village. Within half an hour of her arrival, the train and the kidnapped engineer were released and traffic resumed, yet she did not leave the area. Instead, she stayed on for the next twenty-four hours to supervise repairs of the embankment. A local minister of Parliament met her and asked, "What are you doing? Have you already penalized the local authorities in this incident?" But she refused to pass on the blame, instead focusing on how best to resolve the grievance. Even the engineer who had been kidnapped came back after he was released and began helping with the repairs. In the end, most of the village worked together with railway employees to repair the embankment. She argues that an incident that could have turned into another Gujjar-type agitation—which blocked traffic in Rajasthan for nearly two months—was resolved through genuine communication and a focus on the problem at hand, enabling those with grievances to be heard.

# SEVEN. RALLIES, PROCESSIONS, AND *YĀTRAS*

## Ticketless Travel and the Journey to "Political Arrival"

Your agitation [*āndōlana*] sounds creative [*srjanātmakangā*]
Our agony [*āvēdana*] looks violent [*himsātmakangā*] —VARAVARA RAO, "Déjà vu,"
1986

No issue. No reason. Just to show our strength. To show we'd arrived. —Dalit professional, explaining why he and his colleagues would travel ticketless to Nagpur each year, April 16, 2009

In April 2009, I mentioned my research work on political uses of the railways to a well-educated Dalit professional from Maharashtra.[1] As I elaborated on my interest in rail roko blockades, alarm chain pulling, ticketless travel, and other creative uses of transportation networks for the purposes of political communication, his enthusiastic reaction took me by surprise but suggested that I was onto something important. "Oh yes, we also did that!" he exclaimed with excitement. "In the 1970s and 80s, I participated in many. About seven to eight thousand would travel from Aurangabad to Nagpur. . . . We did it twice every year—14th April [Dalit leader B. R. Ambedkar's birth anniversary] and 14th October [the anniversary of Ambedkar's conversion to Buddhism in Nagpur].[2] When I asked whether there were specific issues that he and others had been advocating in their twice-annual pilgrimages, he replied, "No issue. No reason. Just to show our strength. To show we'd arrived." My curiosity piqued, I followed up with another question, asking whether everyone had traveled without tickets, to which he replied, "Of course. That was the whole point. And after a while the Railways responded by adding an extra train for us," he continued with pride. "That's when we knew we'd *really* arrived!"

Railway administrators, acting as central government employees, responded to the annual pilgrimages to Ambedkar's Deekshabhoomi (place of conversion) by adding additional bogies or even entire trains to accommodate the large numbers of people traveling *without tickets*. These decisions suggest that, by the 1970s and '80s, government representatives had begun to redefine the collective ticketless travel of Maharashtrian Dalits as a political act rather than as a legal violation, thereby granting the practice a formal legitimacy and allowing Dalits to join the status of other recognized political groups. The recognition of their collective ticketless travel as political rather than criminal was indeed, as my interlocutor so clearly emphasized, a mark of Maharashtrian Dalits' "political arrival." In this chapter, I use the phrase "political arrival" to describe situations in which state officials recognize an action as political, using their discretionary power to decide which actions are political or, in some cases, redefining as political (if sometimes only temporarily) acts that might otherwise be defined as criminal, misdemeanors, or civil offenses.

Ticketless travel, like alarm chain pulling and roko actions, is widely used politically in India, both as a means of collective travel to political rallies and as a public display of identity. While sitting one day in the office of Mr. Das, a senior official in India's South Central Railway, he explained to me that there are two types of ticketless travel: "There are those who are trying to avoid paying. They will be arrested," he said. "And then there are those who will travel en masse when there is a big political meeting. They know no one can touch them. No arrests will be made. It's not possible. Arrests would create more problems, like the destruction of railway property. Unofficially everyone understands."[3] His observations resonated with those of another retired railway official I met in Lucknow, who told me that it is now so well known that the police and railways will accommodate a political group traveling ticketless, without harassing or arresting them, that it is quite common in some parts of India like Bihar for labor recruiters to distribute political flags "from one party or another" to their newly recruited laborers and then take them to the distant worksite on the train without purchasing tickets.[4] Although the first official implied that the threat of violence is an important factor in not contesting ticketless travel, the second suggests that the political dimensions of this type of group travel are not irrelevant to the government's stance. If railway officials were simply afraid of what any large group of travelers might do, then there would be no need for labor recruiters to perform the charade of having their laborers carry political flags.

Another example shared by Mr. Mehta, the Government Railway Police official introduced in chapter 6, makes this even clearer. When more than 600,000 people, most of whom had traveled ticketless, converged on the city of Lucknow for a large political rally featuring India's deputy prime minister and the state's chief minister in September 2002, sixteen people were killed in a stampede at Lucknow's Charbagh Railway Station as rallyists returned to the railway station to make their way home after the event.[5] Following an inquiry, the blame for this incident was placed on the railways for having had insufficient measures in place to handle a crowd of this size, with the divisional railway manager for the Lucknow division of the Northern Railways transferred to a less desirable post as punishment.[6] To prevent such incidents from recurring, political groups routinely inform the railways when rallies are occurring, and in turn, the railways provide additional trains to carry people to and from those rallies.[7] And although we may be tempted to dismiss this example as an illustration of the organizational advantages and disproportionate access to public space of political parties in power, the fact that I was told similar stories of railway accommodation of other groups suggests that this accommodation is not offered only to political parties in power.[8]

Histories of Ticketless Travel

By 1921, when the Non-Cooperation Movement led by M. K. Gandhi was active, ticketless travel became an object of inquiry for the British colonial administration. Officials sought to discover how widespread the problem was and whether isolated reports of its occurrence actually reflected a wider, more systematic problem. In that year, for example, a crowd of ticketless travelers returning from a Non-Cooperation meeting organized in Ludhiana by the Indian National Congress was highlighted in debates in the House of Lords as typical of the wider political uses of ticketless travel in India more generally. In a letter to Lord Lytton, the under secretary of state for India, Sir Michael O'Dwyer described the crowd as one that "was returning from one of Gandhi's great demonstrations," continuing that "as usual on those occasions, [it] invaded the railway station, intimidated the staff, took possession of the train, and travelled without tickets."[9] Virtually identical statements were offered in the House of Lords' debates over whether the existing strength of the British Army in India should be maintained or reduced. One member stated, "That was a crowd which had just been attending one of Mr. Gandhi's great demonstrations, and as so often happens in India now, it took possession of the train, and travelled without taking any tickets," suggesting that this represented a regular pattern rather than an exception and using it to advocate for strengthening the army.[10] Railway officials in the Punjab where the incident took place responded by downplaying it as an isolated one:

> We had no reason to suppose that we had underestimated the amount of interference with railway traffic. The information given by the Railway Board tallied with what we had received ourselves, namely, that occasionally students were carried away by the exuberance of their enthusiasm and more or less raided trains, travelled without tickets and intimidated the railway staff. . . . We have not had from any source any information which would lead us to suppose that the incident described by Sir Michael O'Dwyer's correspondent is in any sense a common incident or one of frequent occurrence.[11]

Their correspondent, C. W. Gwynne, concluded that "we may say quite safely that the occurrence was an isolated one."[12]

Yet ticketless travel continued to be a subject of concern over the next decade and a half, leading to the proposal on March 23, 1936, of a bill to amend the Indian Railway Act to grant railway officials greater power to respond to the problem. The Marwadi Association, a pan-regional organization of traders and merchants with origins in Rajasthan, weighed in on the debate as railway officials conducted a more systematic analysis of the problem of ticketless travel in the wake of the bill's proposal. Strikingly, however, individuals traveling without tickets for political purposes was not included among the five categories of ticketless travel that they identified:

> (i) persons belonging to the professions and the merchants class and others who are obliged to travel without tickets due to late arrival at stations or other similar reasons, or who, having purchased tickets, have lost them in the way; (ii) unemployed persons coming from villages and towns in search of employment or returning disappointed; (iii) vagrants, sadhus, religious or other mendicants and the like; (iv) men drawn from various classes who deliberately travel without tickets; (v) the friends and acquaintances of the Railway staff, who may do so with the assistance or connivance of the latter.[13]

In 1939, with the continued rise of anticolonial nationalist sentiments, however, political motivations for ticketless travel again became a serious object of concern for British administrators. The confidential Andhra Provincial Congress Committee circular of July 29, 1942, cited in chapter 5, names ticketless travel as a key strategy used by the Quit India Movement.

The new post-independence government of India also inherited ticketless travel as a concern. Jawaharlal Nehru, for example, speaking to an audience in Bihar in 1955, said,

> Ticketless travel has become an occupation of the people of Bihar now. I am sure you will earn a great name for yourselves. Some members of your Action Committee had gone to Delhi to meet me, and forgetting that the rest of India is not yet like Patna they travelled without tickets. They were promptly arrested and sent off to jail which surprised them no end. How can we go on like this?[14]

In the wake of Indian independence, acknowledgment of ticketless travel as a political rather than criminal act continued to be a variable and negotiated form of recognition and a mark of "political arrival," as the next section argues.

## Performing "Political Arrival"

As we saw in chapters 5 and 6, the shift from defining an act as criminal to defining it as political is not necessarily permanent and can change depending on who is engaging in a particular action. For many marginalized groups, obtaining recognition as having a legitimate voice in the public sphere is an ongoing project.[15] Thus, pilgrimages, rallies, processions, and other visible collective actions play an important role in constructing, projecting, and protecting the hard-won legitimacy of voices in the public sphere, particularly for members of historically disenfranchised populations. This process involves continual coalition-building, investment in alliances, and the forging of links with a wide range of partners and intermediaries who can facilitate connections, interventions, audiences, and consultations with those in elected and appointed government positions or other positions of authority. I define this process as building "axes of access."

The focus on individual efforts to make connections with intermediaries to gain access to public resources and state recognition—whether directly or through integration into various types of networks—is widespread.[16]

Much less attention has been given, however, to the ways that collective mobilizations are used to establish connections with channels of access to public resources. As the preceding chapters have argued, scholarly analysis of collective actions tends to portray group mobilizations not as efforts to access state resources or otherwise hail the state, but rather as rebellion or opposition to the state, therefore downplaying its role in the amplification of efforts to communicate with the state. Gabrielle Kruks-Wisner, in her work on claims-making in India, argues that "understanding when and how citizens engage rather than exit from or rebel against the state is . . . of critical consequence," opening up exciting new avenues for investigation.[17] She writes, "My central argument . . . is that citizens who traverse local social and spatial boundaries will, all else equal, be more likely to make claims on the state, and will do so through a broader repertoire of practices, than those who remain more constrained."[18] This suggests that access to collective forms of mobilization is dependent on exposure to social differences and broader repertoires of practice—from "direct appeals to officials, to brokerage through third parties, to collective claim-making through associations, and contentious collective action."[19]

Although her focus is on "the micro-determinants of citizen action at the level of the *individual*, asking why people living in the same institutional settings navigate access to the state through different means," her data simultaneously open up important questions about when and how individuals come together with others to engage representatives of the state collectively.[20] She reports, for example, on one interview in which a woman described her efforts to access the government's Mahatma Gandhi National Rural Employment Guarantee Scheme (MGNREGS), which entitles rural residents to one hundred days of guaranteed work per year. "There was the issue of getting documentation so that we could get work," reported the woman. "We went again and again to get our names on the list [for job cards]. So it became necessary to do more. Our whole [women's self-help] group went at once. There were so many of us that we crowded the office, and the officials there finally gave up the papers."[21] Kruks-Wisner reports that despite the fact that "social rights campaigns in India have effectively employed contentious strategies to shape policy at the state and national levels . . . just 17 percent . . . reported that they had participated in a rally, strike, or other kind of protest activity, and just 11 percent were aware of an active social movement organization in their vicinity."[22] Even though their collective action was effective, it is unlikely that the women participating in it would have included themselves in the 17 percent that Kruks-Wisner identifies as having reported participation in a "rally, strike, or other protest activity," and yet they were able to accomplish collectively what they were unable to do as individuals.

This collective effort to get themselves registered is an example of what I refer to as the creation of an "axis of access." An axis of access is a channel—often created collectively—that enables an effective connection with the state. As Ribot and Peluso argue, we can see this as distinct from a right.[23] Even when rights exist, not everyone has the ability to realize these rights or have them recognized. In the case of the women seeking registration in the MGNREGS employment program, this was a channel that was *only* able to be opened collectively. Approached through this lens, individuals approaching the state on their own, individuals seeking out an intermediary to negotiate with the state on their behalf, collective efforts (whether stemming from associational membership or simply shared interests), and social movement mobilization can be seen as different stages within a single process of seeking state recognition or accessing state services or resources. As Kruks-Wisner argues, the repertoire of available actions and customary channels is a product of both local landscapes and individual social and spatial exposure. So, too, is the fact that those who are successful in their initial encounters with the state have little need to escalate their efforts, offering another explanation for why such a small percentage of the population might report having engaged in social movement mobilizations. Not everyone needs social movements or collective action to access the state.

As I argued earlier, rather than seeing individual and collective actions as two distinct categories juxtaposed in opposition to one another, the movement from individual to collective action can be viewed as a way to escalate efforts to gain the attention of state representatives, as can the move from attempts to access local representatives of the state to approaching more distant representatives. Jennifer Bussell, for example, notes that after efforts to gain state recognition are blocked at the local level, citizens often seek out higher-level politicians, located at a greater remove.[24] Her contemporary observations of this are consistent with historical data on India as well.[25]

It is not only those in marginal positions seeking state services or those seeking upward social mobility who recognize the importance of being well connected, however. Those who find themselves in positions of power—administrators, elected officials, or those who are able to compel others to follow their instructions—also recognize the importance of maintaining and continuing to expand their connections in all directions, not simply upward, to preserve crucial access to information. Zeynep Tufekci's observations of the vulnerability of authoritarian regimes to sudden collective assertions point precisely to the importance of being well connected to sources of information from multiple directions (up, down, and laterally). She writes, "Democracies, as imperfect as they may be, tend to be more stable not only because they have more legitimacy than authoritarian regimes, but also because they can engage in self-correction more easily, since voter dissatisfaction with a government leads directly to a change in its leaders."[26] Effective rulers have long recognized the importance of good communication as a means of ensuring their own continuation of power. Tufekci cites, for example, the Ming Dynasty's Emperor Zhu Di, who asserted, "Stability depends on superior and inferior communicating; there is none when they do not. From ancient times, many a state has fallen because a ruler did not know the affairs of the people."[27]

The importance of access to information also helps explain the continued openness of politicians in India to regular face-to-face audiences and direct interactions with their constituents, as discussed in chapter 2.[28] Many elected officials—and political parties more generally—recognize the need to keep their fingers on the pulses circulating more generally to maintain their positions, especially at the local level. The need to be aware of current trends in public opinion also explains why politicians and parties so often try to get out in front of and position themselves as leaders within emerging social movements, as the many examples from the Telangana and other recent movements illustrate.[29]

Yet as we have seen, individual concerns—what some call "claims"—are much more likely to be legible to politicians and less likely to be ignored when communicated collectively. Successful "political arrival" therefore depends on the effective performance of collective identity and shared interests, which in turn, requires the building of alliances and the perception of common cause. When viewed from this perspective, collective identities do not appear to exist naturally prior to processes of political mobilization but rather must be forged. Awareness of the dependence of politicians and political parties on their constituents also raises the important question of the relationships between those who try to act as representatives and those they purport to be representing. In the next section I address portrayals of these two groups and of the relationships between them as they relate to collective identities and forms of assembly.

Those who see themselves as leaders or representatives do not always consider themselves a part of the groups they claim to represent. A likely apocryphal story concerning a Bengali-language film begins by establishing that the film had become an unexpected blockbuster hit. After playing in Kolkata theaters for many weeks to packed houses at every screening, two members of the Bengali *bhadralok* (lit., "respectable people," or the professional salaried Bengali middle class) went to see the film. Afterward, as the two friends were exiting the theater, one of them turned to the other and said, "A truly wonderful film. But, you know, I don't think the public will appreciate it." This story captures a quite common invocation of the concept of the public as an imagined body of people with whom the speaker does *not* self-identify—indeed, *against* whom one can define oneself, one's tastes, and one's sensibilities. There is tremendous power attributed to this type of conjured public and to the media through which they are represented as communicating. In what follows, I intervene within existing theorizations of publics by comparing explicit representations of two types of publics in the context of Telugu-speaking southern India.[30] In doing so, I examine their relationships to one another, to the state and other forms of authority, and, most importantly, to democracy and the various genealogies of its practice in India.

The representation of the first type of public parallels representations of European publics that emerged in relation to the growing circulation of print media (and later other forms of mass media). We might think of it along the lines of the classic bourgeois public sphere described by Jürgen Habermas, albeit in the distinctive version born of the unique pressures and perspectives fostered by a colonial context and celebrated in its later form by Benedict Anderson in his discussion of the rise of new forms of imagined community.[31] In Habermas this begins with face-to-face exchanges in the coffeehouses of the new European mercantile class, whose profits from international shipping and trade (including quite prominently with India) gave them increasing power and prominence in ways that challenged preexisting power structures dominated by the hereditary aristocracy. It then extends to the printed literary sphere. Scholars of South Asia have constructed portraits of Indian variants of the Habermasian public sphere that point to the importance not only of print media and the literate elites who produced periodicals, books, and other publications but also of processions, rituals, and other public performances of power, identity, and public opinion—thereby challenging the portrayal of a single unitary "public sphere" in favor of multiple overlapping and competing spheres.[32] Chris Bayly's "Indian ecumene," which he argues predates the rise of print media, shares with Habermas's portrait of the modern European public sphere an attention to the role played by "its leaders [who] were able to mount a critical surveillance of government and society."[33] Douglas Haynes similarly offers a focus on the role of "notables" in the Indian public sphere.[34] The role of print media in forming new types of linguistic and communitarian identities has also featured prominently.[35] In the context of Telugu-speaking southern India, scholars have written about the emergence of this first kind of public in relation to the library and town hall movements and the new forms of public space created by them, the publication of social reform literature in the latter part of the nineteenth century, the movement for a separate Telugu-speaking state, and activities associated with the rise of the anticolonial nationalist movement.[36]

Yet these analyses do not typically make explicit the dual use of the concept of the "public"—the first to describe a group with which a speaker claims to identify, and the second to describe a group that the speaker seeks to represent but sees as distinct and with which he or she explicitly does not identify. More recent scholarship expands the concept of the public sphere through attention to modern forms of mass media, particularly film and television, and to the role of a wide range of associations.[37] Critics of a single unitary public sphere incorporate recognitions of gender, class, caste, language, and religion within the shaping of multiple, often competing public spheres.[38] New work also gives voice to members of previously marginalized groups and challenges the methods through which members of dominant groups have laid claim to the right to speak for others and project their own identities onto them. Kancha Ilaiah's *Why I Am Not a Hindu*, for example, illustrates the ways that expanded educational opportunities in India have better enabled those from a wide range of economic and social backgrounds to articulate and publicize their own agendas, rather than having dominant groups claim to do so on their behalf.[39]

The wider recognition of previously marginalized or silenced voices has helped make more visible the second commonly represented type of public: that made up of people thought to be distinctively *different* from those doing the representing. This is a public (*prajānīkam* in Telugu) with which one does *not* identify. This second type of public has several characteristic features. First, this public is rarely addressed. Instead, in India (as in other places in the world) it is typically spoken about or on behalf of. It is usually represented by those who mark themselves as different from it in some way, be they political leaders, prominent members of society, journalists, or academics. The affective response of this public, unlike that of the bourgeois public, is rarely anticipated or solicited; instead, it is usually described after the fact. In other words, it is interpreted by those who position themselves outside it as its mediators. The crowd, the mob, the lumpen element, the masses, the people, even the generic "public"—as in the story of the bhadralok and the public's taste in films—all are names for this second type of public. This is the kind of public that is so frequently invoked explicitly by the *word* "public" in South Asia—not as a body being addressed or as a social totality but as an entity *against* which a speaker can define him- or herself. This public sometimes provokes fear, pity, anxiety, or embarrassment and is often assumed to be incapable of speaking for itself. Nevertheless, its acknowledged will and unharnessed power is seen as able to be interpreted by political adepts who claim to channel the meanings of the actions of this voiceless yet active mob.

The movements for new and separate linguistically defined states within the Indian nation that emerged in the first half of the twentieth century offer an excellent example of the dual ways in which Indian publics are often represented. The Telugu linguistic state movement, for example, first emerged in the 1910s, and the many meetings, resolutions, petitions, and public debates, as well as the circulation of printed copies of the minutes, addresses, and proceedings that fueled the movement, span more than four decades, connecting the British colonial era with the immediate postcolonial administration of the newly independent Indian state in 1947.[40] The Andhra movement eventually culminated in the creation of a new Telugu linguistic state in 1953, known then as Andhra State, the first successful movement for a separate linguistic state in independent India. It offered a model for the All-India Linguistic States Reorganisation that took place three years later, when additional regions throughout India were reorganized along linguistic lines and Andhra State was joined with the Telugu-speaking districts of the former princely state of Hyderabad (the Telangana region) to become Andhra Pradesh, making linguistic states the norm in India.[41] Yet most observers would acknowledge that, despite the more than four decades of political activities engaged in by the literate, well-educated Telugu-speaking elites, it was ultimately another, quite distinctive "public" that played the more significant role in bringing the new state into being. However, this public—often described as the masses or subalterns—was represented almost entirely by those who distinguished themselves from it.

Before turning to this second type of public, there are several character-istics of the first public—the one so easily imagined in relation to printed media, town hall meetings, and Habermasian deliberative debate—that are worth emphasizing, particularly for the ways in which these features form a contrast with the second type of public. The first public is a public explicitly addressed. Although its members may be strangers to each other, as Michael Warner suggests in his important book, *Publics and Counterpublics*, those being addressed are already imagined as members of a common group to which the speaker also belongs. In this sense, they are marked by what they are perceived to *share*. The representation of the affective dimension of this public is also significant. Their affect is anticipated and solicited with the intention of channeling it in a disciplined manner toward a particular goal, identity, or shared object, and it is this goal or collective imagining that holds the public together as a coherent form and recognizable entity. In this sense, although such a public is explicitly imagined to already exist, the address to this public is also simultaneously implicitly transformative, seeking to bring into being something that has not previously existed or been recognized.

We see this, for example, in Gurujada Sriramamurti's 1878 *Kavi Jīvitamulu* (Lives of Poets), the first work to use the Telugu language as a foundational organizational category, rather than using a dynastic affiliation, a religious sectarian identity, an intellectual genealogy, a patronage relationship, or a geographic territory as a basis for inclusion or exclusion of authors. In pub-lishing a second edition in 1893, Sriramamurti begins his preface with an ap-peal explicitly addressed to "*telugu dēśa bhāṣa abhimānulu* [those having affection for or pride in the language of the Telugu country]."[42] Rather than assuming the preexistence of a public defined by its shared usage of a com-mon language, his solicitation works to bring into being a public that did *not* already previously recognize itself. This public's uncertain and emergent char-acter is confirmed by Sriramamurti later in the preface to the second edition, when he explicitly states that in publishing the first edition of his *Lives of Poets* fifteen years earlier in 1878, he was not yet certain whether an audience for his publication actually existed or whether readers would support his liter-ary endeavors by purchasing and reading the volume in question.[43]

As mentioned earlier, the second type of public differs from the first primarily in its conceptualization as a body made up of people who are *different* from the speaker who invokes them. This type of public is often represented as "subaltern" and is sometimes framed in relationship to oral networks, rather than the print media thought to be used primarily by members of the first type of public. These oral communicative networks include networks that facilitate rumor, the circulation of messages via drums, or the passing of chapatis (unleavened bread) and other political symbols at speeds that exceeded the movement of the British Indian postal service in the mid-nineteenth century.[44] In southern India, such publics have also been represented as physically emerging around nodal points within larger material networks of communication—particularly those sites and spaces of transportation that connect the local community to the world beyond and so naturally attract people and cause them to congregate at and around them. These spaces include railway stations and streets, newsstands, and tea stalls immediately adjacent to the stations, and, to a lesser extent, bus stations and stands in places that have no railway station.

This kind of public has had little place in existing theoretical characterizations of publics, most of which rely heavily on the concept of address. Michael Warner, for example, who offers us one of the most thorough definitions of a public, identifies three distinct senses of the noun *public* that are often intermixed in popular usage. Significantly, none of his three definitions accommodate an understanding of a public as an entity *against* which speakers can define themselves. Of the first form, which usually appears as "*the* public," he writes, "*The* public is a kind of social totality . . . the public, as a people, is thought to include everyone within the field in question."[45] There is no suggestion of the speaker (or of anyone like him or her) being excluded from this social totality. His second form is "a concrete audience, a crowd witnessing itself in space, as with a theatrical public." He suggests that this public "also has a sense of totality, bounded by the event or by the shared physical space."[46] It is the third sense, however, that Warner is most interested in, identifying it as "the kind of public that comes into being only in relation to texts and their circulation."[47] This public "exists by virtue of being addressed" and is "organized by nothing other than discourse itself."[48]

None of Warner's three publics describe a public *against* which a speaker might try to define himself or herself, even while often simultaneously attempting to represent it from outside. Close attention to specific invocations of the different types of publics can highlight the methods through which people have been narrativized into them, as well as the spaces and communicative channels that scholars have privileged in their representations of publics (coffeehouses, reading publics, media viewers), often at the expense of other spaces like those featured in this book. These different methods, spaces, and communicative channels are apparent in representations of the culminating days of the movement for a separate Telugu-speaking Andhra province in 1952. Elsewhere I have explored these tensions in detail; however, here I want to highlight a brief example to emphasize the constructed nature of this second, invoked public.[49] Despite the regular meetings, letters to the government, editorials, resolutions, and petitions that members of the Andhra movement organized during the first half of the twentieth century to bring a Telugu linguistic province into being, it was the large collective assemblies that massed in and around railway stations along the main Madras-Calcutta railway line in the wake of linguistic state activist Potti Sreeramulu's widely publicized fast-unto-death that ultimately succeeded in bringing the new state into being.

Yet many leaders of the Andhra movement made it clear in interviews with me that even though they acknowledged the undeniably critical role of these crowds, they saw these actors as quite different from themselves and did not recognize them as genuine *political* actors. This was expressed in a range of ways, from dismissing them as "not freedom fighters" to characterizing them as "hooligans," "labourers," or "unruly elements"—as though laborers and those who were "unruly" could not also be politically engaged. Leaders also contrasted these "hooligans" with "students" who "stood in rows," "moved in queues," and were regarded by the narrators as proper political actors.[50] One leader in the coastal city of Nellore made this contrast very clear in his description of the crowds at the railway station on whom the police fired in their efforts to maintain order, killing four and injuring an additional eighteen:

> When *we* came to know that the firing was taking place, *we* ran [to the station]. After knowing. First *we* were not the leaders of that group at the railway station. *We* might have held some meetings in support of Potti Sriramulu, in the town. *We* didn't participate in that attack on the railway station. That was the job of *some others*. So, when *nobody* went to their rescue, *we* went in a group of about four to five hundred, to help *them*—to prevent further firing. . . . After *we* went, *people gathered around us*. There was no more violence, no firing, no tear gas.[51]

It is the explicit marking of difference that I want to highlight here: "we" versus "them" or "some others," "we" versus the "people" who gathered around "us." These and other comments dismiss the political agency of most of the people present at the railway station, including those who fell victim to police bullets.[52] Andhra movement leaders distinguished between those who engaged in orderly processions and chants, wearing armbands and passing out food and fruits to the passengers of a halted train, and the masses or mobs engaged in looting, burning of rail cars, tearing up of railway tracks, or theft. Such references often appeared in a single paragraph, sometimes within the same sentence, and often distinguished different actions within the same crowd. In all of these representations, the "public" engaging in actions in the wake of Potti Sriramulu's death consistently appears *not* to be a unified collective will after all. In short, the "public" appears as a single unified voice only when channeled by adepts—political leaders who claim to interpret the *meanings* of the impassioned violence, "criminal" acts, and public displays of affect while also rendering invisible the communicative efforts of many of those present and their relevance as *political* agents.

## Visibility, Invisibility, and Political Arrival

Lucky
You are born rich
To say in your language
'Born with silver spoon in mouth'

Your agitation [āndōlana] sounds creative [srjanātmakangā]
Our agony [āvēdana] looks violent [himsātmakangā]

You are meritorious
You can break glass of buses
In a shape
As symmetric as Sun rays

You can deflate the tires
With artistic élan
While indulgent police look on
With their jaws rested on rifle butts
. . . . . . . . . . . . . . . . . . . . . . . . . . . .

We are
Rickshaw pullers
Porters and cart wheelers
Petty shopkeepers
And low grade clerks

We are
Desolate mothers
Who can give no milk
To the child who bites with hunger

We stand in hospital queues
To sell blood to buy food

Except for the smell of poverty and hunger
How can it acquire
The patriotic flavor
Of your blood donation?
—From Varavara Rao, "Déjà vu," 1986

As we have seen throughout this book, the same actions frequently evoke quite dramatically different responses from the state, depending on who is engaging in them. Existing scholarship attributes this variation in state reaction to purported differences in the groups themselves (civil vs. political society, elite vs. subaltern, gentlemen vs. hooligans, individuals vs. collectives) or to the categories of practices in which each group is engaging (legal/illegal, civil/uncivil, political/criminal, liberal/illiberal). In the poet Varavara Rao's verses, indulgent police are portrayed as looking on with their chins resting on the butts of their rifles as upper-caste students destroy state-owned buses, engage in gāli tiyaḍam (the deflating of tires) of state-owned buses, and occupy the streets in protest against the expansion of India's affirmative action system for government jobs and educational admissions. This is in sharp contrast to the speedy arrests, police charges with batons, and tear gas used against protests by groups who are not recognized as "having arrived" politically, such as the efforts of poor agricultural laborers to form associations or the examples of Dalit protests in Hyderabad and Tamil Nadu (see chapter 3). However, rather than simply seeing their actions in binary contrast, Varavara Rao's 1986 poem, "Déjà vu," equips us with the tools to identify the waxing and waning visibility of various groups, parties, movements and their specific agendas as *political* actions.

Telugu literature is one forum in which efforts have been made to talk back to dominant forms of historiography and social theory, illustrating how we might use such literary efforts to reframe theory. This book highlights some of the ways in which differences between types of collective assemblies have been inscribed and argues that these portrayals have long been fundamental to projects that seek to set limits on the political and authorize whose actions are able to gain recognition as political.[53] Rather than reinforcing these distinctions, however, one of this book's goals is to locate projects that have sought to delegitimize actions and refuse to recognize them as *political*. A brief historical analysis of the shift in meaning of the Telugu term *āvēdana* illustrates one method for accomplishing this.

In "Déjà vu," Rao draws attention to the ongoing impact of the distinctions made in authorizing whose voices count as political and therefore as legible and able to be heard. He contrasts the performative acts of prosperous upper-caste students protesting the Mandal Commission's recommendations to expand affirmative action quotas with the similar processions of impoverished laborers, road workers, sweepers, and leather workers. He writes, "Your agitation [āndōlana] sounds creative [srjanātmakangā], Our agony [āvēdana] looks violent [himsātmakangā]." In using the term *āvēdana*, Rao's critical eye captures the widespread perception and assumption of distinctions in practice that enable some to lay claim to the political while denying it to others who are engaged in identical efforts. Instead, their actions are misread as agony, raw affect, anger, violence, or criminality, or they simply fail to be recognizable at all. This phenomenon makes some efforts to intervene politically appear invisible through the framing of the agony of poverty as a personal problem or a narrow self-interest, rather than a universal claim, and through the framing of efforts to communicate or make recognizable this agony as violence, anger, or criminality.

The two terms Rao strategically employs—*āndōlana* (agitation) and *āvēdana* (agony)—are contrasted with one another. *Āndōlana*, a term from Sanskrit that originally means swinging, trembling, or oscillating, is now in widespread use in many Indian languages both to describe political agitation and in the names of civil society organizations that engage in agitation.[54] Rao captures the capacity of āndōlana to be recognized as srjanātmakangā, creative or world changing. But the other term, *āvēdana*, which he perceptively suggests so easily gets read today as violent (himsātmakangā), has undergone a surprising historical transformation that troubles the distinction between the creativity of political agitation and the violence of agony displayed.

Today, *āvēdana* is typically used in Telugu to mean grief, sorrow, agony, distress, or anguish. An earlier documentation of the term's meaning, however, recorded by the nineteenth-century colonial linguist and literary scholar Charles Philip Brown (writing in an era when the category of the political differed from today's), captures a different valence of the term. According to Brown, the noun *āvēdana* means "making known," and its adjectival form, *āvēditamu*, means "made known" or "communicated."[55] This shift in the weight of the complex meanings of āvēdana points to an earlier era that recognized individuals as embedded within social relationships with their rulers, relationships in which the right to "make known" one's suffering was sanctioned and accepted as legitimate within an understanding of good governance or moral rule.[56] With the rise of notions of abstract citizenship, embedded social relationships have come to be seen as corrupting or as self-serving and personal, rather than serving the overall good. Thus, the earlier meaning of "making known" of āvēdana appears to have dropped away, leaving instead an agony or pain no longer seen as located within embedded social relationships in which it can be made known. Instead of a political voice communicated through collective action and the possibility of recognition, only noise, excess, violence, and the raw affect of personal pain and agony are recognizable, demoting actions—as in the example of the Dalit students discussed in chapter 2—to expressions of emotion and expelling them from the category of political communication.

We can speculate that the new limitations placed on political activities—restricting roko agitations to fifteen or twenty minutes and dharnas to officially designated spaces on quiet back streets or eliminating designated protest spaces altogether—may well be yet another strategy for minimizing the visibility of particular groups and their agendas and restricting the impact of the expansion of democracy into new domains and classes of Indian citizens. Yet even in the face of such restrictions, there continue to be movements, factions, and groups who successfully violate these prohibitions, actively blocking roads or rail lines for days, weeks, or even months at a time or sitting in dharna in areas outside those designated for such activity. Looking closely at the forms of state accommodation that are offered or withheld in response to particular actions is an important tool for reading the degree of "political arrival" of a group or agenda, given that continued access to elected officials, media outlets, and spaces for collective assembly is crucial to a vibrant democracy. Attending more closely to the actions of the state and its representatives can help us recenter their roles in denying permission, silencing communicative efforts, and disbanding collective assemblies. Analyzing those who are granted permission or informally allowed to proceed, and tracing their relationships to politicians and government officials, can help make visible both those who have been difficult to see as political actors and the less visible networks of state and society intersections. Such an approach also enables us to move beyond the many static binaries that have been proposed for understanding and analyzing Indian politics and forces us to broaden our recognition of unconventional media. In the process, it decreases the invisibility of those who are attempting to enter public spheres to be recognized and seen, thereby increasing their visibility within our analytic frameworks.

In 2009, a brief news article appeared in *The Hindu* newspaper titled "Somnath Ignites Democratic Values among Students." Somnath Chatterjee, then speaker of the Lok Sabha, the lower house of the Indian Parliament, was reported as affirming the "democratic actions" of a group of five hundred schoolchildren from ten schools who had planned a march from the site of Gandhi's death to Parliament. The schoolchildren had been denied permission to hold the march by the Delhi police, and it was for this reason that the Speaker of the House had come to meet them. The article positively equates marching in the street with the practice of democracy, with Chatterjee remarking that "he was deeply touched by this intervention of the students and felt inspired to work more towards strengthening Parliamentary democracy in the country."[57] His comment emphasizes the idea that parliamentary democracy does not begin and end with elections, but that communicative practices must be continued even in between.

But it is also important to recognize that not all those who seek to engage in democratic communication are granted permission equally, nor is everyone able to access the benefits and protections of existing legal structures equally. Engaging in acts like collective ticketless travel is one way to draw attention to the systemic violence that Dalits have faced, including local-level atrocities, rape, and murder. Such efforts have followed long-standing attempts to draw attention to failures of the policing and judicial systems to prosecute such crimes and continued double standards. As Parthasarathi Muthukkaruppan and Timothy Mitchell show, this gap between the abstract letter of the law and its actual implementation has historically made invisible the violence engaged in by and exceptions to the law granted to dominant groups in ways that have enabled them to maintain their privileged positions.[58] Focusing only on the binary that is produced between legal and illegal actions ignores the way that institutions such as the judicial system and police are themselves implicated in the creation and maintenance of such binaries and discretionary forms of power, with roots in the colonial implementation of a structure of law, as Radha Kumar has shown.[59] The political and narrative strategies discussed earlier, however, can challenge the many discursive and physical obstacles that have impeded and continue to impede "political arrival" in India today.

On January 1, 2019, more than five million women in the south Indian state of Kerala participated in the creation of a *vanitha mathil*, or "women's wall" (*mānavahāram*, "human chain" in Telugu) to support gender equality amidst a controversy over the admission of women of menstruating age into the Sabarimala Hindu temple.[1] The human wall stretched along 620 kilometers (385 miles) of national highways and passed through all fourteen districts of the state, from Kasargod in the north to the state's southernmost district of Thiruvananthapuram. It sought to affirm the Supreme Court's September 2018 revocation of the ban that had prevented women between the ages of ten and fifty from entering the temple and demanded an end to the violent attacks targeting women who attempted to do so.[2] Despite the historic Supreme Court decision, not a single woman in that age bracket who had subsequently tried to enter the temple had been successful, and the state had done little to provide for their protection. The day after the vanitha mathil, however, two women of childbearing age successfully entered the temple, and a third was able to enter and complete her worship of the deity two days later.[3]

The vanitha mathil joins earlier South Asian human chains, including the current Guinness World Record holder organized by opposition parties in Bangladesh on December 11, 2004, to demand new elections. The 2004 human chain stretched 1,050 kilometers (652 miles), from Teknaf, the southernmost point of mainland Bangladesh (on the Burmese border), to Tentulia in the north of the country; it also reportedly involved more than five million people.[4] Human chains were also one of the many strategies that the Telangana movement used to garner attention. A 500-kilometer mānavahāram organized along National Highway 7 by the umbrella organization, the Telangana Joint Action Committee, in February 2010 spanned five of the region's districts, seeking to "send a clear message to the Central government that the people of the entire region were behind the movement."[5]

Other significant human chains have been organized in South Asia against discriminatory policies written into Nepal's new constitution (October 1, 2015), in opposition to India's sudden demonetization (in Kerala on December 29, 2016), and in support of the prohibition of liquor (in the north Indian state of Bihar on January 21, 2017).[6] These, too, were organized across long stretches of South Asia's national highways as efforts to demonstrate the extent of support for the agendas in question, often appealing to the Guinness Book to certify their status as new "world records."[7] Like the examples offered throughout this book, these human chains illustrate how the infrastructures of existing transportation networks play a central role in the organization of collective political actions. But they also show efforts to perform sensational stunts to garner both global and local media attention.

Garnering Attention in South Asia:
Collective Action, Political Parties, and the State

The Kerala women's wall; the human chains in Telangana, Bihar, Nepal, and Bangladesh; and the examples offered throughout this book have all sought the attention of those in positions of authority. Like Bina Bai, the widow in chapter 1 who performed her dharna not in front of her brother-in-law's home but at the local temple, or the expelled Dalit students who staged a hunger strike at Hyderabad's Dharna Chowk in chapter 2, participants in these actions use their visibility to influence public opinion and put pressure on authorities. Attention and the channels through which it flows have been altered by technological innovations—from print media, to mass audiovisual media, to social media—and by the changing communicative uses of transportation networks, prompting shifts in both forms and levels of effectiveness of political communication.[8] These shifting uses of communicative networks and media can help us recognize the importance of placing collective assemblies into longer trajectories of efforts to gain recognition. To conclude, then, I turn to the mechanisms through which "attention" has been channeled within India's changing mediascapes to enable groups to gain audiences with those in positions of authority, and to the influence of these shifting mechanisms on the relationships between the activities of formal political parties and other types of activism in India today.

As the preceding chapters show, collective performances are not uniformly successful, do not always produce the desired recognition (or do so immediately), and do not necessarily bring about sudden or lasting political change. Nor, in India, are many forms of collective action spontaneous, despite sometimes being portrayed as such. Instead, they often develop in the context of purposeful campaigns, building on and intensifying earlier efforts, and mediated by institutions, organizations, political parties, and other intermediaries. Collective assemblies function as efforts to assess, display, and expand levels of popular support, in effect serving as popular referenda for particular agendas, movements, positions, or electoral representatives. A closer look at spectacular attention-garnering strategies, which often require weeks or even months of preparation and large expenditures, reveals their often deep connections with state institutional structures and organized political parties. Yet recent events also suggest that the nature of these relationships between movements and political parties is not unidirectional. If formal political parties (including those in power) once saw themselves as organizing and leading social movements, as well as engaging in formal campaigns to educate and recruit constituents into political subjectivity and support, collective actions today also suggest that political parties follow popular social movements and compete with one another to get in front of them. In doing so they often seek to claim leadership of movements that have much longer histories of painstaking structural building efforts.

Many elected officials and others in positions of authority in India today recognize the importance of maintaining and continuing to expand their connections—in all directions, not simply upward—to preserve crucial access to information.[9] The continued openness of many politicians in India to regular face-to-face audiences and direct interactions with their constituents helps enable this access.[10] To maintain their positions, elected officials—and political parties more generally—need to keep their fingers on the pulse of the public, particularly at the local level. This also explains why politicians and parties so often try to position themselves as leaders within emergent social movements, as the examples of the Kerala women's wall, the Bihar human chain, and the Telangana movement all illustrate.

The successful women's wall in Kerala on January 1, 2019, for example, was not spontaneous but was organized by the state's ruling political coalition—led by the Communist Party of India (Marxist) party—in cooperation with 176 social and political organizations. Yet many women's groups who had devoted themselves to this and related issues for the preceding quarter century were annoyed by the state's late entrance and effort to claim credit for the event and by the diversion of state funds "from the fund earmarked for women's safety" to fund the women's wall event instead. Many were also frustrated by the state's failure to provide police protection to women in the wake of the Supreme Court decision, finding it unsettling that the ruling party would put so much energy into a one-day promotional stunt but not into the day-to-day support and protection of women.[11] The feminist historian J. Devika was one among a number of feminist scholars who found it difficult to celebrate the women's wall; she felt that, rather than marking a significant liberating moment, it served to mask the continuing "insidious presence of modern patriarchy in all institutions in Kerala, including the mainstream Left."[12]

The 2017 Bihar human chain in support of a complete ban on the sale of liquor in the state was similarly led by the state's chief minister, Nitish Kumar, with the support of women's organizations and opposition parties, although it also drew criticism from those who felt the event was used "to promote [the chief minister's] own self and brand" and that it "forced school children" to participate.[13] A similar event the following year, this time in opposition to dowry and child marriage, drew even more criticism and less support from opposition parties.[14] In both cases, an elaborate organizational structure was put into place, making use of the existing network of government officials and encouraging governmental employees and schoolchildren to participate, and tens of millions of rupees of government money were spent to organize, publicize, and document the event.[15] Both the women's wall and the Bihar cases are examples of political parties seeking to belatedly get out in front of and place themselves at the helm of a popular movement that has already gained widespread support.

Jeffrey Schnapp and Matthew Tiews note that "forms of mass assembly and collective social action . . . reached their apogee in the first half of the twentieth century" and "began to attenuate gradually in the second half of the century, particularly in the wake of the protest movements of the 1960s and 1970s, as a result of the proliferation and ever-increasing prevalence of virtual or media-based forms of 'assembly' over physical assemblies in postindustrial societies."[16] Yet the examples offered in this chapter and throughout this book suggest that corporeal presence in public space is actually becoming even more important. Even with the advent of social media and virtual connectivity, physical presence in public space is still a necessary part of the political, reinforcing John Parkinson's observations that physical assemblies in public spaces provide the content for both media reporting and social media posts.[17] The images that dominate media are generated by "real people who take up, occupy, share, and contest physical space," reminding us that democracy depends on the physical presence of people within public space, whether it be at campaign rallies or inaugural events, indoor public meetings to deliberate over policies, or outdoor public events like the ones during the Telangana movement that sought to hold elected officials accountable to their campaign promises.[18]

The examples offered in this book suggest that the accessibility of physical, public space for political uses, even in our increasingly digitally mediated world, is essential to democracy's survival.[19] Yet restrictions on the uses of spaces like Dharna Chowk in Hyderabad and Jantar Mantar in Delhi have grown in recent decades as urban administrators seek to transform urban spaces into their visions of "world-class" cities. Limits on the uses of public space for political purposes can be understood as an assault on democracy and as an effort to prevent participation and silence disparate voices. Those whose views are already audible and recognized have little need to escalate their efforts or act collectively. However, those whose voices are not already able to be heard rely for amplification on access to public buildings, the spaces adjacent to them, and the attention of elected and appointed officials who work in them.

## Placing Collective Actions in the Context of Longer Genealogies

All this suggests that collective public performances are not only still important in attracting the attention needed to be heard in the public sphere—particularly if one is not a member of a historically dominant community—but that they also may be becoming even *more* important than ever. In advocating for a relational approach to the study of Indian democracy—one that takes seriously not only electoral institutions but also the ongoing relationships and interactions connecting voters with elected officials between elections—this book seeks to place each of the forms of political practice analyzed into a longer genealogy of practice. This is not a study of clientelism or patronage that assumes permanent fixed relationships or quid pro quo reciprocal obligations or payments. Instead, it sees collective assemblies as efforts by citizens to amplify voices, perform and strengthen power, gain audience, and create channels that can facilitate communication with elected officials and government administrators. In doing so, the book distinguishes between efforts to incite violence or riots as a way of asserting alternate forms of sovereignty or silencing others, and efforts to seek political recognition and inclusion within existing state decision-making processes. In the case of the Kerala women's wall, the more than five million women who participated stood peacefully, arms linked along the 620 kilometers. Members of political and religious organizations who opposed the Supreme Court's decision to grant men and women equal access to the temple, however, participated in violent reprisals against the women who attempted to enter. These opposition groups also engaged in street fights, arson, attacks on journalists, damage to state-owned buses, and destruction of government offices, buildings, and libraries—violently targeting both those whose views they opposed and the state.[20] Their action was not an appeal to the state for recognition or to adjudicate the dispute, but rather an effort to claim sovereignty and the right to adjudicate for themselves, opposing the state while targeting those with whom they disagreed. This is reminiscent of the distinction made in chapter 4 between the early eighteenth-century Spitalfields weavers—who took the law into their own hands by targeting women wearing imported silks in an era in which representatives of the state were not yet targets of collective action in Europe—and those in the Indian textile industry at the same time who used collective action to bring their grievances to the state-like authorities of the East India Company for adjudication.

Just as the women's wall was a culmination of two and a half decades of organization, the Telangana movement also did not occur spontaneously or in isolation. It built on the legal, social, and political activism of the previous decades, gaining the support of the political parties only after popular support reached a critical mass and it was clear that associating with the movement was in the political interests of the ruling coalition. Similarly, the processions, long-distance yātras, and ticketless travel that have supported collective assemblies and rallies in cities throughout India also have much longer histories that can benefit from the types of close examination and contextualization illustrated in this book.

## Indian Democracy between Elections

Rousseau, in *The Social Contract*, wrote, "The English people thinks it is free; it is greatly mistaken, it is free only during the election of Members of Parliament; as soon as they are elected, it is enslaved, it is nothing."[21] If we take seriously Thomas Jefferson's assertion that "the people are the only censors of their governors" and that "even their errors will tend to keep these to the true principles of their institutions," then we must be willing to closely examine the kind of political activity that occurs between elections, evaluating its role in holding elected officials accountable to their campaign promises.[22] We must also maintain a focus on government efforts to encourage, limit, or constrain such activity.

As I have argued throughout the book, in the context of the world's largest democracy, many—though certainly not all—collective actions are neither efforts to undermine the legitimacy of the existing state nor protests *against* anything; rather, they are appeals *for* something. In the process of making such appeals—for recognition, for equal rights, for full implementation of existing legal structures, for economic equity, or for accountability to electoral promises—such collective actions also often have the effect of reifying and strengthening the power, legitimacy, and authority of the state rather than weakening it. When the state is responsive to those appeals, trust in the state and its representatives is strengthened. In addition, many recent collective actions in India have been performed collaboratively by state and nonstate actors working *together*, as the examples of the women's wall and other human chains make clear.

My goal in this book has been to rewrite the history of democracy by attending not just to the introduction of formal electoral representative institutions but also to the practices that occur between elections. Analysis of the long histories of forms of political practice that use public spaces to engage with authorities, compel recognition, and hold officials accountable show that these continue to play an important role in contemporary Indian politics. A wide range of such practices use road and railway spaces as mechanisms for hailing the state, seeking recognition from electoral representatives, and gaining representation. The preceding chapters see these spaces not only as transportation systems but also as technologized communication networks capable of dramatically amplifying messages by telegraphing them across the length and breadth of the country and from the margins to the center. I also demonstrate that not everyone has equal access to these networks and that a practice regarded as political when undertaken by one group may be deemed criminal when used by others. Over time, collective action can help bring about recognition, even if—as in the Telangana, Dalit, and women's movements—it may require weeks, months, years, or even decades to achieve.

A common strategy for continuing to prevent the recognition of new voices is to expand restrictions on the uses of public spaces by requiring permits, placing restrictions on access, or otherwise limiting collective political occupations of space. Part I places the contemporary practices of sit-ins, hunger demonstrations, rallies, strikes, and other mechanisms for compelling an audience with authorities into longer genealogies of engagements with the state. Part II traces the state's efforts to ban or otherwise restrict such actions. Colonial-era sedition and unlawful assembly legal strictures continue to provide opportunities for police and elected officials to overextend their authority in postcolonial India and to silence both dissent and efforts to give voice to concerns, seek audience, ensure the equitable application of existing laws, enable participation in deliberation and decision making, and hold elected officials accountable. But it is also the case that redefining criminal acts as political can offer sometimes surprising options to authorities for silencing dissent, as the case of alarm chain pulling has shown. These examples highlight the critical role of debates among state officials in defining the line between the criminal and the political and demonstrate the law's sometimes arbitrary origins. This ability to make discretionary decisions about who should be allowed to transgress existing laws while engaging in political communication points to the fuzziness of existing legal structures and their potential for abuse. Authorities can and do use their discretion to restrict collective actions, as recent uses of colonial-era sedition and unlawful assembly laws in India demonstrate.[23] Freedom of assembly, freedom of speech, and freedom of the press have long been held to be essential to a healthy democracy. Yet threats to these freedoms have not disappeared in the world's largest democracy; indeed, recent evidence suggests they are growing.[24] Suspicion and pessimism toward the state on the part of the Left and anarchists, including within academic scholarship, have made it easier for libertarians, small-state conservatives, and advocates of neoliberalism to roll back democratic protections and safeguards, downsize regulatory frameworks and institutions, and limit the role of the state in producing a more equitable distribution of education, employment, property, and income.

The evidence offered throughout this book traces the history of an infrastructure of the political and suggests that more, not less, freedom to use public space for political assembly is fundamental to the process of making social and political structures more equitable. But it also suggests that this is often why those in positions of authority are reluctant to recognize collective action as a form of political communication.[25] This book emphasizes the importance of situating corporeal political practices like sit-ins and hunger strikes, mass outdoor meetings, general strikes, alarm chain pulling, road and rail blockades, ticketless travel, marches, pilgrimages, processions, and human chains within longer genealogies of practice that precede and have shaped the formal introduction of institutions and practices of electoral democracy. It also stresses the importance of attending to the different audiences that such practices seek to address, offering an important intervention and supplement to the ways that democracy is understood today. Such practices cannot simply be described as the practices of a particular segment of the population, subaltern or otherwise, or as representing a "style" of political engagement unique to particular groups, as chapter 2 argues. Instead, they offer recourse for amplification when other methods of engaging with the state and its representatives are unsuccessful. Viewing practices outside the West not as bastardized forms of democracy or as failures to measure up to others' norms, but rather as having a history worth theorizing in their own right, offers new tools for analyzing the uses of public space not only in India but also elsewhere in the world, including in the West. At the very least, such contextualization can help us reevaluate the historical and social scientific categories and oppositions that have been bequeathed to us and recognize forms of collective assembly as fundamental to the infrastructure of democracy—and therefore as essential considerations in approaching decision making related to the creation, protection, accessibility, and maintenance of spaces of assembly.

INTRODUCTION

1 *Jana* (adj., from *janam*, n., people, folk) and *prajā* (adj., people's, public, from *praja*, n., people, folk) are widely used in Telugu in conjunction with the noun *garjana* (roar) to refer to an outdoor collective assembly. Exceptionally large gatherings often also include the adjective *maha* (great or large). For a more detailed discussion of garjana, see chapter 3. Although crowd estimates are notoriously difficult to determine, estimates of attendees ranged from 1.2 to 2.5 million. The *Economic Times* included the December 16, 2010, Telangana Maha Garjana in a list of the largest political rallies in world history, estimating that more people were present than in the 1963 civil rights march on Washington, DC; in Tiananmen Square on June 4, 1989; in the February 15, 2003, antiwar protest in London (described as "the largest-ever political demonstration in UK history"); or in the 2004 Orange Revolution in Kiev ("Largest Political Rallies across the World," *Economic Times*, September 30, 2013). See also "KCR Fails to Roar at Garjana," *Times of India*, December 17, 2010. Numerous other articles (perhaps citing the capacity of the assembly grounds at Prakashreddypeta, Hanamkonda) suggest there were 25 lakhs (2.5 million) in attendance; for example, "TRS Maha Garjana: We Are Losing Our Patience on Telangana," *Siasat*, December 16, 2010.

2 "Traffic Blocked for over 20 km: Half the People on the Roads," *Andhra Jyothi*, December 17, 2010; "Telangana Maha Garjana: Traffic Jam up to 35 km," *Eenadu*, December 17, 2010.

3 Andhra State was formed in 1953 from two predominantly Telugu-speaking regions of the former Madras State (Coastal Andhra and Rayalaseema). A third Telugu-speaking region, Telangana, had been part of the Nizam's state of Hyderabad, India's largest princely state, and was never under direct British rule. After the States Reorganisation Act of 1956, which reorganized many of the states of India along linguistic lines, Hyderabad State was split into three linguistic portions, with predominantly Marathi-speaking districts added to the existing Bombay State, Kannada districts to Mysore State, and Telugu districts combined with Coastal Andhra and Rayalaseema to form the new state of Andhra Pradesh. Widespread opposition to this linguistic merger existed from its very inception, with fears that Telangana, already underdeveloped, would be disadvantaged economically.

Opposition swelled during several periods—especially in 1969, 1985, and 1999—with the most recent efforts occurring in the wake of the formation of the Telangana Rashtra Samiti in 2001. See Seshadri, "Telangana Agitation"; Forrester, "Subregionalism in India"; Gray, "Demand for a Separate Telangana"; Simhadri and Vishweshwar Rao, *Telangana*; Kannabiran et al., "On the Telangana Trail"; and Muppidi, *Politics in Emotion*.

4  Thirmal Reddy Sunkari, "Telangana Roars at Karimnagar," *Mission Telangana*, September 13, 2011, http://missiontelangana.com/telangana-roars-at-karimnagar/. See also Gowrishankar, *Ā 42 Rōjulu*. On the administrative stalling after publicly announcing in Parliament the creation of the new state on December 9, 2009, see Pingle, *Fall and Rise of Telangana*, 1 and 105.

5  Gowrishankar, *Ā 42 Rōjulu*.

6  An electoral promise to create Telangana as one of four new states was first made in the 1999 general election as one among a number of promises made by the Bharatiya Janata Party (BJP)–led National Democratic Alliance (NDA), which included the Telugu Desam Party (TDP) as one of the parties in the alliance. Ultimately, however, the NDA created only three of the four states, leaving the promise of Telangana unfulfilled. In the 2004 general election, the Congress Party–led United Progressive Alliance allied with the newly formed Telangana Rashtra Samiti and "capitalized on the Telangana sentiment to drive the TDP and its ally, the BJP, out of power in the state and at the centre," but they, too, "did not deliver" (Pingle, *Fall and Rise of Telangana*, 100–103). In the 2009 election, all of the major political parties pledged their support and promised to bifurcate the state and create Telangana. But following Home Minister P. Chidambaram's announcement of a resolution to move forward, a backlash from landowners and political leaders in Coastal Andhra caused the government to backpedal on their promise (Pingle, *Fall and Rise of Telangana*, 105; Mahesh Vijapurkar, "Telangana: Of Broken Promises and Congress's 'Catch 22,'" *Rediff News*, December 16, 2009).

7  The day after the Warangal Jana Garjana, on December 17, 2010, Mohammed Bouazizi, a Tunisian street vendor, set himself on fire in response to police harassment, launching what came to be known as the Arab Spring. Just five days after, the Karimnagar Jana Garjana, a group of activists in New York City, took over Zuccotti Park, launching the Occupy Movement. Although both the Arab Spring and the Occupy movements prompted worldwide media coverage and an initial sense of optimism and possibility, their long-term impacts have been less impressive. On the paucity of international media coverage of the Telangana movement, see Muppidi, *Politics in Emotion*.

8  Interview, feminist activist, Hyderabad, August 15, 2012.

9  Pingle, *Fall and Rise of Telangana*, 100–109.

10  On October 31, 2019, the Indian state of Jammu and Kashmir was reconstituted into two union territories, "Ladakh" and "Jammu and Kashmir," removing the former state's government and placing the two new territories under the central administration of the Government of India. This reduced the number of Indian states to twenty-eight.

11 Population data taken from Government of India, *Census of India 2011*. Wealth measured by GDP per capita in 2013 (Parilla et al., *Global Metro Monitor 2014*, 4).

12 Frustrations on the part of local Hyderabadis at their exclusion from government administrative positions first emerged in the mid-nineteenth century, leading to the development of two distinct categories: "non-Mulki" (applied to bureaucrats and administrators recruited from British-ruled North India brought in to help modernize Hyderabad's administrative systems) and "Mulki" (locals or natives). See Leonard, "Hyderabad"; Haragopal, "Telangana People's Movement."

13 Ravinder Kaur, "How a Farmers' Protest in India Evolved into a Mass Movement that Refuses to Fade," *New Statesman*, February 19, 2021.

14 Sukhbir Siwach, "Explained: How Farmers Have Tweaked Protest Strategy to Stay Put at Delhi Borders for Many More Months," *Indian Express*, March 2, 2021.

15 "Farmer Agitation: Centre Issues 'Formal Letter' Agreeing to Farmers' Demands," *Economic Times*, December 10, 2021.

16 The Hindi term *morchā* (lit., a "front" or "battlefront"; *mōracā* in Marathi, "A battery: also fortified lines or fortifications") is also sometimes used to describe rallies, processions, mass public gatherings, and protests, as well as efforts to motivate a meeting with a government official. It also appears in the names of political organizations (in the connotation of a "front'), such as the Maratha Kranti Morcha, the Gorkha Janmukti Morcha, and the BJP Dakshina Kannada Yuva Morcha, which regularly lobby the state and organize such actions. For Hindi definitions, see Bahri, *Learner's Hindi-English Dictionary*, 525; Chaturvedi, *Practical Hindi-English Dictionary*, 622. For Marathi, see Molesworth, *Dictionary, Marathi and English*, 394.

17 For a critique of democracy as an "idea," see Mitchell, *Carbon Democracy*, 2–3.

18 In focusing on acts that hail the state, I am aware of the complexities surrounding the concept of the state (see, for example, Abrams, "Notes on the Difficulty of Studying the State"; and Mitchell, "The Limits of the State"). However, I use the term here to stand in for the range of elected representatives and appointed officials who populate "the State" as defined in the Indian Constitution: "Unless the context otherwise requires, 'the State' includes the Government and Parliament of India and the Government and the Legislature of each of the States and all local or other authorities within the territory of India or under the control of the Government of India" (excerpted from Article 12 of the Indian Constitution).

19 On the panoptic expansion of state power, see Foucault, *Discipline and Punish*. On the ocular capacities of democracies analyzed from the perspective not of states but of citizens, see Green, *Eyes of the People*. Green highlights Max Weber's discussion of the people's role in subjecting elected officials to surveillance that "would render politicians in mass democracy *responsible*" (156, emphasis in original).

20 Althusser, "Ideology and Ideological State Apparatuses," 173–75.

21 Althusser, *Reproduction of Capitalism*, 70; Althusser, "Ideology and Ideological State Apparatuses," 174 (emphasis in original).

22 Althusser, "Ideology and Ideological State Apparatuses."

23 Agha, "Meet Mediatization," 168. My thanks to Indivar Jonnalagadda for drawing my attention to Agha's reading of Althusser (Jonnalagadda, "Citizenship as a Communicative Effect," 541).

24 Agha, "Meet Mediatization," 168 (emphasis added).

25 Foucault, "Governmentality," 102–3 (emphasis added).

26 Foucault, "Governmentality," 100. See also Foucault, *Security, Territory, Population*; *Birth of Biopolitics*; "Subject and Power"; and "Technologies of the Self"; and Burchell, Gordon, and Miller, *Foucault Effect*.

27 Shah, *Nightmarch*, 12–25. However, even the term *revolution*, typically associated with the overthrow of the existing state, is sometimes understood in South Asia as describing the hailing of state attention. Describing the "revolution" declared by the Dalit Panther movement in Bombay, Juned Shaikh writes, "In Bombay, this revolutionary fervor demanded responsiveness from the democratically elected municipal, state, and federal government in meeting Dalit demands, which included housing and employment" (Shaikh, *Outcaste Bombay*, 135).

28 I am grateful to Lisa Björkman, whose essay "The Ostentatious Crowd" offers an excellent model of this type of attention and from whose thinking I have greatly benefited.

29 India's Constitution includes a list of historically disadvantaged groups ("Scheduled Castes," or those once regarded as "untouchable" by orthodox Hinduism, and "Scheduled Tribes" or Indigenous groups) who were designated to benefit from affirmative action quotas in government employment and admission into government educational institutions. Additional groups have lobbied to be included in the expansion of these reserved quotas (see note 48).

30 Hansen, *Wages of Violence*; Mehta, *Maximum City*; Valiani, *Militant Publics in India*; Ghassem-Fachandi, *Pogrom in Gujarat*; Asim Ali, "'Hindu Rashtra': How Hindutva Has Created a Self-Propelled Market of Mobs," *The Quint*, April 19, 2022; Pratap Bhanu Mehta, "With Eyes Wide Open, We're Hurtling into an Abyss," *Indian Express*, April 26, 2022. See Frykenberg, "On Roads and Riots," for an early example of the use of a hartāl by dominant caste groups to prevent lower castes from accessing a "public" road.

31 Govindrajan, Joshi, and Rizvi, "Majoritarian Politics in South Asia"; Anderson and Longkumer, "'Neo-Hindutva'"; Ramdev, Nambiar, and Bhattacharya, *Sentiment, Politics, Censorship*; Rollier, Frøystad, and Ruud, *Outrage*; Hansen, *The Saffron Wave*; Jaffrelot, *Hindu Nationalist Movement*.

32 The widespread protests against the 1990 efforts to implement the Mandal Commission's Report included roadblocks (*The Tribune*, Chandigarh, August 31, 1990), rallies, demonstrations, self-immolations by upper-caste college students, and attacks on government buildings and property (Guha, *India after Gandhi*, 602–4). See also "Mandal Commission."

33 Bedi, *Dashing Ladies of Shiv Sena*; Jaffrelot, "Hindu Nationalist Reinterpretation of Pilgrimage."

34 Taylor, "Politics of Recognition"; Fraser, "From Redistribution to Recognition?" and "Rethinking Recognition"; Glen Coulthard, "Indigenous Peoples and

the "Politics of Recognition,'" *IC*, May 6, 2007, https://intercontinentalcry.org/indigenous-peoples-and-the-politics-of-recognition/.

35  As Charles Taylor famously frames the issue, "Collective goals may require restrictions on the behavior of individuals that may violate their [individual] rights" (Taylor, "Politics of Recognition," 55).

36  *Dalit* is a term "widely used to describe India's former untouchables" (Rawat and Satyanarayana, *Dalit Studies*, 2).

37  See, for example, Elizabeth Povinelli's discussion of the ways that those who have been empowered to act as representatives often seek to protect their own privileged positions by denying recognition to those who do not conform to impossible standards of "authentic cultural tradition" (Povinelli, *Cunning of Recognition*).

38  Mitchell, "Visual Turn in Political Anthropology."

39  The creation of these four smaller states has been widely regarded as a response to economic and cultural marginalization. On the role of the region in cultivating and producing cultural differences among those who appear to be speakers of the "same" language, see Srinivas, "Maoism to Mass Culture."

40  Ortner, "Dark Anthropology," 49–50.

41  Ortner, "Dark Anthropology," 50–51.

42  Ortner argues that the same is true of Marx: "Although there are certain optimistic aspects of Marxist theory, the Marx in play in anthropological theory today is primarily the darkest Marx, who emphasized the enrichment of the wealthy and powerful at the expense of the poor and powerless, and the relentless global expansion of capitalism as a brutal and dehumanizing social and economic formation" (Ortner, "Dark Anthropology," 51).

43  Ortner, "Dark Anthropology," 58–60. See Robbins, "Beyond the Suffering Subject."

44  As the work of Ramnarayan Rawat shows, activism among Dalits in Uttar Pradesh sought recognition outside Dalit neighborhoods from as early as the 1920s but only became more widely visible, audible, and recognized from the 1980s and 1990s (Rawat, *Reconsidering Untouchability*). As a result, many scholars assume that Dalit political activism during the earlier decades was nonexistent, rather than recognizing that it was the "political arrival" of Dalits that enabled recognition by a much wider audience which has only recently become aware of their political activism; see, for example, Jaffrelot, *India's Silent Revolution*.

45  On the placing of limits on violence, see Balibar, "Three Concepts of Politics." On upper-caste violence and the failure of the state to place checks on this violence as an important catalyst for Dalit political mobilization, see Satyanarayana, "Dalit Reconfiguration of Caste," 46; Muthukkaruppan, "Critique of Caste Violence" and "Dalit."

46  Scott, *Art of Not Being Governed*, *Two Cheers for Anarchism*, and *Against the Grain*; Graeber, *The Democracy Project*; Von Mises, *Human Action*; Hayek, *The Constitution of Liberty*; Friedman and Friedman, *Free to Choose*; Friedman, *Capitalism and Freedom*.

47 Such quotas predate independence. For a discussion of the Mulki (local/native) versus Non-Mulki (nonlocal/migrant) employment debates in the Nizam State of Hyderabad going back to the mid-nineteenth century, see Narayana Rao, *Internal Migration Policies in an Indian State*; Leonard, "Hyderabad: The Mulki–Non-Mulki Conflict"; and on the relationship between reservations for local natives and education, Datla, *The Language of Secular Islam*, 125–26.

48 In 1950, the Indian Constitution introduced reservation quotas in government-aided educational institutions and public sector employment for two histori-cally disadvantaged groups—15% for members of designated Scheduled Castes (groups who had been regarded as "untouchable" by orthodox Hinduism) and 7.5% for members of designated Scheduled Tribes (Indigenous groups). In 1991, spurred by the 1980 Mandal Commission Report, an additional 27% of seats in government-aided educational institutions and public sector employment were reserved for Other Backward Classes (OBCs), bringing the total to 49.5%. On January 14, 2019, the 103rd amendment to the Indian Constitution awarded an additional 10% reservations for members of Economically Weaker Sections (EWS) within the general category (communities that had previously been ineli-gible for reservations, including members of upper-caste groups), bringing the total to 59.5%. See Subramanian, "Meritocracy and Democracy"; Nath, "Employ-ment Scenario and the Reservation Policy."

49 Habermas, *Structural Transformation* (see especially sections VI and VII).

50 Fraser, "Rethinking the Public Sphere." For another critique of Habermas, see Lilti, *World of the Salons*.

51 Fraser, "Rethinking the Public Sphere," 68.

52 Fraser, "Rethinking the Public Sphere," 61 (emphasis added). See also Warner, *Publics and Counterpublics*.

53 Nivedita Menon similarly suggests that it is more useful to see differences of "style" not as reflecting "actual empirical groupings" but rather different "*styles of political engagement* that are available to people," and that "the availability is fluid and contextual, not fixed by class." Menon, "Introduction," 11–12 (emphasis in original).

54 Habermas, *Structural Transformation*, xviii.

55 Habermas, "Further Reflections," 456.

56 For a discussion of the role of street politics in the American Revolution and in subsequent decades, see Gilje, *Road to Mobocracy*. On the role of labor strikes, particularly among coal miners, railway employees, and dockworkers, in expanding electoral participation in democracy, see Mitchell, *Carbon Democracy*.

57 Chatterjee, *Politics of the Governed*, 25.

58 Chatterjee, *Politics of the Governed*, 4.

59 Chatterjee, *Politics of the Governed*, 40.

60 Michael Collins, for example, shows that Dalits in Tamil Nadu use disruptions in public space to advocate for "the delivery of basic rights alongside an impartial administration of law," rather than as a form of "availing augmented welfare pro-

visions" or "wrangling tentative concessions from authorities" (Collins, "Recalling Democracy," 71).

61 Attention to the definitions of what constitute "universalist" and "particularist" ideals finds a parallel in Fraser's treatment of the spatial distinctions made between "public" and "private" interests. She writes, "These terms, after all, are not simply straightforward designations of societal spheres; they are cultural classifications and rhetorical labels. In political discourse, they are powerful terms that are frequently deployed to delegitimate some interests, views, and topics and to valorize others" ("Rethinking the Public Sphere," 73).

62 Mitchell, *Carbon Democracy*.

63 Mitchell cautions that this is not simply a replacement of "the idealist schemes of the democracy experts with a materialist account" but rather a careful attention to transformations that "involve establishing connections and building alliances . . . to translate one form of power into another" (Mitchell, *Carbon Democracy*, 7).

64 Mitchell, "Carbon Democracy," 406.

65 Professor G. Haragopal, address given on the one-year anniversary of the closing of Hyderabad's Dharnā Chowk [designated space for political assembly], Press Club, Somajiguda, Hyderabad, May 15, 2018, https://www.youtube.com/watch?v=N8qHBjDrrUs (translated from the Telugu original).

66 My focus not on consensus, stasis, and finality but on contestation, disagreement, and dynamic change has been influenced by Jacques Rancière, *Dissensus*, and Chantal Mouffe, *Chantal Mouffe: Hegemony*.

67 Kohli, "Introduction," 4.

68 Kohli, "Introduction," 4.

69 Jayal, "Introduction," 19–23. Dipesh Chakrabarty's discussion of continuities in political practices offer a notable exception, about which I say more in chapter 7.

70 Municipal and local boards, to which Indians were appointed, were formed in most of the provinces of British India in 1882. The British government's motivation was largely fiscal; it was able to shift financial responsibility for municipalities to Indians while still maintaining significant political control. The Indian Councils Act of 1861 set up provincial legislative councils in Madras, Bombay, and Bengal, and an 1892 act increased the number of nominated India representatives on these councils. See Seal, "Imperialism and Nationalism," 12–14. A Legislative Assembly was created by the Government of India Act of 1919 as the lower chamber of the Legislative Council, implementing the Montagu-Chelmsford recommendations of 1918. For a description of the Indian Legislative Assembly that was elected in British India from 1920 onward, see Indian Statutory Commission, *Report of the Indian Statutory Commission*, 164; Robb, *Government of India and Reform*.

71 Paley, "Introduction," 6.

72 Hansen, "Politics as Permanent Performance," 24. Hansen's characterization of Indian politics as permanent performance offers a very important intervention for understanding democracy not just in India but also elsewhere in the world. At the same time, he grounds his analysis in the Shiv Sena's usage of forms of

political practice that he characterizes as "a politics of spectacle." Approaching their *style* of practice/performance as what sets them apart leaves open the question of whether practices that appear similar across varied contexts can be distinguished through the different audiences they address and the ends toward which they are striving. In the Telangana movement, for example, a similar "politics of spectacle" was used to hold political parties to their campaign promises rather than to assert an alternative sovereignty by displaying the ability to engage in violence with impunity (see note 6).

73  Stern, *The Company-State*.
74  See chapter 4.
75  On the former, see Pandey, *Construction of Communalism*; Ziad, "Mufti 'Iwāz." Ziad offers examples of contemporary historians who have been overly quick to accept colonial representations of the 1816 "Disturbances at Bareilli" as the result of Wahhabism.
76  Shiffman et al., *Beyond Zuccotti Park*; Bayat, *Revolution without Revolutionaries*; Dabashi, *Arab Spring*.
77  For an overview, see Schnapp and Tiews, *Crowds*.
78  Mazzarella, "Myth of the Multitude."
79  Mazzarella, "Myth of the Multitude," 698, 700.
80  Mazzarella, "Myth of the Multitude," 713. Hardt and Negri's more recent book, *Assembly*, published in 2017, could also be included within this latter position.
81  Hardt and Negri, *Multitude*, 357.
82  Mazzarella, "Myth of the Multitude," 727.
83  Manin, *Principles of Representative Government*, 8. For a proposed new model of representative government that addresses this lack, see Landemore, *Open Democracy*.
84  Manin, *Principles of Representative Government*, 1.
85  In public talks, I have repeatedly been asked why I frame practices that predate the formal implementation of electoral institutions in India as part of the history of Indian democracy.
86  Mazzarella, "Myth of the Multitude," 700.
87  Schnapp and Tiews, *Crowds*, xi.
88  Butler, *Performative Theory of Assembly*, 85.
89  Chakrabarty, "Early Railwaymen in India" and "'In the Name of Politics,'" 38.
90  Azzellini and Sitrin, *They Can't Represent Us!*, 41.
91  Frank, "Beyond Democracy's Imaginary Investments."
92  Gilje, *Road to Mobocracy*, 27.
93  Thomas Jefferson to James Madison, January 30, 1787, in Appleby and Ball, *Jefferson*, 108.
94  Thomas Jefferson to Edward Carrington, January 16, 1787, in Appleby and Ball, *Jefferson*, 153. Gilje, *Road to Mobocracy*, 71.
95  Gilje, *Road to Mobocracy*, 42.
96  Gilje, *Road to Mobocracy*, 1–3.

97   James Madison, "Federalist 63," in Hamilton, Madison, and Jay, *Federalist Papers*, 387, quoted in Manin, *Principles of Representative Government*, 2.

98   *Dire De L'abbé Sieyes*, 12, quoted in Manin, *Principles of Representative Government*, 2–3.

99   Manin, *Principles of Representative Government*, 232.

100  Hyderabad, August 21, 2012. In keeping with ethnographic convention, names have been changed to protect the privacy of my interlocutors.

101  Hyderabad, August 21, 2012.

102  Hyderabad, August 20, 2012.

103  For examples of related projects, on Senegal, see Schaffer, *Democracy in Translation*; on Argentina, see Sabato, *The Many and the Few*; on Yemen, see Wedeen, "The Politics of Deliberation."

104  Parkinson, *Democracy and Public Space*, 2, 11. For attention to virtual political mobilization, see Hardt and Negri, *Assembly*. For a nuanced discussion of the historical reconfiguration of the work of politics in an era of networked social media, see Tufekci, *Twitter and Tear Gas*.

105  Parkinson, *Democracy and Public Space*, 4.

106  Parkinson, *Democracy and Public Space*. For a discussion of the former, see his chapter 6; for the latter, see chapter 7.

107  For additional discussion of the relationship between public space and democracy in Western contexts, see Henaff and Strong, *Public Space and Democracy*; and in the context of Latin America, see Avritzer, *Democracy and the Public Space*. From the discipline of geography, see Barnett and Low, *Spaces of Democracy*. Rudolph and Rudolph, *In Pursuit of Lakshmi*; Frankel et al., *Transforming India*; Jayal, *Democracy in India*; Kohli, *Success of India's Democracy*; Chatterjee, "Violence of the State" and *Politics of the Governed*; and Bhargava, *Promise of India's Secular Democracy*, offer an introduction to the vast literature on democracy in India. For anthropological approaches to Indian democracy, see Appadurai, "Deep Democracy"; Gupta, "Blurred Boundaries" and *Red Tape*; Spencer, *Anthropology, Politics and the State*; Banerjee, "Democracy, Sacred and Everyday" and *Why India Votes?*; and Michelutti, *Vernacularisation*. From communication studies, see Gaonkar, "On Cultures of Democracy." On Bangladesh, see Chowdhury, *Paradoxes of the Popular*; and Suykens, "Hartal." On Nepal, see Lakier, "Highway and the Chakka Jam," "Illiberal Democracy," "Public of the Bandh," and "Spectacle of Power"; and Kunreuther, *Voicing Subjects* and "Sounds of Democracy." It is worth considering why theorists have been more interested in the study of public space in the context of processes of democratization than in contexts where democracy is already established.

108  Mitchell, *Language, Emotion, and Politics*.

109  See chapter 5, note 31.

110  According to the Indian Railways, 6.219 billion passengers are transported annually, for an average of 17.04 million per day (Indian Railway Board, *Year Book 2006–2007*, 42); *Guinness World Records 2005*, 93.

111 On "the castefication of wage labor" see Pandian, "Building of Indian Railways." For a discussion of racially based strategies of employment in the Indian Railways, see Bear, *Lines of the Nation.* Prasad, "Tracking Modernity" offers a useful analysis of the ways in which class and identitarian divisions were shaped through the provision of railway facilities for the "traveling public."

112 Campbell, *Glimpses of the Nizam's Dominions,* 144.

113 Committee on Disturbances in Bombay, Delhi, and the Punjab, *Report,* 90.

114 "Mamata Banerjee Appeals to Public—Railway Is 'Your Own Service,'" *India-server.com,* February 24, 2010, http://www.india-server.com/news/mamata-banerjee-appeals-to-public-21780.html.

115 Guha, *Elementary Aspects,* 142–43.

116 As in Telangana, the 2006 Gujjar rail blockades and roadblocks in Rajasthan were a response to the failure of elected officials to implement their campaign promises—in this case, promises by the BJP during the 2003 state assembly elections to confer "Scheduled Tribe" status on the community (entitling them to reserved quotas in government employment and educational institutions).

117 Goswami, *Producing India,* 32–33, 59; Lefebvre, *Production of Space.*

118 Goswami, *Producing India,* 49.

119 For an early example of the relationship between roads and shifting forms of sociopolitical communication, see Frykenberg, "On Roads and Riots." For a more recent analysis of roads as sites for citizens' engagements with representatives of the state, see Annavarapu, "Moving Targets."

120 One example is the Telangana Rashtra Samiti's 250-kilometer "Maha Rasta Roko" event held on December 29, 2006. See "'Maha Rasta Roko' Peaceful," *The Hindu,* December 30, 2006.

121 Anjaria, *Slow Boil,* 8.

122 See also Anjaria and Rao, "Talking Back to the State"; and, in political science, Auerbach and Thachil, "How Clients Select Brokers"; Kruks-Wisner, *Claiming the State*; and Auerbach, *Demanding Development.*

123 Viewed in this way, the Telangana movement, for example, can be understood as a referendum on the inclusiveness of efforts to remake Hyderabad into a "world-class" city.

124 Burghart, "Conditions of Listening."

125 David Hardiman, for example, briefly acknowledges that Gandhi's *satyagraha* practices were influenced by existing Indian forms of protest against and dialogue with the state in India. But ultimately, he characterizes the mass civil resistance that Gandhi led as something associated with complex state systems and locates its emergence "in Europe in the ferment of the post-French revolutionary period." Mass civil resistance, he continues, "came from the sphere of civil society—the site of a free association of individuals in public bodies, associations and the like—which were valorized in the political thought of the Enlightenment as providing a means for checking and correcting the excesses of state power and governmental authority." Hardiman, *Gandhi,* 39. See chapter 4.

126 Manin, *Principles of Representative Government*, 236.

127 Manin, *Principles of Representative Government*, 236.

## ONE. SIT-IN DEMONSTRATIONS AND HUNGER STRIKES

Portions of chapter 1 originally appeared as "Spaces of Collective Representation: Urban Growth, Democracy, and Political Inclusion," White Paper Series for World Urban Forum, University of Pennsylvania, 2018.

1 Hardiman, *Gandhi*; Gandhi, *Gandhi*.

2 Hardiman, *Gandhi* (especially chapter 3); Spodek, "Gandhi's Political Methodology." Although Spodek argues that the political methods that influenced Gandhi were unique to the region in which Gandhi grew up, there is evidence of the long history of similar practices in other parts of the subcontinent as well (see chapter 4). For discussion of hunger strikes in a global context, see Scanlan et al., "Starving for Change"; Grant, *Last Weapons*; Shah, *Refusal to Eat*.

3 Mitchell, *Language, Emotion, and Politics*, 1–2, 16, 22, 90, 189–90, 205–7, 218–19. See also Sreeramulu, *Socio-Political Ideas*.

4 Mitchell, *Language, Emotion, and Politics*, 22. See also the medical report in Murthi, *Sri Potti Sriramulu*.

5 Mitchell, 2009, *Language, Emotion, and Politics*, 205. Many in the town of Nellore where he lived recalled him parading around town wearing signboards declaring the practice of untouchability to be a sin and advocating for inter-caste dining and temple-entry rights on behalf of Dalits, suggesting that his fasts were part of his larger political program.

6 Police statistics show that nearly two thousand protests were held at Dharna Chowk in 2016, of which approximately 1,500 were granted permits. See U. Sudhakar Reddy, "Dharna Chowk out of Hyderabad," *Deccan Chronicle*, February 24, 2017; Yunus Lasania, "In Search of a 'Dharna Chowk' in Hyderabad," *Livemint*, May 4, 2017.

7 "Anganwadi Workers Clash at Dharna Chowk in Hyderabad," *Hans India*, March 17, 2015; K. Sajaya, speech at "Prajā Gontuka Dharnā Chowk Pustakāviṣkaraṇa" [People's Voice Dharna Chowk Book Release], Press Club, Hyderabad, May 15, 2018; D. G. Narasimha Rao, speech at "Prajā Gontuka Dharnā Chowk Pustakāviṣkaraṇa" [People's Voice Dharna Chowk Book Release], Press Club, Hyderabad, May 15, 2018; Aihik Sur, "Thousands Swarm Dharna Chowk against CAA, NRC," *New Indian Express*, January 5, 2020. All speeches translated from Telugu.

8 K. Sajaya, speech, May 15, 2018.

9 Interview, Hyderabad, August 15, 2012.

10 K. Sajaya, speech, May 15, 2018.

11 From the Telugu definition of *dharnācēyu* (intransitive verb), Gwynn, *Telugu-English Dictionary*, 278; and the Hindi definition of *dharnā* (masculine noun), Chaturvedi, *Practical Hindi-English Dictionary*, 337.

12 Naidu was chief minister of the united Andhra Pradesh from 1995 to 2004. During this period, he explicitly sought to turn Hyderabad into another Singapore

while at the same time conceptualizing Indian cities as being in competition with one another. Focused especially on attracting IT, pharmaceutical, financial, health care, and biotech companies, he coined the phrase "Bye-Bye Bangalore, Hello Hyderabad" as part of his efforts to remake Hyderabad as the new Silicon Valley of India. He commissioned McKinsey and Company to produce a policy document, *Vision 2020*, to guide development in the state, implemented numerous market-based reforms, and sought to privatize health care and education. See Aparisim Ghosh, "South Asian of the Year: Chandrababu Naidu," *Time Asia*, December 31, 1999. After the bifurcation of the state in 2014, which resulted in the creation of the new state of Telangana from the districts surrounding Hyderabad, Naidu was elected chief minister of the new, smaller state of Andhra Pradesh from 2014 to 2019.

13  Similar demands for Dharna Chowks have arisen in other cities in Telugu-speaking south India, including Tirupati, Vijayawada (now located opposite Alankar Theatre) and Visakhapatnam (near the Collectorate). See "'Dharna Chowk' in Tirupati Sought," *The Hindu*, April 16, 2011; "Move to Shift Dharna Chowk Opposed," *The Hindu*, July 25, 2017; and Aditya Parankusam, "Vijay-awada to Have Own Dharna Chowk Soon," *Times of India*, September 26, 2015.

14  Whereas the original designated assembly space, Dharna Chowk, was located near Indira Park less than two kilometers from the State Secretariat, the four new sites proposed by Chandrashekar Rao are much farther away. Shamshabad, near the city's new airport, is twenty-seven kilometers south of the State Secretariat, Gandi Maisamma is twenty-six kilometers to the north, and Pratap Singaram is twenty-three kilometers to the east. Jawahar Nagar, the closest at just under twenty kilometers, is also the site of the Greater Hyderabad Municipal Corporation's garbage dump. See Aneri Shah, "Dharna Chowk Shifted to Hyderabad Outskirts," March 10, 2017. More recently, the Saroornagar stadium, a bit more than twelve kilometers from the State Secretariat, has also been proposed. "HC Allows Protests at Dharna Chowk," *Hans India*, November 14, 2018.

15  In April 2015, less than a year after becoming chief minister, Chandrashekar Rao approved plans for the construction of a new government multiplex cultural center opposite Indira Park that would feature four auditoriums, rehearsal theaters, seminar rooms, a library, an art museum, painting and sculpture galleries, restaurants, guest rooms, and extensive parking facilities. In January 2016, fourteen acres across from the park on the Dharna Chowk road were rezoned from open space to public and semipublic use, paving the way for the cultural center. This was done with no public discussion. See Padmaja Shaw, "Is Kalabharati the Real Reason Why the Telangana Government Wants the Dharna Chowk to Go?," *News Minute*, May 17, 2017.

16  This was made evident in the title of the publication released on May 15, 2018. See Dharnā Chowk Parirakṣaṇa Kamiṭī (Committee to Save Dharna Chowk), *Prajā Gontuka*.

17  Chāda Venkaṭareḍḍi, "Nirasana Gaḷāni (Dharnā Chowk)-ki Uccu Bigistārā? (Are You Tying a Noose around the Voice of Dissent [Dharna Chowk]?)," *Sākśi*, May 12, 2017 (reprinted in *Prajā Gontuka*, pp. 15–16). Translated from the Telugu original.

18 "Protests at Hyd's Dharna Chowk Can't Be Banned: HC Pulls up Telangana Govt," *The News Minute*, September 19, 2018.

19 "Telangana High Court Cannot Ban Dharna Chowk: Hyderabad High Court," *New Indian Express*, September 19, 2018.

20 Marri Ramu, "Protests Allowed at Dharna Chowk," *The Hindu,* November 14, 2018.

21 Sagar Kumar Mutha, "Open Dharna Chowk for Protests, Says HC," *Times of India*, November 14, 2018.

22 Mutha, "Open Dharna Chowk."

23 In 1991, a wide range of economic reforms was undertaken by the Indian government, including the lifting of restrictions on foreign direct investment, reductions in tariffs on imported goods, and expansion of licensing across industries. See "Looking Back and Looking Ahead"; Ahluwalia, "The 1991 Reforms"; and Nayyar, "Economic Liberalisation in India."

24 Mohite, "Designated Sites."

25 A. K. Sikri, "Mazdoor Kisan Shakti Sanghatan vs Union of India on 23 July, 2018," *Supreme Court of India*, para. 54, https://indiankanoon.org/doc /80616728/ (emphasis added). See also the Supreme Court judgment in "Anita Thakur vs Govt. of J&K on 12 August, 2016," para. 8, https://indiankanoon.org /doc/139222628/: "The 'right to assemble' is beautifully captured in an eloquent statement that 'an unarmed, peaceful protest procession in the land of "salt satyagraha," fast-unto-death and "do or die" is no jural anathema.' It hardly needs elaboration that a distinguishing feature of any democracy is the space offered for legitimate dissent. One cherished and valuable aspect of political life in India is a tradition to express grievances through direct action or peaceful protest. Organised, non-violent protest marches were a key weapon in the struggle for Independence, and the right to peaceful protest is now recognised as a fundamental right in the Constitution."

26 Delhi Police, Standing Order No. 10/2018, "Guidelines for Organizing Protests or Demonstrations at or Near Central Vista, including Jantar Mantar and Boat Club," November 22, 2018. Assemblies at Jantar Mantar are now limited to one thousand people per day (all groups combined), permission must be obtained in advance, and the temporary erection of tents is no longer permitted. Assemblies of up to 50,000 people may request permission to use the Ram Lila Maidan at Ajmer Gate. In addition, "programmes involving only school children duly escorted by their teachers or other peace loving groups for social, traffic & educational awareness will be allowed in the area of Boat Club"; "Candle vigil by school children . . . only in exceptional circumstances" is permitted, provided that "the gathering should not exceed 100 and participation should be symbolic highlighting social, education, health-related or environmental causes" (pp. 7–8). See also Aniruddha Ghosal, "End of a Protest: The Story of Jantar Mantar as a Protest Site Began in 1993," *Indian Express*, June 26, 2018.

27 Chakrabarty, "'In the Name of Politics.'"

28 Section 508, *Indian Penal Code* (1860), https://indiankanoon.org/doc/1734694/.

29 Sections 141–60, *Indian Penal Code* (1860), https://indiankanoon.org/doc/1569253/.

30 Section 144, *Code of Criminal Procedure* (1973), https://indiankanoon.org/doc/930621/.

31 Hyderabad ranked first on the 2020 JLL City Momentum Index, Kelly and Davies, *City Momentum Index 2020.*

32 Rahuldeep Gill, "India's Incomplete Democracy," *Los Angeles Times,* June 18, 2014.

33 Sikri, "Mazdoor Kisan Shakti Sanghatan vs. Union of India," paras. 53–54, https://indiankanoon.org/doc/80616728/.

34 Sikri, "Mazdoor Kisan Shakti Sanghatan vs. Union of India," para. 54.

35 Shore, "Facts, Customs, and Practices of the Hindus," 344–45. See also how it is altered and generalized in Maine, *Lectures on the Early History of Institutions,* 302–4.

36 Resident of Benares to Governor General in Council, October 11, 1792, Duncan Records, Regional State Archive, Allahabad, Basta 11, No. 63, cited in Singha, *Despotism of Law,* 86–89.

37 Singha, *Despotism of Law,* 88.

38 Singha, *Despotism of Law,* 88.

39 Singha, *Despotism of Law,* 89.

40 Singha, *Despotism of Law,* 89.

41 Monier-Williams, *Sanskrit-English Dictionary,* 515.

42 Hopkins, "Dying to Redress a Grievance," 146–47, n. 1.

43 Hopkins, "Dying to Redress a Grievance," 146.

44 Narayan, "Caste, Family and Politics," 197.

45 Rochisha Narayan, "Dharnas, Bribes and Spells: The Messy 'Business of the Adalat' and Social Relationships in Late Eighteenth-Century Banaras," paper presented in the South Asia Colloquium, University of Pennsylvania, November 21, 2013.

46 Freitag, *Collective Action and Community,* 44, 123.

47 Hopkins, "Dying to Redress a Grievance," 147.

48 Society for the Diffusion of Useful Knowledge, *The Hindoos,* 10–11.

49 Mitchell, "Civility and Collective Action." See also Dharampal, *Civil Disobedience,* and *Dharampal Papers.*

50 Society for the Diffusion of Useful Knowledge, *The Hindoos,* 10–11.

51 Singha, *Despotism of Law,* 87.

52 Maine, *Lectures on the Early History of Institutions,* 302.

53 Maine, *Lectures on the Early History of Institutions,* 304.

54 Shore, "Facts, Customs, and Practices of the Hindus," 332–33.

55 Menon, *Ramayana,* 144.

56 Menon, *Ramayana,* 144.

57 Mitchell, "Visual Turn in Political Anthropology," 539–40. See also chapter 7.

58 Interview, April 22, 2009.

59 Interview, April 21, 2009.

60 Interview, April 21, 2009.

61  Balagopal, *Karamchedu Massacre*, 9.

62  Interview, April 21, 2009. See also Balagopal, "Karamchedu: Second Anniversary."

63  Mohandas Karamchand Gandhi, also known as Mahatma Gandhi (1869–1948).

64  Mitchell, "Civility and Collective Action."

65  Gandhi, *Satyagraha*.

66  Reddy, *Telangāṇā Pōrāṭa Smṛtulu*, 1–3.

67  Reddy, *Telangāṇā Pōrāṭa Smṛtulu*, 1–3.

68  Conversation, Hyderabad, August 21, 2012.

69  Conversation, Hyderabad, August 21, 2012. Others also mentioned 1997 as the year when a critical shift occurred in access to public space (interview with activist from a women's organization, Hyderabad, August 23, 2012).

70  Conversation, Hyderabad, August 21, 2012.

71  Mitchell, "Visual Turn in Political Anthropology," 532–33. See also chapter 6.

72  Shashank Bengali, "In India, Upstart Aam Aadmi Party Is Shaking up Traditional Politics." *Los Angeles Times*, February 15, 2014.

73  Desouza, "Struggle for Local Government," 311.

74  Collins, "Recalling Democracy," especially chapter 3.

75  Lefebvre, *Production of Space*, 53; Butler, *Henri Lefebvre*, 49.

76  Parkinson, *Democracy and Public Space*, 18 (and also his chapter 7).

77  Swatanter Kumar, "Re—Ramlila Maidan Incident Dt . . . vs Home Secretary and Ors on 23 February, 2012," para. 200, https://indiankanoon.org/doc/17021567/.

78  Swatanter Kumar, "Re—Ramlila Maidan Incident," para. 200.

TWO. SEEKING AUDIENCE

1  Sandhya Ravishankar, "No University for Dalits," *The Wire*, January 21, 2016. This article inadvertently places the event in 2001 rather than 2002. See Anveshi Law Committee, "Caste and the Metropolitan University."

2  Aarefa Johari, "How Hyderabad's Ambedkar Students' Association Grew to Establish a National Footprint," *Scroll.in*, January 21, 2016.

3  Podile Appa Rao, the chief hostel warden in 2002, was made the vice chancellor of the University of Hyderabad in September 2015. Conflict between the administration and Dalit students continued under Appa Rao's vice chancellorship, leading to the suspension of Dalit PhD scholar Rohith Vemula and four other Dalit scholars shortly after he took office. In January 2016, following the confirmation of their suspension, Rohith Vemula committed suicide, sparking an international outcry. Appa Rao continued as vice chancellor after being placed on a two-month leave following Vemula's suicide.

4  Interview, February 2002.

5  Anveshi Law Committee, "Caste and the Metropolitan University," 1001.

6  The petition documents the appearance in the mess hall of posters offensive to the Dalit students on November 20 and 21, 2001, as well as their earlier memorandum to the vice chancellor, submitted on November 26, 2001, and asking him to "take action against a group of persons resorting to hate campaign against the deprived

sections and thereby insulting and humiliating the SC/ST students community"
(Petition to the Vice-Chancellor, University of Hyderabad, January 16, 2002).

7  "Castaway in Hyderabad," *The Hindu*, March 3, 2002.

8  Mitchell, *Language, Emotion, and Politics.*

9  Majumdar, *Ancient India*, 146.

10  Majumdar, *Ancient India*, 146.

11  Brown, *Telugu Nighaṇṭu* (1852), 282; Brown, *A Telugu-English Dictionary* (1903), 324; Gwynn, *Telugu-English Dictionary* (1991), 144; Chris Chekuri (personal communication).

12  Cody, *Light of Knowledge*, 174–77. In Telugu, the singular nouns *vijñapti* or *viñāpana[m]* are used for "petition, representation, appeal," as well as "prayer" and "request," as is the similar term *darakhāstu*, "petition, application." Gwynn, *Telugu-English Dictionary*, 257, 483.

13  Bussell, *Clients and Constituents.*

14  "Mahabubnagar Collector Urged to Continue Weekly Grievance Day," *Hans India*, February 3, 2015.

15  Anastasia Piliavsky, "Hierarchy, Democracy, and Political Responsibility," paper presented in the South Asia Colloquium, University of Pennsylvania, November 9, 2016.

16  Piliavsky, "Hierarchy, Democracy, and Political Responsibility."

17  Rao, *News as Culture*, 65–68.

18  Interview with K. Senthil Kumar, cited in Mohite, "Designated Sites of Political Agitations," chap. 3.

19  "Madras HC Asks Tamil Nadu Government to Waive Farmers' Loans in Cooperative Banks," *New Indian Express*, April 4, 2017.

20  A. Mariyam Alavi, "Tamil Nadu Farmers Return to Jantar Mantar with Skulls and Chains," *Hindustan Times*, July 19, 2017; and A. Mariyam Alavi, "TN Farmers Protesting at Jantar Mantar 'Eat' Own Excreta, Say Human Flesh Next," *Hindustan Times*, September 11, 2017.

21  See, for example, Deshpande, "Behind Dalit Anger"; Kalpana Sharma, "Why Are Maharashtra's Dalits So Angry," *The Hindu*, December 2, 2006; Harish S. Wankhede, "Why Are the Dalits of Maharashtra So Angry," *Dalit Perspectives*, December 2, 2006, http://dalitperspectivejnu.blogspot.co.uk/2006/12/why-dalits -of-maharashtra-are-so-angry.html; and Jaoul, "'Righteous Anger.'"

22  Jaoul, "'Righteous Anger.'"

23  I draw the term *illocution* from the speech-act theories of John L. Austin and John Searle, which have been widely adopted by political theorists, including Habermas. For a discussion of how Habermas's use of this term departs from Austin and Searle, see Farrell, *Norms of Rhetorical Culture*, chap. 5; and Young, *Inclusion and Democracy*, 66.

24  Quoted in Blom and Tawa Lama-Rewal, *Emotions, Mobilisations and South Asian Politics*, 3.

25  See, for example, Butler, *Performative Theory of Assembly*; Schnapp and Tiews, *Crowds*; Chakrabarty, "'In the Name of Politics.'"

26  Guha, *Elementary Aspects*, 5–6.
27  Chatterjee, "Violence of the State," 8–9.
28  Scott, "Foreword," xi.
29  Guha, *Elementary Aspects*, 12, 18.
30  Guha, *Elementary Aspects*, 97.
31  Guha, *Elementary Aspects*, 9.
32  Sandhya Ravishankar, "No University for Dalits," *The Wire*, January 21, 2016.
33  Holmes, "Importance of Being Angry," 127.
34  Holmes, "Importance of Being Angry," 127.
35  Spelman, "Anger and Insubordination," 264.
36  Spelman, "Anger and Insubordination," 266.
37  Ring, *Zenana*, 117.
38  Lyman, "Domestication of Anger," 133.
39  Daniel Cefaï, quoted in Blom and Jaoul, "Moral and Affective Dimension," para. 3.
40  Blom and Jaoul, "Moral and Affective Dimension," para. 39.
41  Lyman points to the ways in which the Marxian tradition links anger, subordination injury, and collection action: "Revolutionary political movements must enable unfelt or unconscious emotional responses to injustice to become conscious and articulate. It does so by revealing that one's own anger is shared by other people so that one is not alone; through revolutionary poetry that invents new words to express the meaning of inarticulate feelings; and by showing how collective action can resolve the causes of suffering" (Lyman, "Domestication of Anger," 141). See also Lyman, "Politics of Anger"; and Mitchell, "Participatory and Adversarial Politics."
42  Lyman, "Domestication of Anger," 134. See also Ranulf, *Moral Indignation*.
43  Lyman writes, "The etymological roots of the word *anger* refer to 'affliction,' 'grief' and the feeling of 'strangling.' This is an ancient language that describes the experience of suffering and loss, not the loss of emotional control and aggressive behavior that anger connotes to its critics today. What has caused—or justifies—this shift in the meaning of anger, a shift that suggests a lack of empathy for the experience of loss and attaches an element of blame to suffering?" ("Domestication of Anger," 134).
44  Raman, *Document Raj*.
45  See Bayly, "Meanings of Liberalism."
46  Guha, *Unquiet Woods*.
47  Guha, *Unquiet Woods*, 67.
48  Guha, *Unquiet Woods*, 68 (emphasis added).
49  Guha, *Unquiet Woods*, 68 (emphasis added).
50  Panikkar, *Ideas of Sovereignty and State*, 22, 75. See also Ghoshal, *History of Indian Political Ideas*.
51  Guha, *Unquiet Woods*, 69.
52  Guha, *Unquiet Woods*, 69.
53  Guha, *Unquiet Woods*, 68.

54　Guha, *Unquiet Woods*, 75.

55　Guha, *Unquiet Woods*, 76.

56　Guha, *Unquiet Woods*, 129

57　Quoted in Dharampal, *Civil Disobedience*, 71.

58　Guha, *Unquiet Woods*, 124.

59　Dharampal, *Civil Disobedience*, 15.

60　Tilly, "Collective Violence," 42.

61　Hardiman, *Gandhi*, 42.

62　Hardiman, *Gandhi*, 42.

63　Ziad, "Mufti 'Iwāz," 196.

64　Ziad, "Mufti 'Iwāz," 199–200.

65　G. Pershaud, "Deposition Taken on the 28th March, 1816," *Disturbances at Bareilly, Vol. 3*, Board's Collection, IOR/F/4/641/17693.

66　H. Dumbleton, "Letter to E. Colebrooke and T. Perry," 8 July, 1816, *Disturbances at Bareilly, Vol. 1*, Board's Collection, IOR/F/4/640/17691.

67　W. Bayley, "Letter to E. Colebrooke and C. Elliot," 24 May, 1816, *Disturbances at Bareilly, Vol. 1*, Board's Collection IOR/F/4/640/17691, para. 27; Ziad, "Mufti 'Iwāz," 191.

68　Ziad, "Mufti 'Iwāz," 191.

69　Ziad, "Mufti 'Iwāz," 193.

70　Moon, *British Conquest and Dominion*, 376, quoted in Ziad, "Mufti 'Iwāz," 193–94.

71　Ziad, "Mufti 'Iwāz," 193–94.

72　Bayly, *Empire and Information*, 323.

73　Ziad, "Mufti 'Iwāz," 201.

74　Guha, *Elementary Aspects*, 2, 20.

75　Tilly, "Collective Violence," 10.

76　Muthukkaruppan, "Dalit," 41; Muthukkaruppan, "Critique of Caste Violence."

77　Muthukkaruppan, "Critique of Caste Violence," 49.

78　Muthukkaruppan, "Critique of Caste Violence," 54. Muthukkaruppan goes on to cite the "much-maligned" Louis Dumont as one of the first to recognize caste not in terms of substantive group distinctions but rather as a structural relational system.

79　See note 41 for a discussion of the impact of Marxist theory on this.

80　See, for example, Iris Young's discussion of Habermas in her book, *Inclusion and Democracy*, 65.

81　Habermas, *Structural Transformation*, 36.

82　Habermas, *Structural Transformation*, 37 (emphasis in original).

83　McCarthy, "Introduction," xi (emphasis in original).

84　Habermas, *Structural Transformation*, 29.

85　Cowan, "Masculine Public Sphere," 129 (emphasis added).

86　Schivelbusch, *Tastes of Paradise*, 52. Ellis, *Coffee House*.

87　Fraser, "Rethinking the Public Sphere," 62.

88　Fraser, "Rethinking the Public Sphere," 68.

89　Fraser, "Rethinking the Public Sphere," 61 (emphasis added).

90   Warner, "Publics and Counterpublics," 89 (emphasis added).

91   Laura Penny, "Panic on the Streets of London," *Penny Red* (blog), August 9, 2011, http://pennyred.blogspot.com/2011/08/panic-on-streets-of-london.html (accessed August 10, 2011). Paul Lewis of *The Guardian* similarly places emphasis on the failure of the police to recognize and respond to efforts made to communicate with them. When family members and friends of the victims sought to find out what had happened to Duggan, a large group of around two hundred who had gone to the police station reported that "police failed to engage with them." Lewis reports, "Eventually a chief inspector came out and spoke to Duggan's relatives but, organisers said, he conceded a higher-ranking officer should talk to them. Stafford Scott, a community organiser, said police were 'absolutely' culpable for not responding to their requests for dialogue. 'I told the chief inspector personally that we wanted to leave before nightfall,' Scott said. 'If he kept us hanging around after nightfall, it was going to be on his head. We couldn't guarantee it wouldn't get out of control.' Scott said the chief inspector promised a higher ranking official would speak to the crowd. When no one came, organisers said some younger men turned their anger to two police cars, which were set on fire" (Paul Lewis, "Tottenham Riots: A Peaceful Protest, Then Suddenly All Hell Broke Loose," *The Guardian*, August 7, 2011).

92   Jason Lewis, "The Street Code of Vengeance That Sparked the Riots," *The Telegraph*, August 13, 2011.

93   Paul Routledge, "London Riots: Is Rap Music to Blame for Encouraging This Culture of Violence?," *Daily Mirror*, August 10, 2011. Routledge goes on to write, "Stir into this lethal mixture the fostering of irrational anger against the world and disrespect for others and the end result is self-absorbed young people living at boiling point. . . . But in the end only a change of culture, and the way these kids see the world about them, will work. . . . I would . . . urge—require even—schools to teach that the world is a much better place without pointless rage."

94   David Starkey on BBC's Newsnight, quoted in Lisa O'Carroll, "Hundreds Complain to BBC in Newsnight Race Row," *The Guardian*, August 15, 2011.

95   Cooper, "Understanding the English 'Riots,'" 8.

96   Eric Garner, a forty-three-year-old African American was killed on July 17, 2014, by twenty-nine-year-old white police officer Daniel Pantaleo, in what the medical examiner later ruled was a homicide. Despite Pantaleo's use of a chokehold in direct violation of the New York Police Department's stated policy, a grand jury decided on December 3, 2014, not to indict him, prompting the US Department of Justice to launch an independent investigation. Nearly one thousand separate collective assemblies raising concerns over police violence against African Americans were held in the year following Garner's death. See "At Least 957 Black Lives Matter Demonstrations Have Been Held in the Last 360 Days," *Elephrame*, https://elephrame.com/textbook/protests (accessed July 14, 2015). In the past eight years (July 17, 2014, to July 17, 2022), there have been at least 6,687 Black Lives Matter demonstrations; see *Elephrame*, https://elephrame.com/textbook /BLM/chart (accessed July 18, 2022).

97 Daniel J. Watts, "I Can't Breathe," performed on July 29, 2014, published on You-Tube on July 31, 2014 (https://www.youtube.com/watch?v=FpfTos6NroM). See "Broadway Unites to Protest Police Violence and Honor Eric Garner," *The Grio*, July 31, 2014, http://thegrio.com/2014/07/31/broadway-eric-garner-protest/.

98 See, for example, Collins, "Recalling Democracy," 33.

99 Habermas, *Theory of Communicative Action*, 287.

100 Habermas, *Theory of Communicative Action*, 65.

101 Young, *Inclusion and Democracy*, 56, 58.

102 Young, *Inclusion and Democracy*, 59.

103 Young, *Inclusion and Democracy*, 61 (emphasis in original).

104 Young, *Inclusion and Democracy*, 61. See also Taylor, "Politics of Recognition."

105 Young, *Inclusion and Democracy*, 60.

106 Young, *Inclusion and Democracy*, 58.

107 For a discussion of how various democracies have approached public space, see Parkinson, *Democracy and Public Space*. See also Keller, *Triumph of Order*; Henaff and Strong, *Public Space and Democracy*. See also Ministry of Electronics and Information Technology, Government of India, "E-Governance: Reforming Government through Technology," http://www.digitalindia.gov.in/content /e-governance-%E2%80%93-reforming-government-through-technology (accessed on August 2, 2017); Unique Identification Authority of India, Government of India, "About UIDAI," https://uidai.gov.in/about-uidai/about-uidai.html (accessed on August 2, 2017).

108 Young, *Inclusion and Democracy*, 64–65.

109 See, for example, Bauman and Briggs, *Voices of Modernity*.

THREE. COLLECTIVE ASSEMBLY AND THE "ROAR OF THE PEOPLE"

*Epigraph*: emphasis added to Gwatkin.

1 Telugu was the second most widely spoken language in India according to the 1951 and 1961 censuses, the third most widely spoken language from 1971 through 2001, and is currently the fourth most widely spoken language in India (Government of India, *Census of India 2011*).

2 Andhra State, formed in 1953 out of two regions of the former British Madras State (Rayalaseema and Coastal Andhra), was the first linguistically defined state to be created in independent India. Three years later, during the All India Linguistic States Reorganisation of 1956, the predominantly Telugu-speaking regions of the former Nizam State of Hyderabad, a region known as Telangana, reluctantly joined with Andhra State to create Andhra Pradesh. After decades of protest, Telangana became India's newest state in 2014.

3 Mahesh Vijapurkar, "Telangana: Of Broken Promises and Congress's 'Catch 22,'" *Rediff News*, December 16, 2009; Pingle, *Fall and Rise of Telangana*, 100–105 (see note 6 in the introduction).

4 Thiranagama, Kelly, and Forment, "Whose Civility?," 155. See also Sennett, *Fall of Public Man*; Shils, "Virtue of Civil Society."

5   Thiranagama, Kelly, and Forment, "Whose Civility?," 157–58, 161.

6   Thiranagama, Kelly, and Forment, "Whose Civility?"; Elias, *Civilizing Process*; Balibar, *Violence and Civility*. On struggles for dignity and self-respect in India, see Waghmore, *Civility against Caste*; Muthukkaruppan, "Critique of Caste Violence and "Dalit"; Geetha and Rajadurai, "Dalits and Non-Brahmin Consciousness"; and Hodges, "Revolutionary Family Life."

7   Balibar, *Violence and Civility*, 23.

8   Prabhpreet Singh Sood and Prince Singhal, "Students in Literate States Lead Spike in Indian Protests," *India Spend*, November 30, 2016; Wolcott, "Strikes in Colonial India," 481.

9   Data from the ten districts of Telangana on the "registration of cases during the period from Jan. 2011 to Nov. 2011 in connection with the agitation of Telangana and Samaikya Andhra" were obtained under the Right to Information (RTI) Act of 2005 of Andhra Pradesh State from the Inspector of Police, SCRB, CID, Hyderabad, Government of Andhra Pradesh, January 7, 2012. I am grateful to Gandra Mohan Rao, advocate, for assistance in accessing these records.

10  "Data on Police Organizations," Bureau of Police Research and Development, https://bprd.nic.in/content/62_1_DataonPoliceOrganizations.aspx (accessed April 4, 2020). Although some of this growth may reflect changes in reporting practices, collective assemblies continue to play an important role in everyday politics in India today.

11  "Data on Police Organizations"; population of Uttar Pradesh taken from "A-2 Decadal Variation in Population since 1901," *Census of India 2011*, Office of the Registrar General & Census Commissioner, India, https://censusindia.gov.in /2011census/PCA/A2_Data_Table.html; population of Telangana taken from *Statistical Year Book 2015*, www.telangana.gov.in.

12  Arendt, *Crises of the Republic*; Bilgrami, "Gandhi's Integrity"; Brown, *Gandhi and Civil Disobedience*; Dalton, *Mahatma Gandhi*; Haksar, "Rawls and Gandhi"; Hardiman, *Gandhi*; Mantena, "Another Realism"; Mehta, "Gandhi on Democracy."

13  Kapoor, "Deliberative Democracy or Agonistic Pluralism?"; Kohli, *Success of India's Democracy*.

14  On civil disobedience and strikes originating in the West, see Hardiman, *Gandhi*, 39; Randle, *Civil Resistance*, 21, 36; Tarrow, *Power in Movement*, 38; and Tilly, *Popular Contention*, 15. On elections, see Banerjee, "Democracy, Sacred and Everyday," "Elections as Communitas," and *Why India Votes?*; and Michelutti, *Vernacularisation*.

15  Guha, *Elementary Aspects*; Chatterjee, "Violence of the State," 8–9; Chakrabarty, ""In the Name of Politics,"" 52–53.

16  See Fraser, "Rethinking the Public Sphere," 56.

17  Mouffe, "Agonistic Model of Democracy," 203.

18  Mouffe, "Deliberative Democracy," 16–17 (emphasis added to *collective*).

19  Dryzek, *Deliberative Democracy*, 1. See also Benhabib, "Deliberative Model"; Habermas, *Structural Transformation*, *Facts and Norms* and "Political Communication"; Rawls, *Political Liberalism*.

20  Dryzek, *Deliberative Democracy*, 1.

21  Cohen, "Reflections on Civility"; Farrelly, *Justice*; Fishkin and Luskin, "Experimenting with a Democratic Ideal"; Rawls, "Idea of Public Reason."

22  Farrelly, *Justice*, 206, 209.

23  Shils, "Virtue of Civil Society," 12–13.

24  Shils, "Virtue of Civil Society," 13–14.

25  Shils, "Virtue of Civil Society," 14.

26  Shils, "Virtue of Civil Society," 16.

27  Shils, "Virtue of Civil Society," 13.

28  Boyd, "'Value of Civility,'" 864.

29  Boyd, "'Value of Civility,'" 864.

30  Burghart, "Conditions of Listening," 300.

31  Farrelly, *Justice*, 206.

32  Shils, "Virtue of Civil Society," 13.

33  Here I share Judith Butler's critique of Hannah Arendt. Butler writes, "It is precisely this operation of power—the foreclosure and differential allocation of whether and how the body may appear—that is excluded from Arendt's explicit account of the political. Indeed, her explicit account of the political depends upon that very operation of power that it fails to consider as part of politics itself" (Butler, *Performative Theory of Assembly*, 88).

34  Burghart, "Conditions of Listening," 301–2.

35  Bate, *Tamil Oratory*; Bate, *Protestant Textuality*.

36  Bate, *Tamil Oratory*, 162.

37  Piliavsky, "Where Is the Public Sphere?," 108–9.

38  Piliavsky, "Where Is the Public Sphere?," 107.

39  Piliavsky, "Where Is the Public Sphere?," 112.

40  Burghart, "Conditions of Listening," 310.

41  Burghart, "Conditions of Listening," 318.

42  Satyanarayana, "Dalit Reconfiguration of Caste," 46.

43  Balagopal, *Karamchedu Massacre*, 6. On the failure to arrest or prosecute the perpetrators in the Chundur massacre against Dalits in 1991, see Gossman, *Police Killings and Rural Violence*, 20.

44  See chapter 2 for discussion of the 2011 unrest in the wake of the police shooting deaths of Mark Duggan in the United Kingdom and Eric Garner in the United States.

45  The occasional report of violence during the 2011 Telangana All People's Strike, for example, appears to have consistently been linked to police baton charges and the use of tear gas on those assembled. See "T Comes to a Halt," *Mission Telangana*, September 21, 2011; "Sakala Janula Samme: Day 15 Turns Violent," *Telugu One*, September 27, 2011.

46  Connolly, *Identity/Difference*, "Response," and *Pluralism*; Honig, "Agonistic Feminism" and *Political Theory*; Mouffe, "Deliberative Democracy," "Politics and Passions," and "Agonistic Model of Democracy"; see also Arendt, *Human Condition*.

47  Mouffe, "Politics and Passions," 185; Laclau and Mouffe, *Hegemony and Socialist Strategy*, xvii.
48  Mouffe, "Deliberative Democracy."
49  Dryzek, "Deliberative Democracy in Divided Societies," 218.
50  Kapoor, "Deliberative Democracy or Agonistic Pluralism?," 459. See also Appadurai, "Deep Democracy."
51  Mouffe, "Deliberative Democracy," 2.
52  Dryzek, "Deliberative Democracy in Divided Societies," 218.
53  Fossen, "Agonistic Critiques of Liberalism," 384.
54  Mouffe, "Deliberative Democracy," 16, and "Politics and Passions," 185.
55  Mouffe, "Politics and Passions," 184–85.
56  Mouffe, "Politics and Passions," 184–85.
57  Mouffe, "Politics and Passions," 186.
58  Lakoff, "Civility and Its Discontents," 28.
59  Tannen, *Argument Culture*, 3.
60  Tannen, *Argument Culture*, 2.
61  Tannen, *Argument Culture*, 3, 6.
62  Mouffe, "Politics and Passions," 186.
63  Mouffe, "Deliberative Democracy," 16–17.
64  For more information, see "Andhra Balananda Sangham," http://www .balanandam.co.in/ (accessed May 3, 2021).
65  Interview with Kaloji Narayana Rao, Warangal, April 22, 1997.
66  Pingle, *Fall and Rise of Telangana*. Despite the creation of government policies and programs designed to address these inequities, the repeated failures to see these official measures implemented in practice (Girglani, "Commission on G.O.610"), combined with declining wages and rising debt, have produced an increase in debt-related suicides in Telangana (Revathi and Galab, "Economic Reforms"). The Srikrishna Committee, appointed in 2010 to examine the concerns raised by Telangana advocates, reported, "The analysis of income change in rural areas over a period of one decade suggests that, in Telangana, the relative income growth has occurred only amongst the richest; whereas the poorer and the most deprived have experienced considerably large declines in relative income over the reference period" (*Report*, 119). It also found that real incomes for agricultural wage laborers, marginalized groups, and minorities in the Telangana region declined over the previous decade, while incomes for members of the same communities in coastal Andhra increased substantially (120). The committee concluded, "The Telangana movement can be interpreted as a desire for greater democracy and empowerment within a political unit; cutting across caste, religion, gender and other divisions, the Telangana movement brings a focus on the development of the region as a whole, a focus on rights and access to regional resources and further, it pitches for a rights-based development perspective whereby groups and communities put forth their agendas within a larger vision of equitable development" (413).
67  Bauman and Briggs, *Voices of Modernity*.

68   Girglani, "Commission on G.O. 610."

69   On the rise of Velamas in relation to the economic dominance of the Kamma and Reddy caste groups in Telangana, see Jangam Chinnaiah, "KCR's Telangana Is Utopia for His Caste Group, Land Barons," *The Print*, October 13, 2021.

70   See Chandra, "Maoist Movement"; Kunnath, *Rebels*; Shah, *Nightmarch*; Sundar, "Reflections on Civil Liberties." On Peru, see Kernaghan, "Furrows and Walls."

71   Subramanian, *Caste of Merit*.

72   Rupa Viswanath, "Being Seen and Being Heard: The Depressed Classes, Political Representation, and the Extrapolitical in Colonial Madras," paper presented at the workshop "Extrapolitics," University of Göttingen, December 5, 2012.

73   Letter from A. G. Leach, District Magistrate, North Arcot, dated August 4, 1925, quoted in Viswanath, "Being Seen and Being Heard," 8–9.

74   Viswanath, "Being Seen and Being Heard," 9.

75   Palshikar and Patnaik, "Violence in a University."

76   On the rise of more visible political activism among Dalits, for example, see Jaffrelot, *India's Silent Revolution*; Rawat, *Reconsidering Untouchability*; Rawat and Satyanarayana, *Dalit Studies*; and Collins, "Recalling Democracy."

77   J. Chelameswar, Andhra High Court, Madiga Reservation Porata . . . vs the Commissioner of Police, 13 April, 1999 (AIR 1999 AP 289, 1999 (3) ALT 146).

78   Viswanathan, *Dalits in Dravidian Land*, 95 (first published in *Frontline*, August 28, 1998). I am grateful to Nate Roberts for this example.

79   Rajayya, *Bhūmi: Kathalu*, 8.

80   Rajayya, *Bhūmi: Kathalu*, 8.

81   Rajayya, *Bhūmi: Kathalu*, 9.

82   Gossman, *Police Killings and Rural Violence*, 26–27.

83   Gossman, *Police Killings and Rural Violence*, 26–27.

84   Kling, *Blue Mutiny*.

85   J. P. Grant, "Minute," Bengal Judicial Proceedings, Sept. 1860, No. 238 (IOR p/146/31), para. 5. See also Buckland, *Bengal under the Lieutenant-Governors*, 192.

86   Kling, *Blue Mutiny*, 168.

87   J. P. Grant, "Minute," Bengal Judicial Proceedings, Sept. 1860, No. 238 (IOR p/146/31), para. 5.

88   J. P. Grant, "Minute," Bengal Judicial Proceedings, Sept. 1860, paras. 5–6.

89   Sastri, *Law of Sedition*.

90   Nehru, "Students and Discipline," 29: 70–72, quoted in Chakrabarty, "'In the Name of Politics,'" 35–36.

91   Hardiman, *Gandhi*, 39; see also Tilly, *Popular Contention*, 15; Tarrow, *Power in Movement*, 38.

92   Nehru, "Students and Discipline."

93   J. Gwatkin, Secretary, Board of Trade, Madras, 11th March, 1817, in Madras Proceedings, 19th June, 1817, IOR-P-335-20, pp. 1363–64 (emphasis added).

94   Nehru, "Students and Discipline," 71.

95   Nehru, "Students and Discipline," 74.

96   Nehru, "Students and Discipline," 82.

97  Nehru, "Students and Discipline," 73.

98  Nehru, "Students and Discipline," 76.

99  Balibar, *Violence and Civility*, 22 (emphasis in original).

100 Balibar, *Violence and Civility*, 23 (emphasis in original).

101 Balibar, *Violence and Civility*, 23 (emphasis added).

102 "TNGOs to Organise 'Udyoga Garjana,'" *The Hindu*, October 20, 2009; "KCR, Kishan Reddy to Address Sakala Jana Bheri," *Times of India*, September 28, 2013.

103 *Tamil Murasu* is an evening Tamil newspaper published daily in Chennai, Coimbatore, Salem, Erode, Pondicherry, Madurai, Trichy, and Nagercoil. A second *Tamil Murasu*, published continuously since 1935, is Singapore's only Tamil newspaper and is one of the main sources of information for the Tamil-speaking community in that city. *Malai Murasu* is both a Tamil language evening daily newspaper in Tamil Nadu and a television channel that broadcasts from Chennai.

104 Kunreuther, "Sounds of Democracy," 23–24. On embodied amplification, see also Kelp-Stebbins and Schifani, "Medium Is the Masses."

105 Kunreuther, "Sounds of Democracy," 24. See also Cody, "Populist Publics," on the need to explore "forms of self-abstraction and embodiment . . . that are overdetermined on one end by classical liberalism and by the discourses on totalitarianism or fascism on the other," 62.

106 Kapoor, "Deliberative Democracy or Agonistic Pluralism?," 459.

107 Carter, *Civility*.

108 Burghart, "Conditions of Listening," 300.

FOUR. THE GENERAL STRIKE

1   Thirmal Reddy Sunkari, "Telangana Roars at Karimnagar," *Mission Telangana*, September 13, 2011, https://missiontelangana.com/telangana-roars-at-karimnagar; Gowrishankar, *Ā 42 Rōjulu*.

2   Sharika Thiranagama and Tobias Kelly, "Civility: Trust, Recognition and Co-existence," conference abstract, Stanford Global Studies Workshop, Stanford University, April 17–18, 2015. See also Thiranagama, Kelly, and Forment, "Whose Civility?"

3   Tilly, *Popular Contention*, 15.

4   Tilly, *Mobilization to Revolution*, 159.

5   Shorter and Tilly, *Strikes in France*, 4–5.

6   Carpenter, *Civilisation*; Crook, *General Strike*; Prothero, "William Benbow"; Harman, "What Do We Mean"; Tarrow, "Social Movements" and *Power in Movement*.

7   Tarrow, *Power in Movement*; Diwakar, *Saga of Satyagraha*; Hardiman, *Gandhi*.

8   Dharampal, *Civil Disobedience*.

9   Tilly, *Popular Contention*, 45.

10  Tilly, *Popular Contention*, 46 and "Contentious Repertoires," 272.

11  Tarrow, *Power in Movement*, 38.

12  Thompson, "Moral Economy," 96.

13  Thompson, *English Working Class*, 468, 475–76.

14   Tarrow, *Power in Movement*, 38.

15   Carpenter, *Civilisation*; Crook, *General Strike*; Prothero, "William Benbow"; Harman, "What Do We Mean."

16   Benbow, *Grand National Holiday*, 10 (emphasis in original).

17   Benbow, *Grand National Holiday*, 14.

18   Compare, for example, Engels, "The Bakuninists at Work," written in 1873, with Luxemburg, "The Mass Strike," written in 1906 in the wake of the 1905 Russian Revolution. Engels is skeptical of the effectiveness of mass strikes given their need for extensive organization. If the working classes were already that well organized, then he felt that "it would not need the roundabout way of the general strike to reach its goal" (147).

19   Randle, *Civil Resistance*, 21.

20   Randle, *Civil Resistance*, 36.

21   Diwakar, *Saga of Satyagraha*, 9.

22   Hardiman, *Gandhi*, 39.

23   Hardiman, *Gandhi*, 40.

24   Hardiman, *Gandhi*, 40.

25   Dharampal, *Civil Disobedience*; Dharampal, *Dharampal Papers*; Parthasarathi, *Colonial Economy*; Refai, "Anglo-Mughal Relations."

26   Wolcott, "Strikes in Colonial India," 481.

27   Hardiman, *Gandhi*, 41–49.

28   Refai, "Anglo-Mughal Relations," 135, 132.

29   Das Gupta, "Merchants of Surat," 201; Haynes, *Rhetoric and Ritual*, 37.

30   Haynes, *Rhetoric and Ritual*, 37; Chakrabarti, "Myth of the Date," 489.

31   Refai, "Anglo-Mughal Relations," 132.

32   Refai, "Anglo-Mughal Relations," 132.

33   Dharampal, *Civil Disobedience*; Dharampal, *Dharampal Papers*.

34   Records of Fort St. George, 1680–1681: 28th March (20), 25th June (41), 7th Oct. (71–72).

35   Records of Fort St. George, 1680–1681: 27th Oct. (75).

36   Records of Fort St. George, 1680–1681: 6th Nov. (76).

37   Records of Fort St. George, 1680–1681: 1st Nov. (75), 8th Nov. (76), 15th Nov. (77).

38   Records of Fort St. George, 1680–1681: 29th Nov. (80–81).

39   Records of Fort St. George, 1680–1681: 26th Nov. (79), 9th Dec. (83), 6th Jan. (90); Records of Fort St. George, 1681: 19th, 22nd & 26th Sept. (54–56), 17th Oct. (60), 1st Dec. (69–70); Pringle, *Diary and Consultation Book*, 1682: 2nd Feb. (9), 9th Feb. (13). For further discussion, see Dharampal, *Civil Disobedience*, 14; and Mukund, *Trading World*, 109–12.

40   Dharampal, *Dharampal Papers*.

41   Ahuja, "Labour Unsettled," 394–96.

42   Irschick, *Dialogue and History*, 29–30. For a discussion of similar forms of protest in Southeast Asia, see Adas, "Avoidance and Confrontation."

43   Stern, *Company-State*.

44   "civility, n." OED Online. June 2021. Oxford University Press, I.12.a.

45 "civility, n." OED *Online*. June 2021. Oxford University Press, I.2.

46 See chapter 2.

47 Parthasarathi, *Colonial Economy*, 130.

48 Parthasarathi, *Colonial Economy*, 101.

49 Swarnalatha, "Revolt, Testimony, Petition," 117.

50 Richard Dillon to Benjamin Branfil, January 16, 1798, and Richard Dillon to Cornish Gambier, January 19 and 23, 1798, *Godavari District Records* 847: 168, 263–64, 269, quoted in Swarnalatha, "The World of the Weaver," 357–58.

51 Arasaratnam, "Trade and Political Dominion"; Swarnalatha, "Revolt, Testimony, Petition"; Parthasarathi, *Colonial Economy*; Katten, *Colonial Lists*.

52 Swarnalatha, "Revolt, Testimony, Petition," 117.

53 Dharampal, *Civil Disobedience*; Heitler, "Varanasi House"; Freitag, *Collective Action and Community*, 215–20.

54 East India Company, *Selection of Papers Vol. 2*, 89.

55 Mill, *History of British India*, 467.

56 Mill, *History of British India*, 466.

57 Marx and Engels, *The First Indian War of Independence*; Savarkar, *The Indian War of Independence*.

58 J. P. Grant, "Minute," Bengal Judicial Proceedings, Sept. 1860, No. 238 (IOR/P/146/31), para. 5.

59 Lord Canning, Governor General of India to Sir Charles Wood, Secretary of State for India, October 30, 1860, quoted in Kling, *Blue Mutiny*, 169.

60 Mazzarella, "Myth of the Multitude."

61 Freitag, *Collective Action and Community*, 223.

62 Freitag, *Collective Action and Community*, 220.

63 Dharampal, *Civil Disobedience*; Ziad, "Mufti 'Iwāz."

64 Spodek, "Gandhi's Political Methodology," 363.

65 Wolcott, "Strikes in Colonial India," 475.

66 Wolcott, "Strikes in Colonial India," 460, 481.

67 Wolcott, "Strikes in Colonial India," 468–69.

68 Wolcott, "Strikes in Colonial India," 474.

69 Tilly, "Contentious Repertoires," 272, and *Popular Contention*, 349.

70 Bayly, *Empire and Information*.

71 Quoted in Dharampal, *Dharampal Papers*, 25.

72 Smith, *Consumption*, 53–54.

73 Smith, *Consumption*, 57–58.

74 Page, "Industries: Silk-weaving," 134.

75 Thornbury, *Old and New London*, 152.

76 Parthasarathi, *Colonial Economy*, 101.

77 The Subaltern Studies Collective refers to a group of Indian historians that emerged in the 1980s to examine history from the perspective of nonelites. The collective published a series of 12 volumes of essays between 1982 and 2005.

78 Parthasarathi, *Colonial Economy*, 102.

79 Parthasarathi, *Colonial Economy*, 101.

80　Parthasarathi, *Colonial Economy*, 114.

81　Parthasarathi, *Colonial Economy*, 114.

82　Swarnalatha, "Revolt, Testimony, Petition."

83　Swarnalatha, "Revolt, Testimony, Petition," 113.

84　Swarnalatha, "Revolt, Testimony, Petition," 116.

85　"Petitions from Weavers," in Madras Proceedings, June 19, 1817, IOR/P/335/20.

86　Thompson, "Rough Music"; Tarrow, *Power in Movement*.

87　Smith, *Consumption*, 49.

88　Smith, *Consumption*, 50.

89　Smith, *Consumption*, 50 (emphasis added).

90　Habermas, *Structural Transformation*, 31.

91　Smith, *Consumption*, 51 (emphasis in original).

92　Smith, *Consumption*, 58.

93　Smith, *Consumption*, 59.

94　Cited in Ziad, "Mufti 'Iwāz," 190.

95　J. Gwatkin, Secretary, Board of Trade, Madras, 11th March, 1817, in Madras Proceedings, 19th June, 1817, IOR/P/335/20, pp. 1363–64.

96　J. Gwatkin, Secretary, Board of Trade, Madras, 11th March, 1817, in Madras Proceedings, 19th June, 1817, IOR/P/335/20, pp. 1363–64 (emphasis added).

97　Mitchell, "Carbon Democracy."

98　Mitchell, "Carbon Democracy," 403.

99　Mitchell, "Carbon Democracy," 401.

100　Michelutti, *Vernacularisation*; Piliavsky, *Patronage as Politics*.

101　Thachil and Teitelbaum, "Ethnic Parties," 1390.

102　Björkman, "'You Can't Buy a Vote'"; Björkman, "Ostentatious Crowd."

103　Björkman, "Ostentatious Crowd," 159.

104　On "actually existing democracy," see Fraser, "Rethinking the Public Sphere."

FIVE. ALARM CHAIN PULLING

An earlier version of chapter 5 was previously published as "'To Stop Train Pull Chain': Writing Histories of Contemporary Political Practice," *Indian Economic and Social History Review* 48, no. 4 (2011): 469–95, copyright *Indian Economic and Social History Review*, used by permission.

1　Railway Traffic B, Jan. 1917, 119-T/16/1-2, National Archives of India (NAI).

2　In 2009, a proposal was introduced to replace the existing alarm chain system with "a modern communication system" that would enable passengers to communicate directly with the driver and give the driver the authority to decide whether or not to stop the train. The Passenger Amenities Committee, which raised the proposal, argued that this would eliminate the widespread abuse of the system, with one member commenting, "In most of the incidents, miscreants, robbers and dacoits [bandits] use the system to make good their escape from the train. After carrying out an act of robbery, they simply pull the chain and get away. The system is also misused by common passengers and pranksters, who stop the train whenever they feel like. The Rs 1,000 fine has not been a deterrent because in most cases the person is not found" ("Alarm Chain-Pulling System in Trains Could Be a Thing of the Past," *Indian Express*, December 4, 2009).

3   Railway Traffic B, Jan. 1917, 119-T/16/1–2, NAI.

4   Railway Traffic B, Jan. 1917, 119-T/16/1–2, NAI. The previous letter was sent by Panvalkar on December 23 and received by the Railway Board in Simla on December 25.

5   Letter dated January 26, 1917, Railway Traffic B, Feb. 1917, 119T-16/3–4, NAI.

6   Letter dated January 26, 1917, Railway Traffic B, Feb. 1917, 119T-16/3–4, NAI.

7   "The Right to Resist Overcrowding," *The Mahratta* (Poona), April 4, 1915, Railway Traffic B, March 1916, No. 119T/x, NAI.

8   "The Right to Resist Overcrowding," NAI.

9   "The Right to Resist Overcrowding," NAI (emphasis in original).

10  Routine Notes (*Not to be sent out of the Office or Printed*), May 10, 1915, Railway Traffic B, March 1916, No. 119T/x, NAI.

11  Railway Traffic A, May 1930, 614-T/17–78, p. 1, NAI.

12  Railway Traffic A, May 1930, 614-T/17–78, p. 4, NAI.

13  Railway Traffic B, Aug. 1930, 614-T-I/1–4, NAI.

14  Gandhi, *Third Class in Indian Railways*, 1.

15  Gandhi, "Statement to the Press." He made two more statements in December 1945 and October 1947 condemning the use of alarm chains for any purpose except emergencies or accidents (Gandhi, "Speech at Prayer Meeting, Sodepur" and "Speech at Prayer Meeting, New Delhi").

16  Railway Traffic B, Dec. 1935, 614-T/125–139, NAI.

17  "Notice of Amendments, The Indian Railways (Amendment) Bill (Amendment of Sections 108 and 131)," February 15, 1933, Railway Traffic B, Dec. 1935, 614-T/125–139, NAI.

18  C. P. Ramaswami Iyer, "Proposed Amendment of Section 108 of the Indian Railways Act—Not Proceeded With," July 13, 1932, File No. 321/32 C. & G. Notes, Serial Nos. 1–6; and J. W. Bhore, "Statement of Objects and Reasons," November 22, 1932, Railway Traffic B, Dec. 1935, 614-T/125–139, NAI.

19  Mr. Muhammad Yamin Khan (Agra Division: Muhammadan Rural), "Extract from the Legislative Assembly Debates, Vol. I, No. 4," Serial No. 5, p. 4, Railway Traffic B, Dec. 1935, 614-T/125–139, NAI.

20  Railway Traffic B, July 1943, 614-T/141–164, NAI.

21  "Letter from Andhra Provincial Congress Committee," All India Congress Committee Manuscript Collection, Vol. G-37/1942, pp. 119–21, Nehru Memorial Museum and Library (NMML), New Delhi.

22  Home Political (Internal), 1942, F. No. 3/42/42, NAI.

23  "Mahatma Gandhi's Message to Free India," Home Political (Internal), 1942, F. No. 3/79/42, p. 54, NAI.

24  The East Indian, North Western, and Madras and Southern Mahratta Railways all reported having experienced a recent increase in alarm chain pulling cases—in some cases a considerable increase; the Great Indian Peninsula, Bombay Baroda

and Central India, Bengal Nagpur, Nizam State, and South Indian Railways all stated that, although they had not yet noticed serious increases in alarm chain pulling activity, they anticipated an increase in the near future. Only three railways—the Bengal Assam, Jodhpur, and Mysore Railways—stated that they had neither seen an increase nor anticipated an increase in the near future ("Memorandum for Discussion by the Board," Railway Traffic B, July 1943, 614-T/141–164, p. 27, NAI).

25 "Memorandum for Discussion by the Board."
26 Three relevant cases cited are A.I.R. 1922 Patna 8, Ishwar Das Varshni v. Emperor (Patna High Court); A.I.R. 1930 Bombay 160, Popatlal Bhaichand Shah v. Emperor (Bombay High Court); and Crown v. Sardar Surat Singh son of Sardar Hira Singh, Secretary, District Motor Union, Montgomery and President of the Punjab Provincial Motor Union, 1941 (Montgomery District Court), "Memorandum for Discussion by the Board," 8–10.
27 "Memorandum for Discussion by the Board," 30–31.
28 "Memorandum for Discussion by the Board," 30–31.
29 Railway Traffic B, July 1943, 614-T/141–164, S. No. 156, p. 19, NAI.
30 Interview with male, b. late 1920s, Kavali, Andhra Pradesh, August 12, 1998.
31 Interview, August 12, 1998. The death of Andhra State activist Potti Sriramulu on the fifty-eighth day of his fast on December 15, 1952, and the surge of public outrage that followed prompted Jawaharlal Nehru's declaration of the new state just four days later, on December 19. Police firings occurred in four places in coastal Andhra—Nellore, Anakapalle, Waltair, and Srikakulam, all railway stations—as authorities struggled to maintain order. Mass gatherings also occurred in railway stations in Vijayawada, Navabpalam (West Godavari district), Machilipatnam, Anantapur, Mudanur, Guntur, Rajamundry, Duggirala, Tenali, Ongole, and numerous other cities and towns on the main rail line. Several of the locations are documented in "Situation in Andhra: Police Firings in Three Centres," *The Hindu*, December 18, 1952, p. 8, col. 2 (see Mitchell, *Language, Emotion and Politics*, chap. 6).
32 Interview, August 12, 1998.
33 Interview with male, b. 1932, October 16, 2004.
34 Interview, feminist activist, Hyderabad, April 23, 2009.
35 Chakrabarty, "'In the Name of Politics,'" 37.
36 Nehru, "Students and Discipline," 83, quoted in Chakrabarty, "'In the Name of Politics,'" 37.
37 Nehru, "Policy of India," 22–23, quoted in Chakrabarty, "'In the Name of Politics,'" 37.
38 See the challenge to this position posed by "a Dalit activist" present at a lecture by Partha Chatterjee in Delhi in 2000 regarding the rising pessimism held by "liberal and leftist intellectuals" in stark contrast to the optimism held by Dalits (and one might add, other formerly marginalized groups) regarding the status and direction of Indian democracy at that time, in Chatterjee, *Politics of the Governed*, 24–25.

39  Interview with senior railway official, Lucknow, March 27, 2009.

40  Fraser, "Rethinking the Public Sphere," 71.

41  Goswami, *Producing India*, 32–33, 59; Lefebvre, *Production of Space*.

42  Goswami, *Producing India*, 49.

43  Interview, senior railway official, Secunderabad, January 2, 2009.

44  Interview, feminist activist, Hyderabad, April 23, 2009.

45  Interview, March 27, 2009.

46  Gelder, "Introduction to Part Seven," 375, quoted in Mazumdar, *Bombay Cinema*, 99; Jeffrey, *Timepass*, 93.

47  Jeffrey, *Timepass*.

48  Interview with Indian Railway Traffic Service officer, Lucknow, March 26, 2009.

49  In my earlier work I argued that those in positions of structural marginalization take up available recognizable foundations for collective identification and assertion, such as language, ethnicity, or region (Mitchell, *Language, Emotion and Politics*). This can be potentially liberatory for those in positions of structural marginalization, as in the case of the recent mobilization over regional identity in Telangana. However, an ever-present danger is that such assertions can quickly be reappropriated by dominant interests, evacuating their liberatory potential. This also points to the fact that it is not the form of collective action that determines its liberatory potential but rather the extent to which a particular form enables the inclusion and consideration of marginalized voices.

SIX. RAIL AND ROAD BLOCKADES

1  Interview, Besant Nagar, Chennai, January 22, 2009.

2  See statistics on the destruction of communication and transport links in Home Political (I), 1942, 3/79/1942, National Archives of India; "Provincial Summaries of Events—Disturbances 9 Aug.–31 Sept. 1942," Home Political (I), 1942, 3/30/42, NAI; and "Misc. Reports on Sabotage to Railways," Home Political (I), 1943, 3/86/43, NAI.

3  Q & A in the Legislative Assembly on "the imposition of joint responsibility for safety of communication," Home Political Proceedings (I), 1943, 22/3/43, NAI; "Enhanced penalties for sabotage," Home Political (I), 1942, 25/8/42; "Enhanced penalties for sabotage," NAI and Home Political (I), 1943, 25/10/43, NAI; "Death penalty for sabotage," Home Political (I), 1943, 3/9/43, NAI.

4  "Statement to Defence Council on Congress Disturbances," Home Political (I), 1942, 3/42/42, NAI.

5  Ram and Kumar, *Quit India Movement*, 229.

6  *Harijan*, May 1942, quoted in Ram and Kumar, *Quit India Movement*, Appendix V.

7  Ram and Kumar, *Quit India Movement*.

8  Interview with senior Indian Police Service (IPS) officer, Lucknow, March 27, 2009.

9  Bureau of Police Research and Development, Data on Police Organizations, Annual Reports published January 1 of each year from 2008 through 2017 (covering

2006–7 through 2015–16), New Delhi. Data are available at http://bprd.nic.in /content/62_1_DataonPoliceOrganizations.aspx (accessed March 9, 2018).

10  Bureau of Police Research and Development, Data on Police Organizations. Data show a more than 305% increase in the number of agitations per year between 2006 and 2016. Although the number of agitations dropped 32.2% from 2006 to 2007, they showed a 10.5% increase from 2007 to 2008, a 98.4% increase from 2008 to 2009, a slight 3.3% decrease from 2009 to 2010, a 34.4% increase from 2010 to 2011, a 6.96% increase from 2011 to 2012, a slight 3.13% decrease from 2012 to 2013, a 15.13% increase from 2013 to 2014, a 25.07% increase from 2014 to 2015, and a 5.85% increase from 2015 to 2016, the most recent year for which data are available. The data for 2016 included 8,926 separate agitations in Telangana alone, placing Telangana fourth among Indian states for 2016. Uttarakhand ranked first with 21,966 agitations; Tamil Nadu, with 17,043, ranked second; and the Punjab, with 11,876, ranked third.

11  Interview with senior Government Railway Police official, March 27, 2009. In keeping with ethnographic convention, I have changed the names of railway employees, police administrators, and activists with whom I spoke unless attributing credit for their innovations.

12  For an interpretation of Tocqueville's distinction, see Kaviraj, "Empire of Democracy," 21.

13  Rudolph and Rudolph's distinction between "demand polity" and "command polity" relies on measuring the relative balance of power between the state and society (*In Pursuit of Lakshmi*). For a survey of the debates surrounding the concept of civil society, see Kaviraj and Khilnani, *Civil Society*. For two contrasting understandings of the distinction between civil society and political society, see Chatterjee, "Violence of the State," 8–9; and Bhargava, "Introduction," 18. The distinction between "elites" and "masses" or between "elites" and "the governed" (Alam, *Who Wants Democracy?*) has been difficult to avoid in scholarship on South Asia and has been fundamental to Marxist and Subaltern Studies' approaches and their successors. Too often, these terms are left undefined, and the distinguishing line between these two categories is assumed to be unproblematic. A hallmark of much ethnography has been its efforts to disturb the easy boundaries between such categories. For an early effort to disrupt the boundary between state and civil society, for example, see Gupta, "Blurred Boundaries."

14  The same logic that enabled the British colonial state to generate lists of criminal tribes and castes and to define caste groups in relation to occupational categories or specific practices thought to be unique (e.g., leatherwork) continues to inform many of the contemporary categories available for analyzing Indian democracy. For a critique of the logic that engagement in a particular practice equals identity, see Rawat, *Reconsidering Untouchability*.

15  Alam, *Who Wants Democracy?*, 36.

16  Alam, *Who Wants Democracy?*, 123.

17  Alam, *Who Wants Democracy?*, 122.

18  Alam, *Who Wants Democracy?*, 122.

19   See the introduction to this book.

20   Interview, October 16, 2004.

21   Amba Batra Bakshi, "Rail Roko . . . Roko," *Outlook*, September 8, 2008.

22   Lakier, "Illiberal Democracy," 254–55; Zakaria, "Rise of Illiberal Democracy."
     On rethinking the public sphere "from an illiberal perspective," see also, Cody,
     "Populist Publics," 61.

23   Zakaria, "Rise of Illiberal Democracy," 22.

24   Zakaria, "Rise of Illiberal Democracy," 22.

25   Zakaria, "Rise of Illiberal Democracy," 22–23.

26   Lakier, "Illiberal Democracy," 253.

27   Lakier, "Illiberal Democracy," 253.

28   Lakier, "Illiberal Democracy," 256–57 (emphasis in original).

29   Lakier, "Illiberal Democracy," 261 (emphasis in original).

30   Lakier, "Illiberal Democracy," 263.

31   Lakier's interview with Surya Bahadur Bhattarai, general secretary of the FNTE,
     quoted in Lakier, "Illiberal Democracy," 264.

32   Lakier, "Illiberal Democracy," 262 (emphasis added).

33   Lakier, "Illiberal Democracy," 265.

34   Poudel, "Dealing with Syndicates," *My Republica*, August 26, 2019, https://
     myrepublica.nagariknetwork.com/news/dealing-with-syndicates/.

35   Poudel, "Dealing with Syndicates."

36   Poudel, "Dealing with Syndicates."

37   Poudel, "Dealing with Syndicates."

38   Chakrabarty, "'In the Name of Politics,'" 37.

39   Chakrabarty, "'In the Name of Politics,'" 37.

40   Chakrabarty, "'In the Name of Politics,'" 38.

41   Chakrabarty, "'In the Name of Politics,'" 38.

42   Chakrabarty, "'In the Name of Politics,'" 51–52.

43   Chakrabarty, "'In the Name of Politics,'" 52–53.

44   Chakrabarty, "'In the Name of Politics,'" 52–53.

45   Chakrabarty, "Early Railwaymen."

46   Recorded interview, Secunderabad, January 2, 2009.

47   Recorded interview, Secunderabad, January 2, 2009.

48   Recorded interview, Secunderabad, January 2, 2009.

49   Recorded interview, Lucknow, March 2009.

50   Interview, April 2009.

51   "Ryots Stage 'Rail Roko' at Secunderabad Station," *The Hindu*, September 6, 2008.

52   Recorded interview, Secunderabad, January 2, 2009.

53   Recorded interview, Hyderabad, April 23, 2009.

54   Recorded interview, Warangal, April 22, 2009.

55   Recorded interview, April 21, 2009.

56   "Rail Roko (Stop the Trains), 3 December, 2011," *International Campaign for Justice in Bhopal* (blog), November 15, 2011, https://www.bhopal.net/rail-roko-stop
     -the-trains-december-3-2011/.

57   "Chief Minister Backs Survivors, Rail Roko Ends," *International Campaign for Justice in Bhopal* (blog), December 3, 2011, https://www.bhopal.net/rail-roko-ends -as-chief-minister-supports-survivors/.

58   Recorded interview, Warangal, April 22, 2009.

59   "'Maha Rasta Roko' Peaceful," *The Hindu*, December 30, 2006.

60   "'High Voltage' Protests Jolt Government," *Times of India*, December 27, 2006; "All-Party Panel Formed against Kondayapalem Toll Plaza," *The Hindu*, May 13, 2016; "Maha rasta roko at Utnoor for podu lands," *Deccan Chronicle*, October 6, 2021.

61   "Unique 'Rail Roko' Today," *The Hindu*, March 1, 2011; "Telangana Protests Throw Train Services off Track," *The Hindu*, March 1, 2011.

62   "Unique 'Rail Roko' Today"; "Passengers of Long Distance Trains Affected," *The Hindu*, March 2, 2011.

63   "Protestors Disrupt Rail and Road Transport in Andhra Pradesh," *The Hindu*, January 5, 2010.

64   Bakshi, "Rail Roko . . . Roko"; "Gujjar Stir: Central Forces Rush to Rajasthan," *The Hindu*, December 22, 2010; "Rail Track Siege by Gujjars Continues," *The Hindu*, December 22, 2010; "Gujjar Agitation Enters 13th Day," *The Hindu*, January 1, 2011.

65   "Farmers Stage Rail Roko," *The Hindu*, October 25, 2007; "Onion Farmers Stage Rasta Roko in Nashik," *The Hindu*, February 9, 2011; "Rail Roko Successful, Government Will Have to Repeal Agri Laws: Farm Unions," *Times of India*, February 18, 2021.

66   "47 Trains Cancelled to Foil Telangana Million March," *Hindustan Times*, March 10, 2011.

67   "School Protest Stops S. Mumbai," *Indian Express*, July 29, 2009.

68   "What Are We Teaching Our Children?," *DNA India*, July 30, 2009.

69   Comment, July 30, 2009, "Students and Parents Stage Rasta Roko Protest outside New Era High School," *Daijiworld*, July 29, 2009, https://www.daijiworld.com /news/newsDisplay.aspx?newsID=63334.

70   Omvedt, "Rasta Roko."

71   "Mandal Commission," *Economic and Political Weekly*.

72   "Angry government employees come out of their offices in force to join students" (photograph), *The Tribune* (Chandigarh, India), August 31, 1990; "A big branch of a tree used to block vehicular traffic at the intersection of Sectors 7, 8, 18 and 19 by the anti-reservation activists in Chandigarh on Friday" (photograph), *The Tribune* (Chandigarh, India), August 31, 1990.

73   See, for example, Partha Chatterjee's use of Michel Foucault's concept of governmentality in his distinction between elites who make up what he describes as "civil society" and those who are visible primarily as members of governed populations who can be understood as making up "political society," discussed in the introduction. It is also worth pointing out that nonelite groups are not the only ones who have directly benefited from government schemes, government educational institutions, and state employment opportunities, given that the most coveted employment up until the 1990s was government service. This would suggest that we could view even the bourgeoisie in India as targets of gov-

ernmentality and therefore as governed populations whom Chatterjee suggests participate in political society. Chatterjee, "Violence of the State" and *Politics of the Governed*.

74 Interview, Secunderabad, January 2, 2009.

75 Interview, Secunderabad, January 2, 2009.

76 Interview, Lucknow, March 27, 2009.

77 Interview, Lucknow, March 27, 2009.

78 Kamra and Chandra, "Maoism and the Masses."

79 Kamra and Chandra, "Maoism and the Masses," 193.

80 Kamra and Chandra, "Maoism and the Masses," 213–14.

81 Kamra and Chandra, "Maoism and the Masses," 217.

82 Sundar, "Reflections on Civil Liberties," 366.

83 See, for example, Suykens, "Diffuse Authority"; Kunnath, *Rebels*.

84 Chakrabarty, "'In the Name of Politics.'"

85 Richard Kernaghan, "Furrows and Walls: On the Legal Topography of a Frontier Road," paper presented at the Annual Meeting of the American Anthropological Association, Philadelphia, December 2, 2009; and personal conversation.

86 Interview with Ashima Singh, Divisional Railway Manager, Northeastern Railways, Lucknow, March 2009.

SEVEN. RALLIES, PROCESSIONS, AND *YĀTRAS*

*Epigraph:* The English translation of Varavara Rao's poem from Telugu is by the author himself (accessed July 30, 2011, http://www.varavararao.org/en/poetry/deja_vu.html; no longer available). Rao wrote this poem in the context of the widespread upper-caste protests against the Mandal Commission's expansion of affirmative action quotas for government jobs and admission into government-aided educational institutions.

1 At the time, I was splitting my time between the archives of the National Rail Museum and the National Archives of India where I was examining Railway Board, Public Works Department, Home Department, and Political archival collections.

2 Interview, April 16, 2009. Dalit leader and chairman of the committee that drafted India's Constitution, Dr. Bhimrao Ambedkar (1891–1956), continues to be held in high regard by Dalits, and the anniversaries of his birth (April 14), death (Dec. 6), and conversion to Buddhism (Oct. 14) are widely observed with processions and pilgrimages. See Rao, *The Caste Question*, 184.

3 Interview, senior railway official, January 6, 2009.

4 Interview, retired senior railway official, March 26, 2009.

5 "Fatal Stampede after Lucknow Rally," BBC *News*, September 29, 2002.

6 Interview, senior railway official, March 25, 2009.

7 Interview, senior Government Railway Police official, March 27, 2009.

8 Interview, senior railway official, Secunderabad, January 9, 2009.

9 Letter from Michael O'Dwyer to Lord Lytton, April 26, 1921, Home Political 1921, File No. 111, p. 1, NAI.

10 "The Army in India," Extract from the Parliamentary Debates of the House of Lords, dated Wednesday, May 4 1921, Home Political 1921, File No. 111, p. 3, NAI.

11 Letter from C. W. Gwynne, May 28, 1921, Home Political 1921, File No. 111, pp. 3–4, NAI.

12 Letter from C. W. Gwynne, p. 4.

13 Letter from the Secretary, The Marwadi Chamber of Commerce Ltd. to the Secretary to the Government of India, Commerce Department, Simla, August 6, 1936, Railway Traffic B, 1979-T/44-117, May 1938, No. 19.

14 Nehru, "Students and Discipline," 73.

15 Recent actions by the Indian government to stifle free speech and silence journalists and academics show that this shift from criminal to political can move in both directions, redefining political expression and political action as criminal. See, for example, Ramachandra Guha's discussion of recent applications of colonial-era sedition laws ("Threat to Speech: Law 'Designed to Suppress the Liberty of the Citizen' Used against Gandhi and Indians Now," *Telegraph*, August 3, 2019).

16 On middlemen and intermediaries, see, for example, Reddy and Haragopal, "Pyraveekar"; Phillip Oldenburg, "Middlemen"; Björkman, *Bombay Brokers*.

17 Kruks-Wisner, *Claiming the State*, 11. See also Chandra and Taghioff, *Staking Claims*.

18 Kruks-Wisner, *Claiming the State*, 19. She goes on to qualify this statement: "This prediction, however, is dependent on the underlying policies and presence of the state, which sets the stage for claim-making. Social and spatial exposure can be catalytic—but only where the state is *capable* of delivering a broad array of services but *uneven* in actually doing so. In other words, there must be resources to be had but difficulty in obtaining them" (emphasis in original).

19 Kruks-Wisner, *Claiming the State*, 25.

20 Kruks-Wisner, *Claiming the State*, 11–12, 25.

21 Kruks-Wisner, *Claiming the State*, 108.

22 Kruks-Wisner, *Claiming the State*, 13. Kruks-Wisner's data concerning available repertoires for making claims of the state distinguish between direct and mediated actions, and between state (administrative and representative institutions) and nonstate channels (actors and institutions), rather than between individual and collective activities. She divides the repertoire or range of state-claiming activities into ten categories: "Direct Contacting: Administrative and Representative Institutions" (which includes three subcategories: "Gram Panchayat Members," "Bureaucrats: Block and District Levels," and "Politicians/ Parties") and "Mediated Approaches: Non-State Actors and Institutions" (which includes seven subcategories: "Caste Body," "Intercaste Body," "Individual Broker," "NH [Neighborhood] Association," "Village Association," "NGO," and "Social Movement"), 96.

23 Ribot and Peluso, "A Theory of Access." By focusing on "the ability to benefit from things" rather than on *rights*, they argue that "this formulation brings attention to a wider range of social relationships that can constrain or enable people to benefit from resources" (153–54).

24  Bussell, *Clients and Constituents*, 10.

25  Guha, *Unquiet Woods*, 67.

26  Tufekci, *Twitter and Tear Gas*, 236.

27  Tufekci, *Twitter and Tear Gas*.

28  See also Bussell, *Clients and Constituents*, on the significant amounts of time spent by elected officials in India in responding to citizens' concerns.

29  Pingle, *Fall and Rise of Telangana*. See also my discussion of the "women's wall" in Kerala in January 2019 in the conclusion.

30  On contrasts between South Asian and "European" publics, see Kaviraj, "Filth and the Public Sphere," 108; Perkins, "*Mehfil* to the Printed Word," 52; Piliavsky, "Where Is the Public Sphere?," 107. Here, I am interested in different invocations of the concept of the public within South Asia itself.

31  Habermas, *Structural Transformation*; Anderson, *Imagined Communities*. See also Calhoun, *Habermas and the Public Sphere*; Warner, *Publics and Counterpublics*.

32  For the earliest discussions of Habermas, *Structural Transformation*, by South Asian scholars after its 1989 translation into English, see the special journal issue edited by Sandria Freitag, "Aspects of 'the Public' in Colonial South Asia," *South Asia: Journal of South Asian Studies* 14(1), 1991 (especially Freitag, "Introduction," and Price, "Acting in Public"). See also Breckenridge, *Consuming Modernity*, and the discussion of Freitag's special issue twenty-five years later in Ingram, Scott, and Tareen, *Imagining the Public*.

33  Bayly, *Empire and Information*, 182.

34  Haynes, *Rhetoric and Ritual*, especially chapter 7.

35  Gupta and Sharma, *Print Media and Communalism*; Oberoi, *Construction of Religious Boundaries*; Dalmia, *Nationalization of Hindu Traditions*; Ramaswamy, *Passions of the Tongue*; Pernau, *Ashraf into Middle Classes*; Orsini, *Hindi Public Sphere* and "Booklets and Saints"; Naregal, *Language, Politics, Elites*; Stark, *Empire of Books*.

36  Gurunatham, *Viresalingam*; Āndhra Dēśa Granthabhāṇḍāgāra Sanghamuwāru, *Āndhra Dēśa Granthālaya Caritra*; Narayana Rao, *Emergence of Andhra Pradesh*; Suntharalingam, *Politics and Nationalist Awakening*; Gopinatha Rao, *Library Movement*; Subba Rao, *History of Andhra Movement*; Vaikuntham, *Education and Social Change*; Ramakrishna, *Social Reform in Andhra*; Murali, "Changing Perceptions"; Manohar Reddy, "Modernity of Language."

37  Rajagopal, *Indian Public Sphere*; Srinivas, *Politics as Performance*; Dass, *Outside the Lettered City*. On associational life, see Nair, *Promise of the Metropolis*, chap. 2; Cohen, *In the Club*.

38  For discussions of gender, class, and caste and the public sphere, see Fernandes, "Beyond Public Spaces"; Gupta, *Sexuality, Obscenity, Community*; *Gendering Colonial India*; and *Gender of Caste*; Mitchell, *Language, Emotion, and Politics*, chap. 6; Gundimeda, "Democratisation of the Public Sphere"; Nijhawan, *Women and Girls*; Bagchi, *Beyond the Private World*; Rawat and Satyanarayana, "Introduction, Dalit Studies."

39   Ilaiah, *Why I Am Not a Hindu.*

40   Mitchell, *Language, Emotion, and Politics.*

41   Although language formed a common basis for state reformation throughout the second half of the twentieth century, by 2000, other criteria began to supersede language, including issues relating to economic and cultural marginalization. As outlined in the introduction, the new states of Chhattisgarh, Jharkhand, and Uttarakhand were formed in 2000, and Telangana in 2014.

42   Sriramamurti, *Kavi Jīvitamulu,* 1.

43   In the preface to the second edition of his *Kavi Jīvitamulu,* published in 1893, Sriramamurti wrote of his earlier first edition, published in 1878, that it had been an experiment "in order to see what the reception would be like among my fellow countrymen [*dēśasthulu*]" (Sriramamurti, *Kavi Jīvitamulu,* 1, my translation.)

44   See, for example, Guha, *Elementary Aspects,* 257; Amin, "Gandhi as Mahatma"; and, more recently, Wagner, *Great Fear of 1857.*

45   Warner, *Publics and Counterpublics,* 65.

46   Warner, *Publics and Counterpublics,* 66.

47   Warner, *Publics and Counterpublics,* 66.

48   Warner, *Publics and Counterpublics,* 67.

49   Mitchell, *Language, Emotion, and Politics,* 195–203.

50   Mitchell, *Language, Emotion, and Politics,* 194, 200, 202–3.

51   Recorded interview with former leaders and Telugu linguistic state activists, Nellore town, October 19, 2002 (emphasis added), cited in Mitchell, *Language, Emotion, and Politics,* 199–200.

52   For additional examples, see Mitchell, *Language, Emotion, and Politics,* 200–203.

53   Mazzarella, "Myth of the Multitude."

54   Examples include the Narmada Bachao Andolan (Save the Narmada River Movement), the Chipko Andolan (Hug the Trees Movement), the All-India Kisan Andolan (All-India Farmers Movement), or the Beej Bachao Andolan (Save the Seeds Movement).

55   Brown, *Telugu-English Dictionary.*

56   Guha, *Unquiet Woods.*

57   "Somnath Ignites Democratic Values among Students," *The Hindu,* August 12, 2008, 3.

58   Muthukkaruppan, "Dalit," 41, and "Critique of Caste Violence"; Mitchell, *Rule of Experts,* especially chap. 5, "Nobody Listens to a Poor Man," 127–46.

59   Kumar, *Police Matters.*

CONCLUSION

1   Snigdha Poonam, "Indian Women Just Did a Remarkable Thing—They Formed a Wall of Protest," *The Guardian,* January 3, 2019.

2   "30 Lakh People in Kerala to Participate in 'Wall of Women' Campaign," *The Wire,* January 1, 2019; "Sabarimala Temple: Indian Women Form '620km Human Chain' for Equality," *BBC News,* January 1, 2019.

3 "Third Woman Enters Indian Temple amid Protests at Lifting of Ban," *The Guardian*, January 4, 2019.

4 "Longest Human Chain (Length)," *Guinness World Records*, http://www .guinnessworldrecords.com/world-records/longest-human-chain-(length) (accessed January 5, 2019).

5 Mohammed Siddique, "'Longest Human Chain' Formed for Telangana," *Rediff News*, February 3, 2010, http://news.rediff.com/slide-show/2010/feb/03/slide -show-1-andhra-crisis-longest-human-chain-formed-for-telangana.htm.

6 Amit Ranjan, "Join Madhesh Human Chain," *Madhesi Youth: Grassroots Voice for Marginalized Groups in Nepal*, October 1, 2015, http://www.madhesiyouth .com/news/join-madhesh-human-chain-1st-october-1-pm/; "LDF's 'Human Chain' Protest against Demonetization in Kerala," *Economic Times*, December 29, 2016; Amarnath Tewary, "Bihar Supports Prohibition with 'The World's Longest Human Chain,'" *The Hindu*, January 21, 2017.

7 Sheezan Nezami and Ramashankar, "5 Crore Form 18,034 km-Long Human Chain in Bihar," *Times of India*, January 20, 2020.

8 Zeynep Tufekci argues that we should recognize *attention* as a key resource for social and political movements and that attention should therefore be theorized in its own right. "Attention is oxygen for movements," she writes. "Without it, they cannot catch fire. Powerful actors try to smother movements by denying them attention." She also reminds us just how new the networked public sphere is—Facebook has been around only since 2004, Twitter since 2006, the first iPhone only since 2007, and WhatsApp only since 2009 (*Twitter and Tear Gas*, 29–30).

9 See, for example, the Mumbai municipal water engineers discussed in Björkman, *Pipe Politics*.

10 Bussell, *Clients and Constituents*; Kruks-Wisner, *Claiming the State*.

11 Alice Abraham, "Why Are Some Women against the Kerala Government's Women's Wall?," *FII: Feminism in India*, January 2, 2019, https://feminisminindia .com/2019/01/02/against-womens-wall-kerala/.

12 J. Devika, "A Feminist View: Why I Cannot Celebrate the Success of Kerala's Women's Wall," *Scroll.in*, January 14, 2019.

13 Rohit Kumer Singh, "Bihar Human Chain: BJP Says Children Were Forced to Participate," *India Today*, January 22, 2017.

14 Madan Kumar, "Bihar Government's Human Chain against Dowry System and Child Marriage a 'Super Flop': Opposition," *Times of India*, January 21, 2018.

15 "Bihar's Tryst with Human Chain Today," *Times of India*, January 21, 2017; Vithika Salomi, "13,500 km Target for Bihar's Anti-dowry Human Chain," *DNA*, January 14, 2018.

16 Schnapp and Tiews, *Crowds*, xi.

17 Parkinson, *Democracy and Public Space*.

18 Parkinson, *Democracy and Public Space*, 1, 8. On the role of images within contemporary democracy, see also Strassler, *Demanding Images*.

19 Parkinson, *Democracy and Public Space*, 2, 11.

20   Sreedevi Jayarajan, "Sabarimala Violence: 1286 Cases Registered in Kerala, 3187 People Arrested," *News Minute*, January 5, 2019; "Protests Erupt in Kerala after Two Women Enter Sabarimala; bjp, Congress Attack Vijayan Government," *Indian Express*, January 2, 2019; "Kerala Turns into War Zone after Women's Entry into Sabarimala," *Times of India*, January 3, 2019.

21   Rousseau, "Of Deputies or Representatives," 114.

22   Thomas Jefferson to James Madison, January 30, 1787, in Appleby and Ball, *Jefferson*, 153.

23   Mehta, "Redefining 'Azadi'"; Pooja Dantewadia and Vishnu Padmanabhan, "Sedition Cases in India: What Data Says," *LiveMint*, February 25, 2020; "Use and Misuse of Sedition Law: Section 124A of ipc," *India Today*, October 9, 2019; Ayesha Pattnaik, "The Art of Dissolving Dissent: India's Sedition Law as an Instrument to Regulate Public Opinion," *South Asia Centre Blog*, London School of Economics, October 4, 2019, https://blogs.lse.ac.uk/southasia/2019/10/04/long -read-the-art-of-dissolving-dissent-indias-sedition-law-as-an-instrument-to -regulate-public-opinion/; Swaminathan A. Aiyar, "Why India Needs to Scrap Its Sedition Law," *Economic Times*, February 29, 2020.

24   Lydia Finzel, "Democratic Backsliding in India, the World's Largest Democracy," *V-Dem*, February 24, 2020, https://v-dem.net/weekly_graph/democratic -backsliding-in-india-the-world-s-l. The Democracy Index published by the Economist Intelligence Unit, based on sixty indicators, also shows India falling from the thirty-fifth most democratic country in the world in 2006 to fifty-third in 2020.

25   An example of the shift in positions on the practice of dharna is that of Telangana chief minister K. Chandrashekar Rao (KCR). As the leader of the Telangana Rashtra Samiti political party during the movement for a separate Telangana state, Chandrashekar Rao supported and participated in numerous events at Hyderabad's Dharna Chowk, including events in October 2011 as part of the "Sakala Janula Samme" (All People's Strike), discussed in the introduction. Once the new state was created and he was installed as chief minister, however, his position on dissent shifted, and he sought to close Dharna Chowk, a move that resulted in widespread opposition and legal challenges (see chapter 1). In the wake of his loss in a by-election in the Huzurabad constituency on October 30, 2021, Chandrashekar Rao suddenly embraced the role of dharna once again, leading a farmers' dharna directed at the central Indian government and appearing at Dharna Chowk for the first time in ten years. See "KCR back to Dharna Chowk after 10 Years!," *Telugu360*, November 17, 2021; "K Chandrashekar Rao to Sit on Dharna for First Time after Becoming cm," *Times of India*, November 18, 2021; and a recording of his speech at Dharna Chowk on November 18, 2021, at https://www.youtube.com/watch?v=-b1NRw9iKVI.

Abrams, Philip. "Notes on the Difficulty of Studying the State." *Journal of Historical Sociology* 1, no. 1 (1988): 58–89.

Adas, Michael. "From Avoidance to Confrontation: Peasant Protest in Precolonial and Colonial Southeast Asia." *Comparative Studies in Society and History* 23, no. 2 (1981): 217–47.

Agha, Asif. "Meet Mediatization." *Language & Communication, Mediatized Communication in Complex Societies* 31, no. 3 (2011): 163–70.

Ahluwalia, Montek S. "The 1991 Reforms: How Home-Grown Were They?" *Economic and Political Weekly* 51, no. 29 (2016): 39–46.

Ahuja, Ravi. "Labour Unsettled: Mobility and Protest in the Madras Region, 1750–1800." *Indian Economic and Social History Review* 35, no. 4 (1998): 381–404.

Alam, Javeed. *Who Wants Democracy?* Hyderabad: Orient Longman, 2004.

Althusser, Louis. "Ideology and Ideological State Apparatuses: Notes towards an Investigation." In *Lenin and Philosophy, and Other Essays*, translated by Ben Brewster, 127–86. New York: Monthly Review Press, 1971.

Althusser, Louis. *On the Reproduction of Capitalism: Ideology and Ideological State Apparatuses*. Translated by G. M. Goshgarian. New York: Verso, 2014.

Amin, Shahid. "Gandhi as Mahatma: Gorakhpur District, Eastern UP, 1921–22." In *Subaltern Studies III*, edited by Ranajit Guha, 288–348. Delhi: Oxford University Press, 1984.

Anderson, Benedict. *Imagined Communities: Reflections on the Origin and Spread of Nationalism*. London: Verso, 1991.

Anderson, Edward, and Arkotong Longkumer. "'Neo-Hindutva': Evolving Forms, Spaces, and Expressions of Hindu Nationalism." *Contemporary South Asia* 26, no. 4 (2018): 371–77.

Āndhra Dēśa Granthabhāṇḍāgāra Sanghamuwāru (Andhra Region Library Association). *Āndhra Dēśa Granthālaya Caritra* (History of the Andhra Region Library Movement). Bejawāḍa: Bejawāḍa Vāṇī Mudrākṣaraśāla, 1916.

Anjaria, Jonathan Shapiro. "Is There a Culture of the Indian Street?" *Seminar* 636, no. 50 (2013): 21–27.

Anjaria, Jonathan Shapiro. *The Slow Boil: Street Food, Rights and Public Space in Mumbai*. Stanford: Stanford University Press, 2016.

Anjaria, Jonathan Shapiro, and Colin McFarlane, eds. *Urban Navigations: Politics, Space and the City in South Asia.* London: Routledge, 2011.

Anjaria, Jonathan Shapiro, and Ursula Rao. "Talking Back to the State: Citizens' Engagement after Neoliberal Reform in India." *Social Anthropology/Anthropologie Sociale* 22, no. 4 (2014): 410–27.

Annavarapu, Sneha. "Moving Targets: Traffic Rules, State Authority, and Road Safety in Hyderabad, India." PhD diss., University of Chicago, 2020.

Anveshi Law Committee. "Caste and the Metropolitan University." *Economic and Political Weekly* 37, no. 12 (2002): 1100–1103.

Appadurai, Arjun. "Deep Democracy: Urban Governmentality and the Horizon of Politics." *Public Culture* 14, no. 1 (2002): 21–47.

Appleby, Joyce, and Terence Ball, eds. *Jefferson: Political Writings.* Cambridge: Cambridge University Press, 1999.

Arasaratnam, S. "Trade and Political Dominion in South India, 1750–1790: Changing British-Indian Relationships." *Modern Asian Studies* 13, no. 1 (1979): 19–40.

Arendt, Hannah. *Crises of the Republic.* New York: Harvest, 1972.

Arendt, Hannah. *The Human Condition.* 2nd ed. Chicago: University of Chicago Press, 1998.

Auerbach, Adam Michael. *Demanding Development: The Politics of Public Goods Provision in India's Urban Slums.* Cambridge: Cambridge University Press, 2019.

Auerbach, Adam Michael, and Tariq Thachil. "How Clients Select Brokers: Competition and Choice in India's Slums." *American Political Science Review* 112, no. 4 (2018): 775–91.

Avritzer, Leonardo. *Democracy and the Public Space in Latin America.* Princeton: Princeton University Press, 2002.

Azzellini, Dario, and Marina Sitrin, *They Can't Represent Us! Reinventing Democracy from Greece to Occupy.* London: Verso, 2014.

Baddena. *Sumati Śatakamu: An English Rendering with Notes and Comments.* Translated by E. Nageswara Rao. Hyderabad: C. P. Brown Academy, 2008.

Bagchi, Subrata, ed. *Beyond the Private World: Indian Women in the Public Sphere.* New Delhi: Primus Books, 2014.

Bahri, Hardev. *Learners' Hindi-English Dictionary = Siksarthi Hindi-Angrejhi Sabdakosa.* Delhi: Rajpal & Sons, 1989.

Bajoria, Jayshree, and Linda Lakhdhir. *Stifling Dissent: The Criminalization of Peaceful Expression in India.* New York: Human Rights Watch, 2016.

Bakhle, Janaki. "Savarkar (1883–1966), Sedition and Surveillance: The Rule of Law in a Colonial Situation." *Social History* 35, no. 1 (2010): 51–75.

Balagopal, K. *The Karamchedu Massacre: A Report.* Guntur: Andhra Pradesh Civil Liberties Committee, July 22, 1985.

Balagopal, K. "Karamchedu: Second Anniversary." *Economic and Political Weekly* 22, no. 33 (1987): 1378–81.

Balibar, Étienne. "Three Concepts of Politics: Emancipation, Transformation, Civility." In *Politics and the Other Scene,* translated by Christine Jones, James Swenson, and Chris Turner, 1–39. New York: Verso, 2002.

Balibar, Étienne. *Violence and Civility: On the Limits of Political Philosophy*. New York: Columbia University Press, 2015.

Banerjee, Mukulika. "Democracy, Sacred and Everyday: An Ethnographic Case from India." In *Democracy: Anthropological Approaches*, edited by Julia Paley, 63–96. Santa Fe: School for Advanced Research Press, 2008.

Banerjee, Mukulika. "Elections as Communitas." *Social Research* 78, no. 1 (2011): 75–98.

Banerjee, Mukulika. *Why India Votes?* New Delhi: Routledge, 2014.

Barnett, Clive, and Murray Low, eds. *Spaces of Democracy: Geographical Perspectives on Citizenship, Participation and Representation*. London: Sage, 2004.

Bate, Bernard. *Protestant Textuality and the Tamil Modern: Political Oratory and the Social Imaginary in South Asia*. Edited by E. Annamalai, Francis Cody, Malarvizhi Jayanth, and Constantine V. Nakassis. Stanford: Stanford University Press, 2021.

Bate, Bernard. *Tamil Oratory and the Dravidian Aesthetic: Democratic Practice in South India*. New York: Columbia University Press, 2009.

Bauman, Richard, and Charles L. Briggs. *Voices of Modernity: Language Ideologies and the Politics of Inequality*. Cambridge: Cambridge University Press, 2003.

Bayat, Asef. *Revolution without Revolutionaries: Making Sense of the Arab Spring*. Palo Alto, CA: Stanford University Press, 2017.

Bayly, C. A. *Empire and Information: Intelligence Gathering and Social Communication in India, 1780–1870*. Cambridge: Cambridge University Press, 1996.

Bayly, C. A. "Introduction: The Meanings of Liberalism in Colonial India." In *Recovering Liberties: Indian Thought in the Age of Liberalism and Empire*, 1–25. New York: Cambridge University Press, 2011.

Bear, Laura. *Lines of the Nation: Indian Railway Workers, Bureaucracy, and the Intimate Historical Self*. New York: Columbia University Press, 2007.

Bedi, Tarini. *The Dashing Ladies of Shiv Sena: Political Matronage in Urbanizing India*. Albany: SUNY Press, 2017.

Benbow, William. *Grand National Holiday, and Congress of the Productive Classes. &c.* London: William Benbow, 1909.

Benhabib, Seyla. "Toward a Deliberative Model of Democratic Legitimacy." In *Democracy and Difference: Contesting the Boundaries of the Political*, 67–94. Princeton: Princeton University Press, 1996.

Bhargava, Rajeev. "Introduction." In *Civil Society, Public Sphere and Citizenship*, edited by Rajeev Bhargava and Helmut Reifeld, 13–55. New Delhi: Sage, 2005.

Bhargava, Rajeev. *The Promise of India's Secular Democracy*. Oxford: Oxford University Press, 2010.

Bilgrami, Akeel. "Gandhi's Integrity: The Philosophy behind the Politics." *Postcolonial Studies* 5, no. 1 (2002): 79–93.

Björkman, Lisa, ed. *Bombay Brokers*. Durham, NC: Duke University Press, 2021.

Björkman, Lisa. "The Ostentatious Crowd: Public Protest as Mass-Political Street Theatre in Mumbai." *Critique of Anthropology* 35, no. 2 (2015): 142–65.

Björkman, Lisa. *Pipe Politics, Contested Waters: Embedded Infrastructures of Millennial Mumbai*, Durham, NC: Duke University Press, 2015.

Björkman, Lisa. "'You Can't Buy a Vote': Meanings of Money in a Mumbai Election." *American Ethnologist* 41, no. 4 (2014): 617–34.

Blom, Amélie, and Nicolas Jaoul. "Introduction: The Moral and Affectual Dimension of Collective Action in South Asia." *South Asia Multidisciplinary Academic Journal* 2 (2008).

Blom, Amélie, and Stéphanie Tawa Lama-Rewal, eds. *Emotions, Mobilisations and South Asian Politics*. Delhi: Routledge India, 2019.

Boyd, Richard. "'The Value of Civility?'" *Urban Studies* 43, no. 5/6 (2006): 863–78.

Breckenridge, Carol A., ed. *Consuming Modernity: Public Culture in a South Asian World*. Minneapolis: University of Minnesota Press, 1995.

Brown, Charles Philip. *A Telugu-English Dictionary*. Madras: Promoting Christian Knowledge, 1903.

Brown, Charles Philip. *Telugu Nighaṇṭu/A Telugu-English Dictionary*. Madras: Christian Knowledge Society's Press, 1852.

Brown, Judith M., ed. *Gandhi and Civil Disobedience: The Mahatma in Indian Politics, 1928–34*. Cambridge: Cambridge University Press, 1977.

Buckland, C. E. *Bengal under the Lieutenant-Governors*, vol. 1. Calcutta: Kedarnath Bose, 1902.

Burchell, Graham, Colin Gordon, and Peter Miller, eds. *The Foucault Effect: Studies in Governmentality*. Chicago: University of Chicago Press, 1991.

Burghart, Richard. "The Conditions of Listening: The Everyday Experience of Politics in Nepal." In *The Conditions of Listening: Essays on Religion, History and Politics in Nepal*, edited by C. J. Fuller and Jonathan Spencer, 300–318. Delhi: Oxford University Press, 1996.

Bussell, Jennifer. *Clients and Constituents: Political Responsiveness in Patronage Democracies*. Oxford: Oxford University Press, 2019.

Butler, Chris. *Henri Lefebvre: Spatial Politics, Everyday Life, and the Right to the City*. New York: Routledge, 2012.

Butler, Judith. *Notes toward a Performative Theory of Assembly*. Cambridge, MA: Harvard University Press, 2015.

Calhoun, Craig. *Habermas and the Public Sphere*. Cambridge, MA: MIT Press, 1992.

Campbell, A. Claude. *Glimpses of the Nizam's Dominions: Being an Exhaustive Photographic History of the Hyderabad State, Deccan, India*. Bombay: C. B. Burrows, 1898.

Carpenter, Edward. *Civilisation: Its Cause and Cure and Other Essays*. New York: Charles Scribner's Sons, 1921.

Carter, Stephen L. *Civility: Manners, Morals, and the Etiquette of Democracy*. New York: Harper Perennial, 1999.

Chakrabarti, Phanindra N. "Myth of the Date of Establishment of the First English Factory (1613) and Its Baneful Effect on Mughal Economy." *Proceedings of the Indian History Congress* 40 (1979): 487–90.

Chakrabarty, Dipesh. "Early Railwaymen in India: 'Dacoity' and 'Train-Wrecking' (c. 1860–1900)." In *Essays in Honor of S. C. Sarkar*, 523–50. Delhi: People's Publishing House, 1976.

Chakrabarty, Dipesh. "'In the Name of Politics': Democracy and the Power of the Multitude in India." *Public Culture* 19, no. 1 (2007): 35–57.

Chandra, Uday. "The Maoist Movement in Contemporary India." *Social Movement Studies* 13, no. 3 (2014): 414–19.

Chandra, Uday, and Daniel Taghioff, eds. *Staking Claims: The Politics of Social Movements in Contemporary Rural India*. Delhi: Oxford University Press, 2016.

Chattaraj, Durba. "Roadscapes: Everyday Life along the Rural-Urban Continuum in 21st Century India." PhD diss., Yale University, 2010.

Chatterjee, Partha. "Democracy and the Violence of the State: A Political Negotiation of Death." *Inter-Asia Cultural Studies* 2, no. 1 (2001): 7–21.

Chatterjee, Partha. *Lineages of Political Society: Studies in Postcolonial Democracy*. New York: Columbia University Press, 2011.

Chatterjee, Partha. *The Politics of the Governed: Reflections on Popular Politics in Most of the World*. New York: Columbia University Press, 2004.

Chaturvedi, Mahendra. *A Practical Hindi-English Dictionary*. Delhi: National Publishing House, 1970.

Chowdhury, Nusrat. *Paradoxes of the Popular: Crowd Politics in Bangladesh*. Palo Alto, CA: Stanford University Press, 2019.

Cody, Francis. *The Light of Knowledge: Literacy Activism and the Politics of Writing in South India*. Ithaca, NY: Cornell University Press, 2013.

Cody, Francis. "Populist Publics: Print Capitalism and Crowd Violence beyond Liberal Frameworks." *Comparative Studies of South Asia, Africa, and the Middle East* 35, no. 1 (2015): 50–65.

Cody, Francis. "Publics and Politics." *Annual Review of Anthropology* 40 (2011): 37–52.

Cohen, Benjamin B. *In the Club: Associational Life in Colonial South Asia*. Manchester: Manchester University Press, 2015.

Cohen, Joshua. "Reflections on Civility." In *Civility and Democracy in America: A Reasonable Understanding*, edited by Cornell W. Clayton and Richard Elgar, 119–23. Pullman: Washington State University Press, 2012.

Collins, Michael Adrian. "Recalling Democracy: Electoral Politics, Minority Representation, and Dalit Assertion in Modern India." PhD diss., University of Pennsylvania, 2017.

Committee on Disturbances in Bombay, Delhi, and the Punjab. *Report: Disorders Inquiry Committee 1919–1920*. Calcutta: Superintendent Government Printing, 1920.

Connolly, William E. *Identity/Difference: Democratic Negotiations of Political Paradox*. Minneapolis: University of Minnesota Press, 2002.

Connolly, William E. *Pluralism*. Durham, NC: Duke University Press, 2005.

Connolly, William E. "Response: Realizing Agonistic Respect." *Journal of the American Academy of Religion* 72, no. 2 (2004): 507–11.

Cooper, Charlie. "Understanding the English Riots of 2011: 'Mindless Criminality' or Youth 'Mekin Histri' in Austerity Britain?" *Youth and Policy*, no. 109 (2012): 6–26.

Cowan, Brian. "What Was Masculine about the Public Sphere? Gender and the Coffeehouse Milieu in Post-Restoration England." *History Workshop Journal* 51, no. 1 (2001): 127–57.

Crook, Wilfrid Harris. *The General Strike: A Study of Labor's Tragic Weapon in Theory and Practice*. Chapel Hill: University of North Carolina Press, 1931.

Dabashi, Hamid. *Arab Spring: The End of Postcolonialism*. London: Zed Books, 2012.

Dalmia, Vasudha. *The Nationalization of Hindu Traditions: Bharatendu Harischandra and Nineteenth-Century Banaras*. New Delhi: Oxford University Press, 1997.

Dalton, Dennis. *Mahatma Gandhi: Nonviolent Power in Action*. New York: Columbia University Press, 1993.

Das Gupta, Ashin. "The Merchants of Surat, c. 1700–50." In *Elites in South Asia*, edited by Edmund Leach and S. N. Mukherjee, 201–23. Cambridge: Cambridge University Press, 1970.

Dass, Manishita. *Outside the Lettered City: Cinema, Modernity, and the Public Sphere in Late Colonial India*. New York: Oxford University Press, 2015.

Datla, Kavita Saraswathi. *The Language of Secular Islam: Urdu National and Colonial India*. Honolulu: University of Hawai'i Press, 2013.

Deshpande, J. V. "Behind Dalit Anger." *Economic and Political Weekly* 32, no. 33–34 (1997): 2090–91.

Desouza, Peter Ronald. "The Struggle for Local Government: Indian Democracy's New Phase." In *Local Democracy in South Asia: Microprocesses of Democratization in Nepal and Its Neighbors*, edited by David Gellner and Krishna Hachhethu, 301–26. Delhi: Sage, 2008.

Dharampal. *Civil Disobedience and Indian Tradition: With Some Early Nineteenth Century Documents*. Varanasi: Sarva Seva Sangh Prakashan, 1971.

Dharampal. *Dharampal Papers, Vol. 17, Illustrations of Indian Non-Cooperation, 1700–1850*. Sevagram: Ashram Pratishtan, 2000.

Dharnā Chowk Parirakṣaṇa Kamiṭī (Committee to Save Dharna Chowk). *Prajā Gontuka: Dharnā Chowk* (People's Voice: Dharna Chowk). Hyderabad: Dharaṇi Enterprises, 2018.

Diwakar, R. R. *Saga of Satyagraha*. Bombay: Gandhi Peace Foundation, 1969.

Dryzek, John S. *Deliberative Democracy and Beyond: Liberals, Critics, Contestations*. Oxford: Oxford University Press, 2000.

Dryzek, John S. "Deliberative Democracy in Divided Societies: Alternatives to Agonism and Analgesia." *Political Theory* 33, no. 2 (2005): 218–42.

East India Company. *Selection of Papers from the Records at the East-India House, relating to the Revenue, Police, and Civil and Criminal Justice, under the Company's Governments in India*, vol. 2. London: Court of Directors, 1820.

Elias, Norbert. *The Civilizing Process*. New York: Urizen Books, 1994.

Ellis, Markman. *The Coffee House: A Cultural History*. London: Orion, 2004.

Engels, Frederick. "The Bakuninists at Work: A Memorandum on the Spanish Uprising in the Summer of 1873" [1873]. *The Communist* 17, no. 2 (1938): 143–57.

Farrell, Thomas B. *Norms of Rhetorical Culture*. New Haven: Yale University Press, 1993.

Farrelly, Colin. *Justice, Democracy and Reasonable Agreement*. New York: Palgrave Macmillan, 2007.

Fernandes, Leela. "Beyond Public Spaces and Private Spheres: Gender, Family, and Working-Class Politics in India." *Feminist Studies* 23, no. 3 (1997): 525–47.

Fishkin, James S., and Robert C. Luskin. "Experimenting with a Democratic Ideal: Deliberative Polling and Public Opinion." *Acta Politica* 40, no. 3 (2005): 284–98.

Forrester, Duncan B. "Subregionalism in India: The Case of Telangana." *Foreign Affairs* 43, no. 1 (1970): 5–21.

Fossen, Thomas. "Agonistic Critiques of Liberalism: Perfection and Emancipation." *Contemporary Political Theory* 7, no. 4 (2008): 376–94.

Foucault, Michel. *The Birth of Biopolitics: Lectures at the College de France, 1978–79.* Edited by Michel Senellart. Translated by Graham Burchell. New York: Palgrave Macmillan, 2008.

Foucault, Michel. *Discipline and Punish: The Birth of the Prison.* Translated by Alan Sheridan. New York: Vintage Books, 1995.

Foucault, Michel. "Governmentality." In *The Foucault Effect: Studies in Governmentality,* edited by Graham Burchell, Colin Gordon, and Peter Miller, 87–104. Chicago: University of Chicago Press, 1991.

Foucault, Michel. *Security, Territory, Population: Lectures at the College de France, 1977–78.* Edited by Michel Senellart. Translated by Graham Burchell. New York: Palgrave Macmillan, 2009.

Foucault, Michel. "The Subject and Power." *Critical Inquiry* 8, no. 4 (1982): 777–95.

Foucault, Michel. "Technologies of the Self." In *Technologies of the Self: A Seminar with Michel Foucault,* edited by Luther H. Martin, Huck Gutman, and Patrick H. Hutton, 16–49. Amherst: University of Massachusetts Press, 1988.

Frank, Jason. "Beyond Democracy's Imaginary Investments." *Figurative Publics: Crowds, Protest, and Democratic Anxieties, The Immanent Frame: Secularism, Religion, and the Public Sphere.* Social Science Research Council, February 19, 2020. https://tif.ssrc.org/2020/02/19/beyond-democracys-imaginary-investments/.

Frankel, Francine R., Zoya Hasan, Rajeev Bhargava, and Balveer Arora, eds. *Transforming India: Social and Political Dynamics of Democracy.* Delhi: Oxford University Press, 2000.

Fraser, Nancy. "From Redistribution to Recognition? Dilemmas of Justice in a 'Post-Socialist' Age." *New Left Review* 1 (1995): 68–93.

Fraser, Nancy. "Rethinking Recognition." *New Left Review* 3 (2000): 107–20.

Fraser, Nancy. "Rethinking the Public Sphere: A Contribution to the Critique of Actually Existing Democracy." *Social Text,* no. 25/26 (1990): 56–80.

Freitag, Sandria. *Collective Action and Community: Public Arenas and the Emergence of Communalism in North India.* Berkeley: University of California Press, 1989.

Freitag, Sandria. "Introduction." *South Asia: Journal of South Asian Studies* 14, no. 1 (1991): 1–13.

Friedman, Milton. *Capitalism and Freedom.* Chicago: University of Chicago Press, 1962.

Friedman, Milton, and Rose Friedman. *Free to Choose: A Personal Statement.* New York: Harcourt Brace Jovanovich, 1980.

Frykenberg, Robert E. "On Roads and Riots in Tinnevelly: Radical Change and Ideology in Madras Presidency during the 19th Century." *South Asia: Journal of South Asian Studies* 4, no. 2 (1981): 34–52.

Gandhi, M. K. *Satyagraha (Non-violent Resistance).* Ahmedabad: Navajivan Publishing House, 1951.

Gandhi, M. K. "Speech at Prayer Meeting, New Delhi, October 28, 1947," *Prarthana Pravachan.* In *The Collected Works of Mahatma Gandhi* (ebook), 97: 177–80. Delhi: Publications Division Government of India, 1999.

Gandhi, M. K. "Speech at Prayer Meeting, Sodepur, December 17, 1945," *Amrita Bazar Patrika,* December 18, 1945. In *The Collected Works of Mahatma Gandhi* (ebook), 89: 50–51. Delhi: Publications Division Government of India, 1999.

Gandhi, M. K. "Statement to the Press, January 9, 1946," *Amrita Bazar Patrika,* January 10, 1946. In *The Collected Works of Mahatma Gandhi* (ebook), 89: 204–5. Delhi: Publications Division Government of India, 1999.

Gandhi, M. K. *Third Class in Indian Railways.* Lahore: Gandhi Publications League, 1917.

Gandhi, Rajmohan. *Gandhi: The Man, His People, and the Empire.* Berkeley: University of California Press, 2008.

Gaonkar, Dilip Parameshwar. "On Cultures of Democracy." *Public Culture* 19, no. 1 (2007): 1–22.

Geetha, V., and S. V. Rajadurai. "Dalits and Non-Brahmin Consciousness in Colonial Tamil Nadu." *Economic and Political Weekly* 28, no. 39 (1993): 2091–98.

Gelder, Ken. "Introduction to Part Seven." In *The Subcultures Reader,* edited by Ken Gelder and Sarah Thornton, 373–78. London: Routledge, 1997.

Ghassem-Fachandi, Parvis. *Pogrom in Gujarat: Hindu Nationalism and Anti-Muslim Violence in India.* Princeton: Princeton University Press, 2012.

Ghoshal, Upendra Nath. *A History of Indian Political Ideas: The Ancient Period and the Period of Transition to the Middle Ages.* Madras: Oxford University Press, 1966.

Gilje, Paul A. *The Road to Mobocracy: Popular Disorder in New York City, 1763–1834.* Chapel Hill: University of North Carolina Press, 1987.

Girglani, J. M. "Report of the One Man Commission on G.O. 610." Hyderabad: Government of Andhra Pradesh, 2004.

Gopinatha Rao, C. *Library Movement in Andhra Pradesh.* Hyderabad: Department of Public Libraries, 1981.

Gossman, Patricia. *Police Killings and Rural Violence in Andhra Pradesh.* New York: Human Rights Watch, 1992.

Goswami, Manu. *Producing India: From Colonial Economy to National Space.* Chicago: University of Chicago Press, 2004.

Government of India. *Census of India 2011.* Delhi: Office of the Registrar General and Census Commissioner, 2015.

Govindarajan, Radhika, Bhoomika Joshi, and Mubbashir Rizvi. "Majoritarian Politics in South Asia." Hot Spots, *Fieldsights,* March 16, 2021. https://culanth.org/fieldsights/series/majoritarian-politics-in-south-asia.

Gowrishankar, Juluru. *Ā 42 Rōjulu: Sakala Janula Prajāswāmika Ākānkṣa, Modaṭi Bhāgam and Reṇḍawa Bhāgam* (Those 42 Days: The People's Democratic Aspiration, Vol. I and Vol. II). Hyderabad: Spṛha Sāhitī Samstha, 2012.

Graeber, David. *The Democracy Project: A History, a Crisis, a Movement.* New York: Spiegel & Grau, 2013.

Grant, Kevin. *Last Weapons: Hunger Strikes and Fasts in the British Empire, 1890–1948.* Berkeley: University of California Press, 2019.

Gray, Hugh. "The Demand for a Separate Telangana State in India." *Asian Survey* 11, no. 4 (1971): 463–74.

Green, Jeffrey. *The Eyes of the People: Democracy in an Age of Spectatorship*. Oxford: Oxford University Press, 2009.

Guha, Ramchandra. *India after Gandhi: The History of the World's Largest Democracy*. New Delhi: Picador, 2017.

Guha, Ramchandra. *The Unquiet Woods: Ecological Change and Peasant Resistance in the Himalaya*. Expanded ed. Berkeley: University of California Press, 1990.

Guha, Ranajit. *Elementary Aspects of Peasant Insurgency in Colonial India*. Durham, NC: Duke University Press, 1999.

*Guinness World Records 2005*. London: Guinness Media, 2004.

Gundimela, Sambaiah. "Democratization of the Public Sphere: The Beef Stall Case in Hyderabad's Sukoon Festival." *South Asia Research* 29, no. 2 (2009): 127–49.

Gupta, Akhil. "Blurred Boundaries: The Discourse of Corruption, the Culture of Politics, and the Imagined State." *American Ethnologist* 22, no. 2 (1995): 375–402.

Gupta, Akhil. *Red Tape: Bureaucracy, Structured Violence, and Poverty in India*. Durham, NC: Duke University Press, 2012.

Gupta, Charu, ed. *Gendering Colonial India: Reforms, Print, Caste and Communalism*. Delhi: Orient Blackswan, 2012.

Gupta, Charu. *The Gender of Caste: Representing Dalits in Print*. Seattle: University of Washington Press, 2016.

Gupta, Charu. *Sexuality, Obscenity, Community: Women, Muslims, and the Hindu Public in Colonial India*. New York: Palgrave, 2002.

Gupta, Charu, and Mukul Sharma. *Print Media and Communalism*. Delhi: Progress Publishers, 1990.

Gurunatham, Jonnavitthula. *Viresalingam: The Founder of Telugu Public Life*. Rajahmundry: Chintamani Printing Works, 1911.

Gwynn, J. P. L. *A Telugu-English Dictionary*. Delhi: Oxford University Press, 1991.

Habermas, Jürgen. *Between Facts and Norms: Contributions to a Discourse Theory of Law and Democracy*. Cambridge, MA: MIT Press, 1998.

Habermas, Jürgen. "Further Reflections on the Public Sphere." In *Habermas and the Public Sphere*, edited by Craig Calhoun, 421–61. Cambridge, MA: MIT Press, 1992.

Habermas, Jürgen. "Political Communication in Media Society: Does Democracy Still Enjoy an Epistemic Dimension? The Impact of Normative Theory on Empirical Research." *Communication Theory* 16, no. 4 (2006): 411–26.

Habermas, Jürgen. *The Structural Transformation of the Public Sphere: An Inquiry into a Category of Bourgeois Society*. Translated by Thomas Burger. Cambridge, MA: MIT Press, 1991.

Habermas, Jürgen. *The Theory of Communicative Action: Reason and the Rationalization of Society*. Cambridge: Polity, 1986.

Haksar, Vinit. "Rawls and Gandhi on Civil Disobedience." *Inquiry* 19, no. 1–4 (January 1, 1976): 151–92.

Hamilton, Alexander, James Madison, and John Jay. *The Federalist Papers [1787]*. Edited by Clinton Rossiter. New York: Penguin, 1961.

Hansen, Thomas Blom. "Politics as Permanent Performance: The Production of Political Authority in the Locality." In *The Politics of Cultural Mobilization in India*, edited by John Zavos, Andrew Wyatt, and Vernon Hewitt, 19–36. New Delhi: Oxford University Press, 2004.

Hansen, Thomas Blom. *The Saffron Wave: Democracy and Hindu Nationalism in Modern India*. Princeton: Princeton University Press, 1999.

Hansen, Thomas Blom. *Wages of Violence: Naming and Identity in Postcolonial Bombay*. Princeton: Princeton University Press, 2001.

Haragopal, G. "The Telangana People's Movement: The Unfolding Political Culture." *Economic and Political Weekly* 45, no. 42 (2010): 51–60.

Hardiman, David. *Gandhi: In His Time and Ours*. Ranikhet: Permanent Black, 2003.

Hardt, Michael, and Antonio Negri. *Assembly*. Oxford: Oxford University Press, 2017.

Hardt, Michael, and Antonio Negri. *Multitude: War and Democracy in the Age of Empire*. New York: Penguin, 2004.

Harman, Chris. "What Do We Mean by the General Strike?" *Socialist Worker Review*, no. 72 (1985): 8–9.

Hayek, Friedrich A. von. *The Constitution of Liberty*. Chicago: University of Chicago Press, 1960.

Haynes, Douglas E. *Rhetoric and Ritual in Colonial India: The Shaping of a Public Culture in Surat City, 1852–1928*. Berkeley: University of California Press, 1991.

Heitler, Richard. "The Varanasi House Tax Hartal of 1810–11." *Indian Economic & Social History Review* 9, no. 3 (1972): 239–57.

Henaff, Marcel, and Tracy B. Strong, eds. *Public Space and Democracy*. Minneapolis: University of Minnesota Press, 2001.

Hodges, Sarah. "Revolutionary Family Life and the Self Respect Movement in Tamil South India, 1926–49." *Contributions to Indian Sociology* 39, no. 2 (2005): 251–77.

Holmes, Mary. "Introduction: The Importance of Being Angry: Anger in Political Life." *European Journal of Social Theory* 7, no. 2 (2004): 123–32.

Honig, Bonnie. *Political Theory and the Displacement of Politics*. Ithaca, NY: Cornell University Press, 1993.

Honig, Bonnie. "Toward an Agonistic Feminism: Hannah Arendt and the Politics of Identity." In *Feminists Theorize the Political*, edited by Judith Butler and Joan W. Scott, 215–35. New York: Routledge, 1992.

Hooper-Greenhill, Eilean. *Museums and the Interpretation of Visual Culture*. London: Routledge, 2000.

Hopkins, Washburn. "On the Hindu Custom of Dying to Redress a Grievance." *Journal of the American Oriental Society* 21 (1900): 146–59.

Hurd, John, and Ian J. Kerr, eds. *India's Railway History: A Research Handbook*. Leiden: Brill, 2012.

Ilaiah, Kancha. *Why I Am Not a Hindu: A Sudra Critique of Hindutva Philosophy, Culture and Political Economy*. Calcutta: Bhatkal & Sen, 2001.

Inazu, John. "Unlawful Assembly as Social Control." UCLA *Law Review* 64, no. 1 (2017): 2–53.

Indian Railway Board. *Indian Railways Year Book 2006–07.* New Delhi: Ministry of Railways, Government of India, 2007.

Indian Statutory Commission (Sir John Allsebrook Simon, chairman). *Report of the Indian Statutory Commission, Volume I, Survey.* London: His Majesty's Stationery Office, 1930.

Ingram, Brannon D., J. Barton Scott, and SherAli K. Tareen, eds. *Imagining the Public in Modern South Asia.* London: Routledge, 2016.

Irschick, Eugene F. *Dialogue and History: Constructing South India, 1795–1895.* Berkeley: University of California Press, 1994.

Jaffrelot, Christophe. *The Hindu Nationalist Movement and Indian Politics 1925 to the 1990s: Strategies of Identity-Building, Implantation and Mobilisation.* New Delhi: Penguin, 1999.

Jaffrelot, Christophe. "The Hindu Nationalist Reinterpretation of Pilgrimage in India: The Limits of Yatra Politics." *Nations and Nationalism* 15, no. 1 (2009): 1–19.

Jaffrelot, Christophe. *India's Silent Revolution: The Rise of the Lower Castes in India.* New York: Columbia University Press, 2003.

Jaoul, Nicolas. "The 'Righteous Anger' of the Powerless: Investigating Dalit Outrage over Caste Violence." *South Asia Multidisciplinary Academic Journal,* no. 2 (2008).

Jayal, Niraja Gopal. "Introduction." In *Democracy in India,* 1–49. Delhi: Oxford University Press, 2001.

Jeffrey, Craig. *Timepass: Youth, Class, and the Politics of Waiting in India.* Stanford, CA: Stanford University Press, 2010.

Jonnalagadda, Indivar. "Citizenship as a Communicative Effect." *Signs and Society* 6, no. 3 (2018): 531–57.

Kamra, Lipika, and Uday Chandra. "Maoism and the Masses: Critical Reflections on Revolutionary Praxis and Subaltern Agency." In *Revolutionary Violence versus Democracy: Narratives from India,* edited by Ajay Gudavarthy, 191–221. New Delhi: Sage, 2017.

Kannabiran, Kalpana, Sagari R. Ramdas, N. Madhusduhan, S. Ashalatha, and M. Pavan Kumar. "On the Telangana Trail." *Economic and Political Weekly* 45, no. 13 (2010): 69–82.

Kapoor, Ilan. "Deliberative Democracy or Agonistic Pluralism? The Relevance of the Habermas-Mouffe Debate for Third World Politics." *Alternatives: Global, Local, Political* 27, no. 4 (2002): 459–87.

Katten, Michael. *Colonial Lists/Indian Power: Identity Politics in Nineteenth Century Telugu-Speaking India.* New York: Columbia University Press, 2005.

Kaviraj, Sudipta. "The Empire of Democracy: Reading Indian Politics through Tocqueville." In *Anxieties of Democracy: Tocquevillean Reflections on India and the United States,* edited by Partha Chatterjee and Ira Katznelson, 20–49. Oxford: Oxford University Press, 2012.

Kaviraj, Sudipta. "Filth and the Public Sphere: Concepts and Practices about Space in Calcutta." *Public Culture* 10, no. 1 (1997): 83–113.

Kaviraj, Sudipta, and Sunil Khilnani, eds. *Civil Society: History and Possibilities.* Cambridge: Cambridge University Press, 2001.

Keller, Lisa. *Triumph of Order: Democracy and Public Space in New York and London*. New York: Columbia University Press, 2009.

Kelly, Jeremy, and Rupert Davies. *City Momentum Index 2020: Creating a Resilient and Responsible City*. Chicago: JLL Global Research, 2020.

Kelp-Stebbins, Katherine, and Allison M. Schifani. "The Medium Is the Masses: Embodied Amplification, Urban Occupation." *Media Fields Journal* 9 (2015): 1–14.

Kernaghan, Richard. "Furrows and Walls, or the Legal Topography of a Frontier Road in Peru." *Mobilities* 7, no. 4 (2012): 501–20.

Kling, Blair B. *The Blue Mutiny*. Philadelphia: University of Pennsylvania Press, 1966.

Kohli, Atul. "Introduction." In *The Success of India's Democracy*, 1–20. Cambridge: Cambridge University Press, 2001.

Kohli, Atul, ed. *The Success of India's Democracy*. Cambridge: Cambridge University Press, 2001.

Kruks-Wisner, Gabrielle. *Claiming the State: Active Citizenship and Social Welfare in Rural India*. Cambridge: Cambridge University Press, 2018.

Kumar, Radha. *Police Matters: The Everyday State and Caste Politics in South India, 1900–1975*. Ithaca, NY: Cornell University Press, 2021.

Kunnath, George. *Rebels from the Mud Houses: Dalits and the Making of the Maoist Revolution in Bihar*. Delhi: Routledge, 2017.

Kunreuther, Laura. "Sounds of Democracy: Performance, Protest, and Political Subjectivity." *Cultural Anthropology* 33, no. 1 (2018): 1–31.

Kunreuther, Laura. *Voicing Subjects: Public Intimacy and Mediation in Kathmandu*. Berkeley: University of California Press, 2014.

Laclau, Ernesto, and Chantal Mouffe. *Hegemony and Socialist Strategy: Towards a Radical Democratic Politics*. New York: Verso, 2001.

Lakier, Genevieve. "The Highway and the Chakka Jam: National Development and the Limits of State Sovereignty in Nepal." Paper presented at the conference, "Of Mediums and Motored Ways: The Social Lives of Transit Networks," University of Washington, May 23, 2005.

Lakier, Genevieve. "Illiberal Democracy and the Problem of Law: Street Protest and Democratization in Multiparty Nepal." In *Contentious Politics and Democratization in Nepal*, edited by Mahendra Lawoti, 251–72. Delhi: Sage Publications, 2007.

Lakier, Genevieve. "The Myth of the State Is Real: Notes on the Study of the State in Nepal." *Studies in Nepali History & Society* 10 (2005): 135–70.

Lakier, Genevieve. "The Public of the Bandh: Protest, Performance and National Identity in Nepal," invited lecture, University of Pennsylvania, South Asia Colloquium, 2008.

Lakier, Genevieve. "The Spectacle of Power: Coercive Protest and the Problem of Democracy in Nepal." PhD diss., University of Chicago, 2014.

Lakoff, Robin T. "Civility and Its Discontents: Or, Getting in Your Face." In *Broadening the Horizon of Linguistic Politeness*, edited by Robin T. Lakoff and Sachiko Ide, 23–43. Amsterdam: John Benjamins, 2005.

Landemore, Hélène. *Open Democracy: Reinventing Popular Rule for the Twenty-First Century*. Princeton: Princeton University Press, 2020.

Lefebvre, Henri. *The Production of Space*. Translated by Donald Nicholson-Smith. Cambridge: Blackwell, 1991.

Leonard, Karen. "Hyderabad: The Mulki–Non-Mulki Conflict." In *People, Princes and Paramount Power: Society and Power in the Indian Princely States*, edited by Robin Jeffrey, 65–106. New Delhi: Oxford University Press, 1978.

Lilti, Antoine. *The World of the Salons: Sociability and Worldliness in Eighteenth-Century Paris*. Oxford: Oxford University Press, 2018.

"Looking Back and Looking Ahead at the Liberalisation Process." *Economic and Political Weekly* 51, no. 29 (2016): 38.

Luxemburg, Rosa. "The Mass Strike, the Political Party, and the Trade Unions" [1906]. In *The Essential Rosa Luxemburg: Reform or Revolution and the Mass Strike*, edited by Helen Scott, 111–82. Chicago: Haymarket Books, 2008.

Lyman, Peter. "The Domestication of Anger: The Use and Abuse of Anger in Politics." *European Journal of Social Theory* 7, no. 2 (2004): 133–47.

Lyman, Peter. "The Politics of Anger: On Silence, Ressentiment and Political Speech." *Socialist Review* 11, no. 3 (1981): 55–74.

Maine, Henry Sumner. *Ancient Law: Its Connection with the Early History of Society, and Its Relation to Modern Ideas*. New York: Henry Holt and Company, 1861.

Maine, Henry Sumner. *Lectures on the Early History of Institutions*. London: John Murray, 1874.

Majumdar, R. C. *Ancient India*. Delhi: Motilal Banarsidass, 1997.

"Mandal Commission: Bigoted Protests." *Economic and Political Weekly* 25, no. 40 (1990): 2224.

Manin, Bernard. *The Principles of Representative Government*. Cambridge: Cambridge University Press, 1997.

Manohar Reddy, N. "Modernity of Telugu: Language Politics and National Identity." PhD diss., English and Foreign Languages University, 2015.

Mantena, Karuna. "Another Realism: The Politics of Gandhian Nonviolence." *American Political Science Review* 106, no. 2 (2012): 455–70.

Marx, Karl, and Friedrich Engels. *The First Indian War of Independence*. Moscow: Foreign Languages Publishing House, 1960.

Mazumdar, Ranjani. *Bombay Cinema: An Archive of the City*. Minneapolis: University of Minnesota Press, 2007.

Mazzarella, William. "Figurative Publics: Conclusion," *Figurative Publics: Crowds, Protest, and Democratic Anxieties, The Immanent Frame: Secularism, Religion, and the Public Sphere*. Social Science Research Council, May 14, 2020. https://tif.ssrc.org/2020/05/14/figurative-publics-conclusion/.

Mazzarella, William. "The Myth of the Multitude, or, Who's Afraid of the Crowd?" *Critical Inquiry* 36, no. 4 (2010): 697–727.

McCarthy, Thomas. "Introduction." In *The Structural Transformation of the Public Sphere: An Inquiry into a Category of Bourgeois Society*, by Jürgen Habermas, xi–xiv. Cambridge, MA: MIT Press, 1991.

Mehta, Nalin. "Redefining 'Azadi' in India: The Prose of Anti-Sedition." *South Asian History & Culture* 7, no. 3 (2016): 322–25.

Mehta, Suketu. *Maximum City: Bombay Lost and Found*. New York: Knopf, 2004.

Mehta, Uday Singh. "Gandhi on Democracy, Politics and the Ethics of Everyday Life." *Modern Intellectual History* 7, no. 2 (2010): 355–71.

Menon, Nivedita. "Introduction." In *Empire and Nation: Selected Essays*, 1–20. New York: Columbia University Press, 2010.

Menon, Ramesh. *The Ramayana: A Modern Retelling of the Great Indian Epic*. New York: North Point Press, 2003.

Michelutti, Lucia. *The Vernacularisation of Democracy: Politics, Caste, and Religion in India*. London: Routledge, 2008.

Mill, James. *The History of British India: From 1805 to 1835*. J. Madden, 1845.

Mitchell, Lisa. "Civility and Collective Action: Soft Speech, Loud Roars, and the Politics of Recognition." In "Civility: Global Perspectives," edited by Sharika Thiranagama, Tobias Kelly, and Carlos Forment, special issue, *Anthropological Theory* 18, no. 2–3 (2018): 217–47.

Mitchell, Lisa. *Language, Emotion, and Politics in South India: The Making of a Mother Tongue*. Bloomington: Indiana University Press, 2009.

Mitchell, Lisa. "Participatory and Adversarial Politics: Representing Speech Action, Collective Action and Emotion." In *Emotions, Mobilisations and South Asian Politics*, edited by Amelie Blom and Stephanie Tawa Lama-Rewal, 46–67. London: Routledge India, 2019.

Mitchell, Lisa. "The Visual Turn in Political Anthropology and the Mediation of Political Practice in Contemporary India." *South Asia: Journal of South Asian Studies* 37, no. 3 (2014): 515–40.

Mitchell, Timothy. "Carbon Democracy." *Economy and Society* 38, no. 3 (2009): 399–432.

Mitchell, Timothy. *Carbon Democracy: Political Power in the Age of Oil*. London: Verso, 2011.

Mitchell, Timothy. "The Limits of the State: Beyond Statist Approaches and Their Critics." *American Political Science Review* 85, no. 1 (1991): 77–96.

Mitchell, Timothy. *Rule of Experts: Egypt, Techno-Politics, Modernity*. Berkeley: University of California Press, 2002.

Mohite, Komal. "Designated Sites of Political Agitations: A Study of Jantar Mantar Road, New Delhi." MPhil diss., Jawaharlal Nehru University, 2017.

Molesworth, J. T. *A Dictionary, Marathi and English*. 2nd ed. Bombay: Bombay Education Society, 1857.

Monier-Williams, Monier. *A Sanskrit-English Dictionary*. Delhi: Motilal Banarsidass, 1999.

Moon, Penderel. *The British Conquest and Dominion of India*. London: Duckbacks, 1989.

Morton, Stephen. "Fictions of Sedition and the Framing of Indian Revolutionaries in Colonial India." *Journal of Commonwealth Literature* 47, no. 2 (2012): 175–89.

Mouffe, Chantal. *Chantal Mouffe: Hegemony, Radical Democracy, and the Political*. Edited by James Martin. London: Routledge, 2013.

Mouffe, Chantal. *Deliberative Democracy or Agonistic Pluralism*. Political Science Series 72. Vienna: Institute for Advanced Studies, 2000. https://www.ihs.ac.at /publications/pol/pw_72.pdf.

Mouffe, Chantal. "For an Agonistic Model of Democracy (2000)." In *Chantal Mouffe: Hegemony, Radical Democracy, and the Political*, edited by James Martin, 191–206. London: Routledge, 2013.

Mouffe, Chantal. "Politics and Passions: The Stakes of Democracy (2002)." In *Chantal Mouffe: Hegemony, Radical Democracy, and the Political*, edited by James Martin, 181–90. London: Routledge, 2013.

Mukhopadhyay, Aparajita. "Wheels of Change? The Impact of Railways on Colonial North Indian Society, 1855–1920." PhD diss., School of Oriental and African Studies, 2012.

Mukund, Kanakalatha. *The Trading World of the Tamil Merchant: Evolution of Merchant Capitalism in the Coromandel.* Hyderabad: Orient Longman, 1999.

Muppidi, Himadeep. *Politics in Emotion: The Song of Telangana.* Oxon: Routledge, 2015.

Murali, Atlury. "Changing Perceptions and Radicalisation of the National Movement in Andhra, 1922–34." *Social Scientist* 16, no. 8 (1988): 3–29.

Murthi, Kasturi Narayana, ed. *Sri Potti Sriramulu the Martyr that Fasted for 58 Days to Death from 19-10-1952 to 15-12-1952.* Madras: Antiseptic Press, 1953.

Muthukkaruppan, Parthasarathi. "Critique of Caste Violence: Explorations in Theory." *Social Scientist* 45, no. 1/2 (2017): 49–71.

Muthukkaruppan, Parthasarathi. "Dalit: The Making of a Political Subject." *Critical Quarterly* 56, no. 3 (2014): 34–45.

Nair, Janaki. *The Promise of the Metropolis: Bangalore's Twentieth Century.* New Delhi: Oxford University Press, 2005.

Narayan, Rochisha. "Caste, Family and Politics in Northern India during the Eighteenth and Nineteenth Centuries." PhD diss., Rutgers University, 2011.

Narayana Rao, K. V. *The Emergence of Andhra Pradesh.* Bombay: Popular Prakashan, 1973.

Narayana Rao, K. V. *Internal Migration Policies in an Indian State: A Study of the Mulki Rules in Hyderabad and Andhra.* Cambridge, MA: Massachusetts Institute of Technology, Center for International Studies, 1977.

Naregal, Veena. *Language, Politics, Elites and the Public Sphere: Western India under Colonialism.* London: Anthem, 2002.

Narrain, Siddharth. "'Disaffection' and the Law: The Chilling Effect of Sedition Laws in India." *Economic and Political Weekly* 46, no. 8 (2011): 33–37.

Nath, Paaritosh. "Employment Scenario and the Reservation Policy." *Economic and Political Weekly* 54, no. 19 (2019): 56–61.

Nayyar, Deepak. "Economic Liberalisation in India: Then and Now." *Economic and Political Weekly* 52, no. 2 (2017): 41–48.

Nehru, Jawaharlal. "Policy of India." In *Selected Works of Jawaharlal Nehru*, edited by Sarvepalli Gopal, 29: 22–23. New Delhi: Jawaharlal Nehru Memorial Fund, 2001.

Nehru, Jawaharlal. "Students and Discipline." In *Selected Works of Jawaharlal Nehru*, edited by Sarvepalli Gopal, 29: 68–83. New Delhi: Jawaharlal Nehru Memorial Fund, 2001.

Nijhawan, Shobna. *Women and Girls in the Hindi Public Sphere: Periodical Literature in Colonial North India.* New Delhi: Oxford University Press, 2012.

Oberoi, Harjit. *The Construction of Religious Boundaries: Culture, Identity, and Diversity in the Sikh Tradition*. Chicago: University of Chicago Press, 1994.

Oldenburg, Philip. "Middlemen in Third-World Corruption: Implications of an Indian Case." *World Politics* 39, no. 4 (1987): 508–35.

Omvedt, Gail. "Rasta Roko, Kulaks and the Left." *Economic and Political Weekly* 16, no. 48 (1981): 1937–41.

Orsini, Francesca. "Booklets and Saints: Religious Publics and Literary History." *South Asia: Journal of South Asian Studies* 38, no. 3 (2015): 435–49.

Orsini, Francesca. *The Hindi Public Sphere, 1920–1940: Language and Literature in the Age of Nationalism*. New Delhi: Oxford University Press, 2000.

Ortner, Sherry B. "Dark Anthropology and Its Others: Theory since the Eighties." *HAU: Journal of Ethnographic Theory* 6, no. 1 (2016): 47–73.

Page, William, ed. "Industries: Silk-Weaving." In *A History of the County of Middlesex: Volume 2, General; Ashford, East Bedfont with Hatton, Feltham, Hampton with Hampton Wick, Hanworth, Laleham, Littleton*, 132–37. London: Victoria County History, 1911.

Paley, Julia. "Introduction." In *Democracy: Anthropological Approaches*, 3–20. Santa Fe: School for Advanced Research Press, 2008.

Palshikar, Sanjay, and Arun Kumar Patnaik. "Violence in a University: Defending the Indefensible." *Economic and Political Weekly* 37, no. 16 (2002): 1490–91.

Pandey, Gyanendra. *The Construction of Communalism in Colonial North India*. Delhi: Oxford University Press, 1990.

Pandian, Jacob. "The Building of Indian Railways and the Castefication of Wage Laborers in India." *Anthropology of Work Review* 24, no. 1–2 (2003): 13–18.

Panikkar, K. M. *The Ideas of Sovereignty and State in Indian Political Thought*. Bombay: Bharatiya Vidya Bhavan, 1963.

Parilla, Joseph, Jesus Leal Trujillo, Alan Berube, and Tao Ran. *Global Metro Monitor 2014: An Uncertain Recovery*. Washington, DC: Brookings Institution, 2015.

Parkinson, John R. *Democracy and Public Space: The Physical Sites of Democratic Performance*. Oxford: Oxford University Press, 2012.

Parthasarathi, Prasannan. *The Transition to a Colonial Economy: Weavers, Merchants and Kings in South India, 1720–1800*. Cambridge: Cambridge University Press, 2001.

Perkins, C. Ryan. "From the Meḥfil to the Printed Word: Public Debate and Discourse in Late Colonial India." *Indian Economic & Social History Review* 50, no. 1 (2013): 47–76.

Pernau, Margrit. *Ashraf into Middle Classes: Muslims in Nineteenth-Century Delhi*. New Delhi: Oxford University Press, 1999.

Piliavsky, Anastasia, ed. *Patronage as Politics in South Asia*. New Delhi: Cambridge University Press, 2014.

Piliavsky, Anastasia. "Where Is the Public Sphere? Political Communications and the Morality of Disclosure in Rural Rajasthan." *Cambridge Journal of Anthropology* 31, no. 2 (2013): 104–22.

Pingle, Gautam. *The Fall and Rise of Telangana*. Hyderabad: Orient Blackswan, 2014.

Povinelli, Elizabeth. *The Cunning of Recognition: Indigenous Alterities and the Making of Australian Multiculturalism*. Durham, NC: Duke University Press, 2002.

Prasad, Ritika. "Tracking Modernity: The Experience of Railways in Colonial India, 1853–1947." PhD diss., University of California Los Angeles, 2009.

Price, Pamela. "Acting in Public versus Forming a Public: Conflict Processing and Political Mobilization in Nineteenth-Century South India." *South Asia: Journal of South Asian Studies* 14, no. 1 (1991): 91–121.

Pringle, Arthur T., ed. *The Diary and Consultation Book of the Agent Governor and Council of Fort St. George*, 1682. Madras: Superintendent, Government Press, 1894.

Prothero, Iorwerth. "William Benbow and the Concept of the 'General Strike.'" *Past & Present*, no. 63 (1974): 132–71.

Rajagopal, Arvind, ed. *The Indian Public Sphere: Readings in Media History*. New Delhi: Oxford University Press, 2009.

Rajayya, Allam. *Bhūmi: Kathalu* (Land: Stories). Karimnagar: Karimnagar Book Trust, 1982.

Ram, S., and R. Kumar, eds. *Quit India Movement, 1942–1945*. New Delhi: Commonwealth, 2008.

Ramakrishna, V. *Social Reform in Andhra, 1848–1919*. New Delhi: Vikas Publishing, 1983.

Raman, Bhavani. *Document Raj: Writing and Scribes in Early Colonial South India*. Chicago: University of Chicago Press, 2012.

Rāmāñjanēyulu, Tirunagari. *Saṅgaṃ: Telaṅgāṇā Pōrāṭa Navala* (The Union: A Novel of the Telangana Struggle). Vijayawada: Janasāhitī Sāṃskr̥tika Samākhya, 1986.

Ramaswamy, Sumathi. *Passions of the Tongue: Language Devotion in Tamil India, 1891–1970*. Berkeley: University of California Press, 1997.

Ramdev, Rina, Sandhya D. Nambiar, and Debaditya Bhattacharya, eds. *Sentiment, Politics, Censorship: The State of Hurt*. New Delhi: Sage, 2015.

Rancière, Jacques. *Dissensus: On Politics and Aesthetics*. Translated by Steven Corcoran. New York: Bloomsbury, 2010.

Rancière, Jacques. "Ten Theses on Politics." Translated by Davide Panagia and Rachel Bowlby. *Theory & Event* 5, no. 3 (2001).

Randle, Michael. *Civil Resistance*. London: Fontana, 1994.

Ranulf, Svend. *Moral Indignation and Middle Class Psychology: A Sociological Study*. New York: Schocken, 1964.

Rao, Anupama. *The Caste Question: Dalits and the Politics of Modern India*. Berkeley: University of California Press, 2009.

Rao, Ursula. *News as Culture: Journalistic Practices and the Remaking of Indian Leadership Traditions*. New York: Berghahn, 2010.

Rawat, Ramnarayan S. *Reconsidering Untouchability: Chamars and Dalit History in North India*. Bloomington: Indiana University Press, 2011.

Rawat, Ramnarayan S., and K. Satyanarayana, eds. *Dalit Studies*. Durham, NC: Duke University Press, 2016.

Rawat, Ramnarayan S., and K. Satyanarayana, "Introduction, Dalit Studies: New Perspectives on Indian History and Society." In *Dalit Studies*, 1–30. Durham, NC: Duke University Press, 2016.

Rawls, John. "The Idea of Public Reason Revisited." *University of Chicago Law Review* 64, no. 3 (1997): 765–807.

Rawls, John. *Political Liberalism.* New York: Columbia University Press, 1993.

Records of Fort St. George. *Diary and Consultation Book of 1680–1681.* Madras: Superintendent, Government Press, 1912.

Records of Fort St. George. *Diary and Consultation Book of 1681.* Madras: Superintendent Government Press, 1913.

Reddy, Arutla Ramachandra. *Telangāṇā Pōrāṭa Smṛtulu* (Memories of the Telangana Struggle). Vijayawada: Visalandhra Publishing, 1981.

Reddy, G. Ram, and G. Haragopal. "The Pyraveekar: 'The Fixer' in Rural India." *Asian Survey* 25, no. 11 (1985): 1148–62.

Refai, Gulammohammed Zainulaeedin. "Anglo-Mughal Relations in Western India and the Development of Bombay, 1662–1690." PhD diss., Cambridge University, 1968.

*Report of the Committee for Consultations on the Situation in Andhra Pradesh* (Srikrishna Committee Report). New Delhi: Government of India, 2010.

Revathi, E., and Shaik Galab. "Economic Reforms and Regional Disparities." In *Agrarian Crisis and Farmer Suicides*, edited by R. S. Deshpande and Saroj Arora, 192–218. Delhi: Sage, 2010.

Ribot, Jesse C., and Nancy Lee Peluso. "A Theory of Access." *Rural Sociology* 68, no. 2 (2003): 153–81.

Ring, Laura A. *Zenana: Everyday Peace in a Karachi Apartment Building.* Bloomington: Indiana University Press, 2006.

Robb, Peter. *The Government of India and Reform: Policies towards Politics and the Constitution, 1916–1921.* Oxford: Oxford University Press, 1976.

Robbins, Joel. "Beyond the Suffering Subject: Toward an Anthropology of the Good." *Journal of the Royal Anthropological Institute* 19, no. 3 (2013): 447–62.

Rollier, Paul, Kathinka Frøystad, and Arild Engelsen Ruud, eds. *Outrage: The Rise of Religious Offence in Contemporary South Asia.* London: UCL Press, 2019.

Rousseau, Jean-Jacques. "Of Deputies or Representatives." In *Rousseau: "The Social Contract" and Other Later Political Writings*, edited and translated by Victor Gourevitch, 113–16. Cambridge: Cambridge University Press, 1997.

Rudolph, Lloyd I., and Susanne Hoeber Rudolph. *In Pursuit of Lakshmi.* Chicago: University of Chicago Press, 1987.

Sabato, Hilda. *The Many and the Few: Political Participation in Republican Buenos Aires.* Palo Alto, CA: Stanford University Press, 2002.

Sastri, D. Gopalakrishna. *The Law of Sedition in India.* Bombay: N. M. Tripathi, 1964.

Satyanarayana, K. "Dalit Reconfiguration of Caste: Representation, Identity and Politics." *Critical Quarterly* 56, no. 3 (2014): 46–61.

Savarkar, Vinayak Damodar. *The Indian War of Independence, 1857.* Bombay: Phoenix, 1947.

Scanlan, Stephen J., Laurie Cooper Stoll, and Kimberly Lumm. "Starving for Change: The Hunger Strike and Nonviolent Action, 1906–2004." *Research in Social Movements, Conflicts and Change* 28 (2008): 275–323.

Schaffer, Frederic C. *Democracy in Translation: Understanding Politics in an Unfamiliar Culture.* Ithaca, NY: Cornell University Press, 2000.

Schivelbusch, Wolfgang. *Tastes of Paradise: A Social History of Spices, Stimulants, and Intoxicants.* New York: Vintage Books, 1993.

Schnapp, Jeffrey T., and Matthew Tiews, eds. *Crowds.* Palo Alto, CA: Stanford University Press, 2006.

Scott, James C. *Against the Grain: A Deep History of the Earliest States.* New Haven: Yale University Press, 2017.

Scott, James C. *The Art of Not Being Governed: An Anarchist History of Upland Southeast Asia.* New Haven: Yale University Press, 2009.

Scott, James C. "Foreword." In *Elementary Aspects of Peasant Insurgency in Colonial India*, by Ranajit Guha, ix–xiv. Durham, NC: Duke University Press, 1999.

Scott, James C. *Two Cheers for Anarchism: Six Easy Pieces on Autonomy, Dignity, and Meaningful Work and Play.* Princeton: Princeton University Press, 2012.

Seal, Anil. "Imperialism and Nationalism in India." In *Locality, Province and Nation: Essays on India Politics, 1870–1940*, edited by John Gallagher, Gordon Johnson, and Anil Seal, 1–28. Cambridge: Cambridge University Press, 1973.

Sennett, Richard. *The Fall of Public Man.* New York: Norton, 1975.

Seshadri, K. "The Telangana Agitation and the Politics of Andhra Pradesh." *Indian Journal of Political Science* 31, no. 1 (1970): 60–81.

Shah, Alpa. *Nightmarch: Among India's Revolutionary Guerillas.* Chicago: University of Chicago Press, 2019.

Shah, Nayan. *Refusal to Eat: A Century of Prison Hunger Strikes.* Berkeley: University of California Press, 2022.

Shaikh, Juned. *Outcaste Bombay: City Making and the Politics of the Poor.* Seattle: University of Washington Press, 2021.

Shiffman, Ronald, Rick Bell, Lance Jay Brown, and Lynne Elizabeth. *Beyond Zuccotti Park: Freedom of Assembly and the Occupation of Public Space.* New York: NYU Press, 2012.

Shils, Edward. "The Virtue of Civil Society." *Government and Opposition* 26, no. 1 (1991): 3–20.

Shore, John. "On Some Extraordinary Facts, Customs, and Practices of the Hindus." In *Asiatic Researches; or Transactions of the Society Instituted in Bengal, for Inquiring into the History and Antiquities, the Arts, Sciences, and Literatures of Asia, Volume the Fourth*, 343–64. London: For Vernor and Hood, 1798.

Shorter, Edward, and Charles Tilly. *Strikes in France, 1830–1968.* Cambridge: Cambridge University Press, 1974.

Simhadri, S., and P. L. Vishweshwar Rao, eds. *Telangana: Dimensions of Underdevelopment.* Hyderabad: Centre for Telangana Studies, 1997.

Singh, Anushka. *Sedition in Liberal Democracies.* Delhi: Oxford University Press, 2018.

Singha, Radhika. *A Despotism of Law: Crime and Justice in Early Colonial India.* Delhi: Oxford University Press, 1998.

Smith, Woodruff. *Consumption and the Making of Respectability, 1600–1800.* New York: Routledge, 2002.

Society for the Diffusion of Useful Knowledge, ed. *The Hindoos, Vol. II.* London: Charles Knight, 1835.

Spelman, Elizabeth. "Anger and Insubordination." In *Women, Knowledge, and Reality: Explorations in Feminist Philosophy*, edited by Ann Garry and Marilyn Pearsall, 263–73. Winchester: Unwin Hyman, 1989.

Spencer, Jonathan. *Anthropology, Politics and the State*. Cambridge: Cambridge University Press, 2007.

Spodek, Howard. "On the Origins of Gandhi's Political Methodology: The Heritage of Kathiawad and Gujarat." *Journal of Asian Studies* 30, no. 2 (1971): 361–72.

Sreeramulu, B. *Socio-Political Ideas and Activities of Potti Sriramulu*. Bombay: Himalaya Publishing House, 1988.

Srinivas, S. V. "Maoism to Mass Culture: Notes on Telangana's Cultural Turn." *Bioscope* 6, no. 2 (2015): 187–205.

Srinivas, S. V. *Politics as Performance*. Ranikhet: Permanent Black, 2013.

Sriramamurti, Gurujada. *Kavi Jīvitamulu* (Lives of Poets). 2nd ed. Channapattanamu: Empress of India Press, 1893.

Stark, Ulrike. *An Empire of Books: The Naval Kishore Press and the Diffusion of the Printed Word in Colonial India*. Ranikhet: Permanent Black, 2007.

Stern, Philip J. *The Company-State: Corporate Sovereignty and the Early Modern Foundations of the British Empire in India*. Oxford: Oxford University Press, 2011.

Stevenson, Angus, ed. *Oxford Dictionary of English*. 3rd ed. Oxford: Oxford University Press, 2010.

Strassler, Karen. *Demanding Images: Democracy, Mediation, and the Image Event in Indonesia*. Durham, NC: Duke University Press, 2020.

Subba Rao, G. V., ed. *History of Andhra Movement (Andhra Region)*. 2 vols. Hyderabad: Committee of History of Andhra Movement, 1982.

Subramanian, Ajantha. *The Caste of Merit: Engineering Education in India*. Cambridge, MA: Harvard University Press, 2019.

Subramanian, Ajantha. "Meritocracy and Democracy: Indian Reservations and the Politics of Caste." *Public Culture* 31, no. 2 (2019): 275–88.

Sundar, Nandini. "Reflections on Civil Liberties, Citizenship, Adivasi Agency and Maoism: A Response to Alpa Shah." *Critique of Anthropology* 33, no. 3 (2013): 361–68.

Suntharalingam, R. *Politics and Nationalist Awakening in South India, 1852–1891*. Tucson: University of Arizona Press, 1974.

Suykens, Bert. "Diffuse Authority in the Beedi Commodity Chain: Naxalite and State Governance in Tribal Telangana, India." *Development and Change* 41, no. 1 (2010): 153–78.

Suykens, Bert. "Hartal as a Complex Political Performance: General Strikes and the Organisation of (Local) Power in Bangladesh." *Contributions to Indian Sociology* 47, no. 1 (2013): 61–83.

Swarnalatha, Potukuchi. "Revolt, Testimony, Petition: Artisanal Protests in Colonial Andhra." *International Review of Social History* 46, no. S9 (2001): 107–29.

Swarnalatha, Potukuchi. "The World of the Weaver in the Northern Coromandel, 1750–1850." PhD diss., University of Hyderabad, 1991.

Tannen, Deborah. *The Argument Culture: Stopping America's War of Words*. New York: Random House, 1998.

Tarrow, Sidney. *Power in Movement: Social Movements and Contentious Politics.* 3rd ed. Cambridge: Cambridge University Press, 2011.

Tarrow, Sidney. "Social Movements in Europe: Movement Society or Europeanization of Conflict?" Working paper, European University Institute, Florence, 1994.

Taylor, Charles. "The Politics of Recognition." In *Multiculturalism: Examining the Politics of Recognition,* edited by Amy Gutmann, 25–73. Princeton: Princeton University Press, 1994.

Thachil, Tariq, and Emmanuel Teitelbaum. "Ethnic Parties and Public Spending: New Theory and Evidence from the Indian States." *Comparative Political Studies* 48, no. 11 (2015): 1389–420.

Thiranagama, Sharika, Tobias Kelly, and Carlos Forment. "Introduction: Whose Civility?" *Anthropological Theory* 18, no. 2–3 (2018): 153–74.

Thompson, E. P. *The Making of the English Working Class.* New York: Penguin, 1991.

Thompson, E. P. "The Moral Economy of the English Crowd in the Eighteenth Century." *Past & Present,* no. 50 (1971): 76–136.

Thompson, E. P. "Rough Music Reconsidered." *Folklore* 103, no. 1 (1992): 3–26.

Thornbury, Walter. *Old and New London.* London: Cassell, Petter & Galpin, 1878.

Tilly, Charles. "Collective Violence in European Perspective." In *The History of Violence in America: Historical and Comparative Perspectives,* edited by Hugh Davis Graham and Ted Robert Gurr, 4–44. New York: Praeger, 1969.

Tilly, Charles. "Contentious Repertoires in Great Britain, 1758–1834." *Social Science History* 17, no. 2 (1993): 253–80.

Tilly, Charles. *From Mobilization to Revolution.* Boston: Addison-Wesley, 1978.

Tilly, Charles. *Popular Contention in Great Britain, 1758–1834.* Cambridge, MA: Harvard University Press, 1995.

Tufekci, Zeynep. *Twitter and Tear Gas: The Power and Fragility of Networked Protest.* New Haven: Yale University Press, 2017.

Vaikuntham, Y. *Education and Social Change in South India: Andhra, 1880–1920.* Madras: New Era, 1982.

Valiani, Arafaat. *Militant Publics in India: Physical Culture and Violence in the Making of a Modern Polity.* New York: Palgrave, 2011.

Varavara Rao. "Déjà vu." In *Muktakaṇṭham: Jailu Kavitalu, 1986–1989* (Free Voice: Jail Poems, 1986–1989), 43–49. Hyderabad: Samudraṃ Mudraṇalu, 1990.

Viswanathan, S. *Dalits in Dravidian Land: Frontline Reports on Anti-Dalit Violence in Tamil Nadu (1995–2004).* Pondicherry: Navayana, 2005.

Von Mises, Ludwig. *Human Action: A Treatise on Economics.* New Haven: Yale University Press, 1949.

Waghmore, Suryakant. *Civility against Caste: Dalit Politics and Citizenship in Western India.* New Delhi: Sage, 2013.

Wagner, Kim A. *The Great Fear of 1857: Rumours, Conspiracies and the Making of the Indian Uprising.* Oxford: Peter Lang, 2010.

Warner, Michael. *Publics and Counterpublics.* New York: Zone Books, 2002.

Warner, Michael. "Publics and Counterpublics." *Public Culture* 14, no. 1 (2002): 49–90.

Wedeen, Lisa. "The Politics of Deliberation: *Qāt* Chews as Public Spheres in Yemen." *Public Culture* 19, no. 1 (2007): 59–84.

Wolcott, Susan. "Strikes in Colonial India, 1921–1938." *Industrial and Labor Relations Review* 61, no. 4 (2008): 460–84.

Young, Iris Marion. *Inclusion and Democracy*. Oxford: Oxford University Press, 2000.

Zakaria, Fareed. "The Rise of Illiberal Democracy." *Foreign Affairs* 76, no. 6 (1997): 22–43.

Ziad, Waleed. "Mufti 'Iwāz and the 1816 'Disturbances at Bareilli': Inter-Communal Moral Economy and Religious Authority in Rohilkhand." *Journal of Persianate Studies* 7, no. 2 (2014): 189–218.

*Page numbers in italics refer to illustrations.*

anthropology: dark, 14, 229n42; of democracy, 233n107; of the good, 14; methods of, 17, 21, 25

anticolonial movement: alarm chain pulling during, 34, 152–53, 158–59, 162–70; autobiographies of, 62; commodity chains and, 142; comparisons with postcolonial political tactics, 164, 179–80; Gandhi and, 32, 62, 159; Nehru and, 159, 179–80, 201; public and, 206; rail roko agitations during, 159, 165, 169–70; railway stations and, 32; ticketless travel during, 201

antiviolence (Étienne Balibar), 119

A.P. Express (Telangana Superfast Express), object of roko action, 183

Arab Spring, 2, 24, 226n7

Arthaśāstra (classical Indian text on statecraft), 69

ASA. See Ambedkar Students' Association

assassinations of union leaders (by police), 116

assembly: in Andhra movement, 31, 210; in Black Lives Matter movement, 89, 243n96; British colonial opposition to, 51–52, 116–17, 133, 143–44, 223; Judith Butler on, 26, 246n33; as communicative amplification, 38, 45, 77, 110, 119–20, 218, 220; democracy and, 8, 26–27, 36, 92, 223–24, 245n9; designated space for, 43–45, 48, 50, 53, 63–64, 74, 231n65, 236n14, 237n26; differences in types of, 20, 26, 212; East India Company and, 128, 132–33; freedom of (as basic liberty), 175, 223–24, 237n25; Hardt and Negri on, 232n80, 233n104; illegal, 178; illiberal forms of, 177; institutional role of, 26; majoritarian, 11; mass media and, 18, 219, 233n104; origins of, 38, 125, 132, 137, 141, 143; post-colonial opposition to, 48, 51, 119; recognition and, 204, 214, 217; royal (darbar), 72; spaces of, 1, 43, 224, 225n1; as state-hailing, 2–7, 11–13, 73–74, 76, 105, 110; as "style" of politics, 85, 90; in Telangana movement, 2–7, 95–97, 109–10; in Telugu language, 225n1; theorization of, 16, 25–27, 36, 105, 224; violent and nonviolent, 76, 135. See also bhērī; combination(s); garjana; murasu

audience(s): and civility, 102; as deepening democracy, 120–21, 220; dharna as seeking, 53–54, 56–60; differences in, 11–12, 178, 182, 194, 224, 231n72; as grievance redressal, 45, 91, 165, 181, 195–96, 204, 218; history of granting in South Asia, 69–70, 72, 132, 223; mass media as extending, 62, 72–73, 208–9, 217; with officials as object of collective action, 18, 23, 27, 31, 36, 74, 129, 169; and political arrival, 229n44; refusals to grant, 69, 73, 77–78, 81, 111, 113, 141, 180; tools used by those in asymmetrically less powerful positions to gain, 37, 43, 103, 187, 201. See also Grievance Day

āvēdana: making known, 39, 63, 104–5, 213–14; agony, 197, 211, 213. See also āndōlana; Guha, Ramachandra

axis of access, 39, 201; definition, 203. See also Peluso, Nancy Lee; Ribot, Jesse

Ayodhya: chain pulling by college students in, 166; site of Ramayana, 59

Azzellini, Dario, on logic of political representation, 27

Badrinath (manifestation of deity Vishnu, embodied by king), 81

Balibar, Étienne: on violence, 119, 229n45; on civility, 97

Banaras. See Varanasi

bandh (shut-down or general strike), 8, 36, 162, 164, 172, 175, 185; all-India, 6. See also general strike; saḍak bandh (roadblock)

Banerjee, Mamata (1955-), chief minister of Bengal and former railway minister, on railways, 33

Banerjee, Mukulika, on elections, 233n107, 245n14

Bank of America, office in Hyderabad, 4

Bareilly, house tax protest in, 83–84, 135, 144. See also Banaras

Bayer, company in Hyderabad, 4

Bayly, Christopher Alan: on Bareilly, 84; on Indian ecumene, 206

Bedi, Tarini, on Shiv Sena, 11

Belchi, Bihar, site of Dalit massacre (1977), 105

Benares. See Varanasi

Benbow, William (1787–1841), on Grand National Holiday, 126–27. See also general strike

Chundur, Andhra Pradesh, site of Dalit massacre (1991), 246n43
civility: agonistic pluralism and, 106–7; bourgeois culture and, 86–87, 96, 142; collective action and, 99–100, 123–124; definitions of, 100–102; as effect of being heard, 102, 111, 121, 125, 147; emotion and, 86–87; norms of, 90; order and, 132; "style" of political engagement and, 92; violence and, 85, 97–98, 119–20
civil society: comparison with political society, 38, 76, 172–174, 256n13, 258n73; formation of associations and, 115, 128, 140–42, 213; illiberal democracy and, 175; mass civil resistance and, 117, 122, 128, 234n125; practices of, 19–20, 63, 164, 167, 179; relationship with state, 77, 123, 132; restrained, unemotional speech action and, 86, 98, 100–102. See also political society
coal miners: in Britain, 127; and expansion of democracy, 18, 20, 145–46, 230n56; in 2011 Telangana general strike, 1
coastal Andhra: domination of Hyderabad by migrants from, 4, 95, 108–10; incomes in, compared with Telangana, 247n66; opposition to formation of Telangana in, 226n6; police firing in (1952), 254n31; as site of movement to form Telugu linguistic state, 31, 162, 210, 225n3, 244n2; weavers' collective actions in, 135, 145
Cody, Francis: on petitioning, 240n12; on illiberal democratic politics, 257n22
coffeehouse: as public sphere, 16, 205, 209; railway station as, 32; speech action in, 86–87. See also Habermas, Jürgen
combination(s): British characterization of collective assemblies in India as, 22–23, 83, 117, 130–31, 144; contrast with individual actors, 94, 118, 145
commodity chain(s), 20, 23, 38, 125, 141–42, 146
communication cord, 151, 154–55, 157–58. See also alarm chain pulling
Communist Party of India, roko actions by, 185
Communist Party of India (Marxist), women's wall led by, 218
conditions of listening, 16, 37, 102, 105, 108. See also Burghart, Richard

Constitution of India: adoption of (1950), 21; definition of "state" in, 227n18; reservation quotas introduced in, 228n29, 230n48; rights-bearing citizens imagined by, 76; right to assemble protected by, 49–50, 114, 237n25
Constitution of Nepal, 217
Coromandel Coast, 133, 135–36, 139
cosmopolitanism, feature of strikes, 125, 129, 136, 143. See also Tilly, Charles
Cyclone Nisha, road block for promised compensation, 5, 168–69, 190

Dacca Railway, 118. See also indigo rebellion
Dalit(s): Ambedkar and, 67–68, 77–78, 114, 259n2; atrocities against, 60, 85, 105, 108, 229n45, 246n43; definition of, 229n36; growing visibility of, 111, 217, 222, 229n44, 248n76; identity as a result of collective actions, 12; optimism regarding democracy, 254n38; political arrival of, 197–98, 212, 229n44; representation as angry by others, 74–75; silencing/ignoring of their communicative efforts, 115, 168, 186–87, 214–15; struggle for dignity, 97, 230n60, 245n6; students suspended from Hyderabad University, 43, 68–69, 78, 90, 93, 113, 239n3, 239n6; temple-entry rights for, 44, 235n5. See also Ambedkar Students' Association; caste; Dalit Mahasabha; Dalit Panther movement; dominant castes; Madiga Reservation Porata Samithi
Dalit Mahasabha, 60
Dalit Panther movement, 228n27
darakhāstu (petition), 240n12
darakhāstula dinam (Grievance Day), 70
dark anthropology, 14, 229n42
Defence of India Ordinance, proposal to disable alarm chains, 161
deliberative democracy, 96, 100, 102, 106
deliberative turn. See deliberative democracy
Devika, J. (feminist historian), 219
dhandak, as form of collective communication, 80–81
Dharampal (Indian historian of civil disobedience), 82, 124, 130, 134
dharna (also dharṇā, a sit-in demonstration): Adivasi/Indigenous massacre and,

61; in Banaras/Varanasi, 57; definition and changing meaning of, 8, 36–37, 43, 45, 53–65, 235n11; democracy and, 52–53, 65–66; at Dharna Chowk, 49; escalation and, 60; farmers in Delhi, 74; Gandhi and, 60; Karamchedu massacre and, 60; in Khammam, 7; mass media and, 59, 62; prohibition by British, 51–52, 58, 144, 214; public space and, 65; in the Ramayana epic, 59; state officials' use, 64–65; in Telangana, 30

Dharna Chowk (designated assembly space in Hyderabad), 43–44, 47, 235n6; court judgments on, 50; demand for in other cities, 236n13; dharna at, 49, 217; history of, 47, 50; location of, 47, 53, 63–64, 236nn14–15; as "people's voice," 48, 236nn16–17; protection of, 48, 231n65, 235n7; relay hunger strike at, 45, 46; restrictions on, 220, 264n25

Dhobi Ghat (procession route in Hyderabad), 29. *See also* Indira Park

Dilli Chalo (Let's Go to Delhi), farmer protest, 7

disorder: British perception of collective action as, 82, 132–34; civility as absence of, 123, 132

Disorders Inquiry Committee (1919–1920), attacks on communication, 32

disturbance(s): Bareilly, 83, 143; European, 82; indigo, 116; Lucknow, 170

dominant castes: collective action by, 11, 173–74, 191, 228n30; opposition to inclusion and affirmative action, 93, 111, 115, 190, 212–213, 228n32, 259 (epigraph); quota expansion to include, 230n48; resentment, 68, 113; violent impunity of, 105, 115, 212–213, 229n45. *See also* caste; Dalit(s); *dora*

Do or Die (Gandhi's speech), 170, 237n25

*dora* (landlord or member of dominant caste), 115

Dryzek, John, on deliberative democracy, 100

Duggan, Mark, police shooting of, 89, 243n91, 246n44

Duncan, Jonathan (British Resident, Benares, 1787–1794), on dharna, 55

Dupont, company in Hyderabad, 4

East India Company (EIC): collective actions and, 22–23, 58, 128–34, 138–41, 221; efforts to diffuse collective power, 83, 117–18, 143–45; textile procurement by, 136–37, 142, 146

East India Railways, 159, 253n24

Economically Weaker Sections (EWS), 230n48. *See also* affirmative action; reservation quotas

*Economic Times*, crowd estimates at rallies, 1, 225n1

Egypt (Arab Spring), 2, 26

emergency, chain, 151–52, 155–56. *See also* alarm chain pulling

emergent energies, of crowds, 24. *See also,* Mazzarella, William

emotion: appearance of civility and, 86–87, 101, 111; associations with collective action, 74–75, 106, 241n41, 241n43; crowds and, 24, 134, 145; rationality and, 17, 80, 121; representation of as way of excluding, 69, 92, 112–13, 214; as resource for the dominant, 79, 93; of subaltern actors, 76–77, 79, 85, 104. *See also* agony; anger; *āvēdana*

Engels, Frederick: on false consciousness, 14; skepticism of effectiveness of mass strike, 250n18

Enlightenment, 96, 117, 125, 128, 234n125

Euro-American understandings of democracy, 29, 53, 96, 97

Facebook, 4, 263n8

farmer(s): against indigo cultivation (1860), 116; *āndōlans*, 262n54; appeals to native rulers by, 81; attending Grievance Day, 71; as capitalist class, 190–91; collective actions by, 33, 44, 170, 174, 187, 264n25; dharna by, 74, 264n25; protest against new farm laws (2020–21), 6–7, 15, 178, 189; Shay's Rebellion in America (1786–87), 27

Farm Laws Repeal Bill, 7

Federation of Nepal Transport Entrepreneurs (FNTE), 176. *See also* Lakier, Genevieve

Financial District (Hyderabad), 4

Foucault, Michel, 8, 10, 14, 227n19, 258n73

Frank, Jason, 27

Fraser, Nancy, 17–18, 20, 88, 164–65, 231n61

Freitag, Sandra: on the Banaras house tax protest, 135; on dharna, 57; on "the public", 32

French Revolution, 18, 28, 117, 119, 128, 234n125

*gāli tīyaḍam* (removing air from tires to cause a road block), 34, 166, 185, 212. See also *rāstā roko*

Gandhi, Mohandas Karamchand (1869–1948), 239n63; arrest of, 160, 169–70; campaign against overcrowding third-class rail travel, 153, 158; civil disobedience, 97; criticism of alarm chain pulling, 158; Dalits and, 75; European influences on, 97–98, 128, 234n125; hunger strikes conducted by, 43–44, 60, 62; Indian influences on his practices, 130, 135, 235n2; Nehru and, 117; Non-Cooperation movement (1920–22), 84, 199; passive resistance, 122; Quit India movement (1942) and violence, 159, 170; railway stations as site of speeches, 32; salt march, 62; satyagraha, 60, 62, 234n125; schoolchildren's march from site of his death, 215

garbage dump, Hyderabad municipal, effort to move assembly space next to, 47, 65, 236n14. See also Dharna Chowk

Garhwal, responses of native rulers to appeals in, 80–82, 135

*garjana* (roar), 2, 8, 21, 36, 120, 225n1; Jana Garjana (people's roar), 1, 95–96, 109, 225n1, 226n7; Maha Jana Garjana (great roar of the people), 1, 225n1; Praja Garjana (people's roar), 3. See also assembly; *bhērī*; *murasu*

Garner, Eric, victim of police brutality, 89, 243n96

general strike, 1–2, 6; commodity chains and, 125, 142–43; comparison between Britain and India, 38, 123–28, 138; Engels' view of, 250n18; European origins of (claimed), 98, 123, 245n14; farmers', 7; features of, 126, 129, 136; histories of, 122–24, 223; liberalism and, 176; Rosa Luxemburg's view of, 250n18; Madras, 130–31, 139; Plug Riots (1842 General Strike), 127; Surat, 129, 136, 139. See also *bandh*; Benbow, William; Grand National Holiday; Sakala Janula Samme; Tilly, Charles

Genome Valley (Hyderabad), 4

*gherao* (encircling an official), 8, 172, 175, 179

Gilje, Paul, on street politics in early America, 27–28, 230

Goswami, Manu, 34, 165

Government Railway Police, 36, 159, 171, 199, 256n11

Graeber, David, 15

Gramsci: hegemonic consciousness, 14; influence on Ranajit Guha, 77

Grand National Holiday (general strike), 126. See also Benbow, William

Grant, John Peter (1807–1893; lieutenant governor of Bengal, 1859–1862), 116, 134. See also indigo rebellion

Green, Jeffrey, on surveillance of elected officials, 227n19

grievance(s): British opposition to expression of, 24, 131, 133, 145; civility defined as responsiveness to, 102, 196; dharna or strike as means of expression of, 33–34, 45, 55–58, 63, 104, 128–29, 165; refusal to hear, 73, 85, 180; third-class railway overcrowding as, 158; tradition of expressing through peaceful action, 1, 21, 23, 45, 50, 54, 81, 237n25; weavers', 137, 139, 141, 221

Grievance Day, 70, 71, 72. See also *Hindustan Times* (English daily): At Your Doorstep

Guha, Ramachandra: Mandal protests, 228n32; nonviolent collective communication (*dhandak*), 80–82; sedition laws, 260n15

Guha, Ranajit: peasant insurgency, 76–77; targeting of railways, 33

Guinness World Record, 216–17, 233n110

Gujjar agitation, 175, 189, 196, 234n116

Habermas, Jürgen: bourgeois public sphere, 17–19, 88, 142, 205; coffeehouses, 16, 86–87; communicative action, 18, 86, 121; deliberative debate, 17, 38, 88, 100, 208; Indian versions of public sphere, 205–6, 261n32; salons, 142, 230n50; speech acts, 87, 90–91, 240n23

Hansen, Thomas Blom, 22, 231n72

Haragopal, G., 1, 21, 227n12, 231n65, 260n16

Hardiman, David, 82, 124, 128–29, 234n125, 235n2

Hardt, Michael, on the "multitude," 25, 233n104

*hartāl* (strike or work stoppage), 8, 36, 172, 228n30, 233n107. See also *bandh*; *samme*; *sanketi hartāl* (token strike, Nepal)

Hegel, George Wilhelm Friedrich, *Sittlichkeit* as best equivalent to civility, 120

High Court: Bombay and Patna, on alarm chain pulling, 254n26; Hyderabad, decisions on collective assembly, 48–50, 114, 183; Madras, on farmers, 74

*Hindu, The* (English daily): Dalit students, 69; democratic actions, 215; Dharna Chowk demands in other cities, 236n13

*Hindustan Times* (English daily), At Your Doorstep (biannual grievance program), 73

HITEC City (tech industry hub in Hyderabad), 4

Hobsbawm, Eric, notion of pre-political, 76. *See also* Guha, Ranajit

Home Minister: Aam Aadmi Party dharna in front of office, 64; Telangana creation, 226n6

Hong Kong, Umbrella Revolution in, 24

hooligans: contrast with political actors, 210, 212; Nehru equation with action committees, 118

Hopkins, Washburn, on dharna, 56–57

house tax strike: Banaras (Varanasi), 57, 59, 133, 135, 137, 144; Bareilly, 83–84, 144; Bhagalpur, 135; Murshidabad, 135, 137; Patna, 135. See also *dharna*

human chain(s), 8, 222–23; in Bangladesh, 216; in Bihar, 218–19; in Kerala, 216–17; in Nepal, 217; state and nonstate actors working together to organize, 222; in Telangana, 216–17

hunger strike, 8, 36, 55, 58–59; to compel audience, 222–23; fast-unto-death, 31, 44, 55, 59–60, 210, 237n25, 254n31; Gandhi and, 43–44, 60, 62; genealogies of practice and, 223, 235n2; to hold elected officials accountable, 37; in Mumbai, 190; Jawaharlal Nehru's critique of, 163–64; Arutla Ramachandra Reddy's use of, 62; relay hunger strike, 43, 45, 46, 60; state and, 65; visibility and, 217. *See also nirāhāra dīkṣa*; *nirasana vratam*; Sreeramulu, Potti

Hyderabad: as capital city, 4, 5, 6; *garjana* in, 3; Dalit protests in, 212, 217; democratic spaces in, 29–30, 43–44, 47, 53, 62–63, 65, 114, 220, 236n14, 239n69, 264n25; efforts to create world class city, 30, 35, 52–53, 109, 234n123, 235n12; Mulki (local) vs. Non-Mulki (migrant) politics in, 227n12, 230n47; princely state of, 207, 225n3, 244n2; railways in, 192; *roko* action in, 185, 188–89; Telangana movement in, 15. *See also* Dharna Chowk; Secunderabad (Hyderabad's twin city); University of Hyderabad

ideological state apparatuses (Althusser), 9–10, 14, 35

illiberal democracy, 38, 174–78, 212, 257n22

India Gate, permits for assemblies at, 50

Indian Constitution. *See* Constitution of India

Indian Criminal Procedure Code, declaration of unlawful assembly (Section 144), 52, 144

Indian National Congress, 159–60, 169–70, 199, 226n6. *See also* anticolonial movement

Indian Penal Code (IPC), Sections 141–60, prosecution of assemblies, 52, 144

Indian Railway Museum archives, 36

Indian Railways: alarm chain pulling in, 36, 152, 154, 158–60, 166, 253n24; largest employer in the world, 32, 234n111; sites of political communication, 32–33, 174, 183, 195; statistics on passengers, 233n110; ticketless travel, 159, 200

indignation, political movements and, 76, 79. *See also* anger

indigo rebellion, 77, 116, 128

Indira Park, assembly space behind, 29, 44, 48–49, 63, 236nn14–15. *See also* Dharna Chowk

industrial revolution, 123, 127, 143

informal sector, growth of, 16, 44

Injeram (site of EIC factory), weavers, 137, 140–41

International Campaign for Justice in Bhopal, Union Carbide gas disaster, 186–87

International Monetary Fund, local Transport Entrepreneurs Associations in Nepal and, 176, 178 interpellation (hailing), 9, 76, 103. *See also* Althusser, Louis

'Iwāz, Mufti Mohammad (leader of Bareilly house tax strike in 1816), 83, 232n75

Jaffrelot, Christophe: on Dalit activism, 229n44, 248n76; on majoritarian politics, 11

Jana Garjana (People's Roar), in Telangana movement, 1, 95–96, 109, 226n7

Jantar Mantar (designated assembly space in Delhi), 50, *51*, 74, 220, 237n26

Jaoul, Nicolas, on anger, 75, 79

Jefferson, Thomas, on people as censors of their governors, 27, 221

Jeffrey, Craig, on politics of waiting, 167

Jharkhand: formation of state, 13, 262n41; Maoist Naxal movement in, 192

*julūs* (procession), 8

Kamaiyas (bonded laborers in Nepal), freedom struggle of, 176–79

Kamra, Lipika, on militant Maoism and the deepening of democracy, 192–93

Karamchedu, Andhra Pradesh, site of Dalit massacre (1985), 60, 105, 246n43

Karimnagar: collective assembly in, 1–3; media coverage of, 226n7

Karunanidhi, M. (1924–2018; former chief minister, Tamil Nadu), aid to victims of cyclone Nisha, 168

Kenny, Thomas, indigo factory of, 116

Kerala, 5, Dalit student organization, 68; human chains, 216–20

Kernaghan, Richard, on Maoist movement in Peru, 194

Kilvenmani, Tamil Nadu, site of Dalit massacre (1968), 105

Kohli, Atul, on India's transition to democracy, 21

*koluvu* (audience hall, court, service), 69–70. *See also* audience(s)

Kruks-Wisner, Gabrielle, on claims-making, 202–3, 260n18, 260n22

Kumar, Radha, on discretionary forms of power, 215

Kumaun (also Kumaon), British response to appeals in, 80–82, 135

Lakier, Genevieve, on protest forms in Nepal, 175–78

Lakoff, Robin, on agonism, 107

landlord(s): protest against, 128, 176, 193; violent conflict with laborers, 115–16

Lefebvre, Henri, 34, 65, 165

Legislative Assembly, 112, 157–58, 160, 170, 231n70; as destination of a march or procession or site of political meeting, 4, 29, 53, 63; elections to, 21, 234n116; Rajasthan, 72

Levinas, Emmanuel, political communication, 91

liberalism: blockades and, 175; civic, 100, 106; contradictions within, 79–80; democracy and, 20; populism and, 249n105; subject formation within, 18, 24

liberalization (of economy), 16, 50, 177–78, 183

limits of the state, 227n18. *See also* Mitchell, Timothy

London: British Library in, 36; protests in, 89, 225n1, 243n91, 243n93; spread of strikes in relation to, 137. *See also* Spitalfields

Lower Tank Bund Road (procession route in Hyderabad), 29

Lucknow, 5; rail/road blocks in, 170, 182, 195; railways officials, 36–37, 151, 198–99

Lumbini Park (site of collective assembly in Hyderabad opposite State Secretariat), 47

Lyman, Peter, on anger, 79, 241nn41–43

Madiga Reservation Porata Samithi (Organization Fighting for Increased Reservations for Members of the Madiga Community), 114

Madison, James (1751–1836), 27–28

Madras (renamed Chennai in 1996): death of Andhra State activist Potti Sreeramulu in (1952), 31, 44; High Court and farmer protests, 74; Legislative Council, 112, 231n70; petition to Board of Trade, 94, 145; State (until 1956), 225n3, 244n2; strike (1680), 130–31, 135–36, 139. *See also* Chennai

Madras and Southern Mahratta Railway, 157, 253n24

Madras-Calcutta railway line, 31, 210
Maha Jana Garjana (great roar of the people),
   1. *See also garjana*
Maharashtra, 5, 6; alarm chain pulling in, 151;
   Bunds (bandhs), 82; Dalit ticketless travel
   in, 197; mass movements in, 128; passive
   resistance in, 135; *roko* action in, 190
*Mahratta* (Pune newspaper), report on resistance to overcrowding, 155. *See also* alarm
   chain pulling; overcrowding
Maine, Henry, on *dharna*, 58
majoritarian movements, 11–12, 174
making known, practices of, 37, 39, 63, 104–5,
   213–14. *See also āvēdana*
*mānavahāram*, 8, 216. *See also* human
   chain(s)
Mandal Commission, 11, 213, 228n32, 230n48,
   259 (epigraph)
Manin, Bernard, on representative democracy, 26, 28, 39
Maoism (in South Asia), 11, 110, 179, 192–94
Marwadi Association, on ticketless travel,
   200
Marx, Karl, influences of, 9, 14, 218, 229n42,
   241n41, 242n79, 256n13
mass media: amplification of voice (*āwāj*),
   120; impact on political practices, 44, 59,
   62, 171, 183; public sphere and, 205–6
Masulipatnam (Machilipatnam): gathering
   at railway station (1952), 254n31; targets of
   collective action in, 139; weaver march to
   (1798), 133
Mazzarella, William, on crowds, 24–26
Microsoft, company in Hyderabad, 4
middle class: anxiety over the expansion
   of political participation, 173; Bengali,
   205; European, 79–80; Indian English-
   educated, 128; rail/road blockades and, 172,
   174, 190–91; visions of urban governance,
   35. *See also bhadralok*
Million Man March (Egypt, 2011), 2
Million March (Hyderabad, 2011), Telangana
   movement, 2–4, 96, 189
Mitchell, Timothy: genealogies of democracy,
   20–21, 25, 145–46, 230n56, 231n63; limits of
   the state, 227n18; violence and law, 215
Modi, Narendra (b. 1950; prime minister of
   India since 2014), 73, 74

Monsanto (biotech seed company in Hyderabad), 4
moral economy: *dharna* and, 54; E. P.
   Thompson on, 126
*morchā* (front, battlefront), 227n16. *See also*
   rally/rallies
Mouffe, Chantal, on agonistic pluralism, 99,
   106–7
Mughals, collective action to communicate
   with sovereign, 72, 123, 128–29, 139
Mulki (local/native), in Hyderabad, 227n12,
   230n47. *See also* affirmative action; reservation quotas
*murasu* (drum, voice, roar, mass outdoor
   meeting), 8; newspaper and broadcasting
   outlets named, 103, 120, 249n103. See also
   *bhērī; garjana*
Muthukkaruppan, Parthasarathi, on violence
   against marginalized groups, 84–85, 215,
   229n45, 242n78

Narayan, Rochisha, on dharna, 56–57
National Archives of India, 36, 259n1
Naxalite (Maoist) movement, 11, 192–93
Negri, Antonio, on the multitude, 25, 232n80,
   233n104
Nehru, Jawaharlal: Andhra state formation and, 44, 254n31; in anti-colonial
   movement, 159, 169–70; on postcolonial
   political practices, 94, 117–19, 163–64,
   178–80, 201
Nehru Memorial Museum and Library, 36
Nellore, 6, 31, 36–37, 210, 235n5, 254n31
neoliberalism, 16, 223
Nepal, 5; human chain in, 217; political communication in, 102, 104; public space and
   democracy in, 233n107; road blocks in,
   175–76, 179
*nirāhāra dīkṣa* (hunger strike or fasting vow),
   8, 36; relay hunger strike, 43, 45, 46.
   *See also* hunger strike
*niraśana vratam* (hunger strike or fasting
   vow), *See* hunger strike; *nirāhāra dīkṣa*
Non-Cooperation Movement (1919–1922),
   43, 199

Occupy Movement (2011–12), 2, 24, 226n7
Orange Revolution (Kiev, 2004), 225n1

order: anger and, 78–80, 85; capacity for in
India, 116, 133–34; civility and, 132; contrast
with Spitalfields weavers, 138, 141; danger
to, 143, 172, 174–75, 195; Indian state's effort
to maintain, 31, 51, 65, 114, 210, 254n31;
strikes and, 124, 129, 133–36
Ortner, Sherry, on dark theory, 14, 229n42
Osmania University, Dalit students at, 68;
linguistic domination at, 95
Other Backward Classes (OBC), 114, 230n48.
See also affirmative action
overcrowding (in third class railway travel),
34, 151–61, 165

padayātra (also padayātrā, pilgrimage or
journey by foot, often to a seat of power),
3, 8, 34, 36; majoritarian, 11
Paley, Julia, anthropology of democracy, 21–22
Palle Palle Paṭṭala Paiki (Villages on the Rail
Tracks), Telangana roko action, 187–89
Parkinson, John, on democracy and public
space, 30, 65, 219, 244n107
Parliament: within definition of the state,
227n18; discussion of roko actions in, 174;
members of, 59, 64, 82, 196, 221; Nepali,
176; target of political assemblies, 50, 59,
215; on Telangana formation, 226n4; weavers
protest in London (1765), 138
Parthasarathi, Prasannan, on weaver protests,
132, 139–40
Peluso, Nancy Lee, on access, 203, 260n23
People's War Group (Indian Maoist organization), 11, 110
Permanent Settlement (British reform of
Indian land revenue system), 54
Peru, Shining Path (Maoist organization) in,
11, 110, 194
petition(s): in Andhra movement, 207, 210;
British EIC as recipients of, 77, 83, 94, 116,
118; creation of moral space for amplification of, 105; Curative to Union Carbide,
186; Cyclone victims' to Tamil Nadu government, 169; Dalit students' to University
of Hyderabad vice-chancellor, 68–69, 113,
239n6; emergence in England, 126; long
history of receiving in India, 69–70, 72;
refusal by authorities to hear, 20, 73, 83,
85, 90, 94, 115, 118; in Telugu, 36, 240n12;

weavers', 23, 140–41, 145; writ to Andhra
Pradesh High Court, 114
Piliavsky, Anastasia: on seeking audience, 70;
on speaking in public, 103
Plug Riots (1842 General Strike), 127
police: data on assemblies, 44, 97, 170–71,
235n6, 245nn9–11, 256n10; demands for
accountability of, 60, 64, 105, 112, 226n7,
246n43; discretionary power of, 64, 114,
174, 178, 182–83, 198, 211–12, 215, 223; face-
to-face meetings as more effective than,
195–96; failure to implement law, 218;
hailing by (in Althusser), 9; preventative
prohibition on assembly, 50, 52, 63, 144,
237n26; violence of in India, 31, 77, 82–83,
115–16, 185, 210, 246n45, 254n31; violence
of in US/UK, 89, 108, 243n91, 243n96,
246n44. See also Government Railway
Police; Railway Protection Force
political arrival: recognition as, 13, 35, 39, 198,
201, 204, 229n44; state accommodation
as measure of, 214–215. See also making
known; ticketless travel
political society: definition, 19, 76; necessity
of placing actions within longer histories,
37–38; relationship to civil society, 172–73,
180, 212, 256n13, 258n73. See also Chatterjee, Partha; civil society
pōru yātra (confrontational procession or
opposition march), 8. See also morchā
(front, battlefront)
Poudel, Biswo, on Nepal transport association protest, 177
procession(s), 3, 7–8, 23, 34, 98, 136–38, 147,
162, 171; as building axes of access, 201; as
communicative act, 18–19, 23, 137; histories
of, 221, 223; mocking, as social discipline,
126; mōrcha (front, battlement), 227n16;
Nehru on, 118–19, 164; as performance, 96,
147, 205; permission needed to hold, 63,
114–15; political arrival and, 259n2; publics
and, 210, 213; public space and, 52, 63; right
to hold, 29, 237n25

Quit India Movement (1942–43), railways as
target during, 159–163, 169–170, 201
quotas. See affirmative action; Mandal Commission; Mulki; reservation quotas

radio: children's program in Andhra Pradesh (Balanandam), 108–9; as less trustworthy, 31

*rail roko* (rail blockade), 3, 8, 21, 33, 36; alarm chain pulling and, 165–66; in Belgaum over Cauvery water, 184; in Bhopal for Union Carbide victims, 186–87; central government issues and, 183; comparison with memorandums, 168; definition, 169; escalation and, 186–87; government responses to, 195; Gujjar agitation and, 189; in independent India, 170; liberalism and, 174–75; mass media and changes in, 171, 183; during Quit India movement, 159, 162, 169–70; representations of, 172–80; restrictions on, 214; sabotage and, 166, 181; spontaneous, 191; as state-hailing practice, 181–83; state use of, 189; in Vijayawada over Telangana state formation, 184; villages on the rail tracks, 188. *See also rāstā roko*

Railway Protection Force (RPF), 36, 171

Rajasthan: communicative action, 33, 70, 72; Gujjar rail blockades, 189, 196, 234n116; public spaces, 103; ticketless travel, 200

Rajayya, Allam, *Bhūmi* (short story), 115

Raj Bhavan, as dharna site, 63

rally/rallies: and democracy, 6, 18, 36, 147, 176, 201–3, 219; majoritarian, 11, 115, 228n32; within a series of escalating actions, 59, 96, 162, 221–22; in Telangana movement, 1–3, 18, 96, 171, 225n1; ticketless travel to attend, 8, 34, 39, 198–99. See also *morchā*; *pōru yātra*; ticketless travel

*Ramayana* (Hindu epic), 59

Ram Lila Maidan (Delhi), assemblies at, 50, 237n26. *See also* Jantar Mantar

Ranulf, Svend, on middle-class indignation, 79

Rashtriya Swayamsevak Sangh (Hindu nationalist organization), 11

*rāstā roko* (roadblock), 3, 8, 21, 36, 162; definition, 169; in independent India, 170; local variation in, 185; *mahā rasta roko* (mega roadblock), 34, 187, 234n120; in Maharashtra, 190; state-level issues and, 183. See also *chakka jām*; *gāli tīyadam*; *rail roko*; *sadak bandh*

relay hunger strike, 43, 45, 46, 60. *See also* hunger strike; *nirāhāra dīksa* (hunger strike or fasting vow)

relocation, as collective action, 23

reservation quotas, 16, 70, 230nn47–48; opposition to, 258n72. *See also* affirmative action; Mandal Commission; Mulki

revolution: American, 18, 28, 230n56; Chinese, 30; Dalit Panthers and, 228n27; emotion and, 25, 241n41; French, 18, 28, 117, 119, 128, 234n125; Indian Maoists and, 11, 192–93; industrial, 123, 127, 143; Orange (Kiev), 225n1; Russian, 250n18; television and, 18; Umbrella (Hong Kong), 24. *See also* Arab Spring; Occupy movement

Ribot, Jesse, on access, 203, 260n23

Ring, Laura, on cultivation of masculine anger, 78–79

roadblock. *See rāstā roko*

roar (of the people): as outdoor assembly, 1, 3, 8, 37, 95, 109, 225n1; as voice, 103, 120–121. *See also bhērī*; *garjana*; *murasu*

Robbins, Joel, on the anthropology of the good, 14

Rousseau, Jean-Jacques (1712–78), on representation, 28, 221

Russian revolution (1905), 250n18

*ryots* (peasant cultivators), protests by, 116, 137–38

Sabarimala Hindu temple, human chain in support of entrance of women into, 216

*sadak bandh* (roadblock). See *rāstā roko*

Sakala Janula Samme (42-day All People's Strike), 1, 95–96, 122, 246n45, 264n25. *See also* bandh; general strike; *hartāl*; *samme*

Salgamudia (location of indigo factory), 116

*samāvēśam* (meeting), 36. *See also* audience(s)

*samme* (strike), 8, 36, 172. *See also* bandh; general strike; *hartāl*; Sakala Janula Samme

*sangam* (also *sangham*, association or union), vi, 115–16

*sanketi hartāl* (token strike, Nepal), 104. *See also* Burghart, Richard

Santal rebellion (1855–56), railways as target of, 33

satyagraha: alarm chain pulling in railways as, 157–58; Gandhi and, 60, 62, 234n125; Nehru on, 163; right to assemble and, 237n25

Satyanarayana, K., on Dalit mobilization as spurred by failure to prosecute upper-caste violence, 105, 229n45

Scheduled Caste (SC)/Scheduled Tribe (ST), 72, 114, 228n29, 230n48, 234n116. *See also* affirmative action; Dalit(s); untouchability

Schmitt, Carl, on political activity organized around friends and enemies, 101

Schnapp, Jeffrey, history of mass assembly, 26, 219

Scott, James C.: anarchism, 15; emotions of subalterns, 76. *See also* Guha, Ranajit

Section 144 (Indian Criminal Procedure Code), prevention of assembly, 52, 144

Secunderabad (Hyderabad's twin city), 189; railway station, 171, 183; South Central Railway headquarters in, 36

Self-Respect Movement, in south India, 97

Shay's Rebellion (1786–87 farmers' protests in Massachusetts, 1786–87), 27

Shils, Edward, on civility, 100–101

Shining Path (Maoist movement in Peru, founded in 1969), 11, 110, 194

Shiv Sena (right-wing Marathi regionalist and Hindu nationalist political party, founded in 1966), 11, 231n72

Shore, John (1751–1834; Lord Teignmouth, governor-general of British India, 1793–97), on *dharna*, 54–55, 58

shutdown strike. *See bandh*

Sieyès, Emmanuel (theorist of French Revolution), 28

Simla (Shimla): correspondence with Railway Board, 151, 154, 253n4; forms of protest in, 81

Singha, Radhika, on dharna, 55–57

sit-down strike, 4, 45, 59, 62, 65. *See also* dharna

Sitrin, Marina, on logic of political representation, 27

Spitalfields (London neighborhood), silk weaver violence in, 138–39, 141, 221

Spodek, Howard, on Gandhi's methods, 135, 235n2

Sreeramulu, Potti (1901–1952), Andhra State formation and death of, 31, 44, 163, 210–211, 235n5, 254n31

Srikakulam, police firing at (1952), 31, 254n31

state, as defined in Indian constitution, 227n18

state government: dharna by officials of (New Delhi), 64; located in State Secretariat, 63; refusal to permit assemblies, 48–49; roko agitations responsibility of, 175

strike(s): democracy and coal miners, dockworkers, and railway employees', 18, 20, 145–46, 230n56; distances spanned, 137; escalation and, 77; high frequency in India, 122, 129, 135; history of in South Asia, 22; Madras (1680), 130–31, 135–36, 139; participation in, 202–3; Plug Riots (1842 General Strike), 127; Quit India movement, 160, 162; in Telangana, 95, 109; violence and, 82, 246n45; weavers', 135–37, 139–41, 145. See also *bandh*; general strike; *hartāl*; hunger strike; *samme*

subaltern(s): contrast with elites, 76–77, 84, 172, 212; counterpublics, 17, 88; democracy and, 193; representation of, 207–8; "style" of politics, 37–38, 224

Subaltern Studies Collective, 84, 139, 251n77, 256n13

suicide: *dharna* and, 55–57; farmers' protests and, 74; of Dalit PhD student Rohith Venula (2016), 239n3

Supreme Court: farmer protest, 74; right to assemble, 50, 65–66, 237n25; Sabarimala temple, 216, 219, 221

surveillance: by state, 8; of state officials, 11, 15, 206, 227n19. *See also* Althusser, Louis; Foucault, Michel; Green, Jeffrey

Swarnalatha, Potukuchi, on weaver petitions, 140

Tahrir Square (Cairo, Egypt), site of demonstrations (2011), 26

Tamil Nadu, 5, 6, 36; collective assemblies in, 168–169, 184, 212, 230n60, 256n10; farmer's dharna in Delhi, 74; mass killings of Dalits in, 105; prevention of Dalit political action in, 114–15; term *murasu* in, 120, 249n103

violence: absence of, 30, 81–83; as attribute, 83; caste and, 68, 84–85, 105–6, 108, 116, 215, 228, 229n45, 232n72, 242n78, 245n6; civility and, 97, 100, 102, 105, 119, 123, 152; civil resistance and, 127; "culture" and, 89–90, 92, 135; dharna and, 55; emotion and, 68–69, 78, 85, 92, 113, 197, 213–14, 243n93; efforts to be heard and, 37, 76–78, 82–83, 99, 192, 195, 213, 243n96; Gandhi and, 43, 170; in Indian history, 33, 83, 98, 132, 141; majoritarian, 11, 220; against marginalized groups, 84–85, 132, 181, 215, 216, 221, 232n72; railways and, 31, 33, 171, 182, 191–94, 198, 210–11; reorganization of, 97; revolutionary, 193; as social discipline, 115, 141; state, 15, 84, 144, 246nn44–45

Visakhapatnam (Vizagapatam), 6; demand for Dharna Chowk, 236n13; police firing in Waltair, 31, 254n31; weaver grievances, 94, 118, 137, 145

Viswanath, Rupa, on political representation, 112–13

Viswanathan, S., on Dalit mobilization, 115

Waltair. *See* Visakhapatnam

Warangal, 6; collective assemblies in, 1–3, 48, 59, *188*, 226n7; linguistic domination in, 108

Warner, Michael, on publics, 88, 208–9

Watt, Daniel J., political performance, 89. *See also* Black Lives Matter

weavers: actions of Spitalfields (silk weavers in London), 138–39, 221; collective action by, 83, 131, 133, 136–141; EIC rejection of petitions from, 94, 118, 145

Weber, Max (1864–1920), 79, 227n19

welfare: basic rights vs., 230n60; role of laborers in producing state, 20

West Bengal. *See* Bengal

Wood, Sir Charles (1800–1885), on collective assembly, 1

World Bank, 178

world-class city, remaking Hyderabad into, 30, 47, 52, 109, 220, 234n123

World Trade Organization, protests (1999), 24

*yātra* (also *yātrā*, journey/pilgrimage/ march): actions/practices, 3, 8, 21, 36, 162; histories of, 221; official responses to, 171; political arrival and, 39; in Telangana movement, 34

Young, Iris, on inclusive political communication, 91, 93, 242n80

YouTube: Dharna Chowk speeches, 231n65, 264n25; *roko* footage, 183

Zakaria, Fareed, illiberal democracy, 175–76. *See also* Cody, Francis; Lakier, Genevieve

Ziad, Waleed, Bareilly protests, 83–84, 232n75. *See also* house tax strike